THE
FIRST GREAT CHARITY
OF THIS TOWN

THE
FIRST GREAT CHARITY
OF THIS TOWN

BELFAST CHARITABLE SOCIETY AND
ITS ROLE IN THE DEVELOPING CITY

EDITED BY
OLWEN PURDUE

IRISH ACADEMIC PRESS

First published in 2022 by
Irish Academic Press
10 George's Street
Newbridge
Co. Kildare
Ireland
www.iap.ie

978 1 78855 004 8 (Cloth)
978 1 78855 005 5 (Ebook)

A CIP catalogue record for this book
is available from the British Library.

Typeset in Minion Pro 11/15 pt

Front cover: Image from P. D. Hardy's *Twenty-One Views in Belfast and its
Neighbourhood* (Courtesy of the Linen Hall Library)
Back cover: Clifton House (Courtesy of Belfast Charitable Society)
Cover design by riverdesignbooks.com
Endpaper front: A Map of the Town and Environs of Belfast,
James Williamson © National Museums NI, Ulster Museum Collection
Endpaper back: Belfast, 1860, J. Rapkin, H. Bibby © National Museums NI,
Ulster Museum Collection

Irish Academic Press is a member of Publishing Ireland.

Contents

List of Contributors

৪১

Robyn Atcheson holds a PhD on poverty, poor relief and public health in Belfast in the early nineteenth century from Queen's University Belfast. Her work has won numerous awards, including, in 2015, the Kirkpatrick History of Medicine Award from the Royal College of Physicians of Ireland. She writes and teaches on Irish history, women's history and the social history of medicine as well as consulting on public history projects related to the poor of Belfast.

Kenneth L. Dawson is the joint editor (with Dr Myrtle Hill and Dr Brian Turner) of *1798: Rebellion in County Down* (Newtownards, 1998) and author of *The Belfast Jacobin: Samuel Neilson and the United Irishmen* (Dublin, 2017). Originally from Belfast, he was formerly Head of History and Politics and is currently a vice-principal in Down High School, Downpatrick.

Raymond Gillespie was Professor of History in the Department of History, Maynooth University. He has written extensively on the social, religious, cultural and economic history of seventeenth-century Ireland. A native of Belfast, he has made a number of contributions to the early history of the city, most notably *Early Belfast: The Origins and Growth of an Ulster Town to 1750* (Belfast, 2007).

Christine Kinealy is the founding director of Ireland's Great Hunger Institute at Quinnipiac University in Connecticut. A graduate of Trinity College, Dublin, Christine has researched extensively on Ireland's Great

Hunger and, more recently, the Irish abolition movement. Her publications include *The Hidden Famine: Hunger, Poverty and Sectarianism in Belfast 1840–50* (with Gerard MacAtasney, London, 2000), *Charity and the Great Hunger: The Kindness of Strangers* (New York, 2013) and *Black Abolitionists in Ireland* (Abingdon, 2020).

Gerard MacAtasney is an Irish historian who specialises in the history of the Great Famine, particularly its impact on Ulster. His works include *This Dreadful Visitation: The Famine in Lurgan/Portadown* (Belfast, 1997) and *The Hidden Famine: Hunger, Poverty and Sectarianism in Belfast 1840–50*, co-authored with Christine Kinealy (London, 2000)

Ciarán McCabe is a historian of poverty and welfare in Ireland and Britain between the eighteenth and twentieth centuries. His publications include *Begging, Charity and Religion in Pre-Famine Ireland* (Liverpool, 2018), as well as articles in Irish and international journals. Most recently, he has co-edited (with Emily Mark-FitzGerald and Ciarán Reilly) *Dublin and the Great Famine* (Dublin, 2022). Ciarán has taught in a number of Irish universities and is a fellow of the Royal Historical Society.

Aaron D. McIntyre joined the team at Clifton House, home of the Belfast Charitable Society, as Archive & Heritage Coordinator in 2016. He has undertaken extensive research in the Society's archive, dating back to 1752, to develop a series of unique talks, tours and seasonal events to highlight the history of the charity, its people and its role in Belfast and beyond. He also oversees the Society's outreach activities with local community and voluntary groups. Aaron holds a Bachelor's degree in Archaeology (Queen's University, Belfast) and a Masters in Museum Studies (University of Leicester) and has a particular interest in the social history of Georgian Belfast.

Cathryn McWilliams is Assistant Professor of English at the University of South-Eastern Norway. She defended her doctoral thesis, 'The Letters and Legacy of Mary Ann McCracken (1770–1866)', in June 2021. Her research interests include epistolary studies, life writing, women's history, Irish studies and creative writing. She is creative response editor for the journal *MAI: Feminism and Visual Culture*. Her children's book, *Who Ate All the Pies?*, was published in the UK in 2010, while her poetry has appeared in literary magazines such as *The Honest Ulsterman*.

John J. Ó Neill is Research Manager at Irish Archaeological Consultancy Ltd and a visiting research fellow in the School of Natural and Built Environment, Queen's University Belfast. John has held a number of roles in higher education in Ireland, as a researcher and lecturer in archaeology in QUB and UCD, and in management in lifelong learning in IT Carlow (now South East Technological University) and IT Tallaght (now Technological University, Dublin). His published works cover themes in archaeology (*Lisheen Mine Archaeological Project*, Dublin, 2004; *Burnt Mounds in Northern and Western Europe*, Saarbrücken, 2009) and history (*Belfast Battalion: a history of the Belfast IRA 1922–1969*, Litter, 2018) and include a wide variety of shorter papers and articles in peer reviewed and popular publications. John is currently project-managing research and analysis on the Drumclay Crannóg excavations (funded by the Department for Communities), as well as a variety of other archaeological projects.

Paula Reynolds has been Chief Executive of the Belfast Charitable Society since September 2015, leading the charity's new phase of philanthropic work. She was responsible for the Society's residential home until March 2018 and oversaw its smooth transfer. Since then she has ensured the charity uses its resources to meet the needs of the disadvantaged. She is also responsible for the charity's two successful subsidiaries: Clifton House Centre Limited and the Mary Ann McCracken Foundation. Previously Paula had set up a business services social enterprise supporting the community and voluntary sector, following nine years as Director of Member Services at NICVA and five years in Making Belfast Work – all in North Belfast.

Lauren Smyth is a PhD research candidate from Queen's University Belfast. Her research focuses on the work of the Belfast Charitable Society and child welfare during early nineteenth-century Belfast.

David Watters is a Chartered Accountant with over forty years' experience in practice and advisory roles within the private, public and charitable sectors. David was treasurer and chairman at Extern before joining the board of the Belfast Charitable Society. He was also a trustee of the Spirit of 2012 Trust and a non-executive director of the Northern Ireland Guardian Ad Litem Agency. David continues to sit on the board of several privately owned companies in Northern Ireland.

Sir Ronald Weatherup graduated from the Law Faculty of Queens University Belfast in 1970, practised as a barrister in Northern Ireland, was appointed a High Court Judge in 2001 and later served on the Northern Ireland Court of Appeal to 2017. He has been President of the Belfast Charitable Society since 2018.

Jonathan Jeffrey Wright is a lecturer in history at Maynooth University. His current research has focused on Ulster and the Atlantic World in the Age of Revolution, and his recent publications include *An Ulster Slaveowner in the Revolutionary Atlantic: The Life and Letters of John Black* (Dublin, 2019) and *Crime and Punishment in Nineteenth-century Belfast: The Story of John Linn* (Dublin, 2020).

Foreword

Mary McAleese

I was born, raised and went to primary school a short distance from the impressive Clifton Street buildings that became the heart and the hearth of the centuries-long work of care conducted by the Belfast Charitable Society. I knew very little of the Society's remarkable history but had reason to know its environs well. As a youngster I was an in-patient in the neighbouring Benn Hospital, built by one of Belfast's great and little-known philanthropic benefactors, Edward Benn, who is buried in the Clifton Street Cemetery and who collaborated so effectively with the Belfast Charitable Society. That hinterland of magnificent buildings, built with such attention to the dignity of the poor and the ill, was my familiar, everyday hinterland; and yet how very little I knew of its history or the vision and values of those who created and sustained it, and nurture it still. How little I knew of what a massive debt of gratitude I and generations of Belfast's citizens owe to the Belfast Charitable Society.

Now, thanks to this timely and thoroughly researched collection of essays on the Society's role in the emerging city of Belfast and its connections to the wider world, I feel a deep pride in its narrative, for there is in it a richly textured spirit of egalitarian kindness and decency, and there are wells of spontaneous, neighbourly generosity from which the Belfast of today and tomorrow can draw inspiration and hope. It is a huge pleasure to have been invited to write the foreword to this important book, which has introduced me, and I am certain will introduce many others, to hidden layers of Belfast life that enthral and uplift the reader.

In the 270 years since the establishment of the Society, Belfast has changed dramatically from being a busy market town to a great industrial city and, more recently, a vibrant cultural centre and tourist destination. These developments brought with them significant societal challenges, not least in the extent of poverty and the pressures on infrastructure that increased as the town's population expanded. At the time of the Society's establishment, there was limited engagement in the provision of welfare or other necessary services from those apparently in authority – Belfast's town council or its landed elite – and it would be almost another century before statutory welfare was introduced in the form of the Poor Law. In this vacuum, Belfast Charitable Society played a vital role.

From its foundation in 1752 all the way though to 2022, Belfast Charitable Society has been to the fore in promoting social welfare and providing what we know today as comprehensive wraparound services to meet the multifaceted needs of the city's poorest people. Even before the first foundation stone of its Poorhouse was laid, the Society was proactive in identifying and addressing a range of social and economic needs across four main areas of personal care: diet, health, education and industry for the poor of the town. As many of the chapters in this volume evidence, the opening of the Poorhouse represented a major step forward in the provision of residential welfare for the elderly, children and those unable to care for themselves, while the Society continued to provide for people in their own homes through 'outdoor relief', something that allowed those in need to retain a degree of dignity that would be denied to them under the more severe terms of the Poor Law.

The Society, and particularly those women associated with its work – women such as Mary Ann McCracken, who dedicated her life to addressing social issues – were also to the fore of providing education to the town's poorer classes, something that is particularly dear to my own heart. I feel humbled to be writing this foreword for a book that does something to highlight the life of a woman who has been such an inspiration to me. She fought for the rights of young children to be educated, introduced a more diverse and meaningful education and developed apprenticeships for older children in order that they might be equipped to make their way in the world. The legacy of Mary Ann McCracken and the other women of the ladies' committee was profound not just in shaping educational provision but also in laying the foundations for Belfast's growing success as a producer of textiles.

The legacy of those early founders of the Society is also visible on our city's landscape today. As a child and a young woman living in north Belfast, up the road from Clifton House, the old Poorhouse, situated as it is on the boundary between the city centre and north Belfast, I was always and still remain struck by its elegance and beauty. The fact that they created such a beautiful building for the poor of the town, one that would truly stand the test of time and would remain one of the city's most important landmarks, is testimony to the foresight and the bold vision of those early members of the Society. Not for them the barrack-like workhouses in which the poor would commonly be confined; rather, they built something that spoke of dignity and pride. In a world in which many words are penned and spoken about equality and respect, surely we must appreciate the way in which Belfast Charitable Society placed real equality to the fore of their planning, developing the city's most beautiful building for its poorest people.

It also speaks of the resilience and sustainability of the Society. As other chapters in this volume demonstrate, the Poorhouse and the Society it represented survived violent rebellions and pandemics, as well as the political upheaval that surrounded the partition of Ireland and Northern Ireland's more recent conflict. Much of this is due to the ability of the Society to future-proof its work in light of changing social, political and economic contexts in order to best meet the needs of the disadvantaged. In contrast to the quite ephemeral nature of philanthropic organisations, charities and initiatives today, Belfast Charitable Society has demonstrated exceptional skill and true belief in social enterprise as well as equality in order to survive. Through a spirit of entrepreneurship, it is still meeting needs in North Belfast and beyond. By keeping itself informed and flexible, it has been able to morph and meet the ever-changing needs of the most vulnerable in society.

The Society has also been characterised throughout its noble history by innovation. From the early fundraising efforts using a lottery to raise the money for the Poorhouse, through social innovation in terms of educating and training the young in industry or engineering innovation in bringing fresh water to Belfast, to developing their building, municipal work and remaining assets-based across the centuries, the Society has always responded in the most effective ways to the needs of the time. In building their Poorhouse, they included an elegant and impressive boardroom to attract the wealthy of the day to support their work. In developing a graveyard, they sold off prominent plots around the edge to raise enough money to bury the poor. Today, they are inspiring conversations around philanthropic giving, and addressing disadvantage and funding major programmes through partnership. One example is the Loan Programme (Building Better Futures fund) which encourages, in a low-risk way, other, smaller community-sector organisations across Northern Ireland to re-examine how they fund the work that they do.

As we survey the needs and responses of our society today in the light of the history of Belfast Charitable Society over its 270 years, hard questions confront all of us who inhabit the prosperous Western world. What does disadvantage look like today? Who has the responsibility to care for those whose lives are just plain tough and mired in difficulties for a lot of reasons? And when those less fortunate seek help or advice or services, can we be sure they are met with the dignity and respect their humanity and human rights demand? For all that we have progressed, men, women, children, whole families, even whole communities can still fall through the cracks. Today, this morning, this week, there are many who are reliant on foodbanks or charities, who have to choose whether to turn on the heat or eat, who work grindingly hard but just cannot make ends meet. Theirs is a special form of misery in a world of plenty, and it would be so easy for them to simply drop from view, to feel disempowered, silenced by circumstance. But thankfully Clifton House continues to lead the way in demonstrating real authority by addressing disadvantage in meaningful, intuitive ways that are about empowering people, helping to infuse momentum, energy, choice and independence into their lives. Mary Ann McCracken and the founders of the Charitable Society would surely approve of its recent move to fund a social supermarket in North Belfast so that people can have opportunities to make their own choices around essential day-to-day needs. As this book so clearly demonstrates, the Society that was founded centuries ago to address disadvantage and to assert a responsible civic conscience continues to do so, with authority and determination, to this day. It can only do so because men and women make its work their business. In every generation that baton of care has been quietly, unobtrusively handed on. Thank you to each and every one of those involved. And thank you to all who have given us this marvellous insight into their inspirational work. *Ad multos annos*!

Introduction

Olwen Purdue

On the evening of 21 January 2021, Belfast Charitable Society hosted an important event to launch the Society's new Mary Ann McCracken Foundation, established to celebrate the life and carry on the legacy of the abolitionist, philanthropist and social reformer after whom it was named. At the launch, Professor David Olusoga, award-winning broadcaster and historian, and leading campaigner on issues of racial inequality in today's Britain, delivered a lecture on the 'Legacies of Slavery' to an audience of over 400 people. For those who might have attended public lectures or been otherwise associated with Clifton House in past times, this event would have seemed strange indeed, for this was a year like no other. Belfast, like much of the world, was caught in the grip of a global pandemic and had entered another period of strict lockdown, and the speaker and audience lectured, watched and participated from their homes via Zoom. Yet, alien as this would have seemed to the founders of Belfast Charitable Society and those historically associated with the Poorhouse, the lecture itself, in its content, the themes it addressed, the passion with which it was delivered and the searing intelligence of its arguments, would have resonated powerfully with those involved with the Society during its early years. The lecture's focus on racial inequalities today contained strong echoes of speeches that would have been made in early nineteenth-century Belfast campaigning for the abolition of the slave trade, while twenty-first-century issues of sexual harassment, highlighted

2 ๙ THE FIRST GREAT CHARITY OF THIS TOWN

by the #metoo movement, and of human trafficking, sweatshops and child labour – slavery in another name – resonate with the concerns of people such as Mary Ann McCracken and many others associated with the Belfast Charitable Society, who worked to address issues of poverty and campaigned for greater rights for women, the reform of prisons, the end of the practice of using small boys to clean chimneys and equal political rights for Irishmen of all religions and none.

The radical tone of Belfast's public and political discourse at the end of the eighteenth and into the nineteenth century may surprise those who associate nineteenth-century Belfast with a conservative, even reactionary, political outlook, but Belfast during this period was at the heart of reformist thinking in Ireland. It was, as Jonathan Jeffrey Wright puts it, 'a hotbed of advanced political sentiment'.[1] Much of this political thought emanated from the town's mercantile and professional classes who took a leading role in public life, occupying the vacuum left by the local landowning aristocratic family, the Donegalls. Although early nineteenth-century Belfast was 'universally acknowledged to belong to the Donegalls',[2] the family remained largely absentee, resulting in a dearth of the urban gentry class that would normally connect the rural aristocracy with the town's middling sorts.[3] As W.H. Crawford writes, late eighteenth-century Belfast had 'very few town-gentry but substantial numbers of leisured folk of independent means'.[4] These, along with its merchants, proprietors and public figures, constituted a self-confident body of people, mainly Presbyterians, who, shaped by a combination of Ulster Presbyterian theological radicalism, Scottish Enlightenment ideas and the influence of the American revolution, increasingly challenged the hegemony of the Irish Protestant Ascendancy that prevented both Protestant Dissenters and Catholics from fully engaging in the country's institutions of state.[5]

These radical ideas saw their earliest manifestation in the development of Volunteer activity. Originally raised by Ireland's landed gentry as a local militia to protect the country from invasion, some Volunteer companies, inspired by revolutionary events across the Atlantic, quickly turned their attention to campaigning against the subservient position the Irish parliament held in relation to Westminster, and for free trade between Ireland and Britain. Much of this activity centred around Belfast, with one observer declaring that 'Belfast was a perfect Boston'.[6] S.J. Connolly writes that by 1779 'there were three Volunteer companies in the town. In 1780 and again in 1781 Belfast hosted a major provincial review, when corps from all over Ulster attended to march, fire their cannon, stage mock battles and engage in political debate'.[7] By the end of the century, and inspired by another revolution, this time in France, some of Belfast's leading intellectuals and political activists were openly advocating more extreme action. The fall of the Bastille in revolutionary France was celebrated by parades, a public banquet and an address that denounced the injustice and 'ruinous inequality' of the present political system in Ireland. This, as Connolly argues, was the early manifestation of the move towards militancy in the town that would, disastrously, result in open armed rebellion in 1798.[8]

The liberal ideals of late eighteenth- and early nineteenth-century Belfast's mercantile, professional and industrial classes were not just manifest in their engagement in political activism, but also in civic life. As R.J. Morris has shown, Britain's urban and industrial growth during this period was accompanied by the rapid growth of voluntary societies and improvement bodies, which were dominated by the middle classes, focused on civic improvement through relief of the poor, medical relief, improvements in public health and public order, and the fostering of intellectual and cultural life. They operated very much apart from central government, taking upon themselves the responsibility for improving the public, moral and civic life of their town.[9] Belfast at this time was no exception. It was, as J.R.R. Adams has argued, a reading town, one in which its dominant Presbyterian population, in particular, tended to be highly literate and engaged in intellectual life.[10] Its rising middle classes actively embraced and fostered this associational culture, engaging in philanthropic work such as opening schools or small hospitals for the town's poorer classes, establishing learned societies such as the Belfast Reading Society (later the Belfast Society for Promoting Knowledge) and Belfast Academical Institution, founding the Linen Hall Library and sitting on an ever-expanding number of municipal bodies that included the Chamber of Commerce, the Ballast Corporation and the Police Board. Their involvement in the growth of cultural and intellectual life, and the rapid expansion of societies designed to further scientific and literary interests led to Belfast being dubbed the 'Athens of the north', while their contribution to key bodies connected with Belfast's commercial growth was, as Alice Johnson writes, fundamental to 'forging both commercial success and a new and powerful community spirit'.[11]

Belfast's economic character was also undergoing a significant change as its traditional role as a market town exporting agricultural produce, beer and spirits became superseded by its role as a rapidly expanding industrial centre. The last decade of the eighteenth century saw the establishment of rope factories, sugar refineries, foundries and, most importantly for the town's subsequent growth, cotton factories.[12] This industrial expansion attracted inward migration, and the town's population, which had remained fairly stable until the middle years of the eighteenth century, began its rapid expansion, growing from 8,000 in 1757 to 13,000 in 1782 and 20,000 by 1800.[13] This, of course, was just the early stages of the exponential growth that would see the then city's population reach just shy of 350,000 by the time the census was taken in 1901.[14]

With population growth came increasing problems of overcrowding and disease. The fifth earl (later first marquis) of Donegall, on coming of age, had taken an unexpected interest in the appearance of his town and begun a major project of urban improvements, which included the granting of new long leases on the provision that uniform and visually attractive buildings be constructed on them, the expansion of the town beyond its existing limits, the erection of a new parish church of St Anne's and the building of imposing new Exchange and Assembly Rooms at the end of what was named Donegall Street. In spite of this, the reality for most of Belfast's inhabitants remained substandard housing, inadequate sanitation and no water.[15] For all its aspirations to elegance, therefore, Belfast at the end of the eighteenth century would, in Connolly's words, have seemed to a visitor 'noisy, smelly, and still visibly under construction'.[16] R.W.M. Strain relates the expressed horror of one visitor to the town in 1780, who declared, 'But Oh! Cleanliness, Celestial Maid! What was my surprise at beholding piles of dunghills made up through the middle of the whole town from one end to the other'.[17]

This period also saw an increase in both the extent and level of poverty in the town, exacerbated by the growing number of mendicant poor coming into Belfast in the hope of support. High levels of extreme poverty were common in pre-Famine Ireland, as the limited nature of industrial activity outside Belfast and its hinterland placed intense pressure on the land. Harvest failures caused famine, social dislocation and disease, and drove rural labourers into towns in search of food and shelter. Localised slumps in domestic textile production, the only real manufacturing activity outside the cities, left artisans and their families destitute, swelling the numbers who had to resort to begging.[18] But this increase in mobility among the poorer classes was not confined to Belfast or Ireland; rather it was part of a more general shift in Western society at this time. As D.L. Jones writes of late eighteenth-century Massachusetts, where towns were experiencing an increased mendicancy among the poor and increased economic migration among a diverse section of the population, this was a period of social change, a time of flux in which 'structural change, social values, and personal behavior fluctuated amidst the demands of passage from the more simple, face-to-face society of the seventeenth century'.[19]

The mobility of the poor was a major cause of concern for urban elites and civic authorities, representing what they perceived as a threat to the physical and moral well-being of the town. Mendicants coming into towns and cities were thought to carry disease, and they were highly visible on the streets, both of which issues undermined the civic pride of burgeoning towns. As Ciarán McCabe points out, Irish towns 'were regularly described as being "infested" with "swarms" of mendicants and the use of such language affirmed the widespread association of mendicancy with disease'.[20] The absence, in Ireland, of any form of statutory relief greatly exacerbated the problems of destitution and mendicancy, throwing a largely impoverished rural population on the mercy of charity and encouraging the movement of the homeless poor into towns, where they believed that charity might be more readily found. McCabe quotes Belfast Presbyterian minister Rev. Henry Cooke, who declared in 1814 that 'To every commercial town there is a great influx of strangers and their families, seeking employment. When calamity overtakes them, they have no friend to whom they can look for comfort or relief'.[21]

This, then, was the context within which Belfast Charitable Society was established and in which it developed. Belfast was a rapidly expanding town experiencing industrial and economic growth but also the flip side of such growth: overcrowding, poverty, destitution and disease. It was a proud town, led by a self-assured, confident middle-class coterie who sought to improve its prospects by enhancing its infrastructure, to improve themselves through literary and scientific endeavour, and to improve those less fortunate than themselves through the provision of welfare, healthcare and education. It was a politically vibrant town in which many of those involved in its cultural and philanthropic endeavours were also active in its political life. It was also, as are all urban spaces, a town of contradictions. While much of the philanthropic activity of the period was inspired by an altruistic desire to improve the lot of the unfortunate, it was also driven by a desire for increased economic productivity and civic pride; while some embraced the ideas of the Enlightenment and espoused freedom, equality and justice, others sought to protect the economic and political advantages they enjoyed, even at the expense of others. It was a rapidly expanding and industrialising town, yet one in which the rural was still very much present; it was a provincial Irish town, and yet was connected globally through networks of trade across and beyond the British empire, connections that added a diverse transient element to its population via its port. It was a town in which a small number thrived and many struggled to survive. With all these contradictions, however, by the time the Belfast Charitable Society opened its Poorhouse in 1774, the town had, in Raymond Gillespie's words, 'a clear sense of itself'.[22] There was a well-defined social order, one that had 'a sense of its civic duty to deal with the poor and maintain law and order'.[23] In the context of the rapidly growing town of Belfast, this was no mean task.

The Poorhouse, and the Society that established and managed it, were at the heart of that social order and would do much to provide the foundations from which the late Victorian city of Belfast would emerge. Established in 1752 with the purpose of raising funds to build a poorhouse and hospital for the poor of Belfast, the Society would go on to take on increasing responsibility for a range of matters relating to health, welfare and public order. The small group of Belfast residents who met in the George Inn on 28 August 1752 to discuss the idea of raising funds to establish a poorhouse in the town could never have imagined the changes that poorhouse would witness over the next three centuries, the city that would grow up around it, or the role their nascent Society would increasingly play in that city. Their plans undoubtedly got off to a shaky start – the original scheme to sell tickets for a lottery in order to raise the necessary funds proved to be a failure, while their request to the fifth earl of Donegall, then still a minor, for the grant of a piece of land on which to build a poorhouse was met with resistance.[24] Eventually, however, the funds were raised and a meeting of the 'Belfast Charitable Scheme', held on 17 January 1767, resolved to apply the funds to the building of the poorhouse. Mr Saurin, Anglican vicar of Belfast and a member of the Board, was charged with approaching the earl, who had now attained his majority, with a request for the necessary land and to convey the opinion of the Board that 'the Ground on the North West side of the Road leading to Carrickfergus fronting the New Street is the most convenient Place for erecting the intended Buildings, and where they will be most ornamental to the Town of Belfast'.[25] The land was granted, the foundation stone was laid on 1 August 1771 and the Poorhouse and infirmary opened for the reception of the poor and sick of Belfast in 1774. From there, Belfast Charitable Society would go on to take responsibility for badging and providing for the deserving poor, i.e., those 'found unable to support themselves by Labour', and for restraining from begging the undeserving, i.e., those 'found able to support themselves'.[26]

The Society's remit would gradually expand, taking on responsibility for many of the issues normally dealt with by municipal authorities, including the development of medical provision in the town, new provision for the burial of the dead and the supply of fresh water to parts of the town. It provided outdoor relief for the infirm and, in an effort to remove children from the streets and prepare them for work in the industrial town, it opened a school with a focus on vocational training and developed an apprenticeship scheme for some of the town's poorest children. The Society, and its Poorhouse, would survive divisions over the great issues of slavery and abolition and the United Irish rebellion that could have split it asunder in its formative years. It survived cholera epidemics and the Great Famine, the partition of Ireland and two world wars. It saw Belfast grow from a medium-sized town into Ireland's largest city and an industrial powerhouse at the heart of empire, before it retreated to its position as the regional capital of a devolved state. Today,

Clifton House continues to grace Belfast's urban landscape, and Belfast Charitable Society to pursue its mission to 'promote, protect and enhance the philanthropic heritage of the Society through the direct intervention and collaborative working for the benefit of the community'.[27]

This book seeks to do two things. First of all, it aims to provide a new history of the Belfast Charitable Society, bringing fresh perspectives on those who were associated with it and on the vital and multifaceted role it played in dealing with social issues in the growing town of Belfast. Secondly, it seeks to set the work of this institution within the wider context of urban poverty, welfare and public health provision in late eighteenth- and early nineteenth-century Ireland, exploring the challenges that accompanied urban growth, and the voluntary and official responses to those challenges of which the Society represented an important part. For many years the 1961 history of the Belfast Charitable Society, written by Belfast physician and Society Board member Dr R.W.M. Strain, remained the only reference point for those interested in its rich past.[28] This was followed in 2002 by Jonathan Bardon's official history, commissioned by the Society to mark its 250th anniversary.[29] Rich in detail and full of information as these works are, a scholarly examination of the work of the Society and its place in the wider context of welfare, education, healthcare and public order provision, as well as associational culture and voluntarism, in urban Ireland has yet to be developed. This is reflective of a more widespread tardiness in the development of Ireland's social and urban history compared to elsewhere, particularly Britain, where a very rich vein of scholarship exists in these fields. Scholars working on the history of late eighteenth- and early nineteenth-century Ireland have, naturally enough, tended to focus on the dramatic political developments of those years with the result that, until recently, the experiences of those who struggled to get by along with the development and experience of welfare and healthcare have been largely overlooked.

This is now being addressed and the field of Irish social history has seen rapid growth over the past two decades. Research on the workhouse system established by the 1838 Irish Poor Law, for example, has provided a rich seam of work that uncovers how different groups of welfare recipients engaged with and experienced welfare and healthcare in post-Famine Ireland.[30] The experience of poverty and charity beyond statutory provision is also being addressed through work such as that of Ciarán McCabe on begging and vagrancy in pre-Famine Ireland, or of Maria Luddy, Alison Jordan and others on charity and philanthropy in nineteenth-century Ireland.[31] The history of disease, public health and medical provision in Ireland is the subject of a rapidly growing and rich body of research;[32] meanwhile, scholars are increasingly turning their attention to subaltern groups such as women, children or the aged.[33]

The history of Belfast has also experienced increased scholarly attention over the past two decades, part of a growing interest in the Irish urban experience. Writing in 1986, Mary E. Daly observed that, up to that point, Irish urban history had been sadly neglected. Again, this was a result of the tendency of Irish historians to focus on the political struggles of the past but also because of Ireland's overwhelmingly rural character, which meant the urban experience tended to get overlooked. Since then, however, historical scholarship has shown a very promising change of direction, with a succession of significant works on Ireland's urban past. Jacinta Prunty's important study of Dublin's slums provided the first in-depth analysis of urban poverty and living conditions in Ireland;[34] meanwhile, a number of studies have focused on the impacts of the Great Famine on Irish towns and cities.[35] S.J. Connolly's 2012 edited volume, *Belfast 400: People, Place and History*, and David Dickson's 2014 monograph, *Dublin: The Making of a Capital City*, represent a major step forward in understanding the urban development of Ireland's two leading cities, while a number of other Irish towns have also received scholarly attention over the past two decades.[36] The urban and social history of Belfast is now beginning to attract more detailed scholarly attention, with interest turning to issues such as associational culture, social class, governance, poverty and welfare.[37]

This book contributes to this growing body of scholarship by exploring the role of Belfast's oldest remaining philanthropic organisation in the social, cultural and political life of the emerging city and placing this within a wider discussion of urban growth in Belfast and Ireland as a whole. It opens with a contextual chapter that sets out the legislative context for the establishment and subsequent development of the Poorhouse, taking us through the successive pieces of legislation that have shaped Belfast Charitable Society through the centuries and formed it into the organisation it is today. Of these, the most significant is surely that of 1774, which incorporated the 'President and Assistants of the Belfast Charitable Society' as the body responsible for the upkeep of the poor, the licensing of begging – with power to seize, detain and punish strolling vagrants, beggars and prostitutes – and for the supply of fresh water to the town, which would be formalised in 1800 when they were established as the water authority for the town. Through this, the Society took on the same role for Belfast as the corporations that had been established for cities and county towns across Ireland under a parliamentary act of 1772, therefore assuming significant authority and responsibility.

The two chapters that follow focus our attention on some of the people most closely associated with the Society in its formative years, and on some of the pressing issues and debates in which they were immersed. They remind us of the turbulent political context of late eighteenth- and early nineteenth-century Belfast, and of the extent to which many members of the Society were immersed in these debates, and they demonstrate the extent to which Belfast was connected globally through networks of ideas, travel, trade and, of course, slavery. Kenneth L. Dawson, whose biography of Samuel Neilson uncovers the politically tempestuous world of Belfast during the United Irish rebellion, provides here a valuable analysis of the political allegiances of those connected with Belfast Charitable Society during this period.[38] Importantly, this chapter reveals the diversity of opinion that existed within the Society regarding the pressing political debates of the day and highlights the resilience of the Society in coming through this turbulent period intact. The chapter that follows likewise explores the complex relationship of Belfast and its Charitable Society with a highly contentious and pressing political issue that connected the Atlantic world, that of slavery. It demonstrates the close interest the people of Belfast had in the issue, its institutions benefitting from its connections with the trade in enslaved peoples, while the town was simultaneously a hub of fierce anti-slavery and abolitionist activism. In uncovering the story of William John Brown, an escaped slave from New Orleans whose body ended up interred in Belfast Charitable Society's New Burial Ground on Clifton Street, the chapter explores Belfast as a site of encounter between those who debated slavery and those who experienced it. Jonathan Wright shows us Belfast through the eyes of Brown and other slaves who ended up in the town and reveals the extent to which the people of Belfast at this time would have been very familiar with the harsh reality of the slave's experience.

From locating Belfast Charitable Society and its early members within the political and physical spaces of the late eighteenth- and early nineteenth-century town, the volume turns its attention to the core function of the Society, which was the relief of poverty. As was the case in many countries throughout the West, the growth of towns and 'modernisation' of society during the latter decades of the eighteenth century, combined with successive agrarian crises, brought challenges in terms of large migratory populations moving from town to town in search of work or support in the form of alms. Faced with growing numbers of transient populations, many of whom were very visible on the streets, town authorities were compelled to act to address the growing social problem. Raymond Gillespie's chapter introduces us to the growing problem of poverty in eighteenth-century Belfast, particularly in the wake of successive harvest crises mid-century, and explores the impulses that drove some of its leading citizens to establish an institution for the relief of the poor. Highlighting the important influence of voluntarism and civic responsibility, particularly in the absence of traditional urban leaders in the form of an active parish vestry or local aristocracy, Gillespie locates the establishment of a poorhouse as part of a 'reimagining' of Belfast at this point in time. Both in terms of the democratic principles on which it was founded and the elegance of its construction, Belfast Charitable Society's new Poorhouse embodied a forward-looking Belfast based on the civic values and sense of duty on which the town's elite prided themselves. The chapter that follows examines the various ways in which Belfast Charitable Society sought to relieve poverty beyond the walls of the Poorhouse. Drawing on individual cases who sought and received outdoor relief from 1774 onwards, this chapter demonstrates the nature of poverty in the town, the factors that drove people to seek relief and the various strategies for survival adopted by those in desperate need. It also reveals the diverse ways in which the Society sought to address their needs: in keeping with the spirit of this period, it demonstrated an openness to consider individual cases on their own merit or need, something that stood in sharp contrast with the approach that would be taken by the Irish Poor Law when it was introduced in 1838. Ciarán McCabe's chapter takes the discussion forward into the early nineteenth century and sets the ongoing development of the work of Belfast Charitable Society into the wider landscape of middle-class charity in the town. It also demonstrates the shifting landscape of need in Belfast. As the town's population grew, so did the needs of its 'deserving poor' – those who lived by labour but for a range of reasons could no longer fend for themselves. It highlights the flexibility with which some of the town's charities and civic elites responded to this changing landscape of need, a flexibility that ensured the Poorhouse, unlike many of Belfast's voluntary charities, survived the introduction of the Poor Law in 1838.

A theme that runs through many of the contributions to this volume is the concern of middle-class philanthropy to 'make the working man like me'.[39] This is particularly evident in the chapter on children in the Poorhouse, in which Lauren Smyth explores the various ways in which the role of the Society changed in response to growing pressures of child poverty and industrial growth in nineteenth-century Belfast. Through the membership of its board, and its wider network of support within the town, the Society was closely connected with the network of middle-class industrialists that dominated Belfast's economic, social and political life. Thus, they were not just aware of the growing problem of poor and vagrant children becoming increasingly visible on the streets of the town but saw a need to improve the standards, and the moral values, of the town's labouring classes and enhance the skills of the future labour force. As this chapter shows, the women associated with the Society were particularly efficient in this regard through their work on the ladies' committee. This involvement of middle-class women in voluntary charitable work would expand rapidly over the century; however, it would not be until the very end of the nineteenth century that women were given access to a formal role in welfare provision as guardians under the Poor Law.

Robyn Atcheson shifts the focus of the volume to public health, exploring the significant role of the Belfast Charitable Society in the development of medical welfare and public health. As an industrial town experiencing rapid population growth, Belfast had more than its fair share of public health issues. High levels of inward migration put pressure on sanitation, housing and water supplies, while outbreaks of diseases such as typhus and several cholera epidemics resulted in high levels of mortality. Belfast, like most of the country, lacked adequate structures for the care of the sick, particularly those who could not afford to pay for treatment; the opening of the Poorhouse infirmary represented the first provision for the sick poor in the town and would remain the only form of medical relief available for many years, only gradually being supplemented by the establishment of a fever hospital and dispensary, district lunatic asylum and lying-in hospital. This chapter reveals the extent to which the Belfast Charitable Society was integrated into this emerging landscape of medical and welfare provision, not least through the associational culture of which its board members were a part. In the absence of an overarching public health authority in the town throughout the early part of the nineteenth century, this close co-operation between the main providers would prove to be of vital importance during times of crisis.

From the care for the living, the volume turns its attention to the burial of the dead and the development of Belfast Charitable Society's cemetery on Clifton Street. In 1797, Belfast Charitable Society made the decision to open a new graveyard on a plot of land behind the Poorhouse in an effort to relieve pressure on the existing burial grounds in the town. This space would continue to receive the remains of Belfast's dead for almost 200 years, and all of humanity would be represented there, from some of the most prominent of Belfast's citizens, its religious and civic leaders, through to unnamed paupers and illegitimate infants, victims of cholera and typhus, 'strangers' and suicide victims. In this space, death really was the great leveller. In keeping with the approach of this volume as a whole, this chapter positions the cemetery in the wider landscape of burial in Belfast and brings valuable new perspectives by highlighting its innovative nature as one of the very new landscaped suburban secular cemeteries to emerge in European and North American towns in the late eighteenth century. In its egalitarianism and its civic, rather than religious, nature, the burial ground embodied the enlightened ideas that shaped Belfast's civic elites during this period. In its architecture, as befitting the aims of Belfast Charitable Society and its vision of its place in the growing town, the cemetery was to be at once ornamental and organised, and in its layout it promoted the most up-to-date ideas around public health. As

John Ó Neill argues, this space truly reflected 'Belfast's radical zeitgeist of the 1790s'.[40]

Gerard MacAtasney and Christine Kinealey then take the volume forward to the mid-years of the nineteenth century, examining the impact that the Great Famine of 1845–9 had on Belfast and its welfare institutions. As their chapter demonstrates, the severity of the Famine was not successfully averted by industrial Belfast, as was often imagined, but rather had a devastating impact on its population and on the institutions that sought to relieve destitution and disease in the town. The recently opened Union workhouse, established under the Irish Poor Law of 1838, was particularly badly affected as people, often carrying disease, poured into the towns in search of work, food or medical relief. As other chapters have indicated, the multiple and fragmented nature of the institutions that made up the welfare and public health landscape of the nineteenth-century town often hindered the kind of co-ordinated efforts that the crisis brought on by the Famine demanded. As Atcheson has shown in her chapter, however, Belfast's previous public health crises highlighted the need for a co-ordinating body of medical experts, and so a board of health was once more established in the town. This facilitated a more organised approach to the crisis, enabling institutions such as the Charitable Society's Poorhouse, the general hospital or the emergency fever hospital to share resources. As the numbers of deaths in the town soared in 1847, finding burial space became a major issue. Belfast Charitable Society had no choice but to allow the general hospital to bury those who had died of smallpox and dysentery in their cemetery, despite the fact that it was almost full, and subsequently to open the graves of those buried during the cholera epidemic of 1832–3. The extent of the public health crisis in the town was revealed in the fact that Belfast Charitable Society forbade its inmates from leaving the Poorhouse, something that feels less strange to modern readers than it otherwise might, due to the parallels with our own experiences almost 200 years later.

As the volume draws to a close, Cathryn McWilliams turns our attention to one of the key figures associated with the work and social milieu of Belfast Charitable Society, Mary Ann McCracken, exploring her relationship with the Society and with the town that changed so dramatically over the ninety-six years of her life. Drawing extensively on McCracken's correspondence, the chapter traces her journeys around Belfast in relation to two key spaces which held meaning for her – those associated with the United Irish rebellion that led to her brother being publicly hanged, and the streets she walked for many years in her tireless work for the Belfast Charitable Society. It also provides some fascinating insights into how McCracken viewed the changing town in her twilight years. While it reveals her deep disappointment at the demise of the anti-slavery movement and the fact that 'Belfast, once so celebrated for its love of liberty is now so sunk in the love of filthy lucre',[41] it also reveals the deep pride McCracken had in her town, particularly in the attention that was being paid to improvements in public health and the welfare of its poorest classes, something to which she, herself, had dedicated her life.

The volume concludes with a look at the work that has been carried out by Belfast Charitable Society over the past three decades, a period which has seen, as the authors indicate, a time of change comparable to that experienced by the Society in the opening decades of its existence. The Society is now operating in the context of the large and vibrant city of Belfast, devolved capital of Northern Ireland and home to over 634,000 people. These decades have seen the final throes of a thirty-year conflict, and the hope and promise – and the slow outworking – of a peace process. It has seen the city emerge as a tourist hotspot, as cheap flights bring people to explore what is surely the UK's most exotic city, while the thousand plus cruise ships that have docked in Belfast harbour over the past twenty-five years have brought upwards of 350,000 international tourists annually into the city. The past few decades have seen a diversification of Belfast's population, and while the number of people from minority ethnic groups living in the city remains low, their proportion of the overall population is growing. These decades have also seen the continued struggle of people to get by on a day-to-day basis due to issues of unemployment, in-work poverty, life-cycle challenges, disability or ill health. In all of this, the Belfast Charitable Society has continued to support the communities that live around Clifton House and across the city. As it has always done, the Society has had to adapt and change to meet the challenges of a new era. New challenges will continue to arise; even as this volume is being written, Belfast is struggling to address issues relating to Brexit and to recover from the impact of a global pandemic. Through all the changes that this city has seen, and will see, however, Belfast Charitable Society continues to make an important contribution to its civic life, and its Poorhouse remains one of the finest buildings to adorn its urban landscape.

CHAPTER ONE

Belfast Charitable Society and Legislation: From College Green to Westminster to Stormont

Ronnie Weatherup

⅋

The Belfast Charitable Society was incorporated on 1 June 1774 by an act of the old Irish Parliament.[1] The effect of incorporation was to grant to the Society the powers that had already been granted by parliament in 1772 to corporations formed in the counties, cities and county towns in Ireland for 'the relief of the poor and for punishing vagabonds and sturdy beggars'. These powers had not applied to Belfast as it was then a borough and not a city or county town.[2] The 1772 Act required the building of hospitals to be called workhouses or houses of industry for the relief of the poor, when sufficient funds were available. A system of 'badging' was applied so that the 'helpless poor' were issued with a badge and licensed to beg. Powers of arrest and detention were granted to secure the punishment of those regarded as vagabonds and sturdy beggars.

The general approach of the legislature appears from the recitals that introduced the 1772 Act. Having noted that 'strolling beggars are very numerous', the twin objectives were, first of all, to give assistance to the poor who had been disabled by age or infirmity and to enable them to earn a living and, secondly, to restrain and punish those able to support themselves by labour and industry but who chose to live in idleness by begging. It was considered to be just to call upon the humane and affluent to contribute to the support of those who were regarded as the real objects of charity. The view of the legislators is apparent. Those considered to be deserving of support were described as the truly needy, the helpless poor, real objects of charity, those unable to earn a living. Those considered to be deserving of punishment were described as choosing to be idle, sturdy but preferring begging to working, vagabonds who put a burden on local charity by strolling from one area to another.[3]

This was the first occasion that the Irish parliament made direct provision for the support of the poor in Ireland. Earlier laws had been passed in Ireland to address begging and to provide houses of correction in larger urban areas, but those laws had been aimed at providing a deterrent rather than providing support for the poor. These earlier laws were repealed by the 1772 Act.[4]

Belfast was a small town that relied on voluntary charitable action to develop an institution that would provide support for the sick and needy. Lord Donegall, the town's owner, granted four parcels of land in Belfast for the development of a poorhouse and infirmary. The Poorhouse was constructed to the north of the town outside the seventeenth-century ramparts and beyond the North Gate that was situated at the junction of North Street and what is now Royal Avenue. It opened in 1774 and later became known as Clifton House; it remains the home of the Belfast Charitable Society.[5]

As the members of the Society proceeded with the construction of the Poorhouse, it became apparent that statutory powers were required for it to operate effectively. The opportunity came in 1774 when proposals were made for amendments to the 1772 Act. At a meeting of the Society on 4 January 1774 in Belfast Market House, two members were tasked with preparing a draft petition to parliament to be considered by the board at its next meeting.[6] A petition was then presented to the parliament in Dublin seeking the grant of existing statutory powers to the Society.

THE IRISH PARLIAMENT

The parliament met in College Green, Dublin, at Parliament House opposite Trinity College, and contained a House of Commons and a House of Lords on the English model. The House of Commons comprised 300 members, with two members for each of the thirty-two counties, the 109 boroughs (of which Belfast was one), the eight county boroughs and Trinity College Dublin. The House of Lords comprised eighty-five members, of whom twenty-two were the lords spiritual, being the bishops of the Church of Ireland.[7] Ireland had been a kingdom since 1541, when Henry VIII converted the Lordship of Ireland to the Kingdom of Ireland.[8] The ruling executive, which accounted to London rather than Dublin, was the lord lieutenant together with the members of the Irish Privy Council, the King's advisors in Ireland. The management of the business of government was in the hands of the chief secretary, a member of the House of Commons.

The legislative competence of the Irish parliament was subject to Poynings' Law, passed by the Irish parliament sitting in Drogheda in 1494.[9] This made it necessary to secure the approval of the English privy council for the sitting of a parliament in Ireland and for any legislation passed by the Irish parliament.[10] The subordinate nature of the Irish parliament was reinforced by the passing at Westminster of the Declaratory Act 1719.[11] This act provided that the parliament of Great Britain (after the Union of England and Scotland in 1707) could legislate for Ireland and further that the Irish House of Lords did not have any jurisdiction over the courts in Ireland, thereby affirming the final appellate jurisdiction of the House of Lords in London.

Penal laws applied in Ireland in the eighteenth century were intended to promote allegiance to the monarchy and to advance the established Church of Ireland to the disadvantage of Catholics and dissenters who were not eligible to vote or sit in parliament. The majority of Belfast's population were Presbyterians, with less than 10 per cent Catholics and the remaining population mostly Church of Ireland. An oath of supremacy sought to secure the monarch as head of the Church of England and Ireland; an oath of conformity required the taking of communion in the Anglican Church as a condition of public office; an oath of allegiance sought loyalty to the monarch and extended to declarations rejecting Catholic beliefs in transubstantiation, the invoking of saints and the Mass; an oath of abjuration required rejection of the Stuart succession. Some Presbyterians refused the oath of abjuration, not because of support for the Stuarts but rather because it was regarded as a recognition of the subservient nature of Presbyterianism and also because it implied that the Old Pretender was not the son of James II.[12] Rev. Alexander McCracken, great-uncle of Mary Ann and Henry Joy McCracken, the first minister of Lisburn Presbyterian church, refused the oath of abjuration and spent two years in Carrickfergus prison. There were no Roman Catholics or Presbyterians in the Irish parliament in 1774. While the holding of public office required the taking of the sacrament in the Church of Ireland, some Catholics and dissenters had taken the oath of conformity, with no doubt limited degrees of conviction, and some had adopted the Anglican tradition. In any event, the selection of candidates for parliament was tightly controlled.

In the boroughs of Ireland, control lay with the owners. In Belfast, the owners were the Chichester family, who had taken the title Donegall. Sir Arthur Chichester was granted the lands of Belfast in 1603, lands which had previously been owned by the O'Neills of Clandeboye. Chichester was Lord Deputy of Ireland from 1605–16 and he purchased premises in College Green, Dublin, opposite Trinity College, that served as his office and were named Chichester House. The premises were demolished in 1728 to be replaced by Parliament House. With the grant of a charter to Belfast in 1613, the borough was entitled to return two members to the Irish House of Commons. The charter created a town corporation of Belfast comprising a sovereign and twelve burgesses, who were in effect selected by Lord Donegall. In turn, the sovereign and twelve burgesses formed the electorate for the Belfast seats in the Irish parliament.

Many of the religious restraints of the Penal Laws remained in force when the Society was incorporated in 1774, although undoubtedly there had been uneven enforcement which lessened as time passed and greater leniency extended to the Presbyterian population than the Catholic population.

THE ACT OF 1774 INCORPORATING THE BELFAST CHARITABLE SOCIETY

The Society created in Belfast in 1774 was named 'The President and Assistants of the Belfast Charitable Society'. The assistants were the members of the Society. The lands on which the Poorhouse had been built, and which were owned by trustees, were transferred from the trustees to the president and assistants. An important difference between the corporations established in the counties, cities and county towns in Ireland in 1772 and the corporation now established in the borough of Belfast was the means of financial support. While there was provision for voluntary donations, the national scheme was financed by rates applied to property, as fixed by grand juries at the spring assizes each year. On the other hand, the Belfast scheme was to be financed by membership subscriptions and voluntary contributions, although other sources of income were to develop as later legislation was introduced, as outlined later in this chapter.

The 1774 Act provided for additional funding from sermons preached in support of charity in the established Church of Ireland. However, financial support was not limited to that provided by the established Church. While the report of the Society for 1827 recorded that two 'charity sermons', one at the parish of St Anne's and the other at St George's church, had collected some £200 for the Society, it was also noted that other church collections included the First to the Fourth Presbyterian congregations, who had collected some £230. The committee book for 1817 also recorded a charity sermon to be preached in the Catholic chapel.

The legislation also identified the membership of the Belfast Charitable Society. The president was to be the earl of Donegall, who was given the position for life.[13] Arthur Chichester, 5th earl of Donegall, had succeeded to the title in 1757 and was a member of the Irish House of Lords. He was the largest landowner in Ireland and owned not only Belfast but estates in Counties Antrim, Down, Donegal and Wexford. However, he was not resident in Ireland and lived on an English estate in Fisherwick, Staffordshire. He died in 1799.

In addition, eight specific assistants were named. The first was the sovereign of Belfast, James Lewis, the leader of the town's corporation.

Then there were the MPs for Belfast in the Irish parliament, namely George Hamilton and Henry Skeffington.[14] George Hamilton was MP for Belfast from 1768 to 1776 and then took up a judicial appointment as a baron of the exchequer. Henry Skeffington was MP for Belfast from 1768 to 1797 and became the 3rd earl of Masserene on the death of his brother in 1805. It was George Hamilton MP who, on 7 March 1774, introduced the provisions relating to the Society when the amendments to the 1772 Act were passing through the Irish parliament. The established Church was represented by the vicar and church warden of the parish of Belfast, then William Bristow and Waddell Cunningham respectively, whose church was on the site of what is now St George's Church in High Street, Belfast.[15] Bristow was vicar of the parish from 1772 and sovereign of Belfast on several occasions. Cunningham was a wealthy merchant who had business interests extending to America and the Caribbean. Presbyterians had been closely involved in the development of the Society, and three of their ministers were also named in the act as members of the new corporation – James Makay, James Cromby and William Laird – a significant inclusion given that the Anglican parliament failed to accord validity to the marriages performed by Presbyterian ministers until 1782.[16] Makay (or MacKay) was the minister of First Belfast Presbyterian church, which was founded in 1664 in what is now Rosemary Street and rebuilt in 1783; the church, with its magnificent interior, still stands. Crumby (or Crombie) was the assistant minister and, after the death of Makay, the minister of First Presbyterian, and he became the first principal of Belfast Academy when it opened in 1786. Laird was the minister of Third Presbyterian, also located in Rosemary Street and destroyed in the Belfast Blitz in 1941. In addition, although not named in the act, every person who contributed one guinea was an assistant of the Society for the year they contributed and had equal voting rights with the others.

The act did not specify any Roman Catholic clergy as assistants. The first Catholic chapel built in Belfast was St Mary's in Chapel Lane, Belfast, which, like the Poorhouse, was completed in 1774, with Father Hugh O'Donnell as parish priest.[17] However, the Poorhouse admitted all denominations, and the Catholic clergy were involved with the Society, most notably Dr Cornelius Denvir, who was a member of committees of the Society for many years. Dr Denvir was a professor at St Malachy's

College from 1833 and bishop of Down and Connor for thirty years from 1835.[18]

The 1772 Act provided that houses of industry be erected when funds permitted, and the 1774 Act recognised that in Belfast 'a poor house and infirmary' had already been erected. The president and assistants of the Society were granted the same powers in relation to 'the poor and all idle and sturdy beggars' in Belfast as the 1772 Act had granted to the new corporations. The corporations had powers to seize strolling vagrants, unlicensed beggars and strolling prostitutes, detain them in the house and subject them to hard labour and reasonable corporal punishment, which included restraining offenders for significant periods. The houses were to be divided into four parts, one for poor helpless men, one for poor helpless women, one for men who were vagabonds or sturdy beggars able and fit for labour, and one for idle, strolling and disorderly women who were able and fit for labour.

The licensing of begging was to be carried out by the 'badging' of the helpless poor who had resided in the area for one year. The corporations could empower Justices of the Peace (JPs) to grant licences. If a badge was granted to a person with children under ten years who were not apprenticed or provided for, such children could be added to the licence or sent to the town committee for placement in a school or apprenticed if they were over eight years of age. It was an offence to beg without a licence, and the corporations were authorised to appoint persons with powers to arrest beggars without a licence and bring them before a JP. The treatment was severe for those offending. A male over fifteen years old begging without a badge could be committed to the stocks, and persistent offenders tried by jury were liable to imprisonment for up to four months and to public whipping. From 1 December to 1 March, no one could be committed to the stocks after 4 p.m. or at any time after sunset, unless caught in the act after that time. Females were confined by order of a JP rather than placed in the stocks and persistent offenders dealt with as in the case of men.

The 1774 Act also made amendments to the 1772 Act reflecting the experience in Dublin. Certain occupations of 'young and able-bodied persons' were considered to expose them to idleness and vice, namely news crying, cleaning shoes and carrying baskets from the markets. An amendment ensured that licences for such occupations could be granted by the corporation, but otherwise those so engaged were deemed to be idle persons and liable to be committed as vagabonds. The rationale for this approach appears to have been that such persons could be more usefully engaged in labour and that such occupations could be undertaken by persons who were described as 'partly disabled', who would otherwise be taken into the house of industry. There was also an issue in Dublin with 'indirect begging'. This included those who might avoid 'useful labour' by hawking small wares, by which they could not earn a subsistence but would 'excite compassion'. Another amendment provided that unless granted a licence by the corporation as a hawker or peddler, the person was deemed an idle person and liable to be committed as a vagabond.

THE SOCIETY'S RESPONSE TO THE 1774 ACT

The first meeting of the Society after incorporation took place on 5 July 1774 when the assistants named in the act, other than the president and the two MPs, gathered in the Market House. The meeting adjourned to 14 July to enrol as assistants those who contributed one guinea, of whom there were fifty-one attending that meeting. With some later contributions in 1774, the total number of assistants for that first year was sixty-four. At the adjourned meeting a committee was formed to consider the use of the Poorhouse. The committee met at the Market House on 17 September and resolved that twenty-two beds would be fitted for the poor, four double beds in two small rooms in the under storey would be provided for vagrants and sturdy beggars, and seven beds would be sufficient for the sick. The first meeting in the Poorhouse took place on 26 October 1774, at which it was resolved to recruit a steward, a housekeeper, nurse keepers, a porter and a beadle.[19]

In order to establish a sense of the extent and nature of poverty in the town, the committee immediately set about visiting the poor and recording their details. On 11 February 1775, twenty-five people, as approved by the committee, were admitted to the Poorhouse, the sick being admitted on the recommendation of a doctor. A month later, at a board meeting on 13 March, a new committee of nine was established to manage the Poorhouse. It was also resolved at this meeting that the

Society would 'receive such poor and sick as shall be judged proper for reception into the house and also such vagabonds as may be brought to it'.[20] As will be explained in a later chapter, there was some uncertainty about the position of children, and the first admissions to the Poorhouse were of adults only. By February 1776, however, the Society had resolved to admit children aged seven to twelve to be educated and supported. The first child admitted was Mary Kirkpatrick, whose father had died and whose mother had gone to England.

A spring on the site provided a water supply for the Poorhouse, but the supply available for the town itself was inadequate. In 1795, the Society obtained from Lord Donegall a lease, for sixty-one years, of lands with springs and fountains that provided a water source for the town. A water committee was formed by the Society and works were undertaken, with the laying of wooden pipes to direct water to the residents. Considerable sums were expended by the Society and charges were levied on the recipients of the water. However, as there was no statutory power to raise the water charges against the recipients of the water supply, legislation was required to grant such powers.

THE ACT OF 1800 FOR THE IMPROVEMENT OF BELFAST

In 1800, the Irish parliament passed an act that created commissioners with responsibility for the improvement and policing of the streets of Belfast and granted the powers of a water authority to the Society.[21] The act received the Royal Assent on 1 August 1800 and the next day was the last sitting of a parliament for the island of Ireland. The period from 1774 to 1800 had witnessed tumultuous events in Ireland, from reform to revolution to the Acts of Union of Great Britain and Ireland. While some degree of parliamentary independence had been achieved, the House of Commons was still unrepresentative and the franchise remained limited. In the aftermath of the rebellion of 1798, which impacted on the work of the Society when the military occupied the Poorhouse (they did not vacate the premises until 1802), the union of the kingdom of Ireland and of Great Britain became British government policy. The Acts of Union were passed simultaneously in Great Britain and Ireland, and the United Kingdom came into being on 1 January 1801.[22] With the creation of the

UK, all legislative activity concerning Ireland was now carried out at Westminster.

The bill that became the 1800 Act was proposed by Edward May, MP for Belfast, and William John Skeffington, MP for Antrim.[23] When the 1st marquis of Donegall had died in 1799, he was succeeded as president of the Society by the 2nd marquis, George Chichester, who remained president until his death in 1844.[24] As a young man in England, Chichester lived well beyond his substantial means, and his father disinherited him to the extent that family settlements allowed. Edward May, born in County Waterford and operating as a moneylender in London, lent money to Chichester to help meet his creditors' demands, and in 1795 Chichester married Anna, May's daughter. To avoid his creditors, Chichester moved his family to Belfast in 1802, where he continued to reside until his death. Edward May became an MP for Belfast in January 1800, just in time for the last session of the Irish parliament, which commenced on 15 January 1800; after the Union he remained the sole MP for Belfast until his death in 1814.

The 1800 Act recited that Belfast was a very populous market town and borough, which had greatly increased in buildings, inhabitants, commerce and wealth. The population at that stage was around 19,000. The problem addressed by the act was that the streets were 'extremely ill paved and ill lighted and the passengers are much incommoded by encroachments, obstructions, nuisances and annoyances'. The act adopted a two-tier approach. First of all, it established police commissioners, who were the sovereign and twelve burgesses of Belfast, along with twelve other named individuals, with responsibility for carrying out improvements to the town. The use of the word 'police', however, conveyed wider civic functions than would apply today. Any vacancy that arose in the commissioners, other than the sovereign or burgesses, was to result in the sovereign calling an election by those inhabitants of the town paying £1 in rates. To qualify to be a commissioner, a man had to be a householder and resident in the town for the previous twelve months, and he or his wife had to have property with a value of £100 per annum or personal assets worth £2,000 or be an MP, the heir to a peer or a lord of parliament.

A police committee of between nine and twenty-one members was also established, the membership of which was to be elected by those inhabitants of the town paying £1 in rates in an election called by the vicar or the curate of the parish of Belfast, in vestry. The inhabitants of a parish had civic as well as ecclesiastical duties, which were exercised at meetings in the vestry of the parish church. Members of the established Church voted on church matters in special vestry, and all inhabitants, including non-members of the established Church, voted on civic matters in general vestry. To qualify for election, the candidate required property valued at £1,000. The role of the committee was to assist the commissioners and to superintend works of improvement undertaken in the town. In addition, members were to set the rates to be paid for improvements to the town levied on the property owners 'according to substance or ability'. Those members determining the rates were known as 'applotters', and refusal or neglect to make the applotments rendered the member liable to forfeit £10, should self-interest occasion a failure to arrange for a charge to be levied.

The Society was a beneficiary of some of the fines imposed for offences under the act. Under the new legislation it was an offence to interfere with any of the materials used for improvements in the town, and the theft of lamps could result in public whipping or transportation for seven years. One half of the fine for damage to lighting was paid to the Society for the use of the poor, while any pig found wandering in Belfast could be seized or killed and would belong to the Poorhouse for the use and benefit of the poor. The slaughtering of animals without a licence was also subject to a fine, which was paid to the Society for the use and benefit of the poor. Parliament had set a precedent for such support for the Society when, in 1785, an act established a corporation, known as the Ballast Board, for preserving and improving the port and harbour of Belfast. Any surplus funds from the operation of the port and harbour were to be paid to the Society.[25] Although the Ballast Board did not actually generate any surplus, from time to time they did make donations to the Society.

The 1800 Act also required the committee to appoint scavengers and watchmen. Scavengers were men whose job it was to sweep and clean the streets, and they were provided with horses and carts to remove materials collected. The watchmen signalled the beginnings of a police force for Belfast. They were night watchmen only and were given the power to arrest anyone committing offences. They would bring the arrested person to a watch-house before being taken before a magistrate.

The most significant part of the act for the Society, however, was the granting to it of the powers of a water authority for the town. It empowered the Society to receive an annual rent from the owner or occupier of each dwelling house supplied with water, if the annual value of the property was £5 or more. Twelve inhabitants of Belfast, known as pipe water applotters, who were chosen by the inhabitants in vestry, were to fix a rate as a proportion of the value of the property, to a maximum of £2. As to businesses with any 'extraordinary consumption' of water, an agreement could be reached between the Society and the user for the payment of a sum not exceeding £32 2s 6d per annum. The act set out examples of such businesses: brewers, maltsters, distillers, sugar bakers, tanners, skinners, dyers, butchers, slaughterers and innkeepers. The Society was given power to enforce the water rent by warrant of the sovereign or, in his absence, a magistrate, and to seize goods. The Society was to remain the water authority until parliament established the Belfast Water Commissioners in 1840.

It is noteworthy that it was not simply the town corporation that was granted powers in relation to the improvements and policing of the town but rather an extended group that was partially elected by ratepayers. In the same way, it was not the town corporation or the new commissioners who were granted the powers in relation to the provision of water to the town and the charging of water rates but the Society, which had been to the fore in the earlier development of the water supply. The statutory arrangements did not reflect well on the effectiveness of the town corporation.

The final section of the 1800 Act dealt with the old graveyard beside St George's parish church in High Street in Belfast. When the borough of Belfast was established in 1613, the 'corporation' church had been built on the site in High Street, with an adjacent graveyard, but the church fell into disrepair and was replaced on the same site by the present St George's church in 1816. The 1800 Act declared that, with the overflowing sea, which then extended to the lower section of High Street where ships could tie up, the use of the old graveyard had become a public nuisance and no further use was to be made of it.

Later works at St George's resulted in the recovery of what were said by a leading antiquarian, F.J. Bigger, to be the remains of Henry Joy

McCracken, who had been executed after the 1798 rebellion and interred there.[26] From the lands granted to the Society by Lord Donegall prior to 1774, a portion behind Clifton House had been opened as a graveyard in 1797, known as 'The New Burying Ground'. Eventually, in 1909, the remains recovered from the old graveyard were reinterred in the Clifton Street graveyard with those of Henry Joy's sister, Mary Anne, who died in 1866 and was for many years the secretary of the ladies' committee at Clifton House.[27] Clifton Street graveyard is today maintained by Belfast City Council.

In order to carry out the functions allotted to it by the 1800 Act, the Society established a water committee. The work of this committee was, however, beset with difficulties. In summer the water sources were insufficient, and at all times the higher parts of the town were not supplied with water. A search began for additional springs to supply water and sites for a reservoir to retain the water. Delays were caused by objections from occupiers to the course of the piping and by the contamination of the water. The financial position was precarious. There were difficulties with the collection of the water rates. Society funds were used for the works and money was borrowed to support development. But a greater financial return was required and legislation was necessary to achieve that aim.

THE ACT OF 1817 AND THE MANAGEMENT OF WATER

In 1817, amending legislation was passed by the UK parliament granting the Society the power to appoint a board of commissioners to manage the water supply in Belfast and increase the water rate.[28] The population in the town had continued to increase and was by then around 30,000. The legislators stated that 'it is highly expedient that the improved System of furnishing the Inhabitants of large Towns with Water, conducted through Metal Pipes, should be adopted in the said Town of Belfast'.

After the Acts of Union, Ireland returned 100 MPs to the parliament at Westminster, with two members for each of the thirty-two counties and Dublin and Cork cities, and one member for each of the thirty-one boroughs and Trinity College. The members of the Irish House of Lords elected twenty-eight of their number as 'representative peers' to sit in the UK House of Lords, which was also the final court of appeal for Ireland.

Sir Stephen May MP, who had succeeded his father Edward as MP for the borough of Belfast in 1814, introduced the bill that became the 1817 Act.[29]

Under the act, the Society arranged the election of nine water commissioners to manage the waterworks. Most importantly for the Society, the commissioners were to pay it £500 annually for five years and £750 annually thereafter, or such greater sum as the applotters might determine. At a time when Lord Donegall in effect appointed the sovereign and twelve burgesses to the corporation of Belfast, and they in turn appointed the MP for Belfast, the governance arrangements for the water authority are of interest. The president and assistants of the Society were to call a general assembly each year to nominate and appoint, from the inhabitants of Belfast, the nine commissioners. At the general assembly, the clerk of the Society was to draw the names of three of the existing commissioners, who would then cease to be commissioners and be replaced by three other inhabitants nominated by the Society and appointed by ballot. The Society had the power to replace commissioners who refused to act or who died, and also to remove any commissioner. The commissioners were required to report to the general assembly of the Society and to obey its orders and directions. Here was an electorate that included all those who made the annual subscription of one guinea to become an assistant of the Society, who were not required to satisfy any property qualification in order to exercise their vote and who could issue orders and directions to the commissioners. The commissioners thereafter took responsibility for the management of the waterworks, subject to the oversight of the Society.

Those inhabitants of Belfast who were liable to pay £1 or more for water were to elect twelve inhabitants of the town to be spring water applotters for three years. Responsibility for arranging the appointments fell on the vicar or the curate in vestry. The applotters were tasked with ascertaining the annual value of the properties to which water pipes had been laid and determining the amount of the water rate. The maximum rate for any house was increased to £5 per annum, except where 'extraordinary accommodation' was required, in which case a sum was to be agreed between the owner/occupier and the commissioners.

Under the 1817 Act, any water commissioner or spring water applotter who refused or neglected to act was again liable to forfeit £10, payable to the Society. The enforcement measures directed at the vicar or the curate, if they should fail to carry out their duty to arrange the appointment of the spring water applotters, rendered them liable to forfeit up to £50 to the Society, or their goods and chattels were liable to be seized and the proceeds paid to the Society.

Despite the new legislation, difficulties with the water supply continued. The population of the town was increasing rapidly, and the supply of water was still inadequate and sometimes of doubtful quality. Recovery of the water rate was not always assured. In the 1830s a joint committee was established made up of representatives of the town and of the water commissioners and of the Society, seeking expansion of the water supply and further legislation to grant additional powers. However, the committee fell into dispute with the Donegall family, as owners of the relevant lands and for a time the promoters of a rival scheme. Lord Donegall's son, the earl of Belfast, was to the fore in seeking to advance the commercial interests of the family by placing the management of the water supply outside the control of the inhabitants of Belfast and in the hands of a company. At the same time, Lord Donegall remained president of the Society. Delegations were sent to London, representations were made to a parliamentary committee, counsel were engaged. Eventually, however, agreement was reached and responsibility for water was to pass altogether from the Society.[30] Once again the changes required legislation.

A POOR LAW FOR IRELAND AND THE REFORMS OF 1840

The necessary legislative intervention occurred in 1840. The UK parliament had introduced Catholic emancipation in 1829 and parliamentary reform in 1832. Irish representation in the House of Commons increased by five seats to 105 and Belfast acquired a second seat. Boroughs such as Belfast, where the town corporation had once elected the members of parliament, became subject to the franchise for males owning property valued at £10 per annum, the franchise that already applied in the counties.[31]

The year 1840 saw the reform of local government in Ireland. Fifty-eight borough corporations were dissolved and another ten were reformed. Belfast was one of the ten reformed corporations.[32] The first election to the new Belfast Town Council was on 25 October 1842. The sovereign and twelve burgesses previously appointed by Lord Donegall were replaced by an elected mayor, ten aldermen and thirty councillors. The duties of Belfast Town Council included the establishment of a 'Committee on Police Affairs', which took over responsibility for the police force that had developed from the night watchmen.[33]

The legislative changes in 1840 directed at the Society were divided into two acts of parliament. One act granted the Society the power to lease or devise property for ninety-nine years, the previous limit of thirty-one years set down in 1774 having inhibited the income potential of property. This power did not extend to the grounds of the Poorhouse itself.[34] The act contained additional measures relating to subscriptions and voting and the meetings of the Society.

The second act was the Belfast Water Act 1840, which transformed the arrangements for the waterworks of Belfast.[35] The act named eight of the existing elected commissioners and two others as the Belfast water commissioners with responsibility for the waterworks. Accordingly, the Society transferred all property in the waterworks to the Belfast water commissioners in exchange for a payment of £800 per annum and a further £5,000 to discharge certain debts. The Society was also to receive water free of charge and exemption from any rate chargeable under the act. The payments were designed to compensate for the expenditure undertaken by the Society in establishing the system of waterworks for the town. The £800 per annum continues to be paid to the Society.

A potential challenge to the role of the Poorhouse arose from the introduction of the workhouse system in Ireland with the passing of the Poor Relief (Ireland) Act 1838.[36] The act created Poor Law commissioners, Poor Law unions, of which initially there were 130 in Ireland, a 'Board of Guardians' for each union, a workhouse built in each union and a Poor Law rate. Of most concern to the Society was the prospect that all its property would be vested in the Poor Law commissioners. Section 34 of the 1838 Act provided that 'every House of Industry, Workhouse, and Foundling Hospital which has been either wholly or in part supported by Parliamentary Tax, Grant, Grand Jury Aid, or by any compulsory Rate or Contribution ... shall vest in the Poor Law Commissioners'. Was the Poorhouse a workhouse or house of industry that was 'in part supported ... by any compulsory Rate or Contribution'? If that were the case, the assets of the Society would pass to the Poor Law commissioners under section 34. While the Society received subscriptions and voluntary donations, indirect public funding might be said to have arisen from the receipt of fines imposed under the 1800 Act and of forfeits imposed under the 1817 Act and the provision for profits from the Ballast Board under the 1785 Act. The Society also received the annual payment of £750 from the water commissioners under the 1817 Act, although the payments were seen by the Society as a return on prior investment in the water supply.

At a special meeting of the Society on 10 February 1838, a petition to parliament was drafted seeking the insertion of a clause to protect the property of the Society. Writing on 5 March 1838 to the chief secretary, Lord Morpeth, the Society sought the express exclusion of the Poorhouse from the Poor Law Bill.[37] There was to be no clause in the act that excluded the Society, and its position remained uncertain when section 34 of the 1838 Act came into force. A draft amendment to exclude the Society had been prepared but did not survive consideration by a committee of the House of Commons. The Society sought counsel's opinion as to the impact of the 1838 Act on the Poorhouse, and the minutes of the board meeting of 14 February 1839 record the opinion that the Society was not affected by the 1838 Act.[38] This opinion was furnished by William Curry, MP for Armagh, and Richard Warren, who both held the position of serjeant.[39] A serjeant was a barrister who, while in private practice, was retained as a legal representative for the government. The office of serjeant ceased to exist in Ireland, north and south, after partition.

However, the introduction of the Poor Law system was not without impact on the Society. A workhouse was constructed in Belfast on what is now part of the site of the Belfast City Hospital and opened in 1841 with a capacity for 1,000 people.[40] Contributions to the Society fell and its services had to be reduced. The returns for 1839 show a total of 486 residents in the Poorhouse, of whom 238 were adults and 248 were children. With the introduction of the Poor Law workhouse scheme, the Society sought to reduce the number accommodated and its outgoings, and in 1845, at the commencement of the Famine, the total accommodated in Clifton House had reduced to 191, 110 adults and 81 children.[41]

There was also a diminution in the role of the Donegall family in the town. A loss of parliamentary control followed the Great Reform

Act of 1832, and loss of municipal control followed the reform of local government in 1840. In addition, there was diminished control of tenants with the increase in the grant of long leases, and a reduction in the scale of the Donegall estate with the sale of land by the 3rd marquis of Donegall to pay the debts of his father on his death in 1844.[42]

It would be a century and a half before there was any further legislative intervention on behalf of the Society. In 1879, when the population of Belfast had reached 210,000, and with additional requirements being imposed and alternative provision becoming available for children, it was resolved by the Society that it should provide 'solely for the aged and infirm', and the final provision for children within Clifton House was in 1882.

BELFAST CHARITABLE SOCIETY ACT 1996

The Belfast Charitable Society Act 1996 was passed at Westminster to modernise the objects, powers, constitution and management of the Society.[43] The Society continues as a body corporate as established in 1774 and continues to hold the formal title of 'The President and Assistants of the Belfast Charitable Society'. The objects of the Society today are to engage in and encourage charitable activity for the benefit of the disadvantaged. It has wide-ranging powers and may do all that is necessary to achieve its objects, but as a charitable organisation it is subject to the regulation of the Charity Commission for Northern Ireland. The membership of the Society comprises the officers, the board and other members elected by the Board of Management of the Society in accordance with regulations adopted by the Society.

The 1996 Act provides that any future amendment of the legislation may be made by order of the Northern Ireland Department of Health upon the application of the Society. The act also provides that an order made by the Department of Health shall be laid before the Northern Ireland Assembly, and if the Assembly resolves that the order should be annulled, it becomes void. No such application or order has been made.

The parliamentary landscape was transformed with the partition of Ireland. In Northern Ireland certain powers transferred to the devolved institutions at Stormont, with other powers reserved to Westminster.

While the 1996 Act was passed at Westminster, any further legislation concerning the Society has been moved to the devolved institutions.

The five phases of parliamentary activity in relation to the Belfast Charitable Society reflect five different legislative arrangements applicable in Ireland over the last 250 years. The 1774 Act was passed by an Irish parliament at College Green that was constrained by the Great Britain Privy Council and Parliament. The 1800 Act was passed during the limited degree of legislative independence from 1782 to the Acts of Union. The 1817 Act was passed at Westminster prior to Catholic emancipation in 1829 and the reform of the franchise by the Great Reform Act 1832. The 1840 Acts were passed at Westminster by the increased electorate achieved by the extended franchise. Not until the 1996 Act was legislation concerning the Society passed by a parliament elected under a universal franchise. The 1996 Act also concerns devolved powers to Stormont, with future legislative intervention to be undertaken by a devolved government department, subject to the approval of the devolved assembly.

CHAPTER TWO

A House Divided:
The Belfast Charitable Society
in the Age of Revolution

Kenneth L. Dawson

⅋

The weekly committee meeting of the Belfast Charitable Society on Saturday 17 December 1791 was brought to order by Gilbert McIlveen junior, who had assumed the chair for the sparsely attended session. Also present were Robert Stevenson, the physician whose contribution to the workings of the Poorhouse over many years was inestimable, and Thomas Milliken, a prominent Belfast merchant. Samuel Neilson, who owned the Irish Woollen Warehouse in Waring Street, was also in attendance and he was accompanied by a visitor to the town, Olaudah Equiano, the former slave whose *Interesting Narrative* detailed his early life, capture, servitude and eventual liberation.[1] Equiano had arrived in Ireland in May, and his stay in Belfast was spent at the Neilson home, selling copies of his book from Thomas Mullan's shop on the quay and at local booksellers. The evangelical content of Equiano's *Interesting Narrative* would certainly have struck a chord in the mainly Presbyterian town. Equiano noted that 'I found the people extremely hospitable, particularly in Belfast, where I took my passage on board of a vessel for Clyde, on the 29th of January

[1792].' We know little of the detail of his stay in Belfast, but Equiano must have been fully aware of the support shown there by political reformers in July 1791 for the campaign to abolish the slave trade.[2] Five years earlier, the watchmaker and cotton manufacturer Thomas McCabe had publicly scuppered plans by the wealthy merchant Waddell Cunningham to establish a slave trading company in Belfast. At a meeting in the town's Exchange in 1786, McCabe had proclaimed, 'May G[od] eternally damn the soul of the man who subscribes the first guinea.'[3] Like Neilson, McCabe was associated with the work of the Belfast Charitable Society, serving on its committee during the time in which he was trading in Belfast.

The involvement of many of the town's radical citizens in the Society's affairs during the politically explosive final decades of the eighteenth century is, at first glance, suggestive of an institution with a particular 'world view', while the success of Equiano's book sales – and his visit to the Poorhouse – confirm a progressive tendency in the town.[4] This was not always the case, however, as enlightened views often competed with more conservative positions among Belfast's most influential citizens.

SUBSCRIPTION DEMOCRATS

The assertion of colonial nationalist aspirations in the North American colonies in the 1770s provided an opportunity for constitutional grievances in Ireland to be aired, while the events in Paris from 1789 introduced terms such as 'democracy' and 'republicanism' into a new political lexicon, especially among those who railed against the exclusive nature of the Protestant Ascendancy and the unrepresentative composition of the Irish parliament in Dublin. This chapter seeks to consider the 'Age of Revolution' in Belfast through the lens of the Charitable Society, just one of the many improvement bodies established at this time of significant demographic growth and economic transformation.

In political terms, Belfast was a corporation borough, its two MPs being selected by the town sovereign and twelve burgesses. This level of disenfranchisement bred a lingering resentment, and an emerging Presbyterian bourgeoisie sought ways to develop a participative role. In his pioneering study of English urban voluntary associations, R.J. Morris explored how middle-class professionals were able to achieve their social and political goals outside formalised governmental authority. Belfast was no exception to this trend, as affluent, socially responsible entrepreneurs and professionals established themselves as improvers of society.[5] Civic pride was evidenced by the raising of subscriptions to pay for the construction of the White Linen Hall in 1783, the same year as the formation of the Belfast Chamber of Commerce. An outward-looking town, Belfast emulated Dublin, Glasgow, Edinburgh and Liverpool in establishing vehicles for social improvement. The Reading Society, founded in 1788, became the Belfast Society for Promoting Knowledge, with the town's intelligentsia providing additional funds for an organisation originally set up by – in their own words – 'worthy plebians [sic]'.[6] Wealthy and influential members of Belfast's urban elite such as Robert Callwell, Rev. William Bruce, Dr Alexander Haliday, Waddell Cunningham and Narcissus Batt later assumed leadership of the society. These men were among the members of many interlocking associations that focused on mutual economic benefit, public education, philanthropy and, as events elsewhere unfolded, political advancement.

Support for the Belfast Academy, which opened in 1785 as a school for the children of the town's aspirant population, was provided by wealthy subscribers such as Cunningham, his wife's brother-in-law Thomas Greg, Haliday, John Brown of Peter's Hill, the banker Charles Ranken, William Sinclaire, the brothers Robert and William Simms and the printer William Magee.[7] Educating the children of those poorer families unable to access the Academy was also a priority for the circle of affluent improvers. Plans for the establishment of a Sunday school for the instruction of working children originated in the town's Amicable Society in January 1786, and it opened in March with over 100 children receiving instruction 'under the patronage of the benevolent inhabitants of the town'.[8] Of course, such bourgeois endeavours were not entirely altruistic, as summed up by the *Belfast Evening Post*'s editorial in June: 'If these institutions should become established throughout the kingdom, in all probability they will produce a happy change in the morals of the vulgar, and make the execution of criminal justice less necessary.'[9]

A similar outlook can be seen in the deliberations of the Belfast Charitable Society, with subscribers looking for solutions to the problems associated with urbanisation. From the opening of the Poorhouse in 1774, governance was provided by a general board, consisting of subscribers who met quarterly to address items of business before devolving responsibility to a committee which gathered weekly and was refreshed regularly by the replacement of three of its members. The Society's president was the marquis of Donegall, with the town sovereign fulfilling the more active role of vice-president. Discussions centred on the employment and conduct of staff, the provision of coal and food for those forced into indoor relief, actioning medical help for those taking refuge in the Poorhouse, the education of children, ruling on eligibility for relief and raising the finances needed to run an organisation that required the collective administrative know-how of Belfast's nascent urban elite. The minutes of both the general board and the committee are revealing in showing the creative responses to the challenges faced as well as giving an insight into the personalities and dispositions of those who emerged as social leaders despite the political disabilities imposed by the Ascendancy and the restricted franchise in the borough.

The early proceedings of the Belfast Charitable Society reveal the civic leadership offered by personalities such as Rev. William Bristow (the town's sovereign on eleven occasions), Henry and Robert Joy (owners of a paper mill in the Cromac district and sons of Francis Joy, the founder of the *Belfast News-Letter*), Waddell Cunningham, Dr William Drennan, Stewart Banks, Samuel McTier, John Galt Smith and Samuel Hyde (Cunningham's father-in-law). Raising finances was the single greatest challenge for the Society. Subscribers were obliged to pay one guinea annually, with a number contributing significantly more than this.[10] Wealthy merchants like Cunningham provided oatmeal 'of excellent quality at a moderate price', and donations helped to manage the growing cost of providing support for those in the Poorhouse and those receiving relief out of doors.[11] Private donations and bequests were essential, and the Society was grateful to benefactors such as the Right Honourable John O'Neill (then member of parliament for Randalstown), who contributed £20 in 1778. Significant donations were received from Robert Hyde and a Mrs Clark of Castle Street.[12] Generous bequests were left to the Society by some of its greatest advocates: the merchant and banker William Brown left the Society £300 in his will, Thomas Greg £50, Rev. James Hamilton £50 and Waddell Cunningham £200.[13] Charity sermons, society balls and theatre performances added much-needed funds to cover the expenses of the Poorhouse. The Belfast Charitable Society accounts for 1785–6, for example, reveal that two balls held during the Volunteer review of that year contributed £33, while a performance by the celebrated actress Mrs Siddons raised £94 for the Society's work.[14]

Despite these sterling efforts, the vast costs of administering the Poorhouse, infirmary and the poor on out-relief were far in excess of the income received by the general board. Victualling expenses alone in 1785–6 amounted to £470, and the costs of medicines, coal, clothing and outdoor relief had still to be taken into account.[15] The Society's treasurer at this time, John Galt Smith, had advanced his own money and was owed £174.[16] The collective imagination of Belfast's business elite was required to sustain the Poorhouse, especially after the Society embraced the great responsibility for supplying the town with water.

At various stages, the committee attributed its economic shortfall to the increase in the number of strolling beggars, which made potential supporters of the Poorhouse disinclined to subscribe. Its chairman, Samuel Neilson, considered it necessary to 'badge' some of the poor of the town and parish to convince wealthy citizens of the need to donate. Indeed, Neilson's *Northern Star* later congratulated the Society for taking up the idea of confining or expelling strolling beggars. The paper also noted the 'shameful reflection' on the town that so many of the wealthy did not subscribe to the Society. An editorial suggested that publishing a shaming list of non-subscribers to the Society might, in fact, lead to an increase in the funding required to address the problems of a growing town.[17] In a later editorial, Neilson commented that while there had been loud and sustained protests about the number of 'idle and strolling vagrants who infested this town', their removal from the streets – and the increase of out-relief – had addressed the complaint. An 'immediate and liberal subscription' was the only way in which begging would be stopped.[18]

Neilson resigned as treasurer of the Charitable Society in the spring of 1792. His United Irish activities and the editorship of the *Northern Star* were undoubtedly significant factors in his decision, but so, too, was a frustration with the lack of generosity shown by some towards the objective of providing relief. As a Presbyterian who saw himself as championing the right of Catholics to political representation, Neilson was critical of the fact that so few of the town's Catholic population contributed to the running of the Poorhouse. At a meeting of the Charitable Society committee in March 1791, it was decided that Robert Stevenson and James Munfoad would be deputed 'to work on some of the respectable Roman Catholics of this town in order to know why their congregation contribute nothing to the society and to inform them that we make no distinction of Religions in our distributions'.[19]

ATLANTIC REVOLUTION

The political backdrop to the Society's operation during the last three decades of the eighteenth century was spectacular. The grievances of the American colonists against English rule revealed political and economic parallels with Ireland. The small patriot opposition in the Dublin parliament, with Henry Grattan as its leading advocate, was sympathetic to the American cause, just as Whigs in Westminster railed against the policies of Lord North's Tory government. Ulster Presbyterians, while loyal to the King, attested to the justness of the colonists' cause and admired the bold stance taken by those of Irish origin, many of them their co-religionists, in the fight against British rule. French entry into the American War of Independence on the American side in 1778, combined with the reduction in the numbers of troops garrisoned in Ireland, prompted the formation of Volunteer units across the island to protect its shores against an expected French landing now that France had entered the war on the side of the colonists. These Volunteer companies were particularly prevalent in Ulster, and while many such bodies were officered by gentry, the first company was formed in Belfast on St Patrick's Day 1778 and led by many of the business and professional class, who, having sampled positions of civic responsibility, now demonstrated leadership in a new and exciting sphere.[20]

The Volunteers were fiercely independent in make-up, and membership appealed to those who could purchase weapons, devote time to meeting and drilling, and afford the ceremonial uniforms that were a statement of respectability. As the threat of invasion receded, Volunteer companies threw their support behind the minority in the

Irish parliament which called for the removal of punitive restrictions on trade and a greater degree of independence from Westminster for the legislature on College Green. Political muscle was in evidence at the Ulster Volunteer Convention in Dungannon in February 1782, at which a series of resolutions confirmed armed – but respectable – support for the patriot position, and even a tentative endorsement of the gradual relaxation of the Penal Laws.

In Belfast, volunteering was another vehicle for the involvement of respectable Presbyterians in a participative role. Many Volunteers were active in the Charitable Society, and committee members included leading Volunteer figures such as Dr William Drennan, Thomas McCabe, David Tomb, Samuel McTier and Hugh Crawford. Volunteer reviews in Belfast saw the Poorhouse being used to accommodate visiting companies. Before the July review in 1781, the billeting committee requested that twelve loads of oaten straw be laid on the grounds as bedding. Lord Glerawly and his battalion were accommodated within the building itself at a cost of five guineas.[21] A ball was held every night during the review and 400 tickets were printed for these occasions, with proceeds going to the Poorhouse.[22] The following year, Volunteer delegates at the St Patrick's Day celebration in Belfast presented Henry Joy with the sum of £52 for the Poorhouse, and John Crawford sought permission for the Bangor Volunteers to be billeted there during the Belfast Review in July.[23]

As the emergency ended with the end of the American War of Independence in 1783 and the decade progressed, the Volunteers became less formidable, with many of their patriot allies in College Green fearing the consequences of calls for a reform of parliament and internal divisions becoming apparent over the Catholic question. Despite the progressive *Belfast Mercury*'s valiant efforts to convey the continuing relevance of the Volunteers, the numbers of companies and members declined, and Irish politics entered a period of quiescence.[24] That is not to say that the desire for reform had been extinguished completely. The parliamentary election of 1783 had witnessed the success in Lisburn of the independent interest, with William Sharman and William Todd Jones defeating the candidates sponsored by Lord Hertford. Many of Belfast's reformers backed their campaigns and were enrolled in the Constitution Club of Lisburn.

Waddell Cunningham's address to the electors of Lisburn stressed the need for Ireland to be emancipated through 'an equal representation of the people'. The fifty-four inhabitants of Belfast who endorsed this address included many who were attached to the Charitable Society.[25] Cunningham himself was elected to a vacant seat in Carrickfergus in 1784 and took his place for a short time in the Irish parliament before being removed by a petition lodged by the defeated establishment candidate, citing the undue influence of the Constitution Club in the election. In the ensuing poll, Cunningham was defeated by Ezekiel Davys Wilson, whose candidacy was supported by the powerful combined influence of the Lords Hillsborough and Donegall.[26]

Beyond politics, the Charitable Society's general board and committee continued with its activities as before, facing the inevitable challenges of balancing the books and maintaining its good work, both within the Poorhouse and among the impoverished of the town. The continued philanthropic response by the merchant class to the growing pains of industrialisation was reinforced by the involvement of younger men in the work of the Society such as Samuel Neilson, his brother Thomas, Robert and William Simms, William Sinclaire, William Tennent, Gilbert McIlveen junior, Francis McCracken and James Hyndman. All the above were later distinguished by their membership of the Society of United Irishmen.[27]

The outbreak of the French Revolution in 1789 disrupted Ireland's relative political tranquillity, as the ecclesiastical and aristocratic orthodoxies of the *ancien regime* were challenged by the aspirations of the Third Estate. Edmund Burke's skilful invective against this assault upon the established order in his *Reflections on the Revolution in France* and Thomas Paine's powerful rejoinder in *The Rights of Man* saw the battle lines drawn in a pamphlet war about a revolutionary upheaval that, in the words of the young Dublin barrister Theobald Wolfe Tone, 'became the test of every man's political creed'.[28] Nowhere was this more evident than in Ireland. Calls from within a section of the Anglican elite for a revision of the Anglo-Irish relationship and from many Volunteers for an end to the Ascendancy's monopoly of power had generally been frustrated by fears that parliamentary reform, coupled with the extension of Catholic rights, would lead to a wholesale change in the character of Irish politics, something that would alarm as many reformers as it would inspire. Events in Paris, however, challenged the prejudices that existed about equipping Irish Catholics with political citizenship. In his influential pamphlet, *An Argument on Behalf of the Catholics of Ireland*, Tone argued persuasively that by embracing liberty French Catholics had shown that they were not emasculated by the teachings of their Church. Granting the elective franchise would be a panacea for the Irish body politic by creating a representative legislature, a cordial union of Irishmen capable of defying English profligacy and an end to the corruption that characterised the Dublin parliament and executive. 'In a word,' he said, 'we shall recover our rank, and become a nation in something beside the name.'[29]

As an Irish interpreter of the French Revolution, Tone was writing for a northern audience, for he recognised the progressive nature of many Protestant reformers, especially among those Ulster Presbyterians politicised by volunteering and energised by their civic participation, business acumen and philanthropy. They were, however, theologically critical of Catholic teaching and suspicious of Jacobitism. Tone's *Argument* challenged these traditional prejudices. In the words of Kevin Whelan, it 'released this sectarian gridlock on Irish politics, hitherto immobilised by the intransigent Protestant conviction that Catholics were inherently *incapaces libertatis*.'[30] Tone's new-found celebrity in Belfast dovetailed with William Drennan's notion of a secret society, 'a benevolent conspiracy – a plot for the people – no Whig Club – no party title – the Brotherhood its name – the rights of man and the greatest happiness of the greatest number its end – its general end, real independence to Ireland and republicanism its particular purpose.'[31] But it was the Belfast merchant Samuel Neilson, the co-ordinator of a small and confidential group of radical Belfast Volunteers, whose practical and organisational abilities were required to distil these ideas into something tangible: the Society of United Irishmen, founded in Belfast in October 1791.[32] The Dublin society was formed the following month. Meanwhile, the Belfast pioneers established the *Northern Star* newspaper to propagate their cause, with Neilson becoming the editor and leading shareholder.

On 23 January 1792, fifty-three prominent inhabitants of Belfast published a request for a town meeting to discuss petitioning parliament on the Catholic question. The United Irish influence was obvious:

> As MEN and as IRISHMEN, we have long lamented the degrading state of slavery and oppression in which the great majority of our Countrymen, the ROMAN CATHOLICS, are held – nor have we lamented it in silence – we wish to see all distinctions on account of Religion abolished – all narrow, partial maxims of policy done away – we anxiously wait to see the day when every Irishman shall be a Citizen – when CATHOLICS and PROTESTANTS, equally interested in their country's welfare, possessing Equal Freedom and Equal Privileges, shall be cordially UNITED, and shall learn to look upon each other as BRETHREN, the Children of the same God, the Natives of the same land.[33]

Of these signatories, at least twenty-nine were active in the Belfast Charitable Society, either attending meetings of the general board or as active members of its committee.[34] Of course, this is not to say that guardians of the Poorhouse were all United Irishmen.

The deliberations of this, one of the largest meetings ever held in the town, were presided over by the minister of the Third Presbyterian church in Rosemary Lane, Rev. Sinclare Kelburn, who was sympathetic to the United Irishmen. Members of his congregation included the United Irishmen Robert Simms, Henry Joy McCracken and Neilson. It soon became apparent, however, that not all of those in attendance agreed with the sentiments of the resolution that Catholics were in a 'degraded situation' and that all restrictive legislation must be repealed. Also present in the Town House were those who, while proclaiming themselves as reformers – and many of them were members of Volunteer companies – felt that the motion was premature and argued for a more gradualist approach. Dr Alexander Haliday, one of the town's most distinguished personalities, who was present at the inaugural meeting of the Charitable Society's general board on 5 July 1774, opined that:

> He had a high regard for the Roman Catholics, that he had always looked upon the penal code as an abominable system that he

wished to see entirely abolished, that however as to their admission to the elective franchise, he thought they were not prepared for it, they must be farther enlightened and less under the dominion of the priesthood, ere that step ought to be taken.

His friend, Rev. Dr William Bruce, the minister of the First Presbyterian church also in Rosemary Lane, used the meeting to attack the United Irishmen and their attempt to coerce the gathering, prompting an angry response from Neilson and Samuel McTier.[35]

The resolutions were passed, but not without the significant opposition of those who remained to be convinced by the arguments set out by Tone in his pamphlet and were concerned by the bold exhortations of the United Irishmen. An advertisement was placed in the *Belfast News-Letter* by those who dissented from the final resolutions, proclaiming that rather than the immediate enfranchisement of Catholics, such a measure must be 'from time to time and as speedily as the circumstances of the country, and the general welfare of the whole kingdom will permit'. Among the many moderates who put their name to this statement of clarification were prominent subscribers to the Charitable Society, including Rev. Bristow, Haliday, Revs Bruce and Vance (minister of the Second Presbyterian church), Waddell Cunningham, Henry Joy, Narcissus Batt, John Ashmore, Robert Holmes, Dr Robert Apsley (one of the physicians associated with the Poorhouse), George Black, John Galt Smith, Robert Bradshaw, Samuel Hyde, Robert Stevenson, Charles Brett and Francis Turnley.[36]

Just as Belfast's prominent citizens were divided in their approach to the Catholic question, these divisions were replicated among the membership of the Charitable Society. To their credit, these members were able to rise above the differences in political outlook to concentrate on the best interests of the poor. The revival of the Volunteers in the period after 1789 and the obvious similarities between some units with the French National Guard were, however, bound to create a degree of tension within the ranks. At a committee meeting of the Society, attended by Volunteer members Samuel McTier and Thomas Neilson (brother of Samuel), it was resolved that the chairman 'do in the most respectful manner inform the commanding officer of each of the Volunteer corps in town that they should desist from exercising in the Poorhouse green'.

The reason for this was to prevent the 'mob' accompanying the armed citizenry from damaging the hedges 'so necessary to keep the poor of the House from stroling [*sic*] through the town'.[37]

In Belfast, the more radical sections of the Volunteers aligned with the United Irishmen. With a review planned to coincide with the third anniversary of the fall of the Bastille approaching, the fault lines across the town's urban elite, exposed during the January town meeting, again came into focus. The United Irishman and committee member of the Charitable Society, Gilbert McIlveen Jr, was appointed secretary to the group responsible for planning the review. In terms of the review and its choreography, the wording of the political resolutions threatened to dampen the festivities. Drennan and Tone had prepared addresses to the French National Assembly and the people of Ireland respectively. Tone's recent appointment as agent and assistant secretary to the Catholic Committee had rendered him suspicious to those Volunteers of a more gradualist persuasion on the Catholic issue. Consequently, his address was quite deliberately moderate to avoid public shows of dissension during the festivities. In the early hours of 14 July 1792, Tone, in Belfast for the review, was awakened by Neilson who told him that he had heard Waddell Cunningham attempting to persuade provincial Volunteer leaders in a local inn against immediate Catholic emancipation. Neilson had burst into the packed room to admonish him, quite a spectacle since Cunningham was the commanding officer of Neilson's Volunteer regiment (the First Volunteer Company). Tone's account of the incident and his assessment of Cunningham, 'a lying old scoundrel', is indicative of the divisions within the Belfast Volunteers, the business community and – more particularly – those closely associated with the Poorhouse.[38] After the procession, both resolutions were carried at a meeting in the White Linen Hall, although Henry Joy junior, editor of the *News-Letter*, had proposed an alternative resolution to the one written by Tone, believing that it implied that emancipation was desired immediately, something for which they were not yet prepared. The *Northern Star*, in its summary of Joy's case, stated, 'He thought that members of that community were by no means capable of liberty, and therefore thought it rash and dangerous to emancipate them at present, though he hoped to see the day when it could be done with safety.'[39]

It is, perhaps, too tempting to view the United Irishmen in terms of an initial constitutional phase followed by a militant and republican one. While the outbreak of war with France in 1793, subsequent government repression and the frustrations felt by the absence of meaningful reform accelerated the move towards rebellion, there existed a strand within the society's Belfast leadership which was not pushed into such a strategy against its will. On the other hand, some United Irish figures who were zealous in the cause during the early 1790s began to retreat from militancy as the rebellion came closely into view. During this momentous decade, those of both viewpoints were able to set aside differences to work together in looking after the town's poorer residents, as were those subscribers to the Charitable Society who were downright hostile to the United Irishmen and their designs. The minutes of both the general board and the Poorhouse committee offer no clues to the political dynamics of the 1790s (there are no extant committee minutes for the 1794–98 period); however, it is possible to identify advocates of the three broad positions among those who held responsibility for the Society's administration during that decade.

THE REPUBLICANS

Samuel Neilson's influence was critical in the formation, development and revolutionary preparations of the United Irishmen. On top of his business interests and his consuming role as editor of the *Northern Star*, he was instrumental in forging the alliance with the Catholic Defenders and, despite his imprisonment between September 1796 and February 1798, continued his revolutionary activities as part of Lord Edward Fitzgerald's entourage while the rebellion was being planned in the spring of 1798. Before his arrest, he had been treasurer of the Belfast Charitable Society (1790–2) and had served on the committee tasked with investigating the best means by which to provide Belfast with a fresh water supply.[40] Another leading radical in Belfast was Henry Joy McCracken, whose father, Captain John McCracken, and brother, Frank, served as members of the Belfast Charitable Society's committee at various times. His sister, Mary Ann, was perhaps the most remarkable individual associated with the Poorhouse during its long history. Henry Joy McCracken worked closely with Neilson as Belfast republicans moved towards the idea of rebellion and he, too, was imprisoned in Dublin. Upon his release, he continued to prepare for the insurrection, and he seized control of the military committee before leading the United Irishmen at the Battle of Antrim on 7 June 1798. There is no direct evidence that McCracken was himself deeply involved in the running of the Poorhouse, but his name appeared on the list of those present at a committee meeting held on 29 December 1792.[41]

McCracken replaced Robert Simms at the head of the United Irish military structure on the eve of the rebellion. Robert Simms and his brother William were typical of the merchants who contributed much to the development of the town of Belfast. They owned a flour mill in Crumlin and a paper mill at Ballyclare. A prominent Volunteer, Robert was also a foundation member of the Belfast Chamber of Commerce in 1783, an organiser of the Belfast Harpers' Festival in 1792 and one of those who joined the Belfast Society for Promoting Knowledge. He attended the original meetings of the United Irishmen in October 1791 and was one of those responsible for establishing the *Northern Star*.[42] After Neilson's arrest in September 1796, Robert and William Simms took on responsibility for publishing the *Star* and were themselves arrested and imprisoned for a time after an attack on the newspaper's premises in February 1797. According to Samuel Orr, brother of the celebrated United Irish martyr William Orr, Robert Simms was one of a dozen figures present at a meeting held in the home of the Belfast merchant William Tennent towards the end of that year at which Simms agreed to serve as the commander of the rebel army in County Antrim.[43] Simms' resignation on 1 June 1798 was most likely because he was reluctant to take to the field without a successful French landing and also because his wife was expecting their third child.[44] Like his brother, this radical United Irishman had been a loyal and staunch supporter of the Poorhouse, serving on the committee as a nineteen-year-old in 1782–3 and being the treasurer for the funds required for the non-resident poor from April 1793, as well as attending meetings of the general board.[45]

Another great advocate of the Poorhouse with impeccable United Irish connections was William Tennent, one of the most fascinating figures in Belfast's history in the 1790s and during the post-Union period.

His life and legacy have been detailed expertly in recent times by Jonathan Wright.[46] A partner in the New Sugar House in Waring Street during the 1790s, he was another foundation member of the Chamber of Commerce and was later present at the inaugural meeting of the United Irishmen. One of the early proprietors of the *Northern Star*, Tennent's considerable wealth was a significant United Irish resource. One well-placed source within the United Irishmen stated that Tennent had supplied a large sum of money to bribe the gaoler at Carrickfergus (unsuccessfully as it turned out) to permit the escape of William Orr in 1797.[47] Belfast's postmaster, Thomas Whinnery, was convinced that Tennent kept important seditious papers upstairs in the sugarhouse. Another hostile source alleged that he was attempting to smuggle a Corporal Burke, a deserter from the Limerick Militia who had been involved in the murder of suspected informers, out of Belfast before his arrest.[48] Whinnery was well known to Tennent, and both men had attended meetings of the Charitable Society's general board between 1796 and 1798. Tennent was arrested on 6 June 1798, on a charge of aiding and assisting the rebellion, but evidence was hard to come by and no one was prepared to testify.[49] He refused to take up the offer of banishment and was sent on board the prison tender, the *Postlethwaite*, where he suffered a broken leg. Tennent was then imprisoned in Fort George, where he was reunited with Neilson and Robert Simms. Upon his release in 1801, he resumed his business and civic interests and enjoyed considerable wealth and success in the years before his death in 1832.

Originally from the district of Limavady, the leading United Irishman Henry Haslett was recorded as an early member of the Belfast First Volunteer Company. A founder of the Chamber of Commerce, he was in partnership with his brother William in the Belfast Woollen Warehouse in Rosemary Lane. Declared bankrupt in April 1789, he bounced back the following year as a shipping and insurance agent.[50] Haslett served on the Poorhouse committee from 1788–9 and at other times attended meetings of the general board. As a founder of both the United Irishmen and the *Northern Star*, Haslett's name appears regularly in radical resolutions throughout the 1790s, and he was arrested on 16 September 1796 alongside Neilson and Thomas Russell. Conveyed to Kilmainham Gaol in Dublin, Haslett cut an isolated figure and allegedly attacked his fellow inmate, Henry Joy McCracken, with a pan of boiling water. Personal tragedy during this time, which included the deaths of two of his children and his sister, most likely convinced him to retreat from the cause.[51] As rebellion raged in Ulster in June 1798, Haslett was advertising his business interests in the *Belfast News-Letter*. Despite his radical associations and imprisonment, he was elected to a committee to oversee clauses in the Police Act respecting the access to spring water at a meeting of the general board in February 1803.[52]

Two of the Charitable Society's appointed medical superintendents were supporters of the revolutionary conspiracy. Dr John Campbell White was a physician who was a frequent attender at meetings of the general board from 1781 to the period just before the rebellion. He was a strong advocate for Catholic rights in the Belfast meeting in January 1792 and was a United Irishman, being described by General Lake, the commander of the northern district, as one of the 'most notorious rebels in this town'. He went into exile in the United States in 1798 and settled in Baltimore, where he continued practising as a medical doctor, dying in 1847.[53] Richard McClelland was appointed as surgeon and apothecary in the infirmary in 1786 and attended a number of committee meetings in 1792–3. He was present at an early meeting of those Belfast citizens pledging to subscribe to the *Northern Star* and, despite adding his name to the list of those calling for a surrender of the Volunteer cannon on 4 June 1798, he was arrested on the twelfth, alongside an apothecary called John Campbell.[54]

THE CONFLICTED

Just as prominent in the Belfast Charitable Society as the supporters of insurgency was a group that had a clear United Irish affiliation but who retreated from this position as the rebellion approached, probably due to their concerns about the organisation's militant trajectory or perhaps the impact that seditious activity would have on their business interests. The records of the general board and committee reveal the names of leading merchants such as Robert Getty, David Bigger, Gilbert McIlveen Jr, William Sinclaire and Hugh Crawford, all of whom seemingly rejected thoughts of rebellion in favour of demonstrable acts of loyalty. Getty was a successful importer and well-known radical, supporting Catholic emancipation throughout the 1790s. He had also been an active Volunteer from as early as 1784, and while his role – if any – within the United Irishmen is unclear, his name was on a partial list of members of the Jacobin Club (a shadowy group that existed as part of – or alongside – the United Irishmen in Belfast) which landed on the desk of the viceroy, Lord Camden, in 1795.[55] Just days before the rebellion broke out in Ulster, Getty's name was one of 150 attached to an appeal for information on the whereabouts of six Volunteer cannon from the 1780s that were secreted in the vicinity of Belfast (two of the cannon had been kept on Getty's property before their removal on the eve of the rebellion).[56]

Discussions in the town about the creation of a yeomanry company to guard against invasion and revolution generated considerable heat in the period before the outbreak of rebellion, and there was even speculation that United Irish sympathisers were attempting to infiltrate its ranks. A cavalry and infantry were eventually formed, and the town's yeomen performed guard duties at the time of the Battles of Antrim and Ballynahinch. Once the rebellion was over, a number of prominent names 'who are debarred from present service, by inability or indispensable avocations' supported the volunteer [yeomanry] infantry through a subscription fund for members 'as may be reduced to any distress by accident or calamity attending the service'. The names attached included several of those linked to radical politics during the previous decade, including Getty, who contributed £5 15s 9d. Others to subscribe included Sinclaire and McIlveen (founder members of the United Irishmen), William Magee (who was involved in the establishment of the *Northern Star*) and Hugh Crawford, all of whom were frequent attendees at board or committee meetings of the Charitable Society.[57] Getty's retreat from his earlier radicalism may be attributable to fears that a rebellion would be injurious to business. His mentor was the politically moderate entrepreneur John Brown, and he was married to Susanna, daughter of the cotton pioneer Nicholas Grimshaw, whose machinery had been deployed in the Poorhouse in 1779 so that children there could be instructed in the trade under the supervision of Thomas McCabe, Robert Joy and Captain John McCracken.[58]

After the British victory over France's Dutch allies at the Battle of Camperdown in October 1797, several Belfast merchants subscribed to a fund for the wives and children of 'the brave men who fought and fell in the late glorious Action'. It is unsurprising that Waddell Cunningham, Henry Joy, Rev. Bristow, Rev. Bruce and Stewart Banks contributed generously to the fund, but so, too, did others associated with the more radical tendency in Belfast, men like Hugh Crawford and John Tisdall, who, like the former, played leading roles in the workings of the Charitable Society. Crawford's interests were in linen, the flour mill in Crumlin and sugar refining, and he would later be a partner in the Belfast Bank.[59] An active Volunteer, his name generally appeared on resolutions in favour of Catholic emancipation and parliamentary reform. The informer John Hughes, testifying under oath to the Secrecy Committee of the Irish House of Lords on 3 August 1798, named Crawford, Tisdall, Henry Haslett and others as part of the United Irish cell in Belfast two years before. Names were redacted in many published accounts of statements before the Secrecy Committee of the Lords and Commons, but the *News-Letter* printed everything, which no doubt made life uncomfortable for those identified, especially Crawford who had subscribed £11 7s 6d to the yeomanry fund in July.[60] One of Belfast's most civic-minded personalities, Crawford the businessman, Volunteer, member of the Chamber of Commerce and regular attender of meetings of the Charitable Society's general board appeared to be back-pedalling, as were others whose radical credentials were well established. Included in this list was McIlveen, who attended nearly every weekly meeting of the Poorhouse committee during 1791–2. McIlveen was one of the original proprietors of the *Northern Star* and was present for the inaugural meeting of the United Irishmen, but by the year of the rebellion he, too, had withdrawn. Indeed, he subscribed £5 to the fund to support the Belfast yeomanry and later contributed to a collection 'On behalf of the brave fellows who have been wounded, and the widows and orphans of those gallant men who have fallen, gloriously fighting for their KING and CONSTITUTION in the actions with the French and Rebels during the late invasion.'[61]

THE LOYAL

Due to the fact that some long-term supporters of the Poorhouse were in prison and others associated with radical politics seemed to be serving some form of penance, the general board between 1796 and 1798 was dominated by figures such as Bruce, Bristow, Stevenson, Whinnery, John Brown, Francis Turnley and others of a loyal disposition. As one of the supplementary yeomen, Bruce stood sentry guard on the Long Bridge as General Nugent and his men made their way into County Down on the morning of 12 June, en route to engage the United Irish army there. Perhaps the most steadfast supporter of the Poorhouse, as both doctor and committee member in the years preceding the rebellion, was Dr Robert Stevenson, who attended meetings with almost religious regularity. In 1798, he too enrolled in the Belfast Supplementary Yeoman Infantry, 'to act as a surgeon', alongside other prominent members of Belfast society, such as the Revs Bruce and Vance, and the postmaster Thomas Whinnery.[62] Whinnery was a valuable government informer, whose communications with his Dublin counterpart, John Lees, helped keep Edward Cooke, the Dublin Castle spymaster, informed of the unfolding conspiracy. Martha McTier was savage in her denunciation of Whinnery, and she warned her brother, William Drennan, of his fondness for opening her mail, 'for to my hand – his fingers have a strong attraction'.[63] His actions were exposed by the *Northern Star*, which published a short poem in late 1796 ('The Postmaster's Discovery or A Plot in a Packet'), which implored readers to:

> Trust not your letter by the post,
> Howe'r secure the seal, Lest *somebody* should open it –
> And you be sent to jail.[64]

Many of these figures had adopted moderate positions on the Catholic question, were horrified by the excesses of the Great Terror in France and were anxious about the republican trajectory of the United Irishmen in the latter part of the 1790s.

Another stalwart of the Charitable Society, Dr James MacDonnell, had been associated with the radical coterie in the town throughout the 1790s, but he too adopted a conservative position in 1798. He contributed to the yeomanry fund, was unaccountably missing after Henry Joy Mc-Cracken's execution in July, when it was hoped that his unviolated body might be resuscitated, and later betrayed his old friend Thomas Russell in 1803 by contributing to a reward fund for his apprehension in the aftermath of Emmet's rebellion. Martha McTier was scathing of MacDonnell, referring to this 'contemptible cold-blooded Judas', while her brother's hastily penned poem, 'Epigram – on the Living', described him as the man 'Whom future history will describe The Brutus of Belfast.'[65]

AFTERMATH

Of significant concern to the members of the Belfast Charitable Society's general board was the fact that the Poorhouse, with its adequate space and proximity to the town, was taken over by the military as a barrack, and in late July 1798 Robert Stevenson was informed by the inspector general of barracks that the Barrack Board was interested in purchasing the property. Given the context, the general board resolved to co-operate and, providing a fair price was received, the building and adjacent land (bar one field on which a new poorhouse and infirmary would be erected) would be put up for sale. It was agreed to let the Poorhouse for one year at a cost of £500, with the government compensating the Society for any damage caused by the military. However, after hearing nothing for several months, they penned a memorial to the viceroy, Lord Cornwallis, to complain about the fact that the poor had been 'most inconveniently lodged' in inadequate alternative accommodation during the emergency. The board demanded that either the Poorhouse and infirmary be returned to them with the necessary reparation of damage or a fair price be offered so that a new building could be erected. In January 1799, an architect was retained to value the Poorhouse and assess the cost of an alternative. General Thomas Goldie, a senior officer stationed in Belfast, informed the board members that the price being sought – £8,000 – was considered too high, and by 26 January they had reduced this to £6,000 together with a rental charge of £500 per annum to cover the length of the requisition.[66] On 4 March, the governors were informed that the Poorhouse would be returned to them on 1 June, 'there being no further reason for it as a barrack'.[67] This was good news for the general board, which was a body dominated more than ever by the more cautious element within the town's urban elite, men who had sided with the government at a time of rebellion and invasion but who were, at heart, moderate reformers rather than reactionaries.

The convulsions of the 1798 rebellion were felt loud and long in Belfast, even though so few of the urban elite were involved in 'the turnout'. Erstwhile United Irishmen took a step back, leaving less prominent figures to take to the field at Antrim and Ballynahinch and providing credence for Henry Joy McCracken's acerbic observation in the wake of his defeat at Antrim that 'the rich always betray the poor'.[68] For some of those who had flirted with a more dangerous type of politics, however, rehabilitation was permitted in time. Barely one year on from the rebellion, Hugh Crawford, William Magee, Robert Getty, John Tisdall, David Bigger and Gilbert McIlveen Jr were back attending meetings of the Charitable Society's general board. William Sinclaire was appointed to its committee looking at the water accounts in 1801, the same year that Frank McCracken and Henry Haslett resumed their involvement in this important element of bourgeois governance.

The Charitable Society during the Age of Revolution was administered by a remarkable group of businessmen who were dedicated to social improvement. Its deliberations were focused, proactive and free from rancour, despite the obvious internal political differences that were the product of such a defining period in this island's history. The suppression of the rebellion represented the defeat of a temporary republican minority within Belfast's urban Presbyterian elite. But a peaceful attachment by many – the town's 'natural leaders' – to parliamentary reform and Catholic emancipation continued after the Act of Union, and this liberal mentality was perpetuated well into the nineteenth century in the pages of the *Belfast Monthly Magazine*, the corridors of the newly established Belfast Academical Institution and, of course, in the deliberations of the Charitable Society itself.[69]

CHAPTER THREE

From New Orleans to Clifton Street: Slavery and Freedom in Nineteenth-century Belfast[1]

Jonathan Jeffrey Wright

8O

Early in October 1796, on the Caribbean island of Martinique, the Ulster merchant Samuel Cunningham made his will. Hailing from Killead in County Antrim, Cunningham had departed Ireland for the Caribbean in 1792 and had clearly done well for himself.[2] Indeed, the provisions of his will speak eloquently of his success. In the event of his death, Cunningham's brothers, six in number, each stood to receive 'the sum of One Thousand Pounds sterling of good and Lawful Money', while his two sisters were each promised 500 pounds. His father would receive 200 pounds, his mother 400 pounds and the children of his deceased sister, 'or so many as be living at the time of my Death', were each granted 100 pounds. A further 100 pounds of 'Pin Money' would be paid to 'Madamoiselle [*sic*] Harriet Le Duff, of this Towns [i.e., Saint Pierre in Martinique]', and sums were assigned to a James Campbell, resident in St Vincent, and to the will's executors – that is, Cunningham's father, his uncle (James Barber) and two Belfast merchants, Thomas Brown and John Cunningham (most likely a brother).

Here, then, we have a document in which a successful merchant made generous provision for his family and friends. In this, there is nothing remarkable: Cunningham's family might be said to have possessed a legitimate 'claim' to his largesse. But as he sat in Martinique and contemplated the dispersal of his wealth, Cunningham's thoughts ranged beyond his immediate friends and relations, and he made further provision for those of his home country whose lives had not been so markedly blessed with success. Sums of 200 and 100 pounds respectively were assigned to 'the poor of the Parish of Killead in the County of Antrim' and 'the poor house of Belfast'. Although modest when compared to the generous bequests Cunningham showered upon his siblings, these smaller sums were nevertheless carefully protected: 'should it happen that my Estate is not worth the sum I have will'd by this Testament', he stipulated, 'the deficiencies are to be deducted from the Legacys in Proportion to the sum will'd or left each and the sum deficient except that left my Mother and Madamoiselle [sic] Le Duff, these two are not to be affected by any deficiency, neither the Fifty Pounds left each and every of my Executors nor the £300 left the Poor'.[3] Clearly, Cunningham was determined that the poor should receive their money, and he would have been frustrated had he known that a portion of the 200 pounds intended for the poor of Killead was later used to fund a 'handsome monument' erected in his honour in the graveyard of Killead Presbyterian Church.[4] It appears, however, that the monies assigned to Belfast's Poorhouse were disbursed as intended, and thus, as Nini Rodgers has noted, Cunningham's 'name appears among the benefactors to the poorhouse, publicly displayed on the oak boards which until the 1960s covered the walls of the Charitable Institution'.[5]

Cunningham's bequest highlights neatly the connections and entanglements that bound Belfast and its Charitable Society to the wider Atlantic World of the late eighteenth and early nineteenth centuries, and to the institution of slavery that was so central to the working of that world and its economy. Not simply a philanthropically minded merchant, Cunningham was a merchant active in the sugar islands of the Caribbean, whose property is known to have included 'four slave sailors'.[6] And he was not the only slave owner among the benefactors of the Belfast Charitable Society. In another will dating from 1796, the Belfast merchant Thomas

Greg – co-owner with Waddell Cunningham (likely a relative of Samuel Cunningham) of a Dominican sugar plantation named 'Belfast' – left 'to the Trustees of the Belfast Charitable Society the Sum of fifty pounds Sterling'. In turn, Waddell Cunningham bequeathed 200 pounds to the Belfast Poorhouse in his will of December 1797, though he is better-known today for his unsuccessful attempt to establish a slave-trading company in Belfast in 1784.[7]

There was nothing unique in any of this. The now infamous Bristol slave trader Edward Colston – whose statue was dramatically toppled in June 2020 – was a major philanthropist, albeit a decidedly partial one who, in the words of Kenneth Morgan, 'laid down strict conditions for his public charities'.[8] For such men, slavery and the slave trade were facts of economic life – necessary evils, perhaps, but ultimately defensible. They saw no contradiction in making provision for the needy of their home communities while profiting from the sale and exploitation of enslaved Africans overseas.

Of course, there were others in the eighteenth and early nineteenth centuries who considered slavery to be indefensible and who, recognising its barbarity and inhumanity, campaigned for abolition – first of the slave trade and then, later, of slavery itself. Such figures can also be counted among the ranks of the Belfast Charitable Society's supporters. The obvious and oft-invoked example here is Mary Ann McCracken, an ardent abolitionist and active member, during the period 1827 to 1851, of the Charitable Society's so-called 'Ladies Committee'.[9] But we might also point to Thomas McCabe or Samuel Neilson. Both men were members of the Charitable Society's managing committee and both were opponents of slavery. Indeed, their names feature in two of the best-known episodes in the history of anti-slavery in Belfast: while McCabe is said to have been central to defeating Waddell Cunningham's attempt to establish a slave-trading company in the town in 1784, it was with Neilson that the abolitionist activist Olaudah Equiano boarded when he visited Belfast in 1791 in order to promote his influential abolitionist text, *The Interesting Narrative of the Life of Olaudah Equiano or Gustavus Vassa, the African.* While in Belfast, Equiano sold copies of his narrative, moved in radical political circles (Neilson was a founding member of the United Irishmen) and, on 17 December 1791, attended one of the Belfast Charitable

Society's committee meetings.[10] Thus the society supported by wealthy slave-owning merchants was also the society that welcomed a formerly enslaved man who ranked, by the time of his death in March 1797, as 'the most famous person of African descent in the Atlantic world'.[11] Such were the unsettling complexities brought about by Belfast's connections with slavery.

Some forty years after Equiano visited Belfast, in November 1831, a second individual who had experienced slavery would encounter the Belfast Charitable Society, albeit in a very different way. In the mid-1790s, the society had assigned land at the rear of its Poorhouse for use as a burial ground. Better known today as Clifton Street Cemetery, this so-called New Burial Ground was ready for interments by March 1797 and was initially intended for use by those who had purchased burial plots: as R.W.M. Strain has noted, it 'was opened for the primary purpose of raising money'. However, by April 1799 its remit had expanded. Space was assigned for the burial of the poor as well as the wealthy and, in the decades that followed, the Clifton Street Cemetery provided a final resting place for thousands of Belfast citizens.[12] Included among their number was William John Brown, who was buried in November 1831. By no means a long-established resident, Brown had appeared in Belfast just over a year previously, having arrived as a stowaway, fleeing from slavery in New Orleans.

Until recently, Brown's presence in Belfast and his posthumous encounter with the Belfast Charitable Society has been overlooked.[13] This is hardly surprising, for his archival 'footprint' is faint: a single entry in the register of the New Burial Ground and a few newspaper reports, published in August 1830, are the only sources that offer evidence of his presence in Belfast. Added to this, the avenues of enquiry that might be expected to have uncovered and shed light on Brown's story – those concerning Belfast's relationship with slavery and the presence of people of African descent in Ireland – remain somewhat undeveloped. To be sure, important studies have been produced on anti-slavery in Belfast, and scholars such as Nini Rodgers, Norman Gamble and Thomas Truxes have highlighted the city's links, both direct and indirect, with slavery, and identified Belfast slave owners.[14] Nevertheless, much remains to be uncovered – not least concerning the ways in which slavery was encountered in Belfast. Likewise, while W.A. Hart established the presence of an African community in eighteenth-century Ireland some twenty years ago, little comparable work has appeared, though Mark Doyle's recent examination of the case of 'King Billy's African Son' – a Black man named George Henry Thompson who was brought to court following the Belfast riots of 1872 – demonstrates that revealing stories wait to be uncovered.[15] One such story is that of William John Brown, and the discussion that follows will seek to explore its nuances and place it in context. As will become clear, Brown's is a story of individual enslavement and escape, but it is also one that intersects with the story of abolition in Belfast and that draws our attention to the appearance, within the town, of enslaved people.

THE ENSLAVED MAN ARRIVES

Viewing Belfast today, it is difficult to envisage the town as it appeared in the opening decades of the nineteenth century. From 1801–32 the town's population ballooned, growing from approximately 19,000 to over 50,000; cotton manufacturing boomed, before being surpassed in the 1830s by linen spinning, and streets of cramped houses were thrown up to accommodate an expanding urban workforce.[16] In physical terms, the town remained small, but as it morphed into a centre of manufacturing and industry, its boundaries began to stretch. To the south, streets were developed on unused land between the White Linen Hall and the Blackstaff River, while textile mills clustered in the area around Smithfield to the west, creating a distinctive, industrialised urban space.[17] By contrast, Belfast was bounded on its eastern flank by the River Lagan, and there a very different urban space could be found.

Running north from the foot of Waring Street and south from the foot of High Street was Belfast's dockland, a busy network of quaysides, docks and adjacent streets and lanes.[18] This was a polyglot, multi-ethnic and, at times, unruly urban quarter. During the night of 20–21 August 1812, for instance, Belfast's night watch dealt with a 'Lascar' who reported that he had been 'robbed and abused in Matthew Weir's [probably a tavern or drinking den] on the quay'. That same night a group of Portuguese seamen were discovered 'fighting with their knives' on Waring Street and one of their number, 'a Black', was apprehended. Several weeks later, in October 1812, the night watch dealt with another 'Black sailor', who disembarked late at night from his ship, and in November 1816 assistance was given to 'an intoxicated Swedish Sailor' who had clearly strayed far from the docks, making it to Carrick Hill in the west of the town, where he was discovered in a tight spot, having attracted the attention of a crowd which, he claimed, 'evinced a disposition to maltreat him'.[19] Belfast's dockland thus provided a point of contact with the wider world. It was a space where a transient seafaring community could be encountered and an entrance point through which visitors and strangers passed into the town's streets. William John Brown was among their number.

Brown stepped onto a Belfast quayside early in August 1830, having arrived on board the *Planter*, a 'first class brig' of 274 tons, which had sailed from New Orleans.[20] The *Planter*'s arrival in Belfast was by no means unusual. Owned by John Vance, Robert Gamble and a number of 'others', whose names are unknown, it was one of sixty-one Belfast vessels engaged in the so-called 'foreign trade' in 1830 and had been crossing the Atlantic from Belfast to New Orleans since 1826.[21] If not among Belfast's more prominent merchants, its owners appear to have been reasonably successful. Newspaper advertisements record that Vance lived in Donegall Place, the fashionable street occupied in the early decades of the nineteenth century by 'merchants of the town, or country gentlemen who came to Belfast for society in winter'.[22] Gamble, on the other hand, lived in Waring Street, though he, too, appears to have been comfortably off. In 1830, the year in which the *Planter* arrived in Belfast with Brown on board, he was serving as a board member of the Belfast Charitable Society and donated the sum of £1 10 shillings to its funds.[23] As for the *Planter*, it carried both goods and passengers, and its owners boasted that it was a fast-sailing ship that offered 'excellent accommodation'.[24] This might well have been so, but it made little difference to Brown, who crossed the Atlantic as a stowaway, concealed in the *Planter*'s hold with its cargo of cotton.[25]

That the details of Brown's voyage are known is purely the result of chance. Upon the *Planter*'s arrival in Belfast, Brown succeeded in slipping ashore unnoticed. However, in New Orleans his 'owner' had put him to work as a stevedore and, before stowing himself away on the *Planter*, Brown had been employed in loading its cargo. As a result, he was known to the ship's crew, and at some point after he stole ashore he was spotted by one of their number on a Belfast street. Thanks to this, his story has survived. The *Planter*'s crewman, whose name is not recorded, reported that Brown was present in the town. This resulted in his arrest, and on 12 August 1830 he appeared in Belfast's Police Office, where Cortland Skinner, a justice of the peace and, since 1827, the superintendent of the town's police, investigated his case.[26]

The precise chronology of these events is unclear. The *Planter* docked in Belfast on 4 August 1830, some eight days prior to Brown's appearance in the Police Office, but we do not know when he disembarked from the ship, when he was recognised or when he was arrested.[27] In all likelihood he spent several days at liberty before his presence in Belfast was discovered, but this cannot be said for certain. Equally unclear are the particular circumstances of Brown's arrest. Who made the decision that he should be apprehended? Was he detained at the request of the ship's captain? Or was his presence reported to a police officer who acted independently, assuming that some wrongdoing had been committed? And what of Brown himself, did he make any attempt to abscond or avoid arrest? The surviving sources offer no answers to these questions, but what is known is that there were no legal grounds on which to detain Brown following his arrest.

In 1772, long before Brown's arrival in Belfast, Lord Chief Justice Mansfield had delivered his verdict in the case – much discussed, both then and now – of *Somerset v. Stewart*. Mansfield ruled that James Somerset, an enslaved man who travelled to Britain from Boston with his owner, a customs official named Charles Stewart, and who had run away, should be considered free, reasoning, as Kenneth Morgan has put it, that 'English law did not support the keeping of a slave on English soil'. Widely misconstrued at the time, Mansfield's judgment 'was a limited decision', concerning only Somerset; as Morgan notes, 'it did not end slavery in Britain', though it did establish the point 'that slaves could not be forcibly returned to masters in England'.[28]

In 1827, just a few years before Brown arrived in Belfast, the Somerset judgment became the subject of renewed attention when another case concerning an enslaved person – a woman named Grace James – was heard in London. James had travelled to Britain from Antigua with her owner, Ann Allen, in 1822. She returned to Antigua in 1823 and two years later, in 1825, claimed to be free. A customs official intervened, apprehending her 'on the grounds that she had been free once she touched English soil and had therefore been reimported illegally to Antigua', and legal proceedings ensued. James' case was first heard in August 1826, in Antigua's Vice Admiralty court, which ruled that she remain enslaved. But the matter did not rest there. An appeal followed, and in 1827, in the Court of Admiralty in London, Lord Stowell endorsed the original judgment. As Patricia Hagler Minter has explained, Stowell was a man of abolitionist inclinations but felt that it was incumbent upon him 'to clarify what he believed were popular misinterpretations of *Somerset*', which in his view 'implied no more than the suspension of the colonial slave codes during a temporary sojourn to England'.[29] As might be expected, this prompted both criticism and debate, delighting upholders of slavery and dismaying abolitionists.[30] The *Belfast News-Letter* clearly took a dim view. Pushing the logic reflected in the judgment to an improbable limit, it informed readers that 'a slave infant, not manumitted, who, being brought to England from Antigua, attained here (to put extreme cases), the station of Archbishop of Canterbury, or that of Commander-in-Chief might be claimed and reduced to slavery by his master, if he were found in his native island'.[31] But if there was an absurdity at the heart of the judgment, Stowell nevertheless recognised that James *had* been free while in England. His interpretation of Mansfield's Somerset judgment might have been disheartening for abolitionists, but it was nevertheless underpinned by an acceptance that the enslaved person's status as enslaved became legally irrelevant upon their arrival in the United Kingdom. This, of course, had implications for Brown.[32] Although he arrived in Belfast from the United States of America, rather than from a British colony, the point remained that when he stepped onto a Belfast quayside, Brown entered a territory where he was not – indeed, legally could not – be considered as enslaved. There were, therefore, no grounds on which to detain him: he had committed no crime and the logical outcome was that he should be declared free.

THE ENSLAVED MAN TELLS HIS STORY

And so he was. On 12 August 1830, in Belfast's Police Office, Cortland Skinner 'liberated' Brown and 'pronounced him to be a *free man*'.[33] But not before first giving him an opportunity to tell his story. As reported in Belfast's newspapers, Brown's tale was a tragic one.[34] Around fifty years of age in 1830, he was a native of Baltimore in Maryland and had, he claimed, been a 'free black' with 'a wife and family of five children, who resided with him in his own house'. Disaster, however, struck when he fell into the hands of 'some of that class of men styled, in America, *Slave-speculators*, by whom he was kidnapped'. So began the dismal journey that led him, ultimately, to Belfast. He was held by his kidnappers for 'three days without food' before being 'suddenly hurried away by night' and forced to undergo a lengthy and disorientating trek, undertaken 'in such a manner as rendered it impossible for him to form any idea of the route taken'. Following this, Brown 'was put on board of a vessel, in which he remained twenty-five days, at the end of which he found that he had been conveyed to New Orleans'. There, he was 'sold, as a slave, by one King, to a person named Jacob' who put him to work on the docks, 'loading a vessel called the *Planter*'. In so doing, of course, he unwittingly supplied Brown – who was 'indignant … at the fraud which had been practised upon him, and anxious to regain his liberty' – with a means of escape. As Brown explained, he 'purchased a dollar's worth of biscuit' and 'secreted himself' in the *Planter*'s hold. Whether or not he was aware that the ship was destined for Ireland is unknown, but shortly after he boarded, the ship set sail for Belfast. Brown spent the voyage in hiding, 'gliding occasionally out of his retreat in the night time'. On the whole, his attempts at stealth were successful. While he revealed that one member of the *Planter*'s crew, 'whose name he would not divulge', was aware of his presence on the ship, he insisted that 'he was not seen on board by the captain, mates, or any other of the crew'. Thus, known only to one other person, Brown made it to Belfast, where he quietly slipped ashore.[35]

For the historian, evidence generated by legal proceedings can present difficulties. As Edward Muir and Guido Ruggiero have remarked, 'court cases generate evidence that has been polluted by authority'.[36] Granted, Brown was not on trial when he appeared in Belfast's Police Office on

12 August 1830, but he had been arrested and was appearing before a magistrate – Cortland Skinner – who sought to investigate his case. He can be said, therefore, to have spoken while 'under the constraints of authority', and this prompts a range of questions.[37] Belfast's newspapers reported that Skinner investigated Brown's story 'with much patience and strict regard to justice', and they presented the case in such a way as to solicit empathy: Brown was not simply 'kidnapped', for example, he was 'inhumanely torn … from the bosom of his family'.[38] We have no way, however, of knowing how Brown experienced the proceedings in the Police Office. What did *he* make of Skinner's 'regard to justice'? Did he consider himself to be in the hands of a sympathetic magistrate or did he fear that he would be returned to New Orleans? Might this have helped to shape the story he told?

It is worth noting here that there are discrepancies between the newspaper reports that appeared in August 1830 and the sparse details of Brown's life recorded in the registry book of Clifton Street Cemetery. In 1830, for instance, Brown's place of birth was given as Baltimore, in the state of Maryland, but the registry book records that he was born in the state of Virginia. Likewise, while Brown claimed that he had been a free man prior to being trafficked and newspaper coverage makes no mention of his family having been sold into slavery alongside him, the registry book notes that his family were 'in slavery in America'.[39] This latter discrepancy raises the possibility that Brown had not been a free man, though there are other explanations for the apparent inconsistency: it is entirely possible that Brown's wife and children *were* enslaved while he was free. Alternatively, we may be dealing here with a simple error: the individual who recorded Brown's burial, aware of the fact that he escaped slavery, might simply have jumped to the conclusion that his family had also been enslaved. But our questions do not end there. Newspaper reports indicate that Brown did not appear in the Police Office on his own: a group of 'members of the Society of Friends, and others … attended … on behalf of the oppressed man of colour', as also did 'an intelligent and spirited Black, an inhabitant of Belfast, who evinced a lively interest in his behalf, and pleaded his case with an animation and zeal which was honourable to his feelings'.[40] How did Brown view these interested parties and the efforts they made to assist him? And what thoughts crossed his mind when Skinner declared him free? Although liberated, Brown was separated from his wife and children by the vast distance of the Atlantic Ocean. Did he contemplate the possibility of their joining him, or did he despair that such a reunion would prove to be impossible? Intriguing as they are, such questions must remain unanswered. Nevertheless, they serve to foreground the fact that what occurred in Belfast's Police Office was not a straightforward exchange of information and offer a reminder that we can only ever have access to a partial version of Brown's story.

None of this is to suggest that the story Brown told on 12 August 1830 should be dismissed as implausible or unlikely. Quite the reverse, the account he gave of his capture and enslavement is all too credible. By the 1820s, the United States' prohibition on the introduction of enslaved Africans had combined with the expanding cotton industry in the southern states to create an insatiable market for enslaved labour, and this stimulated the development of what Richard Bell has termed the 'Reverse Underground Railroad', by which free Blacks were abducted, trafficked to the South and sold into lives of slavery.[41] According to Bell, there were 'several dozen kidnapping crews active in the mid-Atlantic in the early nineteenth century'. Such 'crews' – or 'gangs' – penetrated as far north as New York and operated wherever significant concentrations of free Blacks could be found.[42] With a Black population that had exploded from around 323 in 1790 to over 10,000 in 1820, Brown's home town of Baltimore – 'the most northern of southern cities' and 'a destination for free black people from throughout the Americas' – was a natural target.[43] Brown, on the other hand, was not. Illegal traders tended to favour youths over those of more mature years, in part because of their inherent value, but also, as Julie Winch has explained, 'because "rapid growth," combined with the hardships of slave labor, often made identification virtually impossible within the space of a couple of years'.[44] That being said, the harsh reality was, as Bell has put it, that 'no one who might conceivably fetch a price as a slave in the South, was ever truly safe'.[45] While Brown's story illustrates this point neatly, it also squares with what is known of the methods employed by 'slave speculators' and chimes with the stories of others who fell into their hands. As has been noted, Brown claimed that following his capture he was briefly 'detained' by his kidnappers, before being 'compelled to cross the country' and placed on a ship destined for

New Orleans.[46] There are echoes here of the modus operandi of Joseph Johnson's gang – in Bell's judgement 'the most successful kidnapping gang in American history' – which is known to have 'warehoused their human cargo in … [an] isolated Delaware farmhouse … before eventually delivering them to waiting vessels ready to sail southward'.[47] Likewise, the particular trajectory of Brown's journey, which carried him from Baltimore to New Orleans, is similar to that, reconstructed by Martha S. Jones, of a man named Jean Baptiste, who was kidnapped in Baltimore in the late 1810s, and who later 'surfaced in the slave markets of New Orleans', where he experienced the 'brutal commodification' of slavery, being 'sold three times in the span of just eight months'.[48]

It has been suggested that Brown faced a similar fate in New Orleans, being 'sold numerous times', but this cannot be said for certain.[49] Indeed, when we turn to consider his sojourn in New Orleans we encounter a further discrepancy in the surviving sources. Brown's appearance in Belfast's Police Office in August 1830, and the account he gave of his story, was first detailed in the *Belfast Commercial Chronicle*, in a report that was republished in the *Northern Whig* on 16 August 1830.[50] Four days later, on 20 August 1830, the *Belfast News-Letter* also covered the case. While the *News-Letter*'s account was largely lifted verbatim from the earlier report, it did introduce some variations. For the most part, these are slight. The *News-Letter*, for example, gave the date on which Brown appeared in the Police Office and omitted some details, included in the original report, concerning his treatment in the days immediately following his capture.[51] More significant, however, is the divergence in the *News-Letter*'s report concerning the amount of time Brown spent in New Orleans. While the earlier report is somewhat oblique, it can be read as suggesting that he spent just a few months in the city.[52] By contrast, the *News-Letter*'s report is clipped and precise on this point, stating that '[a]t this place [that is, New Orleans] he was detained three years and a half'.[53] This divergence could, perhaps, have been the result of a compositional error, though given differences in the sentence structure and the *News-Letter*'s omission of certain details included in the earlier report this seems highly unlikely.[54] More plausibly, it may be suggested that the *News-Letter*'s editor recognised that the original report was unclear concerning the amount of time Brown had spent in New Orleans and sought to clarify matters, perhaps seeking additional information, either from Brown or those who had assisted him. But whatever the explanation, there are reasonable grounds on which to accept the *News-Letter*'s assertion that Brown had spent a number of years in New Orleans. Both reports agree that, while in New Orleans, Brown was 'sold, as a slave, by one King, to a person named Jacob', and there is evidence to suggest that this sale occurred in 1828, for in that year the New Orleans notary William Boswell certified a transaction involving one John W. King (as seller) and a Levy Jacobs.[55] Whether or not this sale concerned an enslaved man is not specified in the index of Boswell's records, but at least three others notaries – Felix De Armis, John W. Duncan and Carlile Pollock – certified sales of enslaved people by King in the same year, and Jacobs is known to have been a player in the New Orleans slave trade during the 1820s and early 1830s.[56]

Brown was thus sold at least once while in New Orleans. But beyond this his story remains patchy. The *News-Letter*'s claim that he spent around three and a half years in New Orleans, before appearing in Belfast in August 1830, suggests that he had arrived in New Orleans at some point early in 1827, but we know nothing about how he had been treated or employed prior to being purchased by Jacobs. Moreover, King remains a shadowy figure. Had he purchased Brown following his arrival in New Orleans, later selling him on to Jacobs, or had he in fact been involved in trafficking Brown? Here, again, we encounter questions which must remain unanswered. We can, however, say something about the character of New Orleans as Brown would have experienced it. Culturally and geographically distinctive, New Orleans was, in Rashauna Johnson's words, a 'polyglot port city' that was 'suspended between the Caribbean and Latin America on the one hand and the US south on the other'. It was a city that grew rapidly in the opening decades of the nineteenth century, emerging as a 'hub of slavery, diversity, and circulation'. In 1803 its inhabitants had numbered around 8,000. By 1820 this figure had risen to 27,000. Around a third of the city's inhabitants were, like Brown, enslaved, though they also rubbed shoulders with a substantial community of free Blacks.[57] They did so literally, for in New Orleans the enslaved experience was characterised by 'slave mobility'. Employed in a range of work settings, the enslaved circulated in the streets of the city. Some were 'hired out' by their owners – this may have been the case with

Brown, whose owner 'employed him in loading the *Planter*' – and it was possible for those enslaved in the urban context to acquire a degree of autonomy, though this is not to suggest that they were in any sense 'free'.[58] Brown's experience provides a case in point. Prior to boarding the *Planter* he 'purchased a dollar's worth of biscuit', an act which suggests that he had both money to spend and the time and freedom to spend it.[59] And, of course, Brown's story also points to the fact that New Orleans was a city that offered opportunities for escape.[60] Indeed, the method he employed in fleeing slavery was by no means unheard of. Recognising the possibility of escape by sea, runaways from the Mississippi Valley are known to have been drawn to New Orleans, and in 1818, some ten years prior to Brown's arrival in Belfast, the *Thomas Jefferson*, a US naval vessel, arrived in Liverpool, carrying with it one John Wild, an enslaved stowaway who had boarded in Louisiana.[61] Whether or not Brown's escape was inspired by the stories of earlier stowaways is unknown, but his seaborne pursuit of freedom was not without precedent.

SLAVERY AND FREEDOM IN BELFAST

Brown's story thus fits against the broader backdrop of slavery in America's antebellum South. But how did it appear in Belfast? Did those gathered in the town's Police Office on 12 August 1830 have any frame of reference within which to locate Brown and his experiences? And what, if anything, can be said of his life in the weeks and months following Cortland Skinner's declaration of his freedom?

Clearly, Brown's case was considered to be of some interest – that it was reported in three Belfast newspapers serves to illustrate this point. But if it was considered worthy of comment, the appearance of an enslaved man in the town was not unprecedented. Newspaper advertisements, for example, point to the presence of the enslaved in the towns and cities of eighteenth-century Ireland, including Belfast, where, in 1766, John Cawdon offered a three-guinea reward for the return of a 'young negro manservant named John Moore'.[62] Moreover, in his *History of the Earth and Animated Nature*, first published in 1774, Oliver Goldsmith detailed a sickening episode that had occurred 'about twenty years ago' when a slave ship 'was, by stress of weather, driven into the harbour of Belfast, with a lading of very sickly slaves'. Observing that his cargo 'took every opportunity to throw themselves over board when brought up upon deck, as is usual, for the benefit of fresh air', the ship's captain selected one of their number – 'a woman slave attempting to drown herself' – in order to make 'a proper example to the rest', who 'he supposed ... did not know the terrors attending death'. Bound by rope and lowered into Belfast Lough, the woman was soon 'heard to give a terrible shriek' – not from 'her fear of drowning', but rather because 'a shark, which had followed the ship, had bit her off from the middle'.[63] By 1830, there were likely few in the town who could recall this event at first hand, though knowledge of the incident was in circulation: as late as 1840, the Belfast clergyman Thomas Drew described the outrage in a public speech, informing his hearers that it had left a 'stain of ... blood ... upon their shores'.[64]

If Brown's appearance in Belfast might have stirred thoughts of the grim incident related by Goldsmith, it would certainly have triggered memories of two more recent episodes. The first had occurred in 1818, in June of which year the *Belfast Commercial Chronicle* publicised the plight of an enslaved girl, 'about fifteen years of age, [who] was lately brought to this country from Jamaica in the service of a *lady* and her husband'. The girl, it reported, was 'subjected frequently to cruel treatment'. What was worse, her owners were set on returning her, against her will, to the Caribbean. There they planned to sell her, dashing her hopes of freedom. As the *Chronicle* explained:

> In this town [Belfast] the girl heard with delight, that by the benevolent laws of our country, when she placed her boot upon Ireland, she was no longer a slave. Blessing the land which bestowed her freedom, she fled from her master, who wanted to compel her to return to the slave market. Her efforts however were in vain; for, as we have heard, her retreat being discovered, she was yesterday (Sunday) forced in a chaise, with the assistance of – an inhabitant, conveyed to the White House shore, and put on board the vessel, about to sail for Jamaica, there again to taste 'the bitter draught.'

This report prompted a brief flurry of activity. Belfast's sovereign 'made enquiry into the nature of the case' and the following day the *Belfast*

News-Letter printed a letter from William Starks, captain of the *Letitia*, the ship on which the girl had been placed. It had all, his account suggested, been something of a misunderstanding. Yes, he had brought the girl from Jamaica when he sailed for Ireland the previous March: she 'came as [a] servant' with 'Mrs Starks'. All had been well for several weeks – the girl 'remained' with Mrs Starks and was 'treated in every respect as a servant ought' – but on Saturday 20 June she had run away 'under very unfavourable circumstances, and secreted herself in a house in town'. Upon tracking her down, Starks 'informed her of the necessity of going home to Jamaica to which she made no objection', until, that is, she discovered that 'her mistress was not going also to return': at that point, Starks conceded, 'she expressed some unwillingness to leave her, but not at all to any extent that required force, as it has been stated, to take her away'.[65]

What was really going on here? While Belfast's sovereign concluded 'that the circumstances represented in the original statement [published in the *Commercial Chronicle*] were quite unfounded', Starks' letter raises as many questions as it answers, and the truth of the case is difficult to discern.[66] Why did the girl run away, and what were the 'unfavourable circumstances' Starks referred to? Other parties were, presumably, involved: who, for instance, owned the house in which the girl 'secreted herself'? Whatever the answers to these questions, it appears that the *Commercial Chronicle*'s initial report frustrated Starks' plan to return the girl to Jamaica, if only in the short term. 'On finding that the matter had been laid before the public under such aggravated circumstances,' he noted, 'I immediately had her brought up to town, when she proceeded directly to Mrs Starks' lodgings, and requested permission to remain with her.'[67] That permission was granted is indicated by a short statement that appeared in the *Belfast News-Letter* several months later, in December 1818. This communicated the fact that three men – Alexander M'Laine, Edward Johnson and John Thompson – had 'at the request of CAPTAIN STARKS ... questioned a Black Girl named SUCKEY, belonging to Mrs Starks, respecting her desire to return to Jamaica' and that the girl had, in their presence, 'solicited Captain S. in the most earnest manner, to take her back to Kingston, in his vessel.'[68] Several weeks earlier, the *Letitia* had returned to Belfast from Jamaica bearing a cargo of 'sugar and mahogany', and by this point preparations were underway for the return journey.[69] Having run into controversy earlier in the year, Starks was no doubt keen to avoid a repeat of the experience. To this end, he sought to place on record the fact that Suckey, who had evidently been permitted to remain in Belfast in June 1818, had now consented to return to Jamaica – though we might reasonably ask how meaningful that consent was. Given the earlier allegations of mistreatment, it is difficult to escape the conclusion that there was a good deal more to this case than is revealed in the columns of Belfast's newspapers.

Some ten years later, in September 1828, a second episode involving slavery occurred when it was discovered that two Bermudian vessels that had recently docked in the town – the *Griffin* and the *Belfast* – were crewed with enslaved men.[70] On 4 September 1828, the men were taken to Belfast's sessions house, where Cortland Skinner and William Clark, a justice of the peace, dealt with their case. Skinner took the lead, but events were shaped, in part, by an initial intervention from a Counsellor Bradshaw. In a clear reference to the Grace James case of 1827, Bradshaw:

> stated to the Magistrates at the commencement of proceedings, that it might be proper, previous to putting any questions to the persons then before them, to acquaint them that it had lately been decided in England, by Lord Stowell, that if a slave claims his freedom on his arrival in Britain, and returns to the island from whence he was brought, he may be reclaimed there as a slave.[71]

Accordingly, Skinner informed the men that 'the very circumstances of their having set foot on Irish ground, or entered an Irish harbour, freed them at once from slavery as long as they remained in these countries'. Following this, they were asked 'whether they would prefer remaining in this country, as freemen, or returning to Bermuda as slaves'.[72] In all, eleven enslaved men answered this question. A twelfth – Thomas Alboy – was 'sent for by order of the Magistrates' but failed to attend, asserting that 'as he intended to go to Bermuda, his appearance before them was quite unnecessary'. Of those present in the sessions office, only three – Joshua Edwards, Robert Edwards and Joseph Rollin – 'declared their wish to remain in Ireland'. The other eight – Benjamin Alick, Richard Pace,

Francis Ramio, Joseph Varman, James Lambert, Thomas Williams, John Stow and George Bassett – 'professed their gratitude ... but explicitly stated, that it was their wish to return to Bermuda': all had either friends or kinfolk that they wanted to return to, and one of their number was overheard explaining 'that his proprietor had himself informed him, that, on his arrival in the British Isles, he might claim his freedom; but, as he had intimated to his master that he would return, he deemed himself bound to fulfil his word'.[73]

At first glance, the case of the enslaved Bermudians appears markedly different from that of William John Brown. Where the latter concerned a single individual who consciously sought to escape slavery, the former involved a group of enslaved men whose owners consented to their travelling to Belfast and the majority of whom rejected the opportunity to claim their freedom. There are, however, a number of similarities between the two cases. Both, for instance, attracted attention far beyond Belfast. While the 1828 case was reported at the national level by the *Anti-Slavery Monthly Reporter* and discussed in the Bermudian House of Assembly – where it was presented as illustrative of 'the benign character of slavery in Bermuda' – the *Belfast Commercial Chronicle*'s report on William John Brown appeared in *The Friend*, a Philadelphia journal, in October 1830.[74] More significantly, each case concerned the same legal question – that of the status of an enslaved person upon arrival in Belfast – and the involvement of Belfast's police magistrate, Cortland Skinner, in investigating and resolving both cases is noteworthy. Indeed, Skinner's handling of Brown's case in 1830 was no doubt informed by his earlier involvement in the case of the Bermudian sailors, though it is worth noting that he was an experienced magistrate and a man who likely knew more than most about the institution of slavery.

The son of Cortland MacGregor Skinner, a leading New Jersey loyalist who moved to Britain following the American War of Independence, Skinner Jr settled near Belfast in the mid-1790s, following twelve years' service in the British army.[75] Employed as an estate agent by Lord Dungannon, he was quickly appointed as a magistrate and chosen, early in 1797, as second lieutenant of the cavalry division of Belfast's recently established loyalist Volunteers.[76] He had no doubt encountered slavery in the New Jersey of his youth, and family connections offered further points of contact, for in November 1797 his sister, Maria, married Major General George Nugent in Belfast, and four years later she accompanied him to the West Indies when he was appointed as governor of Jamaica.[77] There, of course, slavery was ubiquitous. However, as Susan E. Klepp and Roderick A. McDonald have noted, Nugent's 'belief in a hierarchical social order ... blinded her to any connection between her personal rights and freedoms and the subjugation of Jamaica's black population'. Consequently, her 'rich and detailed' account of her time on the island – *Lady Nugent's Journal of her Residence in Jamaica from 1801 to 1805*, first published in 1838 – minimised the mistreatment of the enslaved and reflected a 'benign view of slavery'.[78] Whether or not Skinner shared his sister's views is unknown, but he was the product of the same loyalist milieu, and his connection with Nugent and her husband – who are known to have visited his home in 1808 – remains an intriguing one.[79] At the very least, it suggests that the man tasked with dealing with William John Brown in September 1830 was no provincial innocent, suddenly and shockingly confronted by the reality of slavery.

One further, striking similarity between Brown's case and that of the Bermudian sailors concerns those who offered support to the enslaved men. As noted above, when he appeared in Belfast's Police Office in September 1830, Brown was accompanied by '[s]ome members of the Society of Friends, and others', and 'an intelligent and spirited Black, an inhabitant of Belfast, who evinced a lively interest in his behalf'.[80] Likewise, in 1828, 'a man of colour' and a group of Friends – or Quakers – had advocated on behalf of the Bermudian sailors; indeed, it was thanks to the former that their presence in Belfast had come to light. As the *Northern Whig* explained on 4 September 1828, in a passage that made clear its hostility to slavery:

A few days since, a man of colour who resides in this town, waited on a member of the Society of Friends, and informed him that there were twelve *Slaves* on board the Bermuda vessels. This fact having been communicated to the Moyalen [*sic*] Branch of the London African Anti-Slavery Association, Messrs. Wakefield, Christy, Dawson, and Sinton, members, immediately repaired to Belfast, and waited on several of the Magistrates, and claimed their interference in liberating those unfortunate descendants of the miserable natives of Africa, who had been villainously dragged from their country and their homes, to satisfy the insatiable avarice of some reckless trafficker in human blood and sinews![81]

That Quakers from Moyallon in County Down should have taken an interest in this case requires little explanation. It is well known that Quakers on both sides of the Atlantic played a prominent role in anti-slavery campaigns from the late eighteenth century onwards, and the Moyallon community had petitioned parliament in support of the 'abolition of Slavery in the British Colonies' in the mid-1820s.[82] Of particular interest, however, is the involvement in this case of the so-called 'man of colour who resides in this town' and the 'member of the Society of Friends' who provided the link with Moyallon. Who were these men, and what are we to make of their actions?

In all likelihood, 'the man of colour' mentioned in reports of the Bermudian sailors' case in 1828 and the 'intelligent and spirited Black' who demonstrated such a 'lively interest' in Brown's case in 1830 were one and the same. All reports in which he is mentioned refer to the fact that this man *lived* in Belfast. He was not, therefore, a transient figure, and the *Guardian and Constitutional Advocate* adds the detail that he was 'a very industrious and useful tradesman'.[83] A further reference to 'a respectable looking man of colour resident in this town' appears in an account of an anti-slavery meeting held later in September 1830. If this was the same man then we can add that he was a former soldier who, while freeborn, had witnessed the evils of slavery during a visit to Barbados.[84] Likewise, reference was made to a 'man of colour, named Oveton' in a report of a meeting held in February 1831 'for the purpose of forming an Auxiliary in Belfast to the Hibernian Negroe's Friend Society', though whether this was the same 'man of colour' who assisted Brown and the Bermudian sailors cannot be said for certain.[85] By contrast, the 'member of the Society of Friends' who received news of the Bermudian sailors from the 'man of colour' and sought assistance from the Moyallon Quakers was almost certainly William Bell, a Belfast Quaker who would go on, in 1837, to launch the *Irish Friend*, 'the first proper Quaker periodical in the islands of Britain and Ireland'.[86]

Connected to the Moyallon community through his wife, Hannah Christy Wakefield, Bell is known to have been a committed abolitionist. Moreover, an obituary, published following his death in Richmond, Indiana in 1871, alluded to his earlier involvement in the rescue of enslaved seamen in Belfast – albeit in exaggerated terms that make no mention of the other individuals involved in securing the freedom of the enslaved men:

> in Belfast, he several times discovered on board of West India vessels slaves in the capacity of seamen, who were ignorant of their rights as free men the moment they trod on British soil. These slaves he had brought before a magistrate by writ of Habeas Corpus, had their privileges explained to them, then declared free and assisted them until they could find means of subsistence.[87]

If it is possible to detect a degree of posthumous mythologising here, Bell nevertheless appears to have played a significant role in the events of September 1828, and it is likely that he was also numbered among that group of 'members of the Society of Friends, and others' who accompanied Brown when he appeared before Cortland Skinner in August 1830.

Leaving aside the question of their identity, the activities of 'the man of colour' and the Belfast Quaker in 1828 are significant insofar as they offer a rare glimpse of informal abolitionist activism. Indeed, what emerges from a close reading of newspaper reports concerning the Bermudian sailors' case is a picture, albeit shadowy, of an abolitionist vanguard seizing on a valuable opportunity to bring slavery to public attention. This dynamic was far from unique. Parallels can, for example, be drawn with the development of anti-slavery in America in the 1770s and 1780s, which was pioneered, as Kirsten Sword has demonstrated, by individuals who pursued a project that was 'not politically popular' and 'found a calling in cases … in which messy engagement between people of colour, white activists, and slaveholders was routine'.[88] Of course, the political context in late 1820s Belfast was very different: parliament had passed legislation abolishing the slave trade in 1807 and the establishment, in 1823, of the ponderously named Society for the Mitigation and Gradual Abolition of Slavery Throughout the British Commonwealth had marked the beginning of a revival of mass abolitionist activity.[89] In short, anti-slavery was an altogether more acceptable proposition in Belfast in 1828 than it was in North America in the 1770s and early 1780s. But it does not follow that it was a universally popular one. That William Bell's abolitionist activities were later said to have 'rendered him unpopular among his fellow-merchants and many others, who feared it would tend to injure the West India trade in their town' is telling.[90] Equally so is the fact that news of the Bermudian sailors' presence in Belfast was passed on to the Quakers of Moyallon, who were affiliated with the London African Anti-Slavery Association: as late as 1828, by which point the campaign to abolish slavery in Britain's colonies was well-established, the town of Belfast possessed no formal anti-slavery organisation.[91]

While a petition in opposition to slavery had circulated in the town in 1826, it was not, in fact, until 14 September 1830 that a public meeting was held in the town to facilitate the establishment of an abolitionist society.[92] Coming, as it did, just weeks after Brown's case had unfolded in Belfast's Police Office, the timing of this initial abolitionist overture is suggestive: Brown's story had offered a vivid reminder of the evils of slavery and must surely have contributed to the development of anti-slavery sentiment in the town. But other influences were undoubtedly also at play. Not only had Belfast's newspapers been critical of slavery, but by 1830 the abolitionist campaign was increasingly vociferous, and reports of anti-slavery meetings in Dublin would have alerted readers of the *Belfast News-Letter* to abolitionist activities in the Irish capital.[93] Against this backdrop, at the meeting of 14 September 1830, Belfast's dilatory abolitionists resolved that 'a Society be now formed in connexion with the Anti-Slavery Society in London, to be denominated the Belfast Auxiliary Anti-Slavery Society'.[94] In the weeks and months that followed, this initially moderate society was to become more advanced. As Daniel Ritchie has noted, the moderates were pushed aside, and by August 1832 the society's committee joined those who rejected the gradualist approach to abolition and called, instead, for the immediate emancipation of the enslaved.[95]

This wider context of abolitionist activism is worth bearing in mind when turning, lastly, to consider Brown's experience of Belfast in the period following his appearance in the Police Office. At a time when slavery 'occupied a good deal of the attention of the public' in the town, the nature of Brown's story would have served to mark him out and bestow upon him a degree of local celebrity.[96] Regrettably, the evidence concerning his life in Belfast is scarce, though the registry book for Clifton Street burial ground offers a few details. We know, for instance, that he resided in Long Lane, a narrow thoroughfare in the centre of the town.[97] Likewise, there is evidence to suggest that he found work as a 'labourer', though we know nothing of the type of labouring work he performed, or of his domestic arrangements.[98] In September 1828, Moyallon abolitionists had undertaken to assist the three Bermudian sailors who had chosen to remain in Ireland in securing work, and Brown might well have received similar assistance from local abolitionists.[99] Certainly, it seems unlikely that those who accompanied him in Belfast's Police Office would have left him entirely to his own devices once his freedom had been declared. That being said, it is difficult to escape the conclusion that his life in Belfast must have been a struggle. Separated from his wife and children, he found himself alone in a socially and culturally disorientating urban space. Familiar with Baltimore and New Orleans, American cities with large Black communities, Brown would have been forced to acclimatise to life as one of just a few Black citizens in an overwhelmingly white city. Even had his story not been sufficient to mark him out, his colour would have done so, and anonymity, the chance to disappear into a crowd and be unknown, would have been denied him. He might even have encountered unwelcome scrutiny and attention, for the people of Belfast were not beyond objectifying those they considered as 'others'. Indeed, in January 1826, visitors to Cornmarket had been loudly invited to gawp at 'an exhibition of two persons in Indian dresses, called by their keepers *Malays*'. Local traders had complained to the sovereign: not about the nature of the exhibition, but about the inconvenience it had caused.[100] None of this speaks to Brown having had an easy life in Belfast, let alone a happy one. What can, however, be said for certain is that his struggles were short-lived, for by 17 November 1831 William John Brown had died, and his story – a story of enslavement and escape, which links late Georgian Belfast with antebellum New Orleans – came to an end with his interment in the Belfast Charitable Society's Clifton Street burial ground.

CONCLUSION

William John Brown spent little more than a year in Belfast and appears to have encountered the Charitable Society only in death. Nevertheless, his story reveals much about the world in which the society existed, and it is fitting that he should have been laid to rest in the Clifton Street Cemetery. 'For anyone interested in the history of Belfast', R.W.M. Strain once remarked, 'this place is ... a veritable Westminster Abbey in miniature. Here can be epitomized the history of the town from its beginnings as a place of industry ... It would be impossible to mention the many people of note buried here, but the stones and the monuments speak for themselves.'[101] Fleeting as his time in Belfast was, Brown, too, was a person of note, and his story of enslavement, escape and freedom forms a part of the history of the city. In exploring that story, we encounter a city dense with connections to the wider Atlantic World – a city in which slavery was not simply a subject of debate but an institution that was sometimes encountered directly and in which people of African descent sought to make lives for themselves. Such stories reflect vividly the multifaceted nature of Belfast's connections with slavery and invite us to enlarge our understanding of the city's history.

Left: The Poores Board, originally from the Old Corporation Church, now in Clifton House, records money donated to the poor prior to the Belfast Charitable Society's existence. © Belfast Charitable Society

Below: A lottery ticket from 1753, originally sold to raise money to construct the Poorhouse and Infirmary. © National Museums NI, Ulster Museum Collection

Nº 16m 840. Belfaſt, Anno 1753.

THIS TICKET will intitle the Bearer to Half the Sum, *Iriſh Currency*, ariſing to the ſame Number, if drawn a PRIZE, in the preſent LOTTERY in *England*; to be paid at the Bank in *Belfaſt*, Fifty Days after the Drawing of the ſaid Lottery is finiſhed; purſuant to the Scheme publiſhed here, for erecting a Poor-Houſe and Hoſpital, and for building a Church.

Ex.

The 'Belfast Poor House', *c.* 1785–90 by John Nixon (*c.* 1750–1818).
© National Museums NI, Ulster Museum Collection

View of the Poorhouse North-East Wing addition (1824), constructed due to the
increased need for accommodation. © Belfast Charitable Society

Belfast Charitable Institution (formerly the Poorhouse, now Clifton House), taken by Robert John Welch (1859–1936). © National Museums NI, Ulster Museum Collection

Glenravel Street with a view of the back of Clifton House, the Belfast Mercantile College and the Benn Ears, Nose & Throat Hospital (left).
© National Museums NI, Ulster Museum Collection

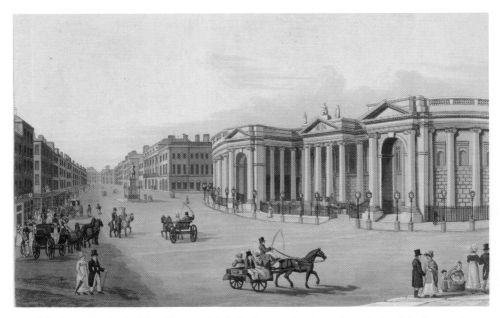

National Bank, Dublin (former Irish Parliament), where four Acts of Parliament governing the Belfast Charitable Society were passed. © National Gallery of Ireland

St Anne's Parish Church, engraving by J. Thomson from *History of the Town of Belfast* by George Benn, 1823.
© National Museums NI, Ulster Museum Collection

Right: Map of the water course (1795) leased to the Belfast Charitable Society.

Below: The Belfast Lying-In Hospital, Clifton Street (1830–1904), built on Belfast Charitable Society land. Both images © Belfast Charitable Society

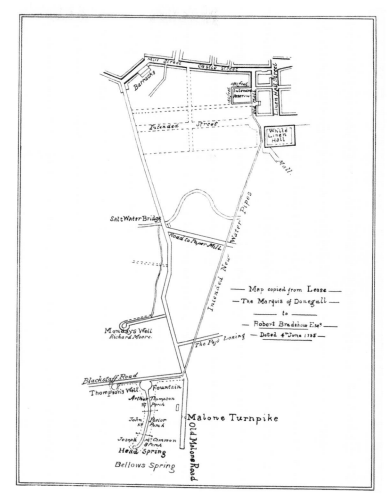

Thomas McCabe denouncing Waddell Cunningham's proposed slaveship company in the Old Exchange, 1786 (1895), by John Carey (*c.* 1860–1943).
© National Museums NI, Ulster Museum Collection

Headstone for Thomas McCabe (1739–1820), Clifton Street Cemetery.
© Belfast Charitable Society

Olaudah Equiano, or Gustavus Vassa, the African.

Publish'd March 1 1789 by G. Vassa

Olaudah Equiano, a freed slave, visited the Poorhouse in December 1791.

© National Portrait Gallery, London

The United Irish Patriots of 1798. © National Portrait Gallery, London

The Poorhouse was taken over as a military barracks in 1798 and was returned to the Belfast Charitable Society in 1800. Image from P.D. Hardy's *Twenty-One Views in Belfast and its Neighbourhood.* Courtesy of the Linen Hall Library

CHAPTER FOUR

Poverty and the Making of the Belfast Charitable Society

Raymond Gillespie

In the summer of 1812, John Gamble, the London-based doctor and litterateur, travelled through his native Ulster. Journeying north from Newry, he came to Belfast where he spent a week. He was impressed with what he saw. It was a 'large and well-built town'. The streets were broad and straight, the houses 'neat and comfortable, mostly made of brick' and the population 'almost entirely working people'. The churches were neat and trim, and there was a new college. In the Linen Hall there was a library, although the practical folk of Belfast had little time for reading. Merchants rather than literary men dominated the town. Card playing was also uncommon, though music was 'their favourite recreation', a trait accredited to Edward Bunting, who had organised the harp festival in the town some thirty years earlier. In the Presbyterian churches, discourse was 'very rational'.[1]

Six years later, the poet John Keats had a very different experience of Belfast. Walking from Donaghadee, he entered the town through its eastern suburbs, where:

we heard on passing into Belfast through a most wretched suburb, that most disgusting of all noises, worse than the bagpipes ... I mean the sound of the shuttle. What a tremendous difficulty is the improvement of such people. I cannot conceive how a mind 'with child' of philanthropy could grasp at its possibility – with me it is absolute despair.[2]

Just how big the problem of industrial poverty was is uncertain, but one letter writer to the *Belfast News-Letter* in 1810 reckoned that some 300 street beggars (excluding their families) received £5,200 annually in donations from residents of the town.[3] The ordered intellectual and commercial world of Gamble seemed never to meet the rapidly industrialising world of the new poor as described by Keats.

THE ROLE OF THE POOR

Part of the explanation for this was a sense that the poor had a limited role to play in the life of the town and represented a problem that was often best ignored. In an article in the *Belfast News-Letter* during 1794, the Belfast Presbyterian minister and intellectual heavyweight William Bruce, together with Henry Joy, had argued that in political life, at least, the poor were irrelevant and required no specific attention, since their best interests lay in supporting property owners who promoted national prosperity and commerce. The working poor would then be employed more regularly and better paid, since 'in a free state the higher ranks of society, as they [the rich] advance, will bring forward the lower ones with them'. The prosperity of merchants and security of property was in the interest of all because wealth trickled down from those who had it to those who did not.[4] In short, poverty was a problem that would take care of itself if the rich prospered and acted in a disinterested way, which their ownership of property would allow them to do. While the radicalism of the United Irishmen, founded in Belfast in October 1791, may have advocated the inclusion of the poor in the political nation, it is difficult to identify those who actively pressed for it apart from a small group of Belfast radicals: Samuel Neilson, Henry Joy McCracken and Thomas Russell.[5] Neilson was actively involved with the Belfast Charitable Society, which was founded to offer poor relief, while Russell preferred a more traditional approach to the poor, based on an English model, which made their home parishes responsible for indigents by issuing them with badges that permitted local begging.[6] For most in the town, Bruce's statement of the position of the poor and the management of their plight remained the orthodoxy.

For all this, there were points at which Gamble's Belfast and that of Keats met. Some regarded the poor as a real problem and a potential danger. In 1809 the House of Industry was established to provide jobs for beggars who, the rules of the institution claimed, infested the streets of Belfast and were unwilling to exert themselves. Relief would be short term, confined to labour-intensive trades such as spinning linen, so that the poor would not become a burden on the town. By this means it was hoped to eliminate poverty: 'to cut it up by the roots, to come at the very source and spring of the evil that rankles in the vitals of every large town'. In addition, moral reform was deemed to be necessary, and this would be provided through 'plain and wholesome' education to prevent children growing up 'in the habits of vice and profligacy exhibited by their parents'.[7] For some, however, the presence of the poor in Belfast was not a problem but an opportunity. Measures for social transformation from the conditions described by Keats to the creation of the polite and rational world of Gamble were an occasion for celebration; such a measure was the Belfast Charitable Society. In 1818 Henry Joy addressed the Belfast Literary Society, a select group of Belfast's elite, on public charity and voluntarism in the town. Joy, a former newspaper proprietor and active local politician through the 1790s, was prominent in a number of Belfast institutions including the dispensary, the fever hospital, the literary society and the Belfast Charitable Society. Joy took the opportunity to celebrate Belfast's achievement in the area of the treatment of the poor. The 'first great charity' of the town was the Poorhouse, and 'the inestimable value of the Poor House requires but little explanation. It feeds, clothes and educates poor children and deserted orphans and it provides board and lodging for those in whom nature is worn out and who might perish in our streets were there not such an asylum to receive them'.

Most importantly, this was not the work of the state but of local voluntarism. As Joy stressed, 'the founders of the first great charity of this town took especial care to avoid everything that would be likely to degenerate to poor's rates, ... [that] has generated an alarming gangrene on the body politic'.[8] Joy's reflections demonstrated that the inhabitants of Belfast had both discharged their Christian duty to relieve the poor and done so in a way that demonstrated their local civic patriotism by their voluntary efforts. In this, the town's citizens had followed the tradition of voluntary association that could be traced back to the Volunteers, founded in the town in the 1770s for fear of invasion, in which Joy had been active. The tradition of bonding together to solve local problems, political and social, had continued through the 1790s and could, Joy implied, be seen as flourishing in the early nineteenth century.[9]

Henry Joy's tract was a clever combination of a number of arguments blended into a carefully constructed package. Relief of the poor was presented as a neatly interlocking structure. Three institutions – the Poorhouse, the fever hospital and the House of Industry – he argued, 'resemble the three columns of a dome, mutually supporting and supported by each other: while some minor and occasional charities fill up the chasm and complete the whole'.[10] In fact, Joy's neat edifice was of very recent creation and had evolved organically rather than being planned. Joy's 'first great charity', the Poorhouse, emerged only slowly and uncertainly. According to an inscription on the foundation stone, the Poorhouse was begun in August 1771, possibly encouraged by a famine early that year, when a town meeting was held to discuss the collection of funds for the purchase and distribution of food to the distressed poor in an attempt to reduce begging on the streets.[11] The wait for the Poorhouse had been a long one since the body behind it, the Belfast Charitable Society, had first met in 1752. Although it was almost twenty years old when the Poorhouse was created, the Charitable Society had no legal form. As a result, when the Society acquired the property on which the building was erected in 1771, it was conveyed not to the Society but to Robert Thompson and others in trust for the Society, and a further part of the property was conveyed to Henry Joy. The issue of legal form would not be resolved until 1774, when a rider was attached to a bill amending a 1772 act establishing houses of industry in county towns. None of this suggests a carefully planned evolution of ways of dealing with the poor.

Rather it suggests tentative steps towards a solution to a problem that was rather nebulous.

THE PROBLEM OF THE POOR

The problem of the poor, both able-bodied and aged sick, was of long standing and well recognised in Ireland. Some contemporaries in eighteenth-century Belfast thought a good deal about this matter. Perhaps the clearest formulation of the position of the poor in the town in the middle of the eighteenth century comes in the sermons of the vicar of Shankill (the parish in which Belfast lay), James Saurin, who was active in poor relief in the middle of the century and a prominent early member of the Charitable Society. For Saurin, the poor were part of the natural order rather than a problem to be solved. As he told his hearers for the first time in 1749, society was unequally divided but ordered by God's providence:

> To consider things as they are now modelled and as the necessities of society now require there is a plain and visible subordination between men. Some are placed upon an eminence, invested with authority and power commanding the service and obedience of other people though in a much less conspicuous station, yet through the easiness of their circumstances and the plenty they are blessed with move on in a lower but still a pleasant sphere, whilst many through necessity, penury and want are obliged through constant drudgery and toil to be instruments and agents in the hands of those above them and to depend on their own industry and the good will of others for their maintenance and support.[12]

'Society', claimed Saurin, was held together by 'a mutual compact and agreement, a reciprocal trust and confidence in each other', but injustice and distrust dissolved that compact.[13] Thus the rich had a duty to relieve the poor but not extinguish poverty, which was both a religious and a social imperative.

This recognition of the existence of the poor and the duty of managing the problem resulted in well-established techniques for poor relief practised both by individuals and through the establishment of institutions. Since charity was primarily a religious duty, it was managed principally in the context of the churches. Belfast Presbyterians, for instance, supported poor children at school and, seemingly, maintained between thirty and forty poor women in the early eighteenth century, as well as making occasional payments to strangers or those in want. Coffins, for instance, might be provided for those who died in poverty. Unfortunately, the loss of the Church of Ireland vestry records for Shankill parish means that nothing can be said about actions by the established church. Poor relief, however, was not confined to the churches. Material wealth held by individuals was deemed to be a gift of God, and hence there was a religious duty to share resources with the less fortunate and help in the preservation of social order. Belfast residents regularly made provision for the poor in their wills, often to be distributed through the churches. From at least 1631, there had been another arrangement whereby the corporation had used the money left to the poor as working capital, and the interest gained was paid to the churchwardens who distributed it to the poor. In rarer cases the corporation might intervene directly to help poor children avail of apprenticeships.[14]

While such well-established techniques for managing the poor proved adequate for most purposes, there were periods of enhanced stress that were much more challenging. Harvest crises or disease pushed some to the margins of society and caused others, balanced precariously on the edge of subsistence, to fall off the edge of the social cliff into destitution or death. Harvest crises, for example, posed problems for grain supply and for feeding the urban population that depended on a rural agricultural surplus for its food. The famine of 1740–1 arose from bad weather in the autumn of 1740, with blizzards in Belfast resulting in food shortages and grain riots. In response, the Presbyterians in the town established a relief committee.[15] Disease, sometimes associated with food shortages, created equally serious problems for both rich and poor, and the large-scale mortality resulting from the severe smallpox epidemic in Belfast in the summer of 1733 was long remembered.[16] Such periods of crisis can be identified from the surges in the number of burials registered in the Belfast parish registers. In the first surviving parish register for Belfast, that for 1745–61, two periods of crisis can be identified: in 1750–1 and again in 1756–7.[17] The crisis of 1750–1 is the less well documented. In 1750, burials, particularly child burials, surged in the summer months of July, August and September, which suggests deaths from an epidemic, such as a return of smallpox, rather than a simple harvest failure with resulting food shortage. A second peak of burials in January, February and March 1751 may well represent the effects of winter on those at the edge of society, weakened by disease over the summer and autumn. In traditional fashion James Saurin, the vicar, mounted the pulpit in Belfast in January 1751 to tell his hearers to accept their lot in a resigned, cheerful and willing way, since it was God's will. Saurin repeated his message the following month. The poor should labour for their goods, shaking off idleness and sloth, since their poverty was more than compensated for by the gifts of God. In February he repeated the message of resignation in the face of providential events in a sermon on the resurrection of Lazarus.[18] However, resignation was not an occasion for exploitation, as Saurin warned in December 1751:

> whether in times of dearth & scarcity we monopolize necessary and useful commodities, and raise their price at pleasure to the ruin & destruction of the poor and needy, or whether knowing the extremity of those we deal with, we beat them down to a low & unreasonable price & force them to come to our own unjust & cruel terms, a species of injustice this particularly observed by Solomon in these strong & emphatical words, 'He that withholdeth corn, the people shall curse him, but blessing shall be upon the head of him that selleth it'.[19]

Much of the detail of this 1750–1 crisis is uncertain, but the crisis of 1756–7, which extended over the entire country, is better documented and the impact on the Belfast poor clearer.[20] Burials surged in the autumn of 1756, typical of mortality linked to harvest failure and a dramatically reduced food supply. A grain shortage is confirmed by other sources, and grain riots in the town were reported by the *Belfast News-Letter*. Grain shortages were exacerbated by speculative activity on the part of merchants, and throughout the winter the grain riots worsened, with an armed guard having to be posted on the Market House to prevent looting and the collapse of order. There was little comfort from elsewhere. The merchant Daniel Mussenden in his Belfast house received letters from all across Ireland detailing a worsening harvest and presaging food shortages. Mussenden himself imported grain from England in the hope of ameliorating conditions in Belfast.[21] Saurin again took to the pulpit in August 1756 to preach the same sermons he had used in January and February 1751 about the need for contentment and resignation in the face of God's will.[22] While the effects of this crisis were felt throughout the economy of Belfast, it was the poor who suffered disproportionately. Burials of those designated 'poor' in the register surged from eight in 1755 to thirty-two the following year and peaked at forty-nine in 1757 before tailing off to twenty-four in 1758. While total burials in 1757 were a quarter higher than in 1758, poor burials were up by more than half.

Enigmatically, in the worst year of the crisis, as measured by burial totals, the poor comprised a smaller percentage of the burials than they did in the following, apparently less severe, year. This suggests that the impact on the poor was not simply starvation. Food shortages undoubtedly weakened the poor and left them vulnerable to diseases that might not have proved fatal in other circumstances, but the general economic dislocation caused by the crisis also had an impact. Such dislocation may well have meant less access to casual labour markets, and this limited the ability of the poor to survive over a number of years with reduced incomes to purchase food. Certainly, the nature of those termed 'poor' who were buried in 1757 was rather different to the burials of poor people in more settled years. In the early 1750s and then again at the end of the decade, between 70 and 80 per cent of the 'poor' burials were women, few of whom were described as widows. However, in 1756 and more markedly in 1757, men assumed a much greater proportion of poor burials: 50 per cent in 1757. It is not difficult to see here a body of men surviving at the edge of society by casual work or begging, but with the dislocation brought by food shortages they had slipped easily into the position of paupers. Weakened by food shortages, both as a result of absolute shortage of food and lack of money to buy what was available, they suffered hunger and succumbed to disease that in other circumstances they might have survived.

SOLVING THE PROBLEM OF THE POOR?

There is no doubt that the crises of the 1750s raised awareness of the challenge posed by the relief of the poor and its associated problem of disorder. As many of James Saurin's sermons stressed, ideas of proper conduct increasingly rested on personal and social morality, and part of that was the ways that people treated each other – including how the rich treated those less fortunate. Traditional ways had clearly proved inadequate in Belfast, and new methods of poor relief were required. There were, it was clear to contemporaries, two issues to be confronted. The first was the poverty generated by irregular societal shocks of harvest failure and epidemic disease. In this case the immediate solution was ad hoc relief through emergency funds to those affected by famine. In October 1756, against the background of the grain riots, Saurin, preaching on the New Testament story of Ananias' gift of land to the early church, had speculated that part of the sale price had gone to relieve the poor since, for Christians, 'assisting their indigent brethren was their indispensable duty' and that the early church 'judged it proper that a public fund should be made for the relief of the poor and indigent brethren and by these means those in more easy circumstances might assist the want of others and by an excellent distribution set then upon a sort of equality'. His hearers clearly took the hint, and such a fund was established a month later.[23] In January 1757, the *Belfast News-Letter* reported that 496 people were being relieved from this fund, and this had risen to 607 by mid-March. By April the numbers had begun to fall but surged again to 635 by the end of May as grain shortages began to bite. Poor harvests in the autumn gave rise to further complaints about 'scarcity and dearness of provisions' and the need for additional subscriptions for poor relief; a parish beadle was also appointed to keep vagrants out of the town.

Such exceptional measures were certainly important in alleviating the poverty generated by crises such as harvest failures, but they did not deal with the long-term problem of structural poverty that had also been raised by the crises of the 1750s. Some argued for traditional measures. In 1763 Henry and Robert Joy, the Belfast printers who were later active in the Belfast Charitable Society, reprinted a pamphlet that argued for a traditional solution by insisting that the poor should be assigned to their parishes and supported by them in a scheme funded by local taxation.[24] In Belfast, the parish, as the fundamental unit of local government, appears to have been moribund at mid-century. While the original vestry books have not survived, it appears from reports in the *Belfast News-Letter* that the vestry did not meet before the middle of the 1760s except in October 1756, when it convened to organise poor relief during the harvest crisis. The absence of the leadership in social matters, which the vestry could have provided, was made worse by a more serious problem: the absence of a landlord who might organise the town. In the early eighteenth century, Belfast was a landlord town, controlled by the largely absentee Chichester family. For some of the inhabitants of Belfast, the town was understood not simply as bricks and mortar but as a set of personal relationships. The first parish register, for instance, showed an awareness of such relationships by recording the names of the parents of many of those buried, yet many of these were clearly not burials of children; others were described in relation to their husband or wife. The genealogical network was impossible to escape in a town of this size.[25] Position in the social order was defined by an individual's dependency on others and, as it was strongly hierarchical with Donegall at its paternalistic head, a person's position was fixed in relation to him. The merchant John Black wrote to his son in 1765 expressing rather old-fashioned views that he had heard from one of Donegall's supporters: 'his lordship Donegall hath intimated to him his sure intention of paying a visit soon to his vassal Belfastians where I am sure he will be heartily welcome and I pray to God to give him his grace that he may make a proper and good use of a valuable talent committed to him by Almighty Providence for his own good and others welfare.'[26]

In this hierarchical world everyone had their place, even the poor; indeed, some Ulster parishes even claimed their own poor by issuing them with badges.[27]

Those higher in the traditional social order were perceived to have a responsibility for the less fortunate. At least one group of Belfast linen weavers during the 1756 crisis thought so, condemning the actions of socially negligent profiteers and 'the distress to which many of the poor are reduced by the cruelty and oppression of hucksters, regraters and forestallers of the market'.[28] As a sign of their social concern they presented a silver bowl to the sovereign of the town, Stewart Banks, 'in grateful acknowledgement of his extraordinary care of the markets and impartial administration'.[29] Lord Donegall, as landlord of Belfast, had some measure of moral responsibility for the town's poor; he was responsible for protecting them from exploitation by others and providing limited relief where possible. Thus, the family's departure from the town after the burning of their castle in 1706 caused distress, since they would no longer be available either as employer or as a last resort for aid. As the vicar, William Tisdall, put it:

> [T]he unhappy effects descended to all the inferior ranks of people, especially the poor of the parish, insomuch as some tradesmen were obliged to leave the town, others fell into great want whilst a number of the common poor were reduced to the last necessity, all this for want of that employment and of those charitable supplies which they usually had from that great and numerous family and their dependicies.[30]

The departure of the family was part of a wider problem. The fire in Belfast Castle was only one difficulty that the family had to face. It was also in dispute with the principal merchants of the town over the port duties and over the control of urban elections. Once sympathetic to Presbyterianism, the family increasingly moved towards the established church, thereby creating further divisions. Within the town itself, early eighteenth-century Presbyterian factions, which formed the greater part of the town's population, were at war with each other over theological questions. These various disputes placed considerable strain on Belfast society, calling into question the whole corporate existence of the town and raising wider concerns about loyalty to the state.[31] All this was played out against a background of economic stagnation, falling trade and urban decay made worse by the absence of the Donegall family and problems with leases in the town. In such a divided town, and in the absence of a landlord, it was clear that a new sort of social policy needed to be devised in the wake of the crises of the 1750s.

New approaches to the problem of the poor were, however, being formulated elsewhere that might have been useful in Belfast, in particular, the idea of delivering poor relief in an institutional setting rather than in the form of payments made by churches or some other local body. In the seventeenth century there had been attempts to establish houses of correction for sturdy beggars in Dublin, but these had little impact outside the capital and did nothing for the sick poor. In the later seventeenth century, migration into Dublin forced the city corporation to take the problem of the poor more seriously with the establishment of a series of workhouses, the most important being that built in 1706, which brought some 324 parish poor and city beggars together under one roof. Apart from the establishment of a poorhouse in Cork in 1735, the idea of poorhouses was not widespread in Ireland until the middle of the eighteenth century when, in the wake of the harvest crisis of 1740–1, the problem of poverty and its relief impinged on contemporary consciousness.[32] The idea was mooted for Belfast in 1752 when plans for the use of money raised by a lottery in the town included a new church, a poorhouse and a hospital that was needed according to the *Belfast News-Letter* 'for the reception of infirm and diseased poor'. The lottery collapsed and the hoped-for funds did not materialise immediately,[33] but the idea did not go away. In 1765, the Belfast merchant John Black imagined the improvements that were necessary to bring the town into line with modern norms, and among these he 'also proposed a poor house or hospital for the Christian and charity relief of the sick and distressed who are seen in such numbers on your dirty streets'.[34]

VOLUNTEERING A SOLUTION FOR POOR RELIEF

There were good reasons why Black should have thought an institution to deal with the poor significant rather than relying on sporadic relief schemes. He may not have realised that Belfast was on the edge of a boom that would result in an influx of people into the town and, for at least some of these, the town would be overwhelming and they would be pushed to the margins of society. Aside from this practical matter, there was another consideration. In the 1760s John Black was not the only person reimagining Belfast. The wider context involved a desire for improvement that was transforming provincial towns both in Britain and Ireland that Peter Borsay has described as an 'urban renaissance' underpinned by civility, voluntary associations and better behaviour, reflected in improved manners. The creation of a polite society in Belfast implied not only the cultivation of polite manners among the mercantile community – or, as one description of the town in 1738 noted, 'trade don't always spoil politeness' – but also that polite and modern society needed to be reflected in an ordered landscape with impressive public buildings in which people could meet each other, reflecting the latest architectural fashions.[35] This view of society, based on voluntary activity by groups of people freely associating together, in contrast to the fragmented patriarchal world of the Donegalls, provided a model for providing poor relief: a world of what Saurin described as society founded on 'mutual compact and agreement' rather than ordered hierarchy in which power flowed downwards from the landlord. Conversation and apparently fussy yet correct manners promoted something deeper. As the Donegall Street resident Martha McTier observed in 1777, 'while the little attentions and tendernesses which are oftenest required to make life agreeable are, thank God, frequently met with ... we aim at unalterable steady friendship where interest of no sort is its foundation'.[36] Such disinterestedness was precisely the quality that promoted independence, identified by those who ruled as the essential quality of the governing elite at both national and local levels. Thus, politeness could be transformed into virtue and provide the rules for an associational culture. It is hardly surprising that Saurin preached on the subject of polite conversation and how to encourage it in Belfast, for the bond of friendship was 'the tie that keeps us together'.[37]

The idea of a voluntary association to deal with the problem of poor relief in a fractured society clearly became a very attractive one for Belfast. In the early part of the eighteenth century there were few, if any, charitable societies in Ireland. It was only in the wake of the severe harvest failures of 1740–1 that the associational impulse of eighteenth-century Ireland spread into the charitable sector. Initially, in Dublin, this took the form of charitable musical societies created to raise money for the poor and prisoners in the capital. By the early 1750s this impulse spread outside the capital into Munster and into other occupational groups, such as merchants, and by the time of the subsistence crisis of 1765–6 such charitable societies were widespread.[38] These were supplemented by government action, most notably the County Infirmaries Act of 1766 and the 1772 legislation establishing houses of industry.[39] This wave of enthusiasm for the better management of the poor, together with the particular local needs of the fractured society in Belfast, provides the context for the effective formation of the Belfast Charitable Society. A meeting was summoned on 28 August 1752, in the wake of the demographic crisis of 1750–1, 'to consider of a proper way to raise a sum for building a poor house and hospital and a new church in or near the town of Belfast'.[40] The scheme was almost stillborn. The lottery which was intended to raise the funds collapsed in disarray. However, the power of the voluntary association, probably together with the impact of the demographic crisis of 1756–7, held the committee together. The early minute books suggest that the committee of 'managers' of the scheme met throughout the 1750s and 1760s. Initially, there was some enthusiasm, with four meetings in 1752, nine the following year and seven in 1755. However, after this, meetings became less frequent, with no more than four a year, and in some years, such as 1756, 1758, 1761 and 1766, there was only one meeting.[41] Additional lotteries were held to supplement existing funds as well as investing existing resources in other lotteries. In addition, comments in the *Belfast News-Letter* suggest that funds may have been raised by collections within the town, with sections assigned to particular managers, possibly the same method as was used for the collection of parish cess or tithes, or possibly the areas used by the town constables.

The cohesion of the committee, comprised of a range of confessional backgrounds in Belfast, though overwhelmingly mercantile in background, held together by its voluntary and improving assumptions, ensured that funds were accumulated and retained, and by the 1760s the possibility of acquiring a site for a poorhouse came into view. Enthusiasm for the project was reawakened in the late 1760s. In 1763 the managers decided to approach Lord Donegall for a site and meetings became more frequent, increasing from one or two a year in the mid-1760s to twenty-three in 1768 and growing each year thereafter. At the start of the century, the Donegall family had retreated to England, leaving their Irish property in the hands of agents. Their absenteeism was complicated by a period in chancery due to the fourth earl's mental incapacity, and the town had decayed both physically and economically. In 1752 the trustees of the fourth earl, in a fit of enthusiasm for urban improvement (and increases in rents) had begun a major overhaul of urban leases. They set out their vision for the new town in a map of 1757. The central organising principle of the transformation was the creation of a new high-status quarter for Belfast focused on a new street, Linenhall Street (now Donegall Street).[42] The fourth earl did not live to see the proposal realised, as he died in the year the survey was made, leaving the fifth earl as a minor.

It was not until 1761 that the fifth earl came of age and could begin to pursue the ambitions of his predecessor by implementing a radical new leasing plan in 1767. Focusing his efforts on this new Donegall Street axis, he began shaping a number of public buildings that would make an architectural statement and would be appropriate to the emerging world of urban politeness. With Donegall Street it was something of a struggle. Not all were pleased with the new development. The merchant John Black grumbled of the new street, 'but why with these angles and curves at each end I leave to the projectors to give a reason.'[43] William Drennan, the Belfast doctor then living in Dublin, writing to his sister in Donegall Street in November 1796, was even more scathing, noting, 'I consider it [Donegall Street] as the bleakest situation of the bleakest street in the bleak North.'[44] Its attractiveness was not enhanced by the concentration of foul-smelling tan yards just to the west in North Street. The first surviving Belfast directory, that of 1807, suggests that the street never really developed the fashionable mix of residents and shopping that those who shaped improving landscapes hoped for.[45] There was a close relationship between leisure, urban improvement and consumption in the eighteenth century, and linking the social and economic strands through smart shops, luxury trades and prestigious residents was a key preoccupation of Donegall's scheme. According to the directory there were certainly a few smart residents, such as clergy, a physician and an attorney, together with a watchmaker, but there were also more mundane trades, such as a starch manufacturer and wholesale woollen drapers and linen merchants. Some of the earlier leases on Donegall Street do betray attempts to introduce smarter trades, such as the bookseller near the Poorhouse.[46] Fundamentally, Donegall did not have the funds to develop on the scale that he wished and had to lease substantial parts of the area, especially the lands behind Donegall Street to speculative builders, such as Hugh Dunlap and Roger Mulholland, who built to much greater densities and in a more prosaic style than Donegall would have wished.[47]

Central to Donegall's plans for this improving landscape was a suite of public buildings, an area in which Belfast was gravely deficient, which would give a concrete form to his grand scheme. As the agricultural improver Arthur Young commented tersely when visiting the town in 1776, 'the public buildings not numerous or very striking'.[48] Charles Abbot in 1792 put it more starkly: 'the public buildings … are all of brick but they are but few and little worth seeing'.[49] More charitably, John Gamble saw that 'neatness and trimness, indeed, rather than magnificence, are the characteristics of all the public buildings'.[50] Young did highlight the new Exchange built as part of this improvement in 1769 at the south end of Donegall Street; an Assembly Room, 'a very elegant room' according to Young, was added as a first floor in 1776 together with a tea room and card room to promote sociability since, as Martha McTier commented in 1784, at the card table 'happilly [sic] all are equal'.[51] Young added other elements of civility that promoted his new area. A new church costing £10,000 was constructed in 1774–6, 'one of the lightest and most pleasing I have anywhere seen', according to Young. A new linen hall was also built, but John Black thought it 'a little too distant from the town's centre to serve as a merchants exchange'.[52]

The opportunity of adding a poorhouse that would also be a significant new public building to this meagre stock clearly chimed with Donegall's agenda and was part of the reason why he was prepared to grant the site; the Charitable Society also wanted their building to be 'most ornamental to the town of Belfast' and chose the location accordingly, closing the vista along Donegall Street.[53] Belfast Charitable Society was certainly concerned that its building should chime with the modern note set by the development as a whole and consulted the London architect Robert Mylne, who had designed the now-demolished City of London Lying-in Hospital, and the Dublin architect Thomas Cooley, who had been involved in works on a number of public buildings in Dublin. However, it was Robert Joy, one of the owners of the *Belfast News-Letter* and brother of Henry Joy, who prepared the final plans drawing on Mylne's scheme. One of the main carpenters on the scheme was the architect Hugh Dunlop, who was an active property developer in Donegall Street.[54] Thus the scheme as it evolved reflected the desire for international fashion and local priorities in shaping the townscape. In the main, Joy followed Mylne's scheme closely, but there was one significant change. Mylne had designed a large dome and lantern over the central block of the building but, in 1773, probably at Joy's suggestion or at least with his consent, this was replaced by a tall octagonal stone tower with a spire rising from the middle of it.[55] The committee managing the building declared this to be 'unanimously and highly approved of'.[56] While the reason for the change was not articulated, it seems clear that the aim of the spire was to make the new building more prominent in the landscape as achieved by the tower on the Market House and the spire on the parish church. Thus, the vista along Donegall Street from the Exchange and Assembly Rooms was closed not simply by a prominent building but with a spire that clearly marked that building out as exceptional. Equally, for those travelling to the city from the north or south, along Queen Street or Carrick Hill, it focused attention on the Poorhouse. It was no accident that, as John Wesley commented on his visit to Belfast in 1778, 'the Poorhouse stands on an eminence, fronting the main street, and having a beautiful prospect on every side over the whole country'.[57] Such attention to vistas incorporated the Poorhouse firmly into Lord Donegall's vision but also served local needs by providing the image of a prosperous and well-appointed town that promoted economic activity and demonstrated civility. By directing attention to the building, it also stressed the virtues that underpinned it, in particular the voluntary nature of the institution and the civic values of the urban elite. The Poorhouse was not just for the poor but was also part of polite society, with balls and Volunteer reviews. The designation of one room as a 'card room' hints at other forms of sociability.[58] The form and shaping of the building reflected the diverse agendas that lay behind its creation.

CONCLUSION

By 1780 the Belfast Charitable Society was well established. Its claim to existence was clear from the newly erected Poorhouse at the end of Donegall Street. However, the hope that this might lie at the core of a new high social status centre of Belfast did not materialise. By 1800 the Poorhouse lay in the suburbs of the town, and a new high-profile residential centre was emerging around the core of the new town centred on Donegall Square. Legally the Poorhouse was secure, being underpinned by legislation, and already, by 1780, new roles were being explored for it. In 1779 Henry Joy proposed to establish a cotton-weaving centre for the children of the poor in the house, and by the 1790s it was already becoming involved in the supply of water to the town. Nor were the dead to be ignored, since in the 1790s, the Poorhouse established a new burial ground because the parish churchyard was overly full. All these were significant developments, and, as Henry Joy in his 1818 'Remarks' stressed, they were achieved by voluntary effort, without state support. Nor had there been any significant landlord involvement apart from the leasing of the site to the society. Joy was right to stress these developments, for they mark a very significant shift in Belfast's perception of itself focused on the question of the poor and how they were to be treated.

In the 1750s Belfast was reshaped, and the founding of Belfast Charitable Society was part of that process. During the late seventeenth and eighteenth centuries it had been a traditional, hierarchical landlord town in which political and social authority had flowed from the Chichesters through the tightly controlled corporation into the wider world. At the start of the eighteenth century, that world had fragmented under a series of political and religious pressures which had led to the withdrawal of the Donegall family from the town and the collapse of the corporation as a governing body. Disputes with Presbyterianism and economic decline in the first half of the eighteenth century, and the economic collapse of the town, prevented any serious attempt to resolve these problems, and the connectedness of Belfast society was exceedingly fragile.

It was only with the demographic crises of 1750–1 and 1756–7 that the middling sort in Belfast began, falteringly, to consider ways of tackling the social problems, notably that of poverty, that the town was experiencing. While not abandoning completely their old assumptions about hierarchy, they tapped into a growing fashion for voluntary associations to transform the relationships that bound people together and, in turn, discovered a new world of associational cultures, manners and politeness that helped to hold civic society together under the broad heading of the desirable quality of natural virtue. It was these ideas that penetrated the Belfast middling sort, and the formation of the Society as a voluntary body was replicated in other aspects of civic life, from the establishment of Freemasons in the town, the patronising of balls, coffee houses and dining clubs, to the creation of the Volunteers and, ultimately, the United Irishmen. From the 1770s the town itself began to develop parallel representative institutions, such as town meetings, a reinvigorated vestry, the Chamber of Commerce of 1783 and the Police Commission of 1800 outside the control of the Donegalls.[59] Moreover, this helped to create a local environment conducive to the dramatic economic expansion of the town in the late eighteenth century. The founding of the Belfast Charitable Society was not simply an isolated philanthropic act intended to relieve the poor but a social experiment that provided a model for tying together the town in dramatically new and innovative ways, with authority travelling from the bottom up rather than the top down. In doing so it provided the mercantile 'middling sort' with a chance to demonstrate their own form of disinterestedness that contemporaries thought led to virtuous leadership and even a sort of gentility. In this context it is easy to see why the development of the Poorhouse was such a long-drawn-out and tentative process, and why Henry Joy would wish to celebrate and insist on the voluntary nature of the Society in his 1818 address to the Literary Society.

CHAPTER FIVE

'Doing the Needful': Belfast Charitable Society and its Outdoor Relief Scheme

Aaron D. McIntyre

℘

In 1837 the Poorhouse was described as 'an ornamental edifice, with a lofty spire, [which] stands in a very conspicuous elevated situation, at the upper end of Donegal-street [sic]'.[1] This institution provided accommodation and support to thousands of people, from the young and the old to passing sailors, all of whom sought sanctuary within its walls. However, this does not reflect the full impact of Belfast Charitable Society's philanthropic activities during its early history. As we have seen in previous chapters, the Poorhouse and infirmary opened in 1774 with provision for approximately seventy individuals. However, there was an acute awareness that the institution could not alleviate all cases of poverty and distress within what was then the town of Belfast. This quickly led to the introduction of a system of outdoor relief to support the poor in their own homes on a scale that had never been witnessed in Belfast before.

As was the case with the running of the Poorhouse, the financial resources for the provision of outdoor relief came from public subscriptions. Subscribers to the Belfast Charitable Society who contributed at

least a guinea were granted voting rights to elect the Poorhouse committee at the general board, as well as the power to sign petitions for admission to the Poorhouse and recommend cases for outdoor relief. This form
of administration has been termed a 'subscriber democracy', where rights
and regulations were clearly defined and membership of the charity was
open to all who could afford the membership fee.[2] This included women,
one such being Barbara Collyer, one of the original subscribers in 1774,
who recommended a number of individuals and families as 'fit objects'
for admission to the Poorhouse, as well as for outdoor relief.[3] She continued to support the charity throughout her life and, following her death in
1788, bequeathed 200 guineas to the poor as part of her estate.[4]

The administration of the outdoor relief scheme mirrored the system
for admission to the Poorhouse. The charity divided Belfast into six districts,
with members of the Society assigned responsibility for overseeing cases
in their respective areas. Those seeking relief had to present a petition
signed by two Belfast Charitable Society subscribers, which were heard
at the weekly committee meetings for discussion and approval. Outdoor
relief cases from areas outside the limits of the town, but within the parish,
were entered on a separate 'Country List'. This list included places such as
Stranmillis, which were ultimately subsumed into Belfast city.[5]

As the outdoor relief scheme continued to grow, the Charitable
Society took steps to demonstrate the importance of the funds subscribed
by the public and encouraged others to support its work. In September
1776 the Society produced an alphabetical 'List of the Poor of this Town
& Parish, who receive Charity', with Robert Joy printing 200 copies to
be circulated to members and the remainder to be made available in
the Poorhouse.[6] The creation of such lists was not without consequence,
however, as some individuals and families, fearing the stigma attached to
receiving relief, were deterred from seeking assistance when they needed
it. One petitioner, Eleanor Stewart, when seeking relief informed the
Society that she would 'accept no charity without secrecy'.[7] The agency
of the poor who petitioned for relief can also be traced in their requests,
in the Charitable Society's responses and in the response of petitioners
themselves. In select cases, petitioners were offered the choice of whether
they would prefer to be admitted to the Poorhouse or to be put on the 'out
poor' list.[8] There were others such as the Taylor family of Saltwater Bridge

who 'would not accept any Relief' but were 'thankful to the Committee for their care of them',[9] or the McMaster family who would 'not accept of relief till they [were] more in need'.[10]

Belfast Charitable Society soon came to realise that it proved 'easier to prevent economic collapse than to raise the destitute', and outdoor relief came to dominate its work.[11] During the 1770s, following the opening of the Poorhouse, petitions to the charity for outdoor relief far outstripped requests for admission to the Poorhouse. In 1776 there was an increase from 130 to 160 'out poor',[12] growing to 263 petitions in 1778 (80 per cent of all petitions presented to the committee).[13] By 1795, 336 families were being supported by the scheme.[14] It should be noted that there were also cases where individuals were refused relief for being 'healthy and able to work' or not having dependents.[15] However, it is clear that the requests for outdoor relief reflected the pressures of daily life in late eighteenth- and early nineteenth-century Belfast, from births, desertions and deaths to unemployment, sickness, rent and issues around migration, all of which are explored thematically below.

THE BADGED BEGGARS

As construction of the Poorhouse was underway, an act of parliament for the badging of the Poor was introduced to give 'countenance and assistance' to those 'disabled by old age or infirmities to earn their living'. Badges were issued to the poor as a licence to beg, within a strict framework of criteria, which included residency in the parish of Belfast for at least a year.[16] In February 1775, following the opening of the Poorhouse, a number of beds were provided for some of the badged poor, with new badges issued to those who could not be accommodated immediately.[17] Although no known examples of the original Poorhouse beggars' badges survive, they consisted of an oval pewter disc with impressed numbers and the seal of Belfast Charitable Society.[18] The motto impressed around the badge read: 'He that giveth to the poor lendth [sic] to the Lord', reflecting both the religious and civic duty to assist the poor by those who had achieved wealth through God's providence.[19]

An advertisement in the *Belfast News-Letter*, published shortly after the opening of the Poorhouse, called on Belfast's citizens to 'direct their attention to those [badged poor] and discourage all public Beggars, who, they may be assured, are not entitled to their Charity', drawing a clear distinction between genuine cases of poverty and those 'strolling beggars' who moved from town to town.[20] In March 1775 the Society resolved to remove the remaining licenses from the badged poor and, in its place, establish an outdoor relief scheme, giving each of the former licensed beggars a fortnightly allowance to be collected from the Poorhouse (see Table 5.1).[21]

The archives held at Clifton House give us an insight into the lives of some of the original badged beggars who became the first 'out poor', the term used by the Charitable Society in this period for those receiving outdoor relief. Grace Sheals, alternatively given as Shiels, for example, continued to receive outdoor relief for several years for herself and her young family. Grace received fortnightly payments until April 1778 when she petitioned for additional help. In order to enable her to provide for her family, she was granted a spinning wheel and a pound of dressed flax and was then struck off the 'out poor' list.[22] The Sheals family continued to receive 12lb of meal each fortnight but it appears that Grace continued to struggle, and in January 1780 she petitioned

Table 5.1 Badged poor moved on to fortnightly outdoor relief payments

Name	Age	Notes	Location
Grace Sheals	–	4 young children	Barrack Street
John Gilliland	80	Old wife	Pound
William Davison	75	Old wife	Pound
Thomas Wynn	75	Old wife and grandchild	Sandy Row
Catharine Gillespy	77	1 grandchild	Millfield
James Jones	80	Old wife	–
Daniel Hagan's wife	–	–	Carrick Hill
Mary McKinney	30	3 young children	Hercules Lane
Ann Campbell	45	Blind with 2 children	Long Lane
Kenith McKensy	80	Old wife	Old Quay
Jane Sands	–	Blind living with sister	Mitchell's Court
Rose Proctor	75	Grandchild who has 'fall fits'	Long Lane

to have two of her children admitted to the Poorhouse.[23] Jane Sands' situation also appears to have deteriorated over time, as her allowance was increased in April 1775 and she was ultimately admitted to the Poorhouse in May of that year.[24] Jane was later recorded as one of the 'finest spinners' in the institution, and the 'finest dressed flax' was procured for her to spin.[25] When John Gilliland passed away in May 1778, his fortnightly payment was transferred to his widow at a reduced rate. She was also given an allowance of 12lb of meal fortnightly in addition to her reduced payment.[26] These few examples of the original badged beggars illustrate the unique circumstances of each individual and their families, as well as the attention paid by the Belfast Charitable Society to each case on its own merits.

OUTPATIENTS

Alongside the beginning of the outdoor relief scheme, 1775 witnessed the birth of public healthcare in Belfast with the opening of the Poorhouse infirmary, which provided inpatient care for those formally admitted by the institution's doctors.[27] Medical provision in the town continued to develop under the auspices of the Belfast Charitable Society, in response to the distress identified by members of its committee and the realisation that the infirmary alone was insufficient to deal with the rising number of medical cases in the town. In July 1776, the charity decided to allot 'a portion of their funds for the benefit of Externs or out-Patients'.[28] This proposal also included a provision for what could arguably be viewed as a predecessor of our modern GP surgeries, with individuals allowed to attend the Poorhouse and seek 'advice & assistance' from the physician and surgeon in attendance each Tuesday and Saturday at 12 o'clock, with cases afterwards reviewed by the Poorhouse committee.[29]

Outpatients were subject to the same rules and regulations that determined eligibility for other forms of assistance from the Society, principally that they had to have been resident in the parish for at least a year and to be a genuine object of charity. Some individuals sought relief from the Poorhouse even though they did not meet the formal criteria. One such individual was Arthur Rippard. Arthur, who was living at Carrick Hill, had recently moved to Belfast from Saintfield, County Down. In January 1778 the Committee reported that he had made several representations for medical provision but was 'inadmissible, as being a foreigner'. However, the charity did what they could to assist Arthur, paying his travel back to Saintfield, where the parish was considered to be responsible for his care.[30] Most of those who became outpatients were individuals who had previously been admitted to the infirmary but had recovered to a sufficient level to be sent home. John McLean was discharged from the hospital in July 1777 but was instructed to attend the apothecary every morning for dressings as an outpatient.[31] John was also granted immediate financial relief on his discharge, with subsequent fortnightly payments through the out poor list.[32] Although we do not know the nature of John's illness, it was not until April 1778 that he had recovered sufficiently to return to work, for which he was granted a one-off payment of 11s 4½d to re-establish his trade.[33]

Due to demand for beds in the infirmary, cases found to be incurable were discharged to live out their final days in their own homes. Two cases of this nature stand out in the archive, both of which fell under the care of Dr Robert Stevenson, a physician renowned for his work on cancers. Widow Collins of Carrick Hill first received temporary outdoor relief in December 1775, the sum of which was later increased 'on account of her sick daughter'.[34] Her daughter, Mary, was subsequently admitted to the infirmary but was found to be incurable by Dr Stevenson. It was therefore recommended that she return to her mother and be 'taken care of there as an Out patient' with a fortnightly allowance.[35] Against the odds, Mary Collins survived; however, she relapsed in May 1777 and her mother petitioned for assistance for 'a cure for dropsy'. This was granted, and Widow Collins' monthly relief was also doubled until such time as her daughter recovered.[36] Others, sadly, were not as fortunate as Mary Collins. In October 1777 Dr Stevenson requested to trial a procedure on Patrick McLaughlin's case of cheek cancer, although the surgeon was 'very doubtful of [a] cure'. The committee granted permission on the condition that, if it was not successful, Patrick would remain in his home and receive a maintenance.[37] By December 1777 Patrick had been discharged as incurable and put on the 'Fortnightly List of Objects [of Charity] at

3s 3d'.[38] He passed away in January 1778 and his death placed his widow in a perilous financial position, so the Society agreed to continue her outdoor relief payments.[39]

The Poorhouse committee also had to deal with cases of sickness and illness which impacted on people's ability to support themselves or their families through employment, but outdoor relief cases of this nature tended to be temporary. In February 1776 two petitions for relief were received from the Old Quay area of the town: John McAlester was 'lame and unable to work' and Donald McIntier 'afflicted & confined with a Rheumatism'. Both men were granted 3s 3d per month 'until recovered'.[40] There was also an acknowledgement of those older residents whose ailments were caused by advancing years and, as such, should be provided for on a permanent basis. In extreme cases immediate relief could be granted by a committee member before a petition was investigated. At the same meeting as the cases from Old Quay were examined, Henry Logan of New Row, who was 'old, sick & in great distress', was granted immediate relief not exceeding 5s 5d, and upon investigation he was granted 2s 2d per fortnight and put on the list of out poor.[41]

Concerns for the cleanliness of the outpatients did not escape the attention of the Belfast Charitable Society and a bathing house was constructed in the grounds of the Poorhouse in 1779. The key to the new addition was available to all subscribers to the charity and 'to such poor patients as may be recommended by any of the medical gentlemen' on the condition that the key was returned immediately afterwards.[42] The growth of medical advice texts in the 1700s contained references to the 'cold regimen', which included cold bathing, and it may be that this helped to inform the decision to construct a bathing house in the Poorhouse grounds.[43] In a later period, bathing fell under the control of the Belfast Charitable Society's 'clothing committee' which granted tickets to both Poorhouse residents and to 'out poor' for use of the facility.[44] This function was ultimately taken over by public baths which emerged in the late Victorian period. The outpatients provided for through the Belfast Charitable Society's outdoor relief scheme were therefore not only supported through their illnesses with medication and healthcare, but were also provided for financially during their illnesses when they were temporarily unable to work.

FROM CRADLE TO GRAVE

Belfast Charitable Society's outdoor relief scheme continued to develop, providing assistance for all aspects of the lives of the labouring classes, from issues relating to life-cycle poverty through to the payment of rent, in order to try and prevent the economic collapse of the cases under its care. One area that came under their attention was the upkeep of motherless infants. In 1793 the Humane Female Society for the Relief of Lying-in Women established a lying-in hospital in Belfast to provide maternity care for the town's pregnant women.[45] However, for the woman and children who survived the immediate perils of childbirth, there were other issues to face. In October 1776, for example, James Mullan came before the committee to petition for help for his 'young Infant Child, a Boy of about Eight months Old, [who is] in a perishing condition by the death of his mother'. The Poorhouse believed it to be 'a laudable Charity' for it to pay half the wages of a wet nurse, which was 'to be Continued for One year, if the child lives so long'.[46] The final phrase is a stark reminder of the levels of infant mortality rates during the period.

Pregnancy could also impact on the household income available to families. The Belfast Charitable Society granted temporary relief to women such as John Butty's wife, who was 'great with child', and he a 'blind fiddler', in order to support them through the pregnancy when she could not work.[47] There were also individuals like Michael McCluskey who had suffered an accident at work in a flax mill and, whilst he had recovered from the accident, it left his hand partly disabled. His petition gives us an insight into his home life, as his wife was 'lying-in' and the family was 'in distress' due to these circumstances.[48] Petitions, as has been established, were granted on the merit of each individual case. Breastfeeding mothers had to remain at home to support their new infant, thus reducing the overall household income in two-parent families. There were also numerous instances of death caused by work-related accidents which fell before the committee. Widow Burns was allowed a monthly payment 'until her child is off her breast', as her husband had perished 'in Mr Cunningham's works'; such was the seriousness of her situation that she was also granted immediate relief in addition to the monthly allowance.[49]

Desertion of wives by their husbands was also sadly an all-too-common occurrence and was something that forced many women to petition for relief. Jane McCullough, whose husband John had deserted her and their family of four young children, one of whom was 'still at its mother's breast and another blind in the Small Pocks', was put on the list of out poor.[50] There is only one recorded petition for a man, George Bell, whose 'wife has deserted him in his distress'.[51] This deserted husband was granted permission to receive his meals from the Poorhouse.[52] Outdoor relief in the form of food was another avenue open to petitioners. The number of those receiving food increased to such an extent by 1776 that it necessitated a weekly report of 'the food delivered daily out of the House for the poor' to be provided to the committee going forward.[53]

The Poorhouse provided other forms of relief, such as paying for lodgings and rents in order to relieve the destitution faced by many families in the town. In addition to their lodgings, some of the poor living in Belfast rented small patches of ground on the edge of town that they could cultivate in order to provide food for their family. However, the payment of the rents due on these additional plots could prove difficult for some, leading to individuals such as Mary Major petitioning 'for some assistance to pay her rent for Potatoe Ground'.[54] After investigating her case, 10 shillings was paid to her landlord directly by the Poorhouse committee so that she could keep the plot.[55] Not only did the Society pay the rents to the landlords, it also supported individuals who took in others viewed as objects of charity. Rose Hamill received half a crown fortnightly for lodging and providing care to Widow Hunt.[56] Even those who lodged foreign sailors were granted relief in times of crisis. In July 1777, for example, John Debutt of Castle Street appeared before the committee and informed them that 'ten days since, a seafaring Danish subject came to his house for lodging, on his way to Newry, where his ship lay, having landed out of the Glorious Memory in this Port – And that he fell sick the same night and still continues – Praying the means of support for the Stranger'.[57] John Debutt was afterwards granted relief 'for subsisting the Swede'.[58] People whose homes were damaged by natural causes could also receive assistance. One such individual was Widow Subridge, who received 5s 5d 'having had her house blown down by the late storm'.[59] Fire was an ever-present danger in the growing market town, as illustrated by the case of James Scott of Ballygomartin who petitioned for relief due to 'the miserable condition to which his family are reduced by an accidental fire, which consumed his house, his loom and a 19 hundred web [of linen]'. Although he only requested 'some blankets to cover his poor distressed family', James was granted half a guinea immediate relief.[60]

Within four months of the Poorhouse opening its doors for the reception of the poor, the committee resolved that 'the Orderly shall take no concern in providing coffins for the poor dying out of the house'.[61] Exceptions to this rule were made, however, such as in January 1776 when the Poorhouse committee agreed to pay the cost of a coffin for the burial of John Graham, who had died after a period of receiving outdoor relief.[62] Similarly, the demands on the committee's time due to the high volume of petitions meant that not everyone received relief in a timely manner. Christian Wright, who had passed away before his petition could be considered by the Charitable Society, was 'furnished with a coffin'.[63] The regulation around coffins for the out poor were difficult to implement, especially when poor families, like James McGane who had five young children, petitioned the Poorhouse for a 'coffin for his old mother' to stop the family sinking further into debt.[64] Ultimately, the 1775 rule became redundant as the Society was forced to face the realities of supporting the poor who had died and the associated costs for those they left behind, who were already struggling without additional funeral expenses.

EMPLOYMENT

Belfast Charitable Society's outdoor relief scheme was responsive to the needs of those of the labouring classes who required support to find employment or to re-establish their trade following periods of illness or injury. Two of the first recipients to benefit from the outdoor relief scheme were Philip Magill and his wife, who were provided with the money to purchase a spinning wheel and a spade 'on a solemn promise not to beg or be troublesome'.[65] Particular care was given to those who demonstrated a willingness to better their situation. Robert Joy recommend William Quig and his wife for a wheel in 1779, describing William as 'a sober, industrious man, & doing what he can for support of his numerous family'. The committee granted William a spinning wheel and half a pound of dressed flax to assist his family.[66] The Society was also aware that wages did not always cover the expenses paid out by families to cover necessities. When cases of this nature were presented before the committee, the outdoor relief payments it granted acted as a top-up to the petitioner's earned income. In July 1775, Mary McKinney was given one of the spinning wheels owned by the Poorhouse and was allowed to remain on the list of out poor at the rate of 1s 1d each fortnight.[67] Other examples of employment support granted to petitioners could include the granting of a room in the Poorhouse to use for industry to support themselves, in essence a rent-free workspace.[68]

There were cases of chronic poverty that the Belfast Charitable Society had to address, with many people petitioning for additional relief, to have children entered into the Poorhouse and for clothing. Ann Curran is one individual who received relief in a myriad of forms over the years. Her case highlights the sheer levels of destitution faced by many. Ann was originally a resident of the Poorhouse who taught some of the young girls to sew;[69] however, in October 1778 she petitioned to be given a house where she could work for the benefit of her children and, in consideration of this relief being granted, she would 'do the work of the house upon very reasonable terms'.[70] The committee granted her a dwelling in Poor House Row, and she continued to produce items for the use of the institution.[71] Ann received additional support over the ensuing years, including a new spinning wheel in 1780, the loan of half a guinea and the admission of her daughter, Sarah, to the Poorhouse in 1781; in 1782, she received new clothes.[72] The final reference to Ann's case was during the crisis of 1783 (discussed below), when she was to receive a shilling a week to support the income from her industry 'during these hard times'.[73]

The Poorhouse directly employed individuals who petitioned for relief if their industry was beneficial to the needs of the institution. In 1777, for example, Captain John McCracken employed Nanny McClelland, 'a poor woman in the neighbourhood who knits for payment', to teach the children this skill.[74] Nancy was employed at the rate of 2 shillings per week, paid for by Belfast Charitable Society.[75] The outdoor relief scheme also provided assistance to former Poorhouse employees who had fallen into poverty and destitution. In 1780 it was reported that William Preston 'who has long served faithfully in this house, is now incapable of labour & is left by his wife's death with three young children'. William was granted 1s 1d weekly to support his family in recognition of his service to the Poorhouse.[76] Outdoor relief was also granted to employees who injured themselves during their employment at the Poorhouse. In 1778 John Baird, an 'old man ... labouring for this house' who got a 'rupture' from straining himself, was granted 1s 1d; the doctor was requested 'to pay such attention to his relief as he thinks necessary & to purchase a Truss & bandage for him', this to be paid for by the charity.[77] In more extreme cases, immediate outdoor relief was granted before a full assessment of the petition was undertaken. Dolly McGarrety of Saltpan Lane was granted such relief in 1779, but, in an attempt to prevent the family's economic collapse, the Society also provided her husband, a peddler, with a sum of money to be 'laid out in peddling goods to enable him to support himself'.[78] Relief was similarly granted to individuals like John Carnaghan, to aid them in establishing themselves in their respective trades; John was granted funds to 'buy some necessities for setting up his loom'.[79]

A number of petitions, invariably, were received from older people who could no longer support themselves through work. John Kane from the Falls had served his working life as a blacksmith, a skilled and respectable trade, but due to old age and health complaints, the minute books describing him as 'asthmatic and past labours', he was granted a monthly allowance to support himself and his wife.[80]

MIGRATION

The Elizabethan Poor Laws that had been implemented in England and Wales were not adopted in Ireland; however, there was some commonality between the two systems, with both based on the view that maintenance of the destitute was a communal responsibility and that 'every pauper belonged to a local community'.[81] This led to a process of 'exclusion and removal', which saw individuals and families removed to their native parishes which were deemed to be responsible for their welfare. [82] This practice occurred in Belfast but on a much smaller scale. The most common reason for removal involved people who came to Belfast and were caught begging. Isabella Goofigan was 'sent to Portaferry from which she came' after being brought to the Poorhouse when she was caught begging in the town.[83] The story of outdoor relief in the form of assisted migration is more nuanced in a Belfast context, with many of the poor petitioning on their own accord to be 'carried' elsewhere, which, as in other forms of petitions for relief, was based on the circumstances of each individual and family.

For many men, military service provided a stable income to support their families, but it also meant that those who signed up for the army and navy could be stationed across the British Isles and, in times of war, across the globe. There are numerous petitions throughout the 1770s and 1780s from the wives of soldiers who petitioned for relief in the form of money to carry them from Belfast to their husbands in England and Scotland.[84] The American Revolutionary War also had implications for soldiers' families in Belfast. In July 1776, John Neddermire, a military musician, had been drafted to serve in America, leaving behind his wife, Elizabeth, with a young child. Elizabeth, facing an unknown future, petitioned to be sent to 'her native place' in Galway.[85] Agnes McCloud, a Scotswoman, whose husband was also serving in America, was given clothes for her family, and her passage was paid to 'carry her away' to Scotland.[86] Once a soldier retired from the military, he would receive his 'Chelsea Pension' for services rendered. The Belfast Charitable Society archives contain one mention of such an individual whose wife, Margaret McGowan, petitioned for outdoor relief. However, on examination, his Chelsea Pension was discovered and relief was refused.[87] Migration was also paid for through the outdoor relief scheme for the wives of sailors in the Navy who wished to go to their husbands.[88]

Migration was influenced by the need for family support, which was key for many facing destitution. The Society regularly supported individuals such as Elizabeth Cochrane who petitioned in 1776, 'setting out her distress … [her] being blind', for financial assistance to move her family to Kirkmaiden, Scotland, 'where her Husband has relations'.[89] Similarly, if the main breadwinner passed away, many women found it difficult to support their families, especially those who had come to

Belfast seeking work but had no relations to support them. Some, like Widow Dougan, who lived at Back Plantation with her three young children, sought assistance 'to carry her to her father in Lisburn'.[90] Even the widows of soldiers petitioned for assistance to go home to their native places, including Widow Mountain, who chose to go back to Limerick following the death of her husband.[91]

One of the most unusual outdoor relief efforts tied to migration was the Belfast Charitable Society's association with the Hibernian Marine School in Dublin. In February 1778 it was resolved that 'any poor children of Deceased Sailors belonging to this town, *that chose to go* [emphasis added], be sent to the Marine School in Dublin at the charity's expense'.[92] The Hibernian Marine School clothed these boys, taught them to read and write, and instructed them in navigation 'so as to be fitted for the Sea Service'.[93] The Society committee members Mr Vaght and Captain McCracken were requested to investigate. In April 1778 the committee agreed 'to do the Needful in forwarding the children to the Marine School', with an additional two boys joining the original cohort in June of that year.[94] As another chapter in this volume examines, this provision for children to be engaged in education and training is one that would become available to many of the children resident in the Poorhouse through its apprenticeship scheme.

TIMES OF CRISIS

Belfast continued to grow and develop as a mercantile port in the closing decades of the eighteenth century.[95] Many came from the rural areas, settling in Belfast with the hope of employment and lodgings. However, this growing population placed an even greater strain on the resources of the Belfast Charitable Society to provide relief to all genuine 'objects of distress', particularly during difficult times. As early as May 1775, the committee requested that 'as many of the poor who are willing to take potatoes in lieu of part of their money be directed to call for a bushel each' to decrease the amount of direct expenditure on outdoor relief.[96] The Society soon developed an awareness of the needs of the poor, studying the requests for outdoor relief, which enabled them to work proactively, not only to support those in need but to make the best use of the Society's funds. One such venture was the procurement of approximately 50–100 tonnes of 'good English coal' when the price fell to 14 shillings per tonne or less, 'to be given to the Poor in lieu of money at first cost in times of scarcity of Coals'.[97] The Poorhouse also had to respond to changes in the markets, in particular the textile industry, providing relief to individual weavers like James Bovile in July 1778 'until the linen trade revived'.[98]

The first major test of the Society's outdoor relief scheme in a time of crisis came in 1783, when the prices of goods, especially grain, shot up and distress and poverty prevailed in the poorer districts of Belfast.[99] The committee acted immediately through its outdoor relief scheme to mitigate against the increased prices. All members of the committee were called upon to go out into the streets of Belfast and identify 'the proper objects' who should receive money 'among the poor industrious families' in the parish.[100] Additional powers were granted, and regulations surrounding the review of petitions were suspended, as the committee members were allowed 'to call upon the treasurer for what money they may think necessary', bypassing the normal procedures. The names and amounts given out during the crisis were to be entered in a book purchased for this purpose and laid before the committee each week 'during the continuance of s[ai]d extraordinary distribution'. The charity also called on its members to 'give very particular attention to their [assigned] districts during these severe times'.[101]

The 1783 crisis continued, with the government stepping in to procure meal 'for the relief of the poor'.[102] Members of the Society made enquiries as to how this would impact Belfast, and the allowance of meal required was confirmed at twenty tonnes. They also engaged with Belfast port in arranging the 'mode of distributing the meal', ordering it to be delivered to the Poorhouse where they calculated the amounts to be given to the out poor over the following three weeks.[103] The Poorhouse committee met and agreed that tickets would be produced to allow the poor to collect up to one stone per person, per week, with a clerk appointed to weigh out the grain and collect the tickets. Additional measures were taken to support the poor, including the establishment of a 150-guinea fund set aside for three months to allow additional purchases of grain if required.[104] During the crisis the charity give cognisance to the recommendation of 'objects [of charity] from the Clergy of this parish of different denominations'.[105] This means of working in partnership would form the basis for relief in the future.

In the lead up to the 1798 rebellion and its ultimate suppression, the Society was placed under immense strain which impacted on its provision of outdoor relief. Payments for the out poor continued until March 1798, the month in which Ireland was declared to be in a state of actual rebellion.[106] It was not until October 1798 that payments were once again recorded for the outdoor relief scheme, which continued at the pre-rebellion level, suggesting that the charity sought out those it had previously been assisting before allowing new petitions to be accepted.[107] By 1800 the weekly payments secured for the out poor totalled five guineas, reflecting the growing extent of poverty within the town in the aftermath of the rebellion.[108]

The financial pressures on the Poorhouse at this time are evident in its minute books, which described the funds as being 'inadequate to the present extraordinary Wants' prevalent in Belfast.[109] The financial difficulties continued to mount, with badges for begging reintroduced as the Poorhouse struggled to accommodate new admissions and the demand for outdoor relief.[110] Although the licenses to beg were withdrawn in 1809, they were issued again in 1815 and continued in use until at least 1817 when the Charitable Society issued a warrant against 'all vagrants and Sturdy Beggars who may be found begging in the Street of this Town without [a] Badge'.[111] These crises set in motion a series of events which ultimately led to the end of the Belfast Charitable Society's outdoor relief scheme.

WIDENING CIRCLE OF PHILANTHROPY

The opening decade of the nineteenth century witnessed growing levels of poverty and destitution due to the upheaval of the 1798 rebellion followed by two years of poor harvests in 1799 and 1800. A number of additional philanthropic endeavours were established to alleviate conditions in the town, the most immediate of which were a 'Public Bakery' in 1800 and a soup kitchen in 1801.[112] Even for those who could work, it was often the case that this money was not enough to support themselves or their families. Some concerned citizens responded to this issue by opening the Belfast Repository on Ann Street for the receiving and selling of work of poor women in the town.[113] However, there was a growing awareness that more organised and permanent forms of charity were required to support the out poor. In 1801 a workhouse committee was established in the town following a call from Belfast Charitable Society, the Fever Hospital and the Public Kitchen to mitigate against the growing numbers requiring outdoor relief and to deal with the ongoing issues around strolling beggars.[114] This workhouse was known as the House of Industry and should not be confused with the later workhouse erected under the Irish Poor Law of 1838. Initially, eight rooms were granted within the Poorhouse 'for the carrying on [of] useful Industry' by the poor so they could earn money to support themselves in their own homes, in contrast to being admitted to the Poorhouse and having accommodation and meals provided.[115] The minutes and newspapers of the period highlight the separation of Poorhouse and Workhouse, which were 'supported by a separate Subscription'.[116]

In 1809 the leading citizens of Belfast met to establish a workhouse with its own premises, relinquishing the rooms in the Poorhouse 'for use during the day by such poor people as had no other convenient place in which to work'.[117] To defray the costs of this new institution, the workhouse merged with the Stranger's Friend Society to form the Society for the Employment and Relief of the Poor in the Town of Belfast. The Stranger's Friendly Society had previously supported those outside the remit of the Poorhouse who belonged to other parishes but were resident in Belfast. The new House of Industry took over many aspects of the Belfast Charitable Society's outdoor relief scheme, including providing equipment for industry, clothing and food.[118] It allowed the poor to maintain a degree of independence by living in their own accommodation whilst providing a space to work and earn a wage.[119] In 1810, only a year after the House of Industry opened, it was providing work for over 500 individuals, with an additional 376 families receiving weekly food rations.[120]

With the opening of the House of Industry, Belfast Charitable Society removed itself from its role in the provision of outdoor relief. With the exception of badging the poor during the crises previously outlined, the charity focused its work on providing for aged and infirm adults, as well as deserted and orphaned children. The widening circle of philanthropy in nineteenth-century Belfast was neatly summed up in the Belfast Charitable Society's 1819 annual report:

> Orphans and deserted children, and superannuated men and women are lodged in the Poor-House; and the out-poor are under the vigorous and benevolent superintendence of the House of Industry: The Hospital and Dispensary provide for the sick, and the Lying-In Hospital for poor women in labour; while the Lancastrian and Sunday Schools take charge of the education of the rising generation. These all mutually co-operate, and every inhabitant of the town should liberally and zealously co-operate with them.[121]

This form of partnership working alongside other charities, hospitals and schools came to dominate how charity operated in Belfast and arguably still forms the basis of the Belfast Charitable Society's work in a twenty-first-century context.

CONCLUSION

The Belfast Charitable Society's outdoor relief scheme began as a response to its legal obligations to care for the parish's badged beggars. However, within months of the official opening of the Poorhouse, the extent of poverty and destitution in the town meant that petitions for outdoor relief far outnumbered those seeking admission to the Poorhouse. Throughout the years the charity's outdoor relief scheme developed in response to the needs and requirements of those in the town; it covered many areas, including medical treatment, provision for the sick and injured, employment and assistance for migration. The petitions, and the Society's responses to them, reflect the everyday struggles faced by the poor of Belfast – from paying half the wages of a wet nurse to providing coffins to offset the costs of burial for the impoverished. The investigation of petitions by committee members assigned to each district ensured the charity could respond to individual need, and each case was assessed on its merits.

The crises faced throughout these early decades of the nineteenth century witnessed the emergence of partnership working, with various organisations coming together to deal with the issues facing a growing town, particularly in times of failed harvests, economic depression and inflation. Ultimately, the role of outdoor relief provision was transferred to the House of Industry in 1809 and would continue, in part, through the Poor Law Unions, established in the 1830s. Nevertheless, for nearly forty years outdoor relief dominated the philanthropic activities of Belfast Charitable Society, which helped thousands of individuals and families through the individual and collective crises faced by many of the labouring class in a growing Belfast.

CHAPTER SIX

Charitable Societies and the Welfare Landscape in Pre-Famine Belfast[1]

Ciarán McCabe

෮

In a charity sermon in December 1814 in aid of the Belfast House of Industry, a voluntary charitable society formed five years earlier to rid the town of street beggars, Presbyterian minister Rev. Henry Cooke reflected on what he perceived to be the causes of poverty in the industrialising town. The supposed cross-generational aversion to labour and self-reliance within many poor families, Cooke told his audience, bred idleness, dependence and other social and moral ills. To counteract these evils, the charity in whose favour he spoke sought 'not a temporary palliative, but a radical cure' to this disease. Child mendicants were acutely vulnerable to the 'contagion of bad example', and their moral health could only be ensured through the use of 'proper remedies'.[2] The 'remedies' championed by Cooke and the House of Industry centred on a system of investigation and inspection of poor persons and their abodes, so as to detect and prevent fraud among applicants to the society. 'This system of visitation', asserted Cooke, 'is a matter of the utmost importance: it is a kind of domestic police, which preserves order, so essential to industry;

promotes cleanliness, so essential to health; and stimulates to diligence, by the dread of censure, and the hope of reward.'[3] Children were required to attend day school or Sunday school, while adult mendicants were not provided with pecuniary assistance but, rather, were put to work in order to support themselves – women spun yarn while men broke stones.

Cooke's sermon was reflective of wider societal views of urban poverty in the early nineteenth century, especially in respect of mendicancy. Beggars posed a threat to 'respectable' society – ranging from artisans and petty shopkeepers to merchants, professionals and the gentry – on a number of fronts. Their idleness, oftentimes seen as voluntary, offended notions of independence and self-reliance, and imposed a burden on members of the public who were pressurised into giving alms in order to be free of a temporary nuisance; mendicants' habits, it was held, tended towards drunkenness and petty crime, and their loitering outside commercial premises intimidated shopkeepers' prospective customers. Furthermore, beggars spread contagion and, throughout the nineteenth century, disease outbreaks in Irish towns and countryside were blamed on the movements of transient mendicants.[4] As such, Cooke's use of the imagery of disease when discussing Belfast's poverty and poor persons appealed to the sensitivities and strongly held fears of the merchant classes, who, most likely, constituted a substantial portion of his audience. In urban centres throughout Ireland and Britain, the failure by local or national government to tackle the problems of poverty and mendicancy drove male elites to form voluntary associations aimed at effecting the moral and social improvement of the poorer classes, protecting the economic interests of the middle classes and preserving the moral and somatic health of the civic body. This chapter will focus on charities engaged in the provision of direct material relief to the poor, thus omitting the wide range of medical and missionary charities, the former being addressed by Robyn Atcheson elsewhere in this volume.

THE WELFARE LANDSCAPE IN EARLY NINETEENTH-CENTURY BELFAST

Belfast in the early nineteenth century was a rapidly growing and industrialising town. Its demographic expansion – with its population more than doubling from 18,000 to 37,000 between 1791 and 1821, and continuing to increase until the turn of the twentieth century, when it totalled 350,000 – was driven by inward migration from its rural hinterland and elsewhere in the north, largely of relatively poor persons.[5] The development of the town in this period was a complex process. Urban improvement in the streetscape complemented increased gentility and refinement among the middle classes in the 'Athens of the North'. Yet, Belfast experienced all of the social problems and challenges of nineteenth-century industrialising urban centres, including overcrowding in working-class housing, outbreaks of contagious disease, public intoxication, prostitution and street begging. Migrants swelled Belfast's labouring and artisan classes, who were accommodated in the expanding terraced housing being constructed on the town's outskirts, as well as the courts and laneways in close proximity to the main thoroughfares.[6] The precariousness and isolation of urban life experienced by many of these newfound migrants were addressed by Cooke in his House of Industry sermon: 'To every commercial town there is a great influx of strangers and their families, seeking employment. When calamity overtakes them, they have no friend to whom they can look for comfort or relief.'[7] The suffering of the non-local poor was a feature singular to urban, in contrast to rural, communities, and one which served as a focus of numerous voluntary charitable societies.

Belfast shared with other urban centres in the early nineteenth century a vibrant welfare landscape. Each of the main denominations provided for the poor of their congregation, overseeing internal systems for identifying and relieving those elements of the poor deemed 'deserving' or redeemable. In the 1820s, the Second Presbyterian congregation in Belfast was raising and distributing between £4 and £6 of 'poors money' each month.[8] The two largest sums of non-capital expenditure undertaken by the town's Church of Ireland parish vestry were the provision of coffins for poor parishioners and the support of deserted children. This mirrored trends evident in parishes throughout Ireland in the pre-Poor Law period, when vestries exerted significant welfare responsibilities.[9] The Anglican parish of Christ Church oversaw a clothing fund for poor children, while two-thirds of the newly built church's pews carried no 'pew rent', thus accommodating poorer parishioners; the parish also established a

Magdalene asylum for 'penitent females'.[10] Ladies from Belfast's Catholic community founded the St Patrick's Orphan Society in 1838, under the patronage of Bishop Cornelius Denvir, to provide 'measures of support to destitute orphans, to bestow upon them a religious education and to implement the seeds of virtue in their tender minds'.[11]

From the middle of the eighteenth century, a number of voluntary charitable societies were formed by members of Belfast's growing middle classes, who embraced the associational culture of the period in their eagerness to demonstrate their civic and Christian duty, and to address 'the problems of urban society, both the specific crisis of epidemic, riot and economic slump, and the longer term trends which worried those with power and authority'.[12] S.J. Connolly has identified the philanthropic vibrancy in late eighteenth- and early nineteenth-century Belfast, specifically in respect of voluntary associations, as being reflective of the subscriber democracy then flourishing across Britain and Ireland: in the absence of interventions from local or central government in response to the growing social problems of urbanisation and industrialisation, groups of urban elites, driven by a 'strong sense of collective social responsibility', took the initiative and founded charities, hospitals, schools and a wide range of welfare and educational institutions.[13] The proliferation of this middle-class voluntarist zeal spoke, as Jonathan Wright observes in his study of late-Georgian Belfast's urban culture, not solely of those classes' self-organisation and philanthropic zeal, but also of 'Belfast's growing need for charitable provision'.[14]

In their relief of the poor, voluntary charities commonly focused on specific categories, distinguished by the binary division of 'deserving' and 'undeserving' poor: into the former category fell unemployed artisans, widows and orphans whose penury was seen as not being self-inflicted; into the latter were placed beggars and vagrants, especially able-bodied and non-local mendicants. Upon its foundation in 1752, the Belfast Charitable Society was envisaged as a multifaceted institution (a poorhouse and hospital) catering for different categories of the urban poor: namely, the 'deserving poor', who were to be relieved; 'idle beggars', who were to be put to work; and the sick and indigent poor. The founding resolution of the Society affirmed that 'a Poor House and Hospital are greatly wanted in the Town of Belfast for the support of vast numbers of real objects of charity in this Parish, for the employment of idle beggars that crowd to it from all parts of the North, and for the reception of infirm and diseased poor'.[15]

The belief that the poorer classes contained both 'deserving' and 'undeserving' elements was asserted by clergymen of all denominations. In a charity sermon in February 1811 for the benefit of the House of Industry, a preacher, Rev. Holmes (probably Church of Ireland), was reported as urging his audience in the town's church of the importance of supporting the institution, whose endeavours had served 'not only to relieve the necessities of real distress, but which effectually discouraged the idle vagrant, with whose incessant importunities the public were formerly so frequent assailed'.[16]

Charities were largely male, middle-class-run organisations. When female-run charities operated, they usually did so as auxiliaries to larger male-run entities. The organisation and provision of relief through voluntary societies was driven by a number of factors. Founders sought to demonstrate their civic duty in voluntarily giving their time and money in effectively organising relief to the local poor. Charities oftentimes operated systems of visitations to the homes of the poor, and inspections of their abodes and circumstances, as a means of rooting out imposters and fraudsters, and ensuring that the voluntary subscriptions and donations of supporters reached the most 'deserving' and were not distributed recklessly. Charities, as middle class-run entities, were also important in those classes' desire to ensure order, civility and restraint amongst the lower orders, who were perceived as prone to idleness, intemperance and other manifestations of immortality. Not just the somatic but the moral health of the poor was attended to, while missionary societies also sought to relieve their spiritual wants.[17]

When the Belfast Charitable Society was established in 1752, the initiative for the project derived not from the proprietor of Belfast (the Chichesters) or the town corporation, but from the ranks of the town's merchants and 'gentlemen'. Decades later, the social make-up of the early nineteenth-century town was similarly reflected in the occupations of the founding members of the House of Industry, a voluntary mendicity society formed for the primary purpose of suppressing street begging. The founders were almost invariably merchants (among the occupations were bookseller, draper, tanner, watchmaker, distiller and grocer), whereas the managing committee of Dublin's equivalent charity, the Mendicity Society, established just a few years later, was more likely to comprise men higher up the social ladder, such as medical practitioners, lawyers, judges and bankers.[18] These differences reflect the contrasting dominance of the public sphere by the manufacturing middle classes in Belfast and the town-gentry in Dublin at a time when, in the early post-Union years, Belfast's star was in the ascendant, while Dublin's descent into a 'deposed capital' had commenced.[19]

Among the other charitable institutions formed in the late eighteenth and early nineteenth centuries, and which contributed to the town's vibrant welfare landscape, were the Belfast Marine Society 'for the relief of unfortunate seamen, their widows & families' (1784), a dispensary (1792), a fever hospital (1793), Society for the Relief of Lying-in Women (1793), the Asylum for the Blind (1801), House of Industry (1809) and the Night Asylum (1841), not to mention a plethora of Sunday and day schools.[20] Most charitable societies existed precariously, arising from their dependence on voluntary sources of income, most commonly one-off donations, regular subscriptions, bequests, charity sermons, court fines and the sale of items produced by the organisation and its beneficiaries. For instance, the Belfast House of Industry was funded through the usual voluntary sources – donations, subscriptions and bequests – as well as magistrates' fines.[21] The Belfast Charitable Society's income also came from these sources and was supplemented by funds raised through charitable balls, theatrical and musical performances, and (at various times) from interest on the 'poores money' held in trust by Belfast Corporation and from water rates.[22]

Occasionally, the town's charities benefitted from unorthodox sources of income. In 1817, the House of Industry received a donation of £1 from a travelling group of 'Indian jugglers' who had been performing on Belfast's streets, while in 1831 half the proceeds of a ventriloquist's show was gifted to the charity.[23] Charity sermons were common in urban centres and were among the most visible demonstration of the vibrancy of the welfare landscape in an early nineteenth-century town or city. Non-denominational charities oftentimes benefitted from charity sermons held in the churches or meeting houses of different religious communities.[24] Organisations which benefitted from income raised through charity sermons included the Strangers' Friend Society,[25] the House of Industry,[26] the town's lying-in hospital,[27] the dispensary and fever hospital,[28] and also Sunday schools.[29]

An early contributor to the town's welfare landscape was the Strangers' Friend Society, a charity founded by members of Belfast's Methodist community to alleviate the suffering of the typically industrious, yet unemployed, poor. The 'deserving' poor who were thus relieved included poor artisans who had pawned their tools, as well as widows and others whose indigence arose not from their own moral failings. The society distributed clothes, blankets, food, fuel and money to those poor persons deemed likely to return to habits of industry. In June 1809, a notice promoting a charity sermon in aid of the Strangers' Friend Society (SFS) assured the public that 'the funds are expended upon those only who are real objects of charity'.[30] The Belfast charity was part of an SFS movement which spread within Irish and British Methodism in the quarter of a century after 1785, when the first SFS was founded in London. Later societies were established in Bristol (1786), Leeds (1789), Liverpool (1789), Bath (1790), Dublin (1790), Manchester (1791) and Edinburgh (c. 1815), as well as in Bradford, Burnley, Hull, Rochester and York. In Ireland, in addition to the Belfast and Dublin entities, Strangers' Friend Societies were founded in Armagh, Cork and Waterford.[31]

The Belfast SFS was operating in the 1790s[32] but appears to have declined substantially before being revived in 1808. Its rekindling, however, was short-lived. With the establishment the following year of the House of Industry, the members of the Methodist charity co-operated in its establishment and dissolved their own body, so as to prevent duplication of relief to the poor and subscriptions from the public.[33] The minute books of the Belfast Charitable Society reveal a rare reference to the SFS: in June 1809, the former body resolved that 'a Female Lunatic, name unknown, recommended by the Strangers' Friend Society, be admitted into this House'.[34] While we must be wary of drawing too much from this admittedly brief minute, it suggests a level of co-operation between the two charities at a time when the absence of co-ordination amongst charities in urban centres frequently attracted criticism from social commentators, as this practice pointed to inefficiencies within a community's welfare landscape.[35] Furthermore, there were direct links between the SFS and the new House of Industry, in that a number of the House's managing committee had previously been involved with the SFS: Alex Blackwell (a linen draper at 38/9 High Street), Lawson Annesley (of Arthur Street), Thomas Whinnery and John Lyle (possibly a grocer at Merchant's Quay) had all collected subscriptions for the SFS prior to their election to the committee of the House of Industry.[36] A Belfast branch of the SFS was extant again in the late 1820s and into the 1830s, but little is known of its establishment, activities or the duration of its operation.[37]

RESPONSES TO BEGGING AND VAGRANCY

Control of the movements of the mendicant poor was of significant importance to the workings of charities and civil authorities in this period. Since the early modern period, the mobility of the vagrant poor alarmed communities. In urban centres, this manifested itself in the inward migration of the non-local poor. When civic authorities failed to provide for sufficient measures to mitigate this and related problems, especially vagrancy and mendicancy, middle-class men (local merchants and residents) and local elites took the initiative and implemented their own systems. From the mid-eighteenth century, with the expansion of middle-class associational culture, this was carried out through voluntary charities. For example, among the officers employed by the Belfast Charitable Society in the mid-1770s, shortly after the house opened, was a beadle 'for locking up the Beggars & Vagrants, and acting as Porter to the House'.[38] In 1775 'Dudley the Bang beggar' – possibly the same beadle referred to above – was paid 1s 1d 'for bringing a Beggar to the Poor House'.[39]

The Society also oversaw a system of badging those local poor persons deemed 'deserving' of the public's alms. Badges, typically made of tin, copper or pewter, served as licences to beg, identifying to passers-by whether a soliciting mendicant was deemed by the relevant authorities to be worthy of assistance; it had the additional effect of identifying the fraudulent, 'undeserving' mendicant, by the very fact of them not displaying a badge. The badging of the meritorious poor had been practised throughout Europe since the medieval period, with both parishes and secular authorities overseeing badging regimes. Steve Hindle's analysis of badging in early-modern England points to the complexities in excavating the perceptions of the poor persons who received badges: some sources record paupers' resistance to badge wearing arising from pride or suspicion, while others suggest a resignation (or even perhaps a willingness) on the part of beggars to wearing parochial badges, as such licences could demonstrate respectability within the community.[40] In Ireland the practice, whenever it was implemented (with instances being recorded as early as the 1630s), was undertaken by parish vestries, usually as a short-term measure in response to an acute crisis such as famine or epidemic: evidence as to badging is concentrated, for instance, in the early 1740s, 1799–1801, 1817–19 and the early 1820s. The houses of industry legislation passed by the Irish parliament in the 1770s facilitated the establishment of multifaceted poorhouses, funded through a peculiar mixture of local taxation (through the grand juries) and voluntary sources, to cater within their walls for 'poor helpless' men and women, as well as 'vagabonds and sturdy beggars' and 'idle, strolling and disorderly women'. These houses of industry were also empowered to implement localised systems of badging the meritorious poor, with the most evidence being available for the Dublin institution.[41]

The Belfast Charitable Society introduced its own badging system in March 1775, when 'Badges and Licences to Beg for a limited time [were] granted both to the Beggars with Children, and to the Infirm Husband or Wife'; sixteen badges were initially granted to local paupers.[42] In doing so, the Society was exercising powers created by the 1772 Act for badging the poor and which were extended to the newly incorporated Belfast entity in a separate statute of 1774.[43] The practice of badging the poor gradually declined in the following decades, as badging evolved as a short-term relief measure in times of acute crisis; in September 1809 the Society recalled all of its badges formerly granted to beggars.[44] It is striking that the issue of badging the mendicant poor arose again in the spring of 1817, amidst the social upheaval that followed the end of the Napoleonic Wars, when Irish society, and much of Europe, was struck by successive seasons of poor harvests, inclement weather, famine and disease. The most reliable contemporary estimate put the mortality figure across Ireland during this crisis at up to 65,000. In towns and cities throughout the island, measures were enacted to protect local populations from wandering beggars who were widely targeted as propagators of contagion: for example, in the midlands town of Tullamore, military guards were stationed on all access roads, preventing entrance to 'sickly itinerants', while the town's trade in woollen and cotton goods was suspended, for fearing of introducing contagion.[45] Across Ireland, local authorities – most commonly parish vestries – responded to this crisis by reviving the former practice of badging the local poor, as a means of protecting the local population from the intrusions of itinerant mendicants who were seen as likely disseminators of contagion.[46] The Ballymoney parish vestry spent 10s on 'Printing Handbills relating to Beggars' in 1817 and, the following year, an additional £1 was expended on 'printing Lists of badged and other Poor'.[47] Elsewhere in County Antrim, the Dunluce parish vestry spent £1 6s 8d on 'Badges for the Poor of this Parish'.[48]

Belfast's civic leaders were also active in protecting the town from the vagrant poor. In March 1817 the marquis of Donegall signed a warrant 'authorizing Arthur Bradford, & his assistants to take up all Vagrants & sturdy Beggars who may be found begging in the streets of this Town without a Badge, & deal with them according to Law'.[49] One month later, the Belfast Charitable Society sought for the town's newly formed police to exercise their powers:

> to apprehend all Beggars & strolling Vagrants and Prostitutes (excepting such Beggars as shall be badged & licenced to beg by the Belfast Char. Society) found on the streets of Belfast and within one mile thereof of the Lamps in all directions, & to commit them to the House of Correction, or to said other place or places of confinement, as may be under the care of the Belfast Incorporated Charitable Society, for a term not exceeding two calendar months for the first offence, 4 months for the 2nd offence, & twelve months for the Third offence.[50]

The tiered nature of the punishments for recidivist migrant beggars reflects the justifiable fears of the civic community regarding the health of the town's population, at a time when (typhus) fever 'was uncommonly prevalent and destructive': between July 1817 and July 1820, an estimated

3,000 persons (10 per cent of the town's population) were annually 'attacked' with fever.[51]

Corporate responses to mendicancy in Belfast changed drastically with the foundation of the town's House of Industry. Despite its name, this institution is not to be considered as part of the network of houses of industry established under the 1770s legislation.[52] Twelve such houses of industry were established between 1771 and the early 1800s, and these largely operated as multifaceted institutions, offering a range of welfare services, while incorporating involuntary confinement for 'sturdy beggars' – crucially, they were funded largely through either local or central taxation. Instead, the Belfast House of Industry was the pioneer of the Irish mendicity societies, a transnational movement of voluntary charitable societies focused on suppressing street begging and vagrancy. In the first half of the nineteenth century, mendicity societies were established throughout Ireland, Britain, and western and central Europe – the best known within these islands being the Dublin and London entities – and the Irish movement comprised at least fifty-two such charities.[53]

The Belfast House of Industry, located in the Smithfield market area, defined its 'principal object' as being 'to remove all pretexts for begging'.[54] It is significant that the initiative for the foundation of this institution came just weeks after a significant downturn in the town's manufacturing base. According to one contemporary estimate, as many as 2,000 calico looms in Belfast and its hinterland 'were struck idle in five weeks'.[55] It may be suggested that many of those labouring poor took to begging from the town's inhabitants. The House of Industry's founding proposals were published and circulated throughout the town, under the name of a 'Society for the Abolition of Mendicity, and for the Relief and Encouragement of the Industrious Poor of the Town of Belfast',[56] and the rules and regulations spoke of its driving principle being 'not merely to check the growth of mendicity at present, but to cut it up by the roots, to come at the very source and spring of the evil that rankles in the vitals of every large town'.[57] Poor Law Commissioner George Nicholls distinguished between the Belfast House of Industry, comparing it to the mendicity societies, and the town's Charitable Society or 'Poor House', which he perceived as being akin to the Dublin House of Industry. The Belfast House of Industry was founded, Nicholls said, 'expressly for the suppression of mendicancy, and it has strong rooms to which persons found begging are committed, under sanction of the local authorities'.[58] The Poor Inquiry of the 1830s also located the Belfast House of Industry within the mendicity society movement, describing it as 'the first society established in Ireland for suppressing mendicity'.[59] The organisation's first report saw its work as 'the result of an experiment hitherto untried in Ireland', emphasising the innovative nature of the society at a time when houses of industry had been established throughout the country and mendicity societies were absent from the welfare landscape.[60] A public campaign in Kilkenny city for the establishment of a mendicity society hailed the Belfast House of Industry as the first Irish mendicity society.[61] Widespread support and enthusiasm for this new initiative is evident from the appointment of the committee of the Belfast Charitable Society and the clergy of the town (of all denominations) as honorary members.[62] Also, as noted above, the Methodist-run Strangers' Friend Society took the decision to dissolve itself so that public efforts and money would be focused on the new charity.[63]

The House of Industry adhered to the general mendicity society model by providing only day accommodation for the poor – namely, 'that class of poor who have no place of residence convenient for working in'.[64] A number of persons closely linked to the House of Industry – Rev. Cooke, Catholic parish priest Rev. William Crolly and Presbyterian philanthropist and reformer Robert Tennent – expressed their belief that the external relief provided by the institution was preferable to any provision of internal relief, as the former fostered independence and self-reliance, while the latter was conducive to the spread of immoral conduct.[65] The institution encouraged industrious individuals to engage in employment, mostly the spinning of flax or wool (either on-site or at the paupers' abode), knitting and picking oakum; one year after its opening, 309 spinners of linen yarn were employed, as well as stocking knitters and oakum pickers.[66] The destitute poor were also incentivised away from mendicancy by the House of Industry's provision of food, fuel and straw to 'deserving' cases approved by visitors. Despite its founding objective to rid Belfast's streets of habitual beggars, the House of Industry later shifted its attention and resources to the 'deserving', 'respectable' poor. By the time of the Poor Inquiry's account of the institution in the mid-1830s, the type of persons being relieved had been revised from being 'merely mendicants in the streets' to 'widows of tradesmen, and even tradesmen themselves, who had at once an opportunity of earning as much as would provide for their old age'.[67] Such persons were thus distinguished from the idle and improvident mendicants who habitually sought alms in the public street; instead, the House of Industry's more recent cohort of paupers had 'been reduced by circumstances beyond their control' and 'would rather starve in their houses than go out to beg'.[68] Jonathan Wright correctly observes that this instance reveals the pragmatism and adaptability of the welfare landscape in Belfast, as the providers of assistance shifted their focus to a broader cohort of the distressed poor.[69]

IMPACT OF THE 1838 POOR LAW

The introduction of the statutory system of poor relief in Ireland with the 1838 Poor Law impacted greatly on the existing welfare landscape throughout Ireland. The imposition of a poor rate on householders impacted on the giving of charity by individuals, churches and voluntary charitable societies. Throughout the protracted Poor Law debates of the 1830s, charities, whose precarious existence depended on the voluntary income from the urban middle classes, warned of the dangers they faced should a nationwide rate-based welfare regime be introduced. This argument was based on the expectation that individuals would be less likely to voluntarily part with portions of their disposable income in addition to the compulsory rates they were obliged to pay, especially given that the charities and the Poor Law system aspired to achieve the same goal – namely, the relief of the destitute poor. Despite these concerns, a common refrain within the Poor Law debates was that the introduction of a statutory system of relief, based on general taxation, would result in a more equitable division of the burden of funding poor relief: those householders who avoided contributing to voluntary funds could not, it was hoped, escape the poor rates. The hardship involved in securing voluntary contributions from large sections of the wealthier inhabitants of a town or city was a common complaint of charities. In 1831 the Belfast House of Industry took the step of publishing in the local newspapers the names of all subscribers, thereby implicitly identifying (and, it was hoped, embarrassing) those who did not subscribe. The difficulty in collecting contributions from non-subscribers was such that when the House of Industry's committee designated districts to collectors, 'each person shrinks from undertaking that district in which the most respectable class of inhabitants reside'.[70]

The introduction of the Poor Law system constituted a significant shift in Ireland's welfare landscape, from a largely voluntary ethos to the state-centred system of compulsorily funded, institution-based relief. This is not to deny the continued existence in the post-1838 period of voluntary relief provided through churches, charities and – arguably the most common source of poor assistance – interactions that did not lend themselves to the creation of source material: kin, friends, community and strangers. Philanthropists feared that the sensibility that was such an integral element of voluntary charity would be lost in the harsh, dehumanising workhouses of the Poor Law system. Just two months after the Poor Law's enactment, Belfast's citizens became concerned about conflicting accounts of the future of the town's Charitable Society. Capturing the opinion of Belfast's elites, the *Belfast Commercial Chronicle* opined that the operation of 'this expensive and objectionable [poor] law' would undermine the 'devoted and unpaid superintendence under which that excellent establishment, the [Society's] Poor House, has been carried on'. Noting the Poor Law commissioners' determination that no new workhouse structure be built where existing institutions were located, the *Chronicle* asserted that the commissioners intended 'to appropriate the present Poor House, with any required additions, to the use of the [Poor Law] Union'.[71] As it transpired, this was not carried out: the Society's Poorhouse continued to exist and function independently from the Poor Law system, and a new union workhouse was constructed on the town's southern Lisburn Road, opening in May 1841.

The introduction of the Poor Law had the effect that so many philanthropists feared: it dealt a hammer blow – in some instances, fatal – to many charities across Ireland. Evidence for Dublin city reveals that charities specialising in the provision of material assistance to the poor, in the form of food, clothes and small sums of cash, saw their income levels plummet, requiring these societies to either close or reform their operations.[72] In the case of the mendicity societies, the movement was largely wiped out within three or four years of the Poor Law's enactment.[73] The impact of the Poor Law was also felt by Belfast's voluntary charitable societies, most notably the House of Industry, which suffered the fate of other mendicity societies. It witnessed a significant decline in income received and, subsequently, relief given in 1838 and the ensuing three years – that is, in the period between the passing of the Poor Law and the tangible realisation among the population that the Poor Law system was operational, evinced by the commencement of rate collection and the opening of the workhouse. In spring 1839 the *Northern Whig* urged its readers to continue financially supporting the House of Industry, as the anticipated introduction of poor rates 'within a short period' had led to reductions in voluntary contributions. The *Whig's* appeal to the public was in response to a notice published by the town's Poor Law board of guardians, claiming that the collection of the first poor rates was imminent and that subscribers to the Belfast House of Industry and other charities ought not to pay their regular contributions, 'as another species of relief for the indigent will come into operation with the new Poor Law'.[74] As with the fears just five months earlier in respect of the future of the Belfast Charitable Society, this episode revealed the fears and confusion felt by some of Belfast's citizens arising from the significant shift occurring in the town's welfare landscape. As expected, houses of industry suffered a similar decline to other mendicity societies and lost the financial and moral support of their subscribers owing to the introduction of the Poor Law: for example, a meeting of the Newry Mendicity Society, shortly before its dissolution, was described as being 'miserably and disgracefully attended'.[75] Only twelve persons attended a well-advertised public meeting in autumn 1839, convened to address the fate of the Belfast House of Industry. Those that did attend heard that 'many wealthy individuals had refused their annual subscription, because the Poor Laws were to be in operation, though it was known that no rate could be levied till the work-house was built, which, in all likelihood, would not be for a year to come'.[76]

The first poor rate for Belfast was finally declared on 22 December 1840 and the first paupers were admitted into the town's workhouse on 11 May 1841.[77] The decision to close the Belfast House of Industry was taken at a meeting on 31 May 1841, less than three weeks later.[78] At the time of its closure, the Belfast institution was providing permanent relief to 900 families, as well as approximately fifty 'weekly applicants', while sixty-six children were fed daily 'to enable them to attend school'.[79] The closure of the institution had been anticipated some time in advance, as in December 1840 the institution's premises were advertised as being for sale.[80] A newspaper notice in late 1842 records a bequest of £100 to the charity, 'which institution being dissolved' the legacy was appropriated to the Surgical Hospital with the sanction of the Commissioners of Charitable Bequests.[81]

Despite the fatal consequences to the House of Industry, the introduction of the Poor Law did not have such a devastating effect on the Belfast Charitable Society. The Society did experience a significant drop in income in the late 1830s and early 1840s, as did most charities in this period whether they survived into the post-Poor Law period or not. Its survival, however, centred on the fact that the Society adapted its rules in respect of the type of poor persons it would thenceforth admit into the Poorhouse. The distinction between the 'deserving' and 'undeserving' poor framed this decision, as displayed in an 1841 committee resolution: paupers 'whose claims upon the Charity were the least strong' were discharged, as they 'were considered proper objects for the Work House'. As such, persons whose penury and destitution were self-inflicted, such as the idle able-bodied poor, were appropriate for the latter institution.[82] The Society's Poorhouse, in contrast, now focused its resources on assisting the honest, elderly poor, who were regarded as incontestably 'deserving':

> your Committee would recommend the admission of individuals who are natives of the Town or Parish, who have not been reduced to poverty by their own bad conduct or dissipation, and who do not belong to that class that are admissible into the Work House, so that, in a few years, the House will become an Asylum for persons who had seen better days, & for whom the Charity was originally founded.[83]

Despite the opening of the Poor Law workhouse, the dissolution of the House of Industry and the continued, yet modified, operations of the

Belfast Charitable Society, a strong demand remained in pre-Famine Belfast for temporary shelter for the destitute poor. This was driven by the continued flow of poor migrants into the burgeoning town, where the population grew from around 37,000 to 75,000 between 1821 and 1841.[84] The foundation of the Night Asylum for the Houseless Poor in 1841 aimed to address this need. As with the Bow Street Night Asylum founded in Dublin just three years earlier, the Belfast Night Asylum (located at Poultry Square, later renamed Victoria Square) provided only shelter and did not feed, clothe or train its inmates. Dormitories accommodating up to eighty persons were provided, divided between the two sexes, and paupers could use an open fire to cook what food they brought into the institution, most commonly potatoes; a pauper's average stay in the asylum was three days. The asylum's first report recorded a total of 17,282 individuals using the institution in the year ending December 1842, of whom 5,830 (34 per cent) were 'natives of Belfast'.[85] The instance of the Night Asylum, which closed in 1847, again illustrated the initiative of Belfast's urban elites in combatting an acute and growing social ill (the penury of non-local paupers) that was not being addressed by either local or central government. The model provided by the House of Industry and the associational culture which drove that institution was applied successfully to the Night Asylum; however, its ultimate decline was caused by the asylum's inability to cope with the sheer numbers of fever-stricken paupers congregating therein at the height of the Great Famine.[86]

Voluntary charitable societies constituted just one element of the vibrant welfare landscape of pre-Famine Belfast. Charities emerged in the town from the mid-eighteenth century as part of the merchant classes' embracing of the associational culture of the period as a means to mitigate the pressing social problems increasingly evident in the expanding and industrialising town. Involvement in, and support for, charitable societies allowed Belfast's rising middling classes to shape the town's public civil society. The instance of Belfast fits with Robert Morris' argument that the use of collective action helped the formation of the group identity of urban elites, who spearheaded initiatives to relieve destitution when the responses of officialdom were insufficient: for example, the actions of Belfast's urban elites in founding numerous charitable societies, catering for a wide range of groups designated 'deserving', were somewhat driven by the absence of sufficient action by government, whether locally or through parliament.[87] When state intervention manifested in the 1838 Poor Law, the town's welfare landscape did not escape the drastic impact of the new system of poor relief – a pattern mirrored in urban centres throughout the island. However, while the House of Industry ceased to operate, as its voluntary income shrank, the Belfast Charitable Society ensured its survival by adapting its approach to poor relief, focusing on categories of paupers not catered for in the newly established Poor Law Union workhouses and, thus, carving out its corner in Belfast's crowded and complex welfare landscape.

CHAPTER SEVEN

Child Welfare and Education in the Industrialising Town

Lauren Smyth

౭౦

On Monday 6 November 1775, having previously requested permission to leave the institution, Ann Curran applied to remain within Belfast's Poorhouse and to be allowed to bring her youngest child, aged two and a half, with her into her room.[1] The Belfast Charitable Society's committee decided that, on account of Ann Curran's 'extraordinary good behaviour', she would be permitted to remain within the Poorhouse and to take her daughter into the same room as herself, provided that she did not make another such request in the future.[2] Curran's daughter was to become just one of many children admitted by the Belfast Charitable Society into the Poorhouse in the decades to come, as they sought to provide for the poor of the town and to remove the indigent from the streets.

The historiography of children and charity has been well-developed within a British context. In exploring the history of the London Foundling Hospital, for example, historians have focused on the characteristics of the abandoned infants, the role of external wetnurses and the efforts made by officials to recreate the foundlings' identities so that they could become accepted members of wider society.[3] Lesley Hulonce's research on child welfare in nineteenth-century England and Wales highlights the relationship that existed between poor children, charitable institutions and state relief, while Katrina Honeyman has explored parish factory apprenticeships during the early stages of industrialisation in late eighteenth- and early nineteenth-century Britain.[4] In comparison, the historiography of children and charity within an Irish context is at a much earlier stage of its development. Maria Luddy's noteworthy research on women and philanthropy during the nineteenth century explores women's involvement in helping children, prostitutes and prisoners.[5] Olwen Purdue's work has explored the experience of children from Belfast's Union workhouse, who were boarded out to rural communities, and the attitudes of these local populations towards them, while Sarah-Anne Buckley's research has extensively focused on the history of childhood and child welfare in Ireland during the late nineteenth and twentieth centuries, in particular through the role of the NSPCC.[6] This chapter seeks to add to this growing body of work by exploring the work of the Belfast Charitable Society to improve child poverty during the late eighteenth and early nineteenth centuries. It will examine how the Society provided pauper children with an education, secured them apprenticeships and maintained their welfare outside the Poorhouse, with the intention of making the future working classes more respectable and giving them the skills necessary to contribute to Belfast's industrial economy.

THE DEVELOPMENT OF PAUPER EDUCATION IN CHARITABLE INSTITUTIONS

As previous chapters in this volume have established, the Belfast Chari-table Society was founded in 1752 in response to the growing poverty in late eighteenth-century Belfast.[7] In 1774, the Poorhouse was constructed; its declared purpose was caring for the 'infirm and diseased poor' of the growing town of Belfast.[8] Accommodation within the institution was prioritised for the deserving poor, those of decent character who could not provide for themselves due to misfortune, whilst vagrants considered capable of providing for themselves were not given such preferential treatment.[9] Although the Society had not originally planned for the admission of children, its role in this regard began in 1775, when it permitted two children to stay in the Poorhouse with their single mothers.[10] Whilst residing within the Poorhouse, the children were cared for and provided with a rudimentary education.[11] It was hoped that giving poor children an education would provide them with the skills necessary to live independently from the Poorhouse and create hardworking workers useful to the town's industrial economy.

The first half of the nineteenth century saw growing debates over the role of education for children of the poor. Education and training were seen by many as a means by which to break the cycle of child poverty – not only would it would give pauper children gender-specific vocational skills which would enable them to make a living, it would also instil those behaviours such as hard work and domesticity so valued by the rising middle classes.[12] It was for this reason, for example, that the Irish Poor Law of 1848 included basic provision for the education and training of children admitted to workhouses.[13] The admission of children to the Poorhouse also helped address the problem of poor children on the streets of towns and cities, something that represented a real and present threat to the civic ideal, as well as a potential future threat to the moral health of society and the political health of the nation.[14] One government inspector of factories, delivering his report in the 1850s, styled children who were neither employed nor at school as potentially a menace to society, 'a floating capital of ignorance, idleness and incipient vice, giving to the public an annual interest under the designation of vagrants and criminals'.[15] There were many, however, who held that the education of the children of the poor should remain at a very basic level in order to avoid a poor child becoming 'dissatisfied or discontent with the station in life in which God had been pleased to place him'.[16] Therefore, the level to which pauper children were educated within institutions often depended on the views and opinions of governors, subscribers and donators.[17]

As Alysa Levene points out, some working-class parents were reluctant to have their children educated as they often could not afford the loss of income that would involve. This, therefore, highlights that children represented an important element of the household economy.[18] However, some parents may well have taken a longer-term view, recognising the benefits of educating their children in making them more employable.[19]

Consequently, parents often employed a strategy of compromise to balance the immediate gain of early employment with the longer-term advantages of education. This usually involved providing children with a rudimentary education before they started work. Some factory owners established schools attached to their factories in order to have the children close at hand, though these varied greatly in their effectiveness and the standard of education they offered.[20]

Numerous institutions emerged for the education and training of working-class children in British and Irish towns from the late eighteenth century, including Sunday schools, schools of industry and charter schools. Sunday schools for working-class children existed from the eighteenth century and were often the sole providers of education as they fitted in with children's working patterns, with most children working or in education from Monday through to Saturday each week.[21] These institutions taught children how to read and write as well as offering spiritual guidance to help them live their lives in a manner that was considered respectable and virtuous.[22] Indeed, as Elaine Brown notes, Sunday schools were important for many of the working-class children who attended them, making a 'significant contribution to the decline of illiteracy in areas lacking any other forms of educational provision'.[23]

Schools of industry became available to working-class children in the 1790s and are considered to have represented a 'concerted attempt to reconstruct the lives of the poor'.[24] In addition to teaching children literacy, mathematics and religion, they also ensured that pauper children acquired a trade or handicraft such as spinning, generally relevant to the industrial context in which they lived.[25] Malcolm McKinnon Dick notes that the purpose of this industrial focus within schools of industry was to 'establish social harmony by encouraging self-sufficiency and respectability in the working-class family'.[26] These characteristics were held in high regard for the urban elite and were ones they tried to instil in the working classes.

In addition to schools of industry, the eighteenth century saw the establishment of charter schools in Ireland by the Incorporated Society in Dublin for Promoting English Protestant Schools in Ireland, as an attempt to meet the country's needs.[27] These institutions gained the support of various groups of people but for a range of different reasons. As Kenneth

Milne argues, 'The improving landlord, perhaps a trustee of the Linen Board, saw in them a means to breed good habits of good husbandry; the clergymen of the Established Church viewed them as an antidote to a still virulent popery; the politician looked to them to inculcate right thinking and loyalty.'[28]

The first charter school was established in Castledermot, County Kildare, in May 1734.[29] Children of both sexes were taught how to read, how to speak English and the basics of the Protestant religion.[30] Boys were also taught cultivating skills whilst girls were employed in spinning and learning domestic skills.[31] Thus, the education received by working-class children was influenced by the views and requirements of the institution's supporters.

Clearly, then, the lives of poor and working-class children were shaped by the education they received and the standard of education on offer to them. Deborah Simonton shows that schools of all types usually taught children how to read and spell, so that children could receive moral instruction learning the scriptures.[32] Furthermore, education was seen as a means through which governing bodies could define ideas of gender.[33] Simonton argues that 'while assumptions about social order shaped education, concepts of women's nature and her relative place in society clearly distinguished girls' education from that of boys. In the same way as occupational divisions were gender determined so were assumptions about what skills and knowledge a girl needed.'[34]

Since society held the view that a woman's place was within the domestic sphere, a working-class girl's education focused on preparing her for a career in domestic service or being a good wife, promoting management skills, productiveness and parsimony. Meanwhile, a boy's education emphasised obtaining a trade so that he had the income ready to become the breadwinner for his future family.

PAUPER EDUCATION IN BELFAST POORHOUSE

The educational role of the Belfast Charitable Society was deemed important in improving the lives of the Belfast's vagrant children, along with providing them with accommodation, food and clothing. Occasionally, the committee would record the specific kind of assistance a particular child required. For example, on 3 August 1776 it was recorded that Mary Kelly, who resided with a shoemaker on Donegall Street, was permitted entry into the Poorhouse to be educated and for nourishment.[35] The education of impoverished children was frequently deliberated by the upper and middle classes, who were primarily concerned with whether or not poor children should receive an education and, if so, to what level. Despite possible apprehensions surrounding the education of Belfast's poor child inhabitants, the Belfast Charitable Society saw in it a means to mould the working-classes in ways they deemed respectable and industrious.

Moral Behaviour

The system of rewarding and punishing pauper children was part of the prevailing approach taken by middle-class authorities towards what were considered 'deviant' children. Destitute and criminal children were seen as a problem for local authorities, and were both pitied and feared. The vagrant child was occasionally sympathised with by the wider community as they were unable to find work, were often homeless and had no respectable role models to influence them. As Harry Hendrick has shown, poor or 'deviant' children were often regarded as 'victims' of neglect or circumstance; however, he argues that they were also commonly regarded by society as representing a threat.[36] They threatened the future health of the nation, and they threatened the Victorian ideal of domesticity and the 'ideal family' due to what Heather Shore calls the 'casual assumption that the very poor were corrupted from birth'.[37] These children were perceived as challenging the Victorian ideal of a stable family in which the parents, particularly the mother, were responsible for the moral behaviour and upbringing of their children. Vagrant children were consequently seen as a risk to society as children were seemingly innocent, but they posed a danger because they were the future working-class adults who would pass on these qualities to their offspring. There was the possibility that they could lead other innocent children astray, further exacerbating the problem of immorality amongst the working classes. Therefore, by educating and correcting the moral behaviour of the children, the Belfast Charitable Society was attempting to make the future working class respectable and industrious. This fits with the overall Society's ethos of civil pride – the idea of having 'pride and self-confidence (of a town or city) conferred by prosperity, social improvement and administrative autonomy'.[38] This would have involved reducing the levels of urban poverty seen on the streets of Belfast.

Throughout the late eighteenth and early nineteenth centuries, the Belfast Charitable Society placed a strong emphasis on the moral behaviour of its child inhabitants. The children were rewarded if they were well-behaved and industrious, qualities that the Society thought of as desirable for the working-class populace. The rewards the children received were basic – often a bushel of apples was split amongst them, while on one occasion John Vaght, a Poorhouse orderly and member of the committee, provided a dance for the children.[39] From 5 October 1776, the schoolmaster could hand out premiums to the children in the form of a ticket up to the value of 13d weekly, the exact amount to be determined by the extent of individual children's accomplishments.[40] As well as rewarding the children, the Society punished them for behaviour which they deemed unacceptable in order to prevent repeated offences. For example, on 16 September 1815, six boys were 'severely flogged' for running away to Carrickfergus after having broken a pane of glass in the schoolroom.[41] Some of the chastisements that the children received were particularly harsh. George Brown, who had absconded and later returned, was ordered to be flogged and detained in the 'Black Hole' for seven nights.[42] The 'Black Hole' was a place of solitary confinement used by the committee members to punish unruly inmates of the Poorhouse.

However, it should be noted that the Belfast Charitable Society was not always consistent in instilling the appropriate moral qualities in their child inhabitants. Mary Kirkpatrick, a young, orphaned girl who first entered the Poorhouse in April 1776, was never punished by the committee members despite having run away on three separate occasions.[43] This may have been because the committee members simply did not record the punishments she received; however, it was more likely that they could not afford Mary Kirkpatrick to leave the institution permanently, as she was a skilled textile worker. She was often commended for being industrious and skilled in cotton manufacturing and was regularly supplied with the necessary tools of her trade: 'Mr Bray is ordered to buy six combs, one sheet of pins and half a hundred needles for Mary Kirkpatrick, and allow her four candles weekly if she demands them.'[44] This suggests that, while concerns for the moral health of Belfast's future citizens may have been a strong motivation for the society's work, practical economic concerns could, and did, override more noble sentiments.

Religious Education

Religious education formed another important aspect of pauper education in the Poorhouse. This heavy emphasis on religious education provided another avenue through which the Society could instil those morals valued by the rising middle classes. This type of education was similar to that available in the Sunday schools which were established throughout England during the late eighteenth century.[45] In England it was feared by the urban elites that the lower orders would organise political groups and demand reform, potentially disrupting social order in the country. Similarly social division was apparent in early nineteenth-century Belfast as relations between Catholic and Protestant communities deteriorated, with violent outbursts occurring in 1813, 1822, 1824 and 1825.[46] Due to an awareness of the potential threat of the working classes, education (which comprised basic literary, religious and social knowledge) was seen as an important means by which to 'remodel attitudes and behaviour to recreate a society where mutual harmony prevailed'.[47] The children in the Poorhouse, both boys and girls, were tested almost weekly on how well they could memorise and recite various verses from the New Testament and the Catechism. The various orderlies documented how well children performed to track their development. On 3 November 1810, William Clarke records that he had 'examined a number of the boys and girls in reading and heard them repeat Psalms and Hymns which they did talently well for the first time'.[48] As well as receiving religious instruction, the children were sent to 'Public Worship' on a Sunday with their teachers.[49]

The religious education received by the children was unique in that Roman Catholic children were allowed to learn religion within their own denomination. This was particularly interesting given that, while the Society was comprised of middle-class men from a mix of religious backgrounds, the Poorhouse had an overall Protestant ethos. On 26 June

1813, the Society gave William Crolly, a priest, permission to take the Catholic children resident in the Poorhouse to chapel.[50] However, this permission was granted on the provision that various conditions were met: for example, that the committee would send a chaperone with the children to take and return them to and from public worship.[51] This was unusual for its time and took place in a context where many Protestant-based schools in Ireland, such as charter schools, were considered to have used education as a means to convert and anglicise Catholic children to Protestantism.[52] Even within Europe more widely, it was not until 1850 that non-denominational education institutions began to emerge in Switzerland.[53] Before the establishment of the 1831 National System of Education in Ireland, it was only in Irish 'hedge schools', which were small informal schools illegally established in the eighteenth century by the Irish Catholic Church, that children could receive an education within a Catholic setting.[54]

It would therefore appear that, in its early years, the Belfast Charitable Society showed a high degree of tolerance towards Catholicism and the education of Catholic children. This was due partly to the liberal traditions on which the Charitable Society was founded but also to the proportionately low numbers of Catholics who lived in Belfast during the late eighteenth century – S.J. Connolly records that in 1757 there were only 556 Catholics in a total population of 8,549.[55] However, as the Catholic population began to rise with the increasing industrialisation of Belfast, and as the events of the Irish Rebellion 1789 highlighted issues of denominational difference, the Belfast Charitable Society became increasingly conscious of the confessional divide within the town. In 1829, for the first time, the committee began to record the child's denomination in the admission records, and in cases where no preference was given, the child was to be brought up as a Protestant.[56] Pauper education within the Poorhouse was, therefore, influenced by the surrounding events within Belfast as town officials became more aware of a potential Catholic threat and their campaign for relief.

Literacy and Numeracy

The early years of the nineteenth century saw a new emphasis by the Belfast Charitable Society on educating its children in literacy, rather than preparing them solely for manufacturing. From 1812 the Society began to use, and frequently purchased, both the Universal and Manson's spelling books and the Assembly's Catechism to teach the children how to read and write.[57] Just as was the case with regard to their religious education, the children were frequently tested on their literacy skills. On 21 May 1803, the orderly examined the boys in reading and spelling, 'in neither of which did they miss a word'.[58] Likewise, the girls read a chapter from the Gospel 'very much to [his] satisfaction' and could 'spell without a mistake'.[59] Some of the children clearly benefited from their education – William Bruce, an orderly, noted on 27 September 1817 that James Sinclair 'read & gave out the Psalm, read a chapter & a prayer, concluded with a Lord's Prayer all with great propriety'.[60]

This emphasis on educating poor children in literacy and mathematics was not uncommon in such institutions. English factory schools during the nineteenth century taught child workers arithmetic and literacy following the passing of the Preservation of the Health and Morals of Apprentices Act (1802).[61] Education was deemed important to improve the working classes, as having skills and knowledge would allow vagrant children to gain jobs and lead respectable lives. Harry Hendrick argues that children were seen as 'investments' in which the 'health, welfare and rearing of children have been linked to the destiny of the nation'.[62] However, the level to which the children were educated within these institutions, and the focus of that education, often depended on those who ran them and their views on child education. On 15 August 1812, Henry Joy, a member of the committee, stated that he thought that the children should focus on learning vocational, rather than literary, skills, as he deemed the former more useful.[63] He possibly felt that the children would find it easier to get an apprenticeship or find employment if they had the necessary skills. The written sources record no reaction from the other committee members with regard to Joy's comments, although it would be surprising if there was not some form of verbal reaction, as some of the members were particularly attentive to the children's education. For example, on 14 April 1810, William Berwick (an orderly of the Poorhouse) encouraged other members of the committee to visit the schoolroom to report on the progress of the children's studies,[64] while Robert Tennent, another committee member, issued regulations for the girls' school and regularly noted if the children were in need of more books in order to continue their lessons.[65] Alternatively, the silence of the committee could imply that its members did not take Joy's views seriously or had other, more important matters to deal with than child education. In England, Elaine Brown notes how some employers of children in factories ignored the 1802 Act or allowed them to attend school on a part-time basis.[66] Therefore, despite the view that children within institutions were better educated than those outside, conflicting ideas of pauper education means that the level of education varied between institutions.

Vocational Education

In addition to learning literacy and mathematics, the Belfast Charitable Society taught the children vocational skills and often employed inmates within the Poorhouse to teach them. There was a particular focus on the vocational training of the girls, something that helped reinforce prevailing gender norms at the time. A report from the Committee of Industry in May 1813 reveals that a Miss Elder taught two classes of girls how to sew on alternating days.[67] The class that was not with Miss Elder would then perform chores around the Poorhouse, such as helping the younger children make their beds and cleaning rooms.[68] Between eight and nine in the morning, the girls would be split amongst the reading school and the writing school.[69] Then, after breakfast, the entire class would be engaged in sewing, knitting and spinning until dinner, after which they were to return to the reading school until night-time.[70] Female education during this period often centred around domesticity as girls were taught skills such as housekeeping and morality to prepare them for their future roles as domestic servants and mothers, albeit with a better professional and moral education than that of most existing domestic servants and working-class women. It should be noted that there are no extensive records to indicate that the boys would have been taught a vocational skill to the same extent as the girls. Regardless, these skills would prove to be particularly useful during the middle of the nineteenth century, as many young women migrated to America in the hope of securing jobs in domestic service and making adequate lives for themselves.[71]

PAUPER APPRENTICESHIPS

In April 1783 the *Belfast News-Letter* carried the following announcement made by the Poorhouse:

> There are at present several boys and a few girls in this house fit to be apprenticed out. They have been carefully educated and have all along been trained up to habits of industry. An account may be had of their behaviour and abilities, by enquiring at Mr. and Mrs. Carrothers, who superintend the School – Application to be made to the weekly committee on any Saturday at 12 o'clock noon.[72]

After a poor child's education at the institution was completed, it was time for him or her to be apprenticed off to further their vocational training. It is unclear from the records when the Belfast Charitable Society's apprenticeship scheme began, as a portion of the committee books have been lost. The earliest records date from November 1778, when Robert Heyburn applied to keep a boy, Hugh Dobbin, for five months at 2/2 per month, promising to care for the child and to return him to the Poorhouse at the end of his term.[73] This does not explicitly state that the boy was apprenticed, but it does give an indication that children were hired from the Poorhouse for work.

The practice of apprenticing destitute children had been around for a very long time. In England it had been made compulsory under the Elizabethan Poor Laws for orphans and poor children to be apprenticed into a trade to provide them with the skills necessary to support themselves in adulthood. The utility of the 'old' poor law to provide destitute children with an apprenticeship depended on a range of factors, including the parish's attitudes towards the poor and regional economic conditions.[74] In the long term, pauper apprenticeships allowed charitable institutions to 'safeguard settlements' and relieve themselves of the responsibility of looking after a large number of children who could be a burden on their resources.[75] During the Industrial Revolution, children were the ideal form of labour as they were a cheap resource who were unlikely to complain about working conditions.[76] There was also the possibility of receiving a financial dividend for taking on a pauper apprentice.[77]

However, in reality, parish apprenticeships were not completely low-cost, as, rather than paying a wage, the master had to ensure that his apprentice was properly cared for and provided with lodgings.[78]

This section of the chapter explores the development of apprenticeships by the Belfast Charitable Society by taking a sample of 157 destitute children admitted into the Poorhouse between 1775 and 1820. It examines all those admitted in the months of April and November each year in order to allow for seasonal variation. More children were admitted in November than in April, which was probably due to the harsher conditions faced by the poor during the winter months than during springtime. This would indicate that the Poorhouse was instrumental in the tactics and resources which the poor used to survive the cruellest of months, a set of tactics described by Olwen Hufton as an 'economy of makeshifts'.[79] From the information contained in the Belfast Charitable Society admissions record books, it appears that fifty-nine out of the sample of 157 children were apprenticed off during the years 1805–24.

The age at which children were apprenticed is worth noting. Firstly, it reveals the attitudes of binding officials and respective masters towards child labour and the extent to which charitable administrators, in Levene's words, 'prioritised the passing on of responsibility for children as early as possible'.[80] The sample taken from the Belfast Charitable Society's records reveals that the average age children were apprenticed was thirteen years old, with the youngest being ten and the oldest eighteen (see Figure 7.1).[81] This average is considerably older than that found in Pamela Sharpe's research, where apprentices in Colyton started their training at ten and a half years of age or in London where they were typically apprenticed at twelve years old.[82] It is important to keep in mind that the age at which a child was apprenticed often depended on the type of trade to which he or she was apprenticed. Low-skilled and less physically demanding jobs, such as domestic service, meant that children could be apprenticed at a younger age.

The Society tended to keep their children until they were in their early teens to ensure that they were properly educated and prepared for their future apprenticeships. A report of the boys' school from 1813 reveals that the boys from class one, aged between ten and thirteen, were ready to start the next stage of their education as they were able to read, write

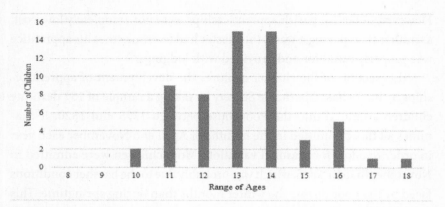

Figure 7.1 The age at which children were apprenticed. (Source: The Belfast Charitable Society Archives)

and count.[83] On the other hand, class two were not quite ready to leave the classroom, as some of the boys, such as William Monaghan (aged ten), were able to write on paper but needed to learn how to count.[84] It is clear that the Society wanted to ensure that each of the children reached a certain level of education before they were apprenticed. This was likely to ensure that the children were not returned to the Society due to their being unable to complete their training.

Equally important is that apprenticeships allowed the Society to reduce the number of children residing within the Poorhouse. It is often recorded that the institution was overrun with poor inhabitants, which made it necessary 'to have several of the oldest boys and girls apprenticed out as soon as possible.[85] Claire Allen points out that the Charitable Society's funds were under strain due to the increasing need for poor relief as a result of Belfast's expansion.[86] In contrast to the Police Board, the Society did not have any constitutional authority to raise money for the Poorhouse.[87] Therefore, it is plausible, as Levene has argued, that apprenticeships allowed charitable institutions to dispose of a large number of children, particularly if space and finances were limited.[88] This could have been at the expense of ensuring children were adequately prepared for apprentice life.

From the sample taken from the Belfast Charitable Society admissions record book, it was recorded that fifty-nine children were apprenticed

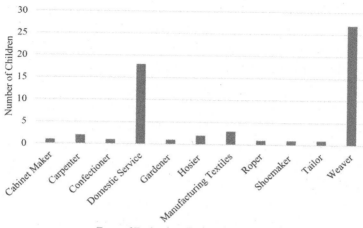

Figure 7.2 Types of trades children from the Poorhouse were apprenticed in from 1805–24. (Source: The Belfast Charitable Society's Archives)

off during the years 1805–24. Most of these children (51 per cent) were apprenticed into trades associated with the industrial sector, such as manufacturing textiles in the surrounding countryside (see Figure 7.2).[89] During the late eighteenth and early nineteenth centuries, Belfast's economy was beginning to flourish due to commercial growth and the cotton industry.[90] Similarly, in London, 76 per cent of parish children were apprenticed within the manufacturing sector, which was thought of as the driving force behind Britain's economic growth.[91] In the rest of Ireland, outside the northeast, and in other less-industrialised countries of Europe, such as Germany, where agriculture was driving their economies, children from welfare institutions were often apprenticed as farm labourers.[92] Therefore, child vocational training was shaped and influenced by the economic context of the surrounding area. Impoverished children had an important part to play in this industrial climate, and the demand for workers increased their chances of getting a job after they completed their apprenticeships.

Children were also apprenticed into traditional sectors. Domestic service was the second-largest sector into which children, particularly girls, were apprenticed, with 31 per cent apprenticed within this area (see

Figure 7.2). Caitriona Clear estimates that in nineteenth-century Ireland over 80 per cent of domestic servants were female, and there was often a blurring of the lines between farmhands and domestic servants on farms.[93] Katrina Honeyman confirms that the gendering of labour was a key characteristic of industrialisation, as boys and girls received different opportunities from apprenticeships and guilds.[94] Boys' apprenticeships were designed to lead to a trade and to emphasise qualities such as proficiency and independence, whilst female apprentices centred around the domestic sphere and they were required to be malleable and contingent.[95]

The purpose of pauper apprenticeships was to give children the necessary skills to make a living but not to elevate them above their social standing. Many of the children from the Poorhouse were apprenticed into trades associated with the working classes, such as weaving, manufacturing and domestic service. A small number of the children were apprenticed in more highly skilled trades, including tailoring and cabinetmaking, which would typically have been jobs for the middling ranks (see Figure 7.2). This indicates that, like pauper education, the nature of apprenticeships was subject to quite localised notions of social class and what kind of work was deemed appropriate for the children of the poor. Levene notes that during the late eighteenth and early nineteenth centuries the London Foundling Hospital faced growing disapproval for allegedly raising its orphans above their social standing.[96] Consequently, the Poorhouse, like other charitable institutions, had to be careful about what type of trades they apprenticed their child inhabitants in. They needed to apprentice their children to give them the opportunity to learn the necessary skills to make a living for themselves and to lessen the pressure of resources within the Poorhouse. Yet, the Society also needed to be aware of any potential public discord from being seen to be raising these children above their social station.

THE WELFARE OF CHILD APPRENTICES

Children were particularly vulnerable during their apprenticeships, as these were often far away from the protection of officials, and cruel masters were rarely punished for their methods of harsh discipline.[97]

Many charitable institutions took measures to try to protect children from mistreatment. The London Foundling Hospital inspected the homes of hired wet nurses to ensure that they 'were not able to perpetrate the worse abuses on the Continent', such as claiming funds for children who had died.[98] Despite the various attempts made by officials, child abuse did still occur without their knowledge.

The Society took certain measures to ensure that children were adequately protected whilst they were apprenticed out. In January 1803, it was agreed that no child was to be apprenticed out on the same day that their potential master applied for them.[99] This gave committee members time to certify if the requested child had received an adequate education as well as checking the suitability of the master and trade for the child.[100] Then an indenture was created to stipulate the terms of each apprenticeship. For example, on 24 October 1801, James Williamson was apprenticed to Thomas Quinn, a master weaver, for five years in Greggs Lane, Belfast. Thomas Quinn was required to 'feed & clothe him [Williamson] – and pay him three guineas at the end of his apprenticeship'.[101] The children were inspected twice a year by a committee member to ensure they were being properly cared for and to collect fees from their masters.[102] Each committee member was assigned to an area and would have had a list of children within that region which they had to check up on. The ladies' committee, established in 1827, also played an important role in checking on the progress and welfare of female apprentices in the surrounding area. It was necessary for the Society to employ these various measures, as pauper children were seen as vulnerable and needed to be protected from exploitation by their masters.

Katrina Honeyman has argued, however, that despite these protective measures, parish authorities were still held accountable for the mistreatment of pauper apprentices, which was apparent in the way in which they forcibly apprenticed them.[103] There is some legitimacy to this statement. Firstly, there is no indication from the sources that the Society did check the reputation of each master. It is possible that when numbers within the Poorhouse were high, the reputation of a prospective master was not considered as much of a priority as the need to remove a large proportion of children from the institution. Secondly, the Society had limited contact time with pauper apprentices, which meant that there was the potential for mistreatment to occur without their knowledge. Those committee members who acted as inspectors of apprenticed children were not employed by the Society, rather they joined the Society as part of their civic duty and their work for the Society was in addition to their professional duties. This would have limited their capacity to check on pauper apprentices on a regular basis. Furthermore, there is no evidence

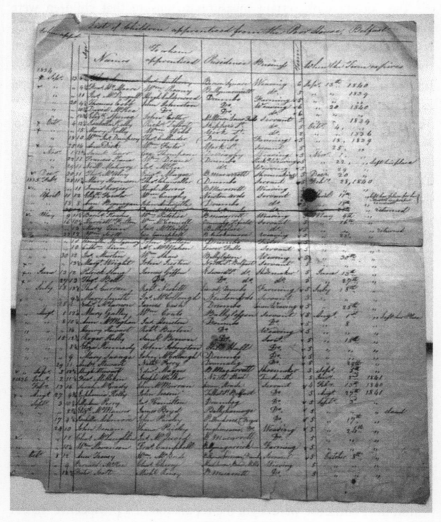

Figure 7.3 A list of children who were apprenticed locally in Belfast which contained details of the child's name, where they resided and information about their indenture. (Courtesy of the Belfast Charitable Society's Archives)

of them having provided written reports of their inspections that might have allowed the Society to keep a record of each pauper apprentice's welfare. The lists of children received by the inspectors were quite extensive (Figure 7.3), which further limited their capacity to adequately report on the conditions of the children's workplace and any improvements that might have been needed. Finally, as is the case today, there could well have been cases of hidden child abuse that went unnoticed by an inspector or where a pauper child would not have approached the Society out of fear of retaliation from their masters.

CONCLUSION

The Belfast Charitable Society served an important role in Belfast during the late eighteenth and early nineteenth centuries, not only practically combatting the growing problem of urban poverty amongst the working class but also moulding the character of poor children through education to create the ideal working-class populace in contemporary society. Apprenticeships were designed to make pauper children useful and give them the opportunity to learn new lifelong skills. This would have helped them find employment once they had finished their training, rather than relying on the assistance provided by welfare institutions. Children from the Poorhouse were often apprenticed into trades that were associated with the working classes, including the industrial and traditional sectors, which would increase the likelihood of them earning a living once they completed their vocational training. Yet, despite being portrayed as a threat to wider society, the Charitable Society took various measures to protect children who were living within the Poorhouse and those who were apprenticed out in the surrounding area. These measures highlight the vulnerability of children, particularly apprentices who were often left at the mercy of their masters and were placed far away from the protection of the Society. The Charitable Society continued its work to combat urban child poverty and mould the character of the future working classes right until the late nineteenth century.

CHAPTER EIGHT

Poorhouse to Pandemic: Medical Relief and Public Health in Early Nineteenth-century Belfast

Robyn Atcheson

&

By the opening years of the nineteenth century, it was becoming apparent that public health was an area in need of improvement in the growing town of Belfast. Although the population of the town was steadily increasing, housing had not grown in proportion and sanitary facilities were grossly inadequate.[1] Sanitation failed to keep pace with social and economic growth during the early years of the nineteenth century, with housing conditions being cramped, overcrowded and mostly without yards or lavatories.[2] In 1831 James Butler Bryan wrote of Belfast, 'Disease, and all the enfeebling attendants of poverty, are busy amongst them; winter and its miseries are approaching, and without adequate food, raiment, or covering: their circumstances present a picture at which humanity shudders.'[3] This chapter will investigate the landscape of medical relief available to the sick poor in Belfast in the early nineteenth century by examining how and why a range of different organisations developed to cater to specific groups of the poor. Although focusing mainly on the early nineteenth century, the chapter will cover the period from the opening of Belfast's Poorhouse in 1774 to the opening of the workhouse in Belfast in 1841.

Existing scholarship on the social history of medicine in Belfast can be placed within the 'grand narrative' approach, identified by Catherine Cox, that predominantly focuses on the twentieth century and institutional case studies.[4] Institutional histories, written by physicians, exist for the town's major hospitals in this period but treat each of them in isolation.[5] Local histories on medicine tend to fall into the trend identified by Laurence Geary for Ireland as a whole, whereby the historiography of the medical aid network of the eighteenth and early nineteenth centuries is often celebratory, commemorative or local.[6] Geary's work locates the medical history of Ireland within a broader socio-economic history, providing context and showing how medicine fits into wider narratives of poverty and welfare. The social history of medicine in Ireland is a developing field of study, with specialised works looking at the Irish dispensary system, insanity and gender, among other topics.[7] Research on Belfast is also a burgeoning field. However, most research on this period focuses on political, economic, religious and social aspects of the growing industrial town.[8] R.W.M. Strain's thorough volume on the Belfast Charitable Society provides a wealth of information on the Society but is mainly an administrative history and stops short of discussing the Society in the context of other organisations.[9]

This chapter addresses the gap in providing a unified history of public health within the town of Belfast during this period. It will track the evolution of the institutions that treated the sick and provide a combined institutional narrative of Belfast's medical network, placing it within the context of Irish and British norms of the time. It will examine ailments common among the poor, the increasing specialisation of medicine and treatments and ideas held by medical professionals and society at large. After discussing the main organisations devoted to the sick poor, it will then look at times of crisis, namely the public health challenges of fever in 1816–18 and the cholera pandemic of 1832. It will show that Belfast was a distinct town in many ways, including in its development of a medical network.

Medical relief for the poor was rare in late eighteenth-century Ireland. A system of county infirmaries across Ireland, supported by a combination of subscription and treasury funding, had been established under a parliamentary act in 1765. This allowed for an infirmary to be established in every county except Dublin and Waterford, where hospitals were already in existence.[10] Infirmaries offered inpatient and outpatient medical assistance, along with provision for accidents and vaccinations. However, these hospitals were often inconveniently situated, and their capacity was mostly devoted to chronic cases.[11] Some excluded specific groups of the sick poor, such as pregnant women, children under the age of ten, lunatics and cases of infectious disease.[12] By 1771, Ulster had nine of Ireland's thirty infirmaries, with an average of eleven beds in each, and, generally, these were better organised than those in other parts of Ireland.[13] Some of them took over buildings previously used by charitable infirmaries, such as that in Armagh, essentially replacing pre-existing voluntary relief.[14] Between 1767 and 1800, twenty infirmary amendment acts were passed, indicating a growing institutionalisation and professionalisation of medicine.[15] This nationwide system initiated state involvement in healthcare and was unique to Ireland, as nowhere else in Europe had a similar national network.[16]

There was also a system of dispensaries that delivered outpatient advice and treatment; however, it was likewise patchy in its provision to the poor. This was based on an English system and encouraged by legislation in 1805 that allowed grand jury contributions to equal voluntary donations.[17] Dispensaries offered care at the dispensary premises or at the homes of patients, attended accidents, supplied medications and oversaw vaccination programmes, helping to popularise the practice.[18] There were 452 dispensaries across Ireland by 1833, but this was not enough to serve the whole population due to uneven distribution, with some districts being too populous.[19] Fever hospitals were another source of medical care, usually founded in response to outbreaks of infectious disease and likewise funded by a combination of grand jury presentments and subscriptions. The first in Ireland was established in Limerick in 1773, and legislation in 1818 provided for district fever hospitals to serve their surrounding areas.[20] These hospitals were solely devoted to treating infectious diseases and were unevenly distributed, being required only periodically.[21] By 1841, Ulster had twenty-two of Ireland's 101 fever hospitals.[22] This developing system of infirmaries, dispensaries and fever hospitals facilitated the spread of professional medical men throughout Ireland and encouraged professionalisation.[23]

THE POORHOUSE

The provision of medical relief for the poor of Belfast originated with the infirmary of the town's Poorhouse. Providing for the sick poor had been a goal of the Belfast Charitable Society from its establishment in the 1750s. A meeting of the Belfast Charitable Society in September 1774, held upon the opening of the Poorhouse, decided immediately to set aside ten beds for the sick poor and, two weeks later, a nurse keeper and servants to specifically tend to the sick were appointed.[24] Physicians and surgeons agreed to attend patients for free and provided lists of necessary equipment for the infirmary. The first medical report of the Poorhouse, dated 9 May 1775, noted that five patients had been treated, one of whom was still receiving treatment. In addition, the infirmary was organising the visiting of outpatients: four had been visited and treated, of whom two had been cured.[25] The infirmary accommodated both medical and surgical cases, arranged outpatient treatment and supplied medicine. In 1776 the Society was advertising outpatient times at the infirmary for people to come to seek advice from the 'medical gentlemen'.[26] In keeping with the ethos of the Society, priority was given to the resident sick poor who had been in Belfast for a specified period of over one year. However, there were exceptions to this, mostly accidents and urgent cases arriving in Belfast needing immediate medical attention.[27]

Other charitable societies, such as that in Coleraine, which was also founded in the 1770s, did not generally begin with such a focus on medical care, nor were they as effective. By 1790, Coleraine Charitable Society's Poorhouse was only being used as rent-free accommodation for the elderly poor.[28] The House of Industry in Dublin did provide medical relief, with three attached hospitals by the early nineteenth century.[29] However, this, too, was dissimilar from Belfast as these hospitals were funded by government and not primarily through voluntary giving. Thus, from the beginning, the focus on medical relief was distinct in the Belfast Charitable Society. However, it was common across Ulster, following the European trend, for charity to be restricted to locals.[30]

The committee of the Belfast Charitable Society, while keen to develop its provision of medical relief, was happy to leave the running of the medical aspects of the Poorhouse to the medical professionals involved. In 1776 the committee recorded that the medical gentlemen who provided their services could work out their own attendance without interference.[31] The Society committee was also supportive of the treatments the physicians wished to carry out, including the controversial prevention of smallpox, a new and much debated idea within the scientific community. Dr William Drennan, a physician and member of the committee, championed the use of inoculation in 1782 and had a section of the infirmary set aside for that purpose. As early as November 1800, the committee had resolved to trial the method of inoculation recently proposed by Edward Jenner.[32] Much of this enthusiasm for the development of public health was driven by the prominent role of medical professionals within the Belfast Charitable Society. The committee lists, as published in the *Belfast Almanack*, show that 105 men served on the committee between 1809 and 1841. Of these, eight were listed in trade directories as physicians and surgeons, their tenures spread out across the period. This almost constant presence of medical knowledge within the management of the Society contributed to the medical decisions made and goes some way to explain the measures taken by the Society as the public health of the town evolved in later years.

Within the Poorhouse, sanitation and hygiene were constant issues among the resident paupers. Much of the discussion of these matters originated with the ladies' committee. The ladies primarily concerned themselves with the children and women in the Poorhouse, in keeping with philanthropic modes at the time, something that provided middle- and upper-class women with opportunities to participate in society while remaining within the 'domestic sphere'.[33] This was common across Europe, as women were more likely to be the recipients of charity.[34] A small committee of ladies was formed in 1814 to look after the welfare of the women and children and made many suggestions in their first two years of operation.[35] These suggestions were mostly shelved by the men's committee, and the ladies' committee soon disbanded, although the individuals involved remained informally connected with the Poorhouse by helping to find employment for the older girls and requesting admittance for certain applicants. The ladies' committee was revived and reformed in March 1827 with a larger membership who proved rigorous in their duties, immediately appointing four members to visit the Poorhouse daily.[36] The ladies consistently raised concerns over cleanliness within the house, requesting more soap, appealing for a solution to the vermin problem and, in 1830, asking to be allowed to supervise the girls' hygiene, particularly in the combing of their hair which suggests that lice was a common problem in the house.[37] In the early nineteenth century overcrowding and poor hygiene in the Poorhouse had left the rooms of the old people particularly unsanitary, while scrofulous complaints were rampant among the children, leading the ladies to repeatedly request increased allocations of soap and to organise a rotation to inspect cleanliness.[38]

The advice of the ladies' committee was in keeping with medical opinion at the time; they recommended fresh air and exercise, and recorded their concerns about overcrowded sleeping arrangements and the potentially unhealthy working conditions of the girls who were apprenticed as weavers.[39] Apprenticeships were one of the ways in which the Society endeavoured to encourage industrial skills among the children in the Poorhouse and thus break the cycle of poverty. At the age of around eleven, children would be apprenticed out to respectable individuals who would be responsible for their welfare and education in their particular trade. The ladies took on the role of checking on these apprenticeships and ensuring the safety and welfare of the children thus boarded out. Their concerns over the working conditions of some of these trades could have stemmed from the examples in the Society steward's reports, which note the occasions on which children were returned by their masters due to ill health. For example, in March 1814, Mary Ann Brown, an apprentice, was returned by her master Edward Craig, on account of 'tender eyes'.[40] There were also some cases in which apprenticed children were returned on account of infectious ailments they had contracted in the Poorhouse, particularly ringworm, often referred to as 'scaldhead'.[41]

The infirmary of the Poorhouse was essentially the only form of accessible medical relief for the poor of Belfast for almost twenty years and continued to provide medical support throughout the early nineteenth century. Although the infirmary catered for small numbers, the records of the Society provide an insight into the kind of medical work the house was offering. By taking an eighteen-month period between July 1805 and December 1806, we can see that forty-one patients were named in the steward's notebook. Fourteen were discharged and there were six deaths. Of those for whom this information is available, we can see that the average stay in the infirmary was five and a half weeks, and that patients' ages ranged from fifteen to eighty. Unfortunately, details of these patients' ailments have gone unrecorded, aside from a few exceptional cases. One such was John Kinley, who underwent an arm amputation after a work accident in a flax mill in August 1805; another was Charles O'Neill, who was admitted to the infirmary in August 1806 and had to have his leg amputated that December.[42] Accidents would have been common in a burgeoning industrial town, but, in the early years of the century, there was no general hospital to treat such cases; thus, they appear in the earlier records of the Poorhouse infirmary.

Providing free medical care for the Society was, for some physicians and surgeons, an opportunity to hone these more specialised skills. Working for hospitals and medical charities was seen as a way to enhance reputations as well as gain experience.[43] Industrialising towns across Britain witnessed medical men highlighting the specific problems facing these growing urban areas, specifically referring to the health dangers of unguarded machinery, air and water pollution and crowded living conditions.[44] In Belfast's fever hospital, most trauma was a result of industrial accidents, leading to a range of surgical interventions.[45] Likewise, conditions in mills and factories in Belfast led to one physician, Dr Andrew Malcolm, developing a particular interest in respiratory illness, which was frequently seen among his patients.[46] Speciality medicine was in its infancy, with physicians, surgeons and even apothecaries frequently taking on each other's roles, especially within medical charities.[47] Some physicians would have been particularly drawn to their own specialised field of interest, for example, Dr Henry Forcade, a committee member and surgeon who also acted as an accoucheur or 'man-midwife' with an interest in obstetrics. Various physicians would come into contact with the Poorhouse infirmary through the years, whether they were committee members or not, and invariably leave their mark on the kind of relief available, as did Dr Drennan with his advocacy for smallpox inoculation.

Many of the ailments that presented in the Poorhouse were a direct result of poverty. Skin conditions were a frequent complaint, with surgeon John Clarke noting that three of the four cases in the infirmary in August 1775 were there due to sores and ulcers.[48] In Strain's history of the Society he lists several ailments mentioned in the early years of the infirmary, including asthma, dropsy and bloody flux, as well as broken bones and dislocations.[49] The doctors attached to the infirmary also saw outpatients both at the Poorhouse and in the patients' homes.[50] The Poorhouse infirmary sat outside the national county infirmary system and was one of the very few voluntary hospitals in Ireland at the turn of the nineteenth century, along with general infirmaries in Waterford and Cork.[51] The completely free-of-charge medical relief being offered in the Poorhouse infirmary was unusual compared to similar institutions in other British industrial towns, such as Manchester, that had witnessed similar patterns of industrial growth, unemployment and urban poverty; there, paupers were often not taken as inpatients unless special payments were made on their behalf.[52]

Attitudes to the sick poor in the Belfast Poorhouse in general were often considered enlightened for the early nineteenth century. In 1828, for example, the ladies' committee championed the employment of Helena Kelly as schoolmistress in needlework to the girls in the house after she returned from the town's fever hospital having had her leg amputated.[53] Such a traumatic procedure would undoubtedly have left Miss Kelly's circumstances even more dire than they had been previously, but the ladies obviously felt her talents should not be wasted due to her disability. An earlier entry in the orderly book reveals that Helena Kelly had grown up in the Poorhouse; she was noted as being lame and recommended for an apprenticeship to a dressmaker when she was seventeen.[54] A few years later the ladies urged the men's committee to allow a Mary Kelly to teach the infant school and be paid an adequate salary. Mary Kelly was noted as being a lame girl who had been educated in Brown Street Sunday school in the town. Having seen her success, the men eventually agreed and granted Miss Kelly a bonnet and a cloak wide enough to cover her crutch; however, she was offered a paid position elsewhere and left.[55]

The cloak as a form of payment is interesting as it highlights that in much of society at the time, a visible disability would have had negative connotations. Although medical opinion had evolved from the association between sin and health, popular culture was slow to accept that illness and disability could be unrelated to moral character.[56] David Turner has shown that female disabled bodies were seen as more shameful than male bodies, not only making them distasteful but socially, as well as physically, deforming.[57] There was little support for the poor who were permanently disabled or chronically ill, so they were frequently to be found in the Poorhouse, on occasion having been brought there by constables for begging.[58] There were also disabled individuals who were admitted to the Poorhouse with notes of their 'decent character' recorded by the committee.[59]

LUNACY

One of the groups of sick poor that appear frequently in the records of the Belfast Charitable Society were those recorded as 'lunatics'. Lunacy was generally applied to anyone suffering from mental health issues and embodied a wide range of conditions including melancholy, mania, learning difficulties and dementia.[60] Oonagh Walsh noted that within institutions, causes of insanity were often categorised under 'moral' and 'physical', with moral causes including grief, anxiety and poverty, while physical causes included intemperance, brain damage and injury.[61] Alice Mauger further expanded the root of moral causes as psychological, revealing perceptions of how life events and circumstances could lead to mental illness.[62]

There was no official provision for lunatics and, while there were private asylums for the wealthy, poor lunatics often ended up in the Poorhouse. 'Madwomen' are mentioned in Society records for the first time in 1782, and in 1791 the Society agreed to admit women of this description, allocating separate spaces at various times, such as the lower rooms or the belfry, thus allowing for them to be separated from the general population.[63] An investigation into institutions housing lunatics in 1812 showed that only nine counties in Ireland had any provision, most of which was in institutions similar to the Poorhouse.[64] Admitting lunatics to the Poorhouse was problematic as there was an absence of resources for these paupers. The committee therefore tried to impose limits on the number of lunatics in the house, but this policy was quickly abandoned as there was simply nowhere else for them to go.[65] From 1810 to 1814 there were twenty-one lunatics identified in the steward's notebook, most of them recorded as being 'confined' to a cell or room in the spire of the building. Two were also chained or handcuffed.[66] The majority of recorded lunatics in the Poorhouse were eventually discharged once they were considered to be sufficiently recovered; the average stay of lunatic paupers in this sample was around nine weeks. A few of the names appear repeatedly, for example Andrew Cochran who was admitted in 1811, 1812 and 1813 for one or two weeks at a time before being discharged as recovered.[67] Existing residents of the Poorhouse who exhibited signs of insanity were often separated and confined until they were deemed well again. In some cases, a period of rest was enough to restore mental and physical health.[68]

For those found to be too unruly for the Poorhouse to cope with, there were occasional arrangements to transport them to the Dublin House of Industry. The Dublin House of Industry had opened in 1773, with additional buildings being added over the following decades, including the Hardwicke Fever Hospital with a courtyard set with lunatic cells.[69] Five paupers from the Poorhouse were sent to Dublin in 1810, six in 1811 and four in 1812, along with two other lunatics from the town that year. We have no surviving record of whether the individuals in question had any choice in this, but a note in June 1810 states that Widow Abernathy left the Poorhouse with her 'Idiot' daughter rather than have her sent to Dublin.[70] In some cases, the name of the individual was not identified, but even these unnamed paupers could be sent to Dublin, as one 'unknown Idiot' was in July 1814 after being unruly and having to be confined to a cell every night.[71] The Dublin House of Industry then developed a separate asylum, the Richmond Lunatic Asylum, in 1815.[72]

Realising that facilitating the lunatic poor was a significant problem for the town, the Belfast Charitable Society called a special meeting in 1818 to apply to the Lord Lieutenant for a lunatic asylum to be erected in Belfast. The Lord Lieutenant replied that commissioners had scoped the possibility of opening an asylum and looked at various proposals for sites. However, despite 'the number and urgent distress of the lunatic poor in Belfast', they were unable to proceed.[73] Several attempts to secure an appropriate site were unsuccessful.[74] In 1825 a further deputation, with allies from the town's fever hospital and the House of Industry, was successful, and the Belfast District Lunatic Asylum was opened in 1829.[75] The Belfast asylum catered for Counties Antrim and Down, with admission strictly controlled, requiring both a medical certificate of insanity and an affidavit of poverty.[76] It was originally built to accommodate 100 but soon held more, with a staff of twenty-seven, including domestic servants, nurses and keepers.[77] The Belfast asylum was built with a twenty-one-acre farm to provide employment and food for the patients and was funded through taxation.[78] It was part of a national system, recommended in 1817, that was based on a belief in 'moral treatment'.[79]

'Moral treatment' was the practice of gentle treatment, aiming to appeal to the individual's humanity, grounded in quiet, comfort and a supportive environment as opposed to restraint and cruelty. This European movement was influenced by French physician Philippe Pinel and introduced to the British Isles by the York Retreat in the late 1790s. District asylums across Ireland followed this method, depending on treatment incorporating work, rest and leisure with minimal drug therapy and moving away from coercive therapy.[80] Indeed, there are very few references to restraint in the records of the Belfast asylum, with the board actually condemning the use in English workhouses in 1845 'where restraint had been carried out to a most pernicious, inhuman, and disgraceful extent'.[81] However, general institutions that housed lunatics, such as the Poorhouse, often used restraint, confinement and other coercive measures. In the district asylum, restraint was usually only applied to suicidal and criminal patients; in such cases, the use of straitjackets was the most common method of restraint for particularly violent patients, for example in the case of a female patient in 1842 who was breaking windows, doors, stripping, striking attendants and encouraging others to violence.[82] Contemporary statistics compiled by Dr Andrew Malcolm in the late 1840s show that mania was the most common form of insanity among patients, accounting for 60 per cent of cases.[83] This tallies with an analysis of Irish asylums in the second half of the century by Alice Mauger, with mania having been identified as the leading diagnosis and encompassing a wide range of symptoms and behaviours.[84]

By October 1830 the Belfast asylum was already full, with space for extra patients being created by converting various rooms in the building to provide accommodation.[85] The overcrowding was explained in 1833 as being due to the fact that around two-thirds of the patients were 'incurable' and therefore could not be expected to be discharged.[86] Again, Belfast followed European models by housing incurables in separate wards for long-term residence.[87] Along with the ever-growing problem of insufficient accommodation, the asylum also had to deal with criminal and dangerous lunatics. Dangerous lunatics were usually admitted from gaols, later legislated under the Dangerous Lunatics Act of 1838, and deemed insane, sometimes with a previous record of insanity.[88] Criminal lunatics were more controversial, having been found guilty of a crime but acquitted due to insanity. In 1828 the board recorded the compulsory admittance of criminal lunatics as 'a great evil experienced in the discipline and proper management of the asylum'.[89] While the numbers remained relatively low, between six and ten a year, the majority of criminal lunatics admitted in the period 1829 to 1850 were women, often those who had been found guilty of infanticide. Due to this, the Belfast asylum was the first to raise the subject of separate lunatic asylums for criminals in 1833.[90] In 1843 a government committee recommended the establishment of one central asylum for criminal lunatics; the Central Criminal Lunatic Asylum for Ireland was built in Dundrum, County Dublin in 1850, a precursor of the similar Broadmoor established in England in 1863.[91]

The relationship between the asylum and the Belfast Charitable Society became more distant once the asylum was fully operational. There were discussions in 1832 about using the burial ground of the Society for patients from the Belfast asylum, but the cost was considered too high.[92] The asylum was, however, managed by a board of governors drawn mainly from the circle of philanthropic individuals already active in the town. This helped to maintain strong connections between the Society committee, the other medical institutions, charities and civic institutions like the House of Correction and, after 1841, the workhouse. Perhaps due to the medical network or the pre-existing establishment of medical and lay co-operation in the town, the board managing the asylum recognised the need for medical superintendence, appointing a physician to the post of superintendent in 1835 before many other Irish and British asylums followed suit.[93] Visitors to the asylum often remarked on its efficient management and success in moral treatment. Dr Andrew Coombe, a Scottish physician to both the King of Belgium and Queen Victoria, visited in 1844 and commented, 'In cleanliness, good ventilation, and other physical comforts, I have seen no Institution which excels this.'[94] An American doctor from the McClean Asylum for the Insane in Boston also commented that he had not come across any asylum superior to that of Belfast.[95]

CHILDBIRTH

Another specific group of the poor often requiring medical care was women in childbirth. Dublin had pioneered the maternity hospital movement, opening the first in the British Isles in 1745.[96] By the 1830s voluntary maternity hospitals could be found in Cork, New Ross, Limerick, Youghal, Waterford, Wexford and Kingstown, as well as in Dublin and Belfast.[97] Some general hospitals offered maternity wards as the nineteenth century progressed, which was more in keeping with the European trend.[98] In this aspect of public health, Belfast differed from Dublin and elsewhere with the impetus for a specific establishment coming not from physicians but from ladies in the town. The Humane Female Society for the Relief of Lying-in Women was established in 1793, with 180 members. It rented a small house in Donegall Street in 1794 with six beds for poor women in childbirth who would be attended by a midwife and maid. A doctor was to be called in the event of difficulties.[99] The Society and hospital were run entirely by women, unique compared to other lying-in hospitals of the time; however, they had the support of several physicians who would attend in rotation. From 1794 to 1800, annual admissions remained under fifty, but they steadily rose in the early years of the nineteenth century.[100] The hospital treated sixty-one women in 1804, 'chiefly poor tradesmen, labourers and soldiers' wives'.[101] In addition to medical relief, the Society also provided clothes for women and their children, education for girls and some outpatient treatment for women in their own homes, funded entirely through voluntary subscriptions.[102]

The lying-in hospital proved effective in assisting poor women and soon needed larger premises. It moved briefly to temporary premises early in 1830 while completing its new building on Clifton Street, on land owned by the Belfast Charitable Society. The new lying-in hospital opened later that year, with eighteen beds.[103] The relationship between the lying-in hospital and the Society was complicated from the outset, as the Society had denied requests for accommodation in 1793;[104] however, it subsequently agreed to the permanent building on the condition that the hospital was used for no other purpose.[105] Stewards' reports from the Poorhouse show that, on occasion, children were taken into the house while their mother was a patient at the hospital if there was nowhere else for them to go.[106] The ladies running the hospital came under pressure to allow medical students to attend, an initiative that was new and contentious in the early nineteenth century. This was finally permitted in 1852, something that led to further discussions with the Society over how best to manage the hospital. This issue continued throughout the rest of the century, with the Society continually arguing that the hospital was not purely devoted to charitable purposes since it was also acting as a medical school.[107] The hospital expanded in 1862, and negotiations over rent continued until the turn of the twentieth century.[108] Although the Society had no formal role in the running of the hospital, due to the leasing of the land on which it was built, the two were intertwined until the hospital moved to Townsend Street in 1904 and was renamed the Maternity Hospital, eventually being replaced by the Royal Maternity Hospital in 1933.[109] In Manchester, a similar charity had been started in 1790 but had to abandon inpatient treatment in 1813, subsequently providing a purely domiciliary service until 1850.[110]

With no other options for poor women who needed medical relief, the lying-in hospital provided an essential service. Wealthier inhabitants could pay for a midwife or accoucheur, while some might have chosen to patronise the private lying-in hospital run by Professor Robert Little in Castle Street. For the majority of pregnant women, however, childbirth was an experience one went through alone or with untrained assistance.[111] The majority of midwives were self-taught and were usually the only means of support. Geary claimed that obstetrics access varied greatly throughout Ireland, and 'despite their reservations regarding handywomen, many doctors neglected the pregnant poor'.[112] The quality of care given at the lying-in hospital appears to have been of a high standard, with admissions to the hospital peaking at times of epidemic disease in the town, showing that poor women were anxious about giving birth without assistance during outbreaks of fever and cholera.[113]

The doctors attending the hospital would, on occasion, perform surgical procedures – the first Caesarean in the hospital was recorded in 1829 when Dr McKibben attempted it without anaesthesia, ultimately unsuccessfully.[114] Writing in the 1850s, Andrew Malcolm recorded that the hospital treated an average of 191 patients annually, a figure which correlates with the summaries provided in various directories in the early nineteenth century.[115] He calculated that between 1830 and 1851 the hospital had treated 3,832 patients with only eleven deaths, noting how favourably this compared to similar institutions.[116] These figures equate to a maternal mortality rate of 2.9 per 1,000 births. Statistics from the Coombe Hospital in Dublin show yearly mortality rates significantly higher than those of Belfast: 21.7 per 1,000 in 1829–30, 9.7 per 1,000 in 1830–31 and 13 per 1,000 in 1839–40.[117] The Rotunda Hospital in Dublin also had higher mortality, with a rate of 10.6 per 1,000 births in the period 1830–37.[118] The Glasgow Maternity Hospital also recorded a higher mortality rate of 12.8 per 1,000 in 1848.[119] The Belfast Lying-in Hospital was therefore, in many ways, different from its counterparts across Britain and Ireland.

CONTAGIOUS DISEASE

One of the other main medical institutions for the poor in the early nineteenth-century town was the fever hospital and dispensary. The dispensary began operating in 1792 while money was raised to rent houses to act as a hospital; this opened in 1797.[120] The dispensary provided outpatient advice and treatment as well as the co-ordination of a vaccination programme among the poor against smallpox, coinciding with a similar venture in Dublin.[121] The fever hospital specifically treated infectious diseases which were a frequent reality of life, especially for the poor, and was funded through a combination of county presentments and voluntary subscriptions. Outbreaks of diseases such as typhus (generally what was meant by the term 'fever') were becoming increasingly common by the end of the eighteenth century as travel became easier and contact with other countries increased through shipping and the growth of Belfast as a port town.[122] While medical knowledge had not advanced enough to understand the role of micro-organisms in spreading infection, the fear of infection drove society to quarantine the sick in order to try and protect the rest of the population.[123] Public interest tended to wane when epidemics had abated, so the hospital also catered for general medicine and surgery. The hospital and dispensary, as one organisation, also cleansed the houses of those infected, extended vaccination programmes and sought to introduce preventative measures.[124] As the nineteenth century progressed, the hospital needed larger premises and began making plans and fundraising from 1810. However, as was common elsewhere in Ireland, the building of fever hospitals was boosted with each fresh epidemic, and the outbreak of typhus and relapsing fever in Belfast in late 1816 provided the impetus to speed up the erection and opening of the new fever hospital in Frederick Street in 1817.[125]

From its establishment, the dispensary offered general medical relief to the poor in their hundreds.[126] In its early years the hospital was treating approximately 100 patients annually with a low mortality rate.[127] Contemporary reports show that while infectious disease made up the majority of cases, there was a small but steady proportion of chronic illnesses and surgical patients.[128] The *Belfast Almanack* summarised the work of the institution in 1818: 'The number of dispensary or outpatients is unlimited: the children of the poor are vaccinated; instruments for the recovery of persons drowned, are provided. The hospital was originally confined to fever patients; but when there is sufficient accommodation, other cases are admitted; and many surgical procedures are performed.'[129]

The fever hospital was closely connected with Belfast Charitable Society. Just over half (50.5 per cent) of those serving on the Society committee in the period 1809–41 also served on the committee of the fever hospital.[130] Once the dispensary opened, it had an arrangement with the Poorhouse whereby it was provided with a room for consultations and in return supplied medicines for the Poorhouse.[131] This could cause problems at times. Letters were written to the Poorhouse from the fever hospital in 1822, insisting on being given the names of those patients who required medicine, thus highlighting the difficulty of not having a resident physician in the Poorhouse who could oversee the administration of medicine.[132] Arrangements regarding those patients from the Poorhouse who might need hospital treatment were drawn up in 1804.[133] In return for accepting Poorhouse patients, the hospital could send dispensary patients to the Poorhouse infirmary.[134] In fact, of the sixty admissions to the Poorhouse infirmary between 1810 and 1816 for whom the reason for admission was supplied, 58 per cent of cases had been referred from the fever hospital and dispensary. The committees of both institutions worked together regularly, for example when the Belfast Charitable Society appointed four members to help collect subscriptions for the new fever hospital building in 1815.[135] During the outbreak of fever in 1816, the fever hospital asked the Society to take some non-fever patients in order to free up space for fever patients, to which the Society agreed on the condition that they would not accept patients with venereal disease.[136] Venereal patients were seen as 'undeserving' in the eyes of society, as they were deemed to have inflicted disease upon themselves through their own immoral behaviour. For this reason, there were few charitable institutions across Ireland and Britain that would accept people with venereal disease.[137] During the same epidemic, the Society worked with the fever hospital, the House of Industry and other organisations in the town in order to meet the increased need for medical relief in addition to implementing precautions to avoid the spread of infection within the Poorhouse.[138]

Once the fever hospital opened their new premises in August 1817, the number of patients receiving both inpatient and outpatient treatment rose dramatically, as shown in Table 8.1. By 1828 the dispensary was providing advice and treatment for around 5,000 people each year.[139] This was provided by dividing the town into six districts, each one with a medical attendant who worked for free. This was later contested following the outbreak of cholera in 1832.[140]

The hospital building, capable of accommodating 200 patients, had four storeys containing four medical and six surgical wards. It had a very good record of keeping fever out of the general wards.[141] A report in 1836 by one of the physicians, Dr William Mateer, showed that from 1818 to 1835, 9,849 cases of fever had been admitted, of which 648 had resulted in fatality, a rate of 6.6 per cent.[142] This tallies with the statistics collected by Denis Phelan, a County Tipperary surgeon and later assistant Poor Law commissioner who conducted a nationwide statistical enquiry into medical charities in Ireland in 1835, which showed a mortality rate of

Table 8.1 Fever hospital and dispensary patients, 1805–19. (Source: *Belfast Almanack*)

around 6 per cent in the hospital.[143] A separate building was erected in response to the cholera outbreak in 1832; once the crisis had passed, this building was repurposed as a lock hospital to treat venereal disease.[144] Lock hospitals were specialist and separate institutions for the treatment of sexually transmitted diseases, namely syphilis. The first such hospital in Ireland was founded in Dublin in 1755, funded by the government and eventually named the Westmoreland Lock Hospital.[145] On occasion, smaller venereal wards or 'lock wards' would be part of a general hospital, as was the case in Limerick and Cork, but this was not as common, as such wards were difficult to justify to subscribers who held society's view that venereal disease was a self-inflicted indicator of immorality.[146] The fever hospital had started treating women with venereal disease in 1828; statistics compiled from 1833 to 1835 recorded a total of 228 patients in the lock wards during those years.[147] This explains why, when assisting the fever hospital in taking non-fever patients, as noted before, the Society specified that they would not accept venereal patients. Dr Malcolm recorded that syphilis was by far the most common surgical complaint treated, although most surgical deaths were the result of burns.[148]

With the opening of the Union workhouse and subsequent legislation giving workhouse unions responsibility for responding to infectious diseases during the 1840s, the fever hospital raised money to repurpose itself solely as a general medical and surgical hospital. It separated from the dispensary to become two distinct organisations in 1846 with the Belfast General (or Town Hospital) becoming operational in 1847.[149] The co-operation between different organisations continued through the connections of the managing committees and the overlap of doctors working in several charitable institutions throughout their careers.[150] The general hospital was later renamed the Belfast Royal and then the Royal Victoria Hospital before moving to its Grosvenor Road site in 1903.[151]

As mentioned, the outbreak of fever in Belfast in 1816 not only hurried the opening of the new fever hospital building but also brought together several of the town's charities in response to the threat. 'Fever' could be used for a range of illnesses, but those in 1816 were considered to be typhus, with symptoms including congestion of blood vessels, rash, gangrene, pain and vomiting, and relapsing fever, characterised by high temperature, vomiting and exhaustion which reappeared every few days.[152] Excessive rain and cold in 1816 ruined the harvest and potato crop, thus leaving the poor more exposed to disease.[153] The outbreak reached epidemic level in Ulster quicker than in other provinces but declined equally quickly.[154] By the time the epidemic waned in February 1819, an estimated one and a half million had been affected and 65,000 had died of the disease in Ireland.[155] Cases appeared simultaneously in different parts of Belfast in November 1816, and the medical and charitable networks in the town reacted quickly to respond to the high levels of disease. From 1816 to 1818 a total of 3,527 patients were treated by the fever hospital for fever; however, it was estimated that as many as 7,400 had been infected.[156] As the population of Belfast in 1821 was 37,277, this meant that just under 20 per cent of the population had been infected with fever.[157] After this crisis, other less dramatic diseases followed, such as outbreaks of smallpox in the town in 1822 and 1824, and the return of fever, albeit on a smaller scale, in 1826.[158]

As the century progressed, a number of smaller charities were established with some catering for a specific group of the sick poor. The Deaf and Dumb Society was founded in April 1821 as an auxiliary to the National Institution for the Education of the Deaf and Dumb of Ireland.[159] In May 1831 the Society opened its own school, later combining with the Asylum for the Blind in 1835.[160] In this enterprise, Belfast again differed from Dublin and elsewhere by admitting both sexes, a practice adopted by the Cork asylum in 1843.[161] The Society for the Relief of the Destitute Sick was founded in 1826 to attend to the sick poor in their own homes and provide materials to improve health conditions, particularly food and clothing. While this Society did not offer specific medical relief, the 1836 Poor Inquiry noted, 'it affords aid by furnishing the sick poor with the necessaries of life'.[162] Like most charitable organisations, the Society relied on donations which were raised, like others, through charity sermons and congregational collections. A notable aspect of this charity was its reliance on women as visitors and collectors, although they did not sit on the managing committee.[163] Unfortunately, few printed reports of the Society remain, but that of 1829 records the 'deep sense of obligation' to the ladies so active in the organisation's pursuits.[164] It is possible to construct how active the Destitute Sick Society was from newspaper reports and statistics presented in the *Belfast Almanack*, which show that the Society steadily provided relief for over 500 individuals each year, with a peak of almost 1,000 cases in 1832 during the national cholera epidemic.[165]

Like the Destitute Sick Society, other small medical charities were founded in the early nineteenth century but have, unfortunately, left few records. Their role can be pieced together using newspaper reports and the annual lists of public institutions in the *Belfast Almanack*. A dispensary was established in October 1827 in Chapel Lane 'for diseases of children, and diseases of the Eye, and for giving advice to such persons as can afford to pay for medicines, but not for medical or surgical advice – supported by voluntary contributions'.[166] The Poor Inquiry noted that 'All paupers applying are attended to, and tickets for admission of patients are not required.'[167] The dispensary did not make home visits or take any maternity cases but, by 1831, had treated over 20,000 patients.[168] In the first three months of 1830 alone, it had treated 2,133, including 963 adults, 1,001 children and 169 cases of diseases of the eye.[169] Lack of funds necessitated its closure in 1839, although it is estimated that over the eleven years of its existence it treated 74,228.[170] The dispensary also sent the poor to other charities, particularly the Destitute Sick and Ladies' Clothing Society.[171] Two further specialist charities provided advice and medicine for free: the Ophthalmic Institution with Eye and

Ear Dispensary and the Northern Institution for Diseases of the Skin amongst the poor, both located in Mill Street.[172]

THE 1832 CHOLERA PANDEMIC

Asiatic cholera spread globally in the nineteenth century, reaching Ireland in March 1832.[173] Doctors in Belfast were aware of the disease and its spread throughout Europe and began making preparations and publishing medical literature, such as pamphlets, in order to exchange information with other medical practitioners. Surviving letters show that Belfast physicians were in correspondence with colleagues in Scotland and England about their preparations and what symptoms they should be aware of.[174] Dr Henry McCormac wrote in his summary of the disease in Belfast in late 1832, 'The progress of the disease, in other places, had given us sufficient warning, and enabled us to arm for its approach.'[175] Cholera presented with severe dehydration, nausea, vomiting, diarrhoea, weakness, intense thirst and exhaustion, and could strike quickly, with some sufferers dying within twenty-four hours.[176] A framework for relief was based on legislation for fever which had been passed in 1818 and included the establishment of local boards of health answerable to a central board in Dublin.[177] A Belfast board of health was set up in November 1831 to prepare for the approaching disease and was supported by the existing medical and philanthropic network of the town. A separate cholera hospital was built at the back of the fever hospital in February 1832, and nearby houses were rented in order to isolate those with symptoms or who had been in contact with confirmed cases. A programme of street cleansing was also implemented.[178] The well-off were advised that the best means to ensure their own safety was to provide for the poor of their areas and public meetings were held in late 1831 to warn that infection could start among the poor and spread through the whole community.[179] In February 1832, appeals were made to the town's inhabitants to donate to the cholera hospital building fund, with lists of donations printed in local newspapers, a common tactic used to encourage giving.[180] Religious publications encouraged those with symptoms to seek medical assistance, urging people not to give in to prejudice, a sign that the public were generally apprehensive about attending hospital.[181] The preparations

William Drennan, MD,
1754–1820 (*c.* 1790), by
Robert Home (1752–1834).
© National Museums NI, Ulster
Museum Collection

Samuel Neilson, 1761–
1803 (*c.* 1795). © National
Museums NI, Ulster Museum
Collection

Henry Joy Junior (1754–1835), cousin of Henry Joy and Mary Ann McCracken. © National Gallery of Ireland

Henry Joy McCracken (1767–98), by Sarah Cecilia Harrison (1863–1941). © National Museums NI, Ulster Museum Collection

Poor Ground Memorial to the thousands who are buried in unmarked graves, Clifton Street Cemetery.
© Belfast Charitable Society

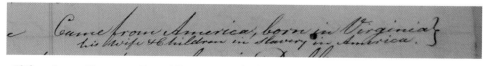

Clifton Street Cemetery Burial Register, with the detail for William Brown's entry below.
© Belfast Charitable Society

Mary Ann McCracken with her niece Maria, *c.* 1801.
© National Museums NI, Ulster Museum Collection

Photograph of Mary Ann McCracken by John Gibson.
© National Museums NI, Ulster Museum Collection

Headstone for Mary Ann McCracken (1770–1866), Clifton Street Cemetery. © Belfast Charitable Society

The Weir tomb, reputedly a fireplace taken from a house on the site of Queen's University. (After Strain, *Belfast and its Charitable Society*, p. 272).

The Luke Mausoleum, designed by Edmund Getty for James Luke in the contemporary Egyptian style, finished in 1857. © J.J. O'Neill

Dr William McGee
1793–1874 (*c*. 1830–35).
© National Museums NI,
Ulster Museum Collection

Rev. Henry Cooke, DD (1788–
1868), by Sir Daniel Macnee
(1806–82).
© National Museums NI, Ulster
Museum Collection

NI Hospice shares its plans with David Watters (Chair, Belfast Charitable Society) after the Society's donation of £250,000.
© Belfast Charitable Society

Barbour Fund Celebration (2019) featuring Sir Ronnie Weatherup (President, Belfast Charitable Society) and Elise Coburn *née* Barbour (back left). © Belfast Charitable Society

Launch of the Great Place North Belfast Project (2018), featuring (left to right) Pleasaunce Perry (Society of Friends), Paula Reynolds (CEO, Belfast Charitable Society) and Angelina Fusco (National Lottery Heritage Fund).
© Belfast Charitable Society

taken in Belfast led Dr Malcolm to reflect that 'we believe that no town of the same magnitude in the three kingdoms was placed in more effective defence'.[182]

The first case of cholera in Ireland appeared in Belfast on 29 February 1832 when Bernard Murtagh, a cooper of Quay Lane, died after nineteen hours. The plans for protecting the town were immediately put into action: his family were quarantined, their bedding and clothes were burned and their house was fumigated and whitewashed.[183] Further cases in March and April could mostly be tracked; for example, a sailor died on 9 April, the woman who dressed his corpse died on 16 April, followed by her husband on 26 April.[184] The Belfast Charitable Society had decided before the first case appeared that they would shut the Poorhouse as soon as cholera appeared in the town. Immediately news of its appearance broke, they erected a wooden gate and barrier to prevent people from entering and leaving.[185] The Society's committee agreed to supply coffins to the board of health and help to convey patients from their homes or watch stations to the cholera hospital and move patients between hospitals. In order to improve the health of the paupers in the Poorhouse, Drs Forcade and McGee advised they be fed a rich meat broth. Anyone who absconded from the house could only re-enter following a period in an isolation unit in one of the Society's small houses, and luxuries like tobacco and snuff were provided to the paupers as they were no longer allowed to leave.[186] It was, incidentally, the opinion of some on the committee that isolation was good for the morals as well as the health of the paupers, as noted by Anglican minister and committee member F.E. Lascelles in September 1832.[187] This policy seems to have been successful in keeping cholera out of the Poorhouse and was particularly effective in the summer months when the epidemic was at its peak. Committee member and surgeon Robert McCluney noted in August 1832 that the Poorhouse was one of the few institutions of the town that was cholera-free. He also noted that the general health of the paupers had improved, with less sickness and fever deaths than usual.[188] However, in October of that year a gravedigger who worked in the burial ground belonging to the Society was infected with cholera and introduced it into the Poorhouse. Thankfully, its impact was limited – Strain notes that there were only four cholera deaths in the house, while others who were afflicted recovered after treatment.[189]

The lunatic asylum also attempted to isolate their institution by freezing admissions in July except in emergency cases; however, by August it had already seen six cases of cholera.[190] At a special meeting in August 1832, the board recorded three patient deaths due to cholera and began to quarantine affected wards and hire additional staff.[191] By the autumn, the asylum had had thirty-six cases among patients and staff, with eleven patient deaths and some servants and patients still convalescing.[192] The lying-in hospital annual report for 1832 does not specifically address the cholera epidemic, noting that two patients died that year of consumption.[193] It is interesting, however, to note that admissions to the hospital spiked in 1832, the highest level since 1817–18, showing that women in childbirth were more likely to seek medical assistance in times of epidemic disease.[194] It is unclear whether this is entirely down to women choosing medical assistance or, rather, was a necessity due to the lack of informal assistance as inhabitants became more cautious about disease transmission.

Calwell estimated that cholera struck nearly 3,000 out of a population of 54,000, killing 500 people in the town.[195] The outbreak peaked in July with over forty new cases a day in the cholera hospital and the death of a physician, Dr Buchanan in Ballymacarrett, who was lauded as a hero in the local press.[196] It had mostly abated by December, when the cholera hospital was closed and the board of health disbanded.[197] Information collected by Dr McCormac on the number of cases and mortality rates in similar cholera hospitals in other towns showed that Belfast had the lowest mortality rate of 24 per cent. In comparison, Edinburgh Cholera Hospital had a 58 per cent mortality rate, the cholera hospital in Glasgow 64 per cent and Dublin, using statistics for the whole city rather than one specific hospital, had a rate of 29 per cent.[198] To put this into context, McCormac noted that cholera had claimed 20,768 victims in Britain as a whole, with a mortality rate of 36 per cent. Other contemporaries reported that Belfast physicians cured more cholera than in other places, but such claims were mostly based on cases in hospitals and not those treated at home or those who paid for treatment.[199] In the aftermath of the epidemic in Belfast, and a further outbreak of fever in 1836–7, there was a growing awareness of the overcrowding and insanitary living conditions of some of the town's population. Efforts were soon being made to improve the health of the town, but individuals involved in the sanitary movement, notably Dr Andrew Malcolm, were frustrated that improvements were only made slowly and usually in times of crisis.[200]

CONCLUSION

The medical network of Belfast had expanded dramatically in the early nineteenth century. Providing care for the sick poor began as a small initiative in the Poorhouse, managed by physicians and surgeons for free and in their own time. As the town and its industries expanded, so, too, did medical provision for the poor, as well as an understanding of public health. This chapter has shown how central the Belfast Charitable Society was to this blossoming network and how with each new organisation and institution for the sick poor, Belfast's network grew as a co-operative. No one organisation had authority over medical matters except in times of crisis, as seen by the role of boards of health during outbreaks of fever and cholera. Instead, organisations often worked together to ease burdens and provide for the sick poor of the town. Such arrangements were not always without friction but were supported by the philanthropic network of men and women who managed and supported the organisations of the town, providing links among the growing middle class that could ease collaboration. The system in existence by the 1830s was not perfect but it was functional, aiding in extending medical aid to the poor of a rapidly changing town. This network was to change with the implementation of the Poor Law in 1838 and particularly an amendment to that law in 1843, giving workhouse guardians responsibility over infectious disease. However, Belfast's medical network was established enough by this stage to simply make space for the board of guardians at its centre, continuing to co-operate throughout the public health crises brought on by the Famine of the late 1840s.

CHAPTER NINE

The New Burying Ground and Burial in Nineteenth-century Belfast

J.J. Ó Neill

❦

'Rattle his bones over the stones, he's only a pauper whom
nobody owns.'

Thomas Noel (1799-1861), 'The Pauper's Drive'

The New Burying Ground off Clifton Street, opened by the Belfast
Charitable Society in 1797, provided an additional space in which
Belfast's dead could be housed at a time when the existing provision for
burial in the town was no longer considered fit for purpose. While burials
continued there until 1984, the sale of all the available grave plots by 1856
prompted expansion elsewhere to provide spaces for burial in Belfast.
In 1864 the civil registration of deaths was introduced and the practices
around death and burial that had become established by then are still
largely those in use today. The lifespan (as such) of the New Burying
Ground thus extends from the end of the eighteenth century through to
the consolidation of modern approaches to death in the last third of the
nineteenth century. This chapter will explore the New Burying Ground
from two perspectives. The first is in terms of cemetery design and its

pioneering position within the Western tradition of non-denominational garden cemeteries (of which Père-Lachaise became the model). The second is to contextualise the new burial space within existing mortuary practices in Belfast at the turn of the nineteenth century and after.

First, as it is such a discomfiting subject, something by way of a preliminary explanation is required. The treatment of the dead and burial spaces occupies a complex and emotive place in the human mind. And the very topic transcends the rational, intermingling the religious and secular, public and private, superstition and regulation. The New Burying Ground emerged from an era before the civil registration of deaths began and amidst emerging public discussion of environmental and public health policies for the disposal of human remains. Religious dogma, folk beliefs and taboos and superstitions around death were largely unconstrained by ethical and regulatory practices. Burial and attitudes towards the interment of the dead in 1800 were often considerably different from those today. A period of transition towards more recognisably modern concepts and ideas therefore coincides with the lifespan of the New Burying Ground. The extent of change is illustrated in this chapter by identifying the eclectic variety of treatments of the dead at the start of the nineteenth century that were to be gradually eradicated by the introduction of civil registration and other standardised approaches to treatment of the dead. Arguably, the New Burying Ground helped articulate and catalyse some of those attitudes through the creation of a new type of space in which the dead could be interred, foreshadowing the type of public provision that was to be put in place in the last third of the nineteenth century.

THE NEW BURYING GROUND: A BRIEF HISTORY

Over the latter half of the eighteenth century, Belfast Charitable Society gradually expanded its footprint within the town.[1] Belfast had rapidly expanded from a nondescript medieval borough to a minor settlement in the sixteenth century and on towards the ranks of Ireland's largest towns by 1800. That swift increase had amplified the dislocation and disruption of family and community networks by industrialisation and urbanisation. Where the local landlords, the Donegalls, and the Belfast Corporation left an organisational and infrastructural void, it was generally the Society

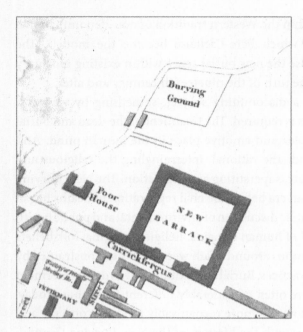

Figure 9.1 The Burying Ground in 1822 (extract from map accompanying Benn's *History of Belfast*).

that offered leadership. One of the areas where this leadership was needed was in the burial of the dead.

At a meeting of the general board of the Society on 27 October 1795, it was 'Resolved that it is recommended to the next general board to consider of appropriating one of the fields up the lane for the purpose of a burying ground,' and the following month it was decided that the field 'lately in the possession of the Rev. Mr. Bristow be enclosed in with a wall and appropriated for a burying ground, and the Committee are hereby empowered to lay it out and dispose of it in such manner as may appear most advantageous to the Society and at the same time ornamental'. [2]

The location and early shape of the New Burying Ground is shown in Figures 9.1 and 9.2. By March 1797 the first adverts had appeared in the local press for the New Burying Ground, saying: 'Poor House, March 1797. The Public are informed that the Burying Ground near the Poor House is now ready, and that Messrs. Robert Stevenson, William Clark, and John Caldwell are appointed to agree with such persons as wish to take Lots.'[3] In April 1799 the Society agreed that 'a portion of the Poor House Burial Ground be laid apart for interring such poor persons as

Figure 9.2 Extract of first edition Ordnance Survey map with Upper Ground and Lower Ground mistakenly labelled as 'New Burying Ground' and 'Old Grave Yard'. The triangular strip alongside the Antrim Road is clearly visible.

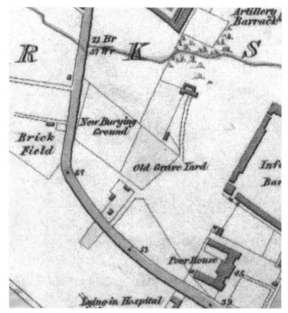

may die not having funds for their interment in the same or some other Burial Ground, the same to be regulated by the Committee for the time being.'[4]

Demand for plots in the New Burying Ground was aided by an act of parliament in 1800 that formally banned further burials in Belfast's High Street burial ground, placing greater pressure on the remaining burial grounds at Shankill and Friar's Bush. By 1802 the sale of burial plots in the Society's New Burying Ground was well in hand, and it was described in a letter from Martha McTier to her brother William Drennan as 'a neat place, well laid out and regular, like a garden'.[5] As the Burying Ground was not consecrated, various other fees were also avoided, and gave it a civic rather than religious character which was a significant innovation. From 1750s onwards, the Society had used lotteries and other somewhat unreliable fundraising schemes to fund the Poorhouse and hospital (and a church). The Burying Ground, it was hoped, would supply a more predictable income stream, at least in the short term; it also chimed with the ideological and intellectual concerns of the Society's members and their peers.

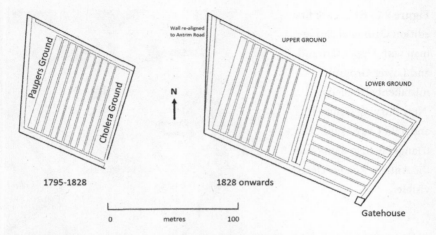

Figure 9.3 The two main phases of development of the New Burying Ground showing locations noted in the text. The first phase is shown on the left and became known as the Upper Ground when the burial ground was extended by 1828. The extended burial ground is shown on the right.

The New Burying Ground began as the field later known as the Upper Ground. This measured roughly 100m (northwest–southeast) by 75m (northeast–southwest). The sections and wall plots were aligned with the pre-existing field boundaries (see Figure 9.3 for the layout). This meant that burial alignments varied haphazardly across the cemetery but explicitly did not facilitate the longstanding Catholic and Anglican prescription for laying out the grave west–east.[6] In November 1819, the Society decided to extend the New Burying Ground with the addition of the field to the immediate southeast, then in the possession of William McClure. A healthy balance sheet for the existing burying ground was produced, presumably to expedite approval of the extension. This included receipts from 1798 onwards and the revenue from cutting hay from 1802 onwards, noting that the profit made on the burial ground to November 1819 was £1,548 8s 1½d. The revenue from cutting hay in the New Burying Ground was to be used for maintenance of the walls.[7]

At the time, a further 224 standard burial lots remained to be sold at two guineas each, as well as twenty-seven burial plots along the wall at eight guineas each. Although both of these were priced in guineas, the paper worth of guineas was higher than the notional value of 21 shillings. In this case, based on the anticipated revenue from the remaining lots of £755 10s, the paper value for a guinea was deemed to be £1 1s 9d. In the same decade, financial uncertainties meant that a guinea had been traded in Ireland for as much as £1 8s in paper money.[8] Thus, the paper value of burial plots priced in guineas had declined by nearly 30 per cent in a decade.

The actual financial value of the New Burying Ground to the Society should probably not be overestimated. In 1819, twenty years after it was established, the total value to the Society was projected at just over £2,200, with under £1,550 already received, averaging £77 10s per year. As recently as 1817, when the Society's hospital was to be opened on 1 August that year, some £3,750 per annum was already being spent providing for the impoverished through the Poorhouse, with a further £5,000 per annum through the House of Industry. So, the New Burying Ground was contributing less than 1 per cent of the revenues needed to keep the Society's other projects going. While this was probably not an insignificant sum and Strain's assertion that the New Burying Ground 'was opened for the primary purpose of raising money' may have some truth to it, it was not to be a major driver of the Society's finances.[9]

McClure's field was subsequently acquired and, by 1828, the New Burying Ground had been extended (the additional space became known as the Lower Ground). The extension included around 700 further standard burial plots and just over 100 wall plots, anticipating a potential revenue over the next decades of around £2,294 12s at 1819 prices. The sale of the last plot was in 1856, so, based on the 1819 balances, the annual revenue from the additional space would have been £82 9s (before costs were deducted which were to include the later construction of a gate house).[10] Those figures clearly represent only a tiny fraction of the Society's annual outgoings, highlighting the extent to which the provision of the New Burying Ground was about more than just raising funds.

Peculiarly, the first edition Ordnance Survey map mixes up the older and newer parts of the New Burying Ground. The original extent is shown on George Benn's 1822 map (these maps are included as Figures 9.1 and 9.2). The laying out of the Antrim Road saw a new wall added at the footpath on the new road in 1831, in what was known as Bachelor's Walk, enclosing a small space alongside the northwestern wall of the New Burying Ground.[11] Plots in the New Burying Ground had been attracting many of Belfast's leading citizens, who added some high-quality monuments, such as the Hyndman Memorial and the Weir Headstone (see the picture section), particularly for those plots along the walls. Another of note is the Luke Mausoleum, in an Egyptian style and topped with an obelisk (see the picture section). This has been attributed to as early as 1809, although its final design and detailing appear to date to the 1850s.[12] Egyptian revival-style monuments were in vogue in the years following Napoleon's Nile expedition of 1798. How early that influenced designs in the New Burying Ground is not clear.

As noted, the last of the burial plots were sold in 1856 (a view of the New Burying Ground at this time is shown in Figure 9.4). In the meantime, burials had continued with considerable pressure on the provisions made for the poor (the Paupers' Ground), as these included burials from the lying-in hospital and Belfast District Lunatic Asylum. As Malcolm noted as early as 1851, Belfast seldom saw a decade without some form of epidemic.[13] The arrival of cholera in 1831–2 saw the erection of a house of recovery in the Burying Ground and the use of the 'Cholera Ground'. While only twenty-three were buried there in 1832, outbreaks recurred in 1834 and again in 1836–7. By 1840 it was proposed to discontinue burial in the 'Paupers' Ground' as it was almost full. But the proliferation of illnesses, now including smallpox, dysentery and typhus in the wake of the potato blight that arrived in 1845, saw the decision made in May 1847 to delay the closure (over 1,000 burials reportedly took place that year).[14] By then none of the Belfast burial grounds had any further capacity, as both Friar's Bush (which had been extended in 1828) and Shankill were considered to be full. The wider need for better burial provision in Belfast was now recognised, although it was not brought to fruition until the Belfast Burial Act of 1866 with the City Cemetery and Milltown opening in 1869.[15]

While the plots in the graveyard continued in use, there were occasional disputes over the ownership of graves and burial rights within families.[16] The grounds received at least one formal set of improvements, with trees and shrubs planted under the supervision of J.J. McCrory in 1874. As has been noted, the construction of the Antrim Road in 1831 had seen the addition of an outer wall alongside the footpath. A dispute in 1875 centred

Figure 9.4 Extract from Connopy's 'Bird's Eye View of Belfast' (1860) with the New Burying Ground and gate house visible to the rear of the Poorhouse.

on the extent to which the space between the old wall and the new Antrim Road wall had been used for burials, with particular reference to mass burials during the epidemics of the 1830s and 1840s.[17] The widening of the Antrim Road had seen an agreement to move the wall constructed in 1831, and, in doing so, soil had reputedly been removed from this space and deposited in Vicinage Park. This allegedly contained bone and coffin fragments. Amongst those interviewed was Alexander Johnstone, a gravedigger, who mentioned that any bones found during work in the graveyard would be redeposited in graves and under memorials. In this case, Belfast Corporation was being prosecuted for causing a nuisance by removing bones and soil, possibly including the bones of cholera victims, from the graveyard, although the use of the Bachelor's Walk space for burial was disputed. During cross-examination of the gravediggers, the prosecutor, Mr McErleane, quoted the following lines from Thomas Noel's poem 'The Paupers' Drive': 'Rattle his bones over the stones, he's only a pauper whom nobody owns'. But incidental details of some significance emerged, particularly how the use of the space between the graveyard wall and Antrim Road wall was actually used. Some witnesses recalled that cholera victims and others had been buried there in 1832; however, mention was also made in court of others who had been buried in that space. A dealer called John Mullan, from Kennedy's Row in Smithfield, committed suicide and was buried in the space between the walls in August 1844. It was noted that this space was regularly used for the interment of suicide victims.[18] Similarly, a saddler called Edward McKeating related how a 'black man' worked in Mr Murphy's in John Street with him and, as a stranger, was buried in the same space.

The burial plots set aside for inmates of the Poorhouse itself continued in use until 1882 when the practice ended. Future burials were now to take place in the recently opened City Cemetery. Many people associate the use of the Burying Ground with lurid tales of bodysnatchers or the lives of its more distinguished residents, stories which have been told elsewhere.[19]

THE NEW BURYING GROUND AS INNOVATION

The creation of the Burying Ground in itself was somewhat of an architectural and social innovation. Existing provision for burial was almost exclusively associated with churches, religious denominations and sites with overt religious associations. Landscaped public cemeteries were just beginning to emerge as urban church graveyards became dramatically overwhelmed by the concentrations of population created by industrialisation. As early as 1711, Sir Christopher Wren had written:

> I could wish that all Burials in Churches might be disallowed, which is not only unwholesom [sic], but the Pavements can never be kept even, nor Pews upright: And if the Church-yard be close about the Church, this also is inconvenient, because the Ground being continually raised by the Graves, occasions, in Time, a Descent by Steps into the Church, which renders it damp, and the Walls green, as appears evidently in all old Churches.

Wren also advocated for burial:

> in Cemeteries seated in the Out-skirts of the Town … This being inclosed with a strong Brick Wall, and having a Walk round, and two cross Walks, decently planted with Yew-trees, the four Quarters may serve four Parishes, where the Dead need not be disturbed at the Pleasure of the Sexton, or piled four or five upon one another, or Bones thrown out to gain Room.[20]

But while Wren was discussing new church graveyards, the provision of landscaped suburban secular cemeteries was to be an innovation of the 1790s, with the pioneering New Burying Ground in New Haven in Connecticut claimed to be the first such burial ground in North America. Construction of the New Burying Ground there was proposed in 1796, and it was then incorporated in October 1797 and development commenced soon after.[21] The first European equivalent of the future generation of landscaped urban cemeteries is often claimed to be Père-Lachaise, opened in Paris in 1804. Earlier examples of landscaped urban cemeteries are known, such as Berlin-Kreuzberg (1739), but in terms of scale and inspiration Père-Lachaise was to inspire many imitators. Père-Lachaise itself was seen as encapsulating the egalitarianism and anticlericalism of the French Revolution. A small number of suburban, secular cemeteries had also been created in Scotland at the likes of Old Calton in Edinburgh (1718) and Gorbals (1786) emerging from a non-conformist tradition that sought 'to rid death and burial of its mystical and Gothic (especially Catholic) elements' in a way that would have resonated deeply with French anticlericalism.[22] James Stevens Curl has also pointed to the broad parallels with large eighteenth-century European colonial cemeteries in India, like Surat and Calcutta.

Almost a decade before Père-Lachaise, in October 1795, Belfast Charitable Society had resolved to create its own burying ground. By the following month the field had been selected and it was agreed that it be laid out 'in such manner as may appear most advantageous to the Society and at the same time ornamental'. The ornamental aspirations for the non-denominational New Burying Ground put it in the earliest phase of the garden cemetery tradition, before New Haven and Père-Lachaise. A comparison with Père-Lachaise may feel indulgent, but, while Père-Lachaise was the inspiration for generations of designed cemeteries in Europe, commentators almost universally note that its creation followed after that of the New Burying Ground in Belfast.[23] Belfast also indulged some of the fashionable trends for Egyptian revivalist designs.

The New Burying Ground, as an unconsecrated graveyard, resonated with those themes evident in the earlier Scottish burial grounds and with ideas developing in revolutionary America and France. The *Belfast News-Letter* in 1793 had reported on directives on graveyards from

France's Committee of Public Safety, which required the secularisation of entrances by using non-religious statements such as 'Here is the abode of the peace and eternal sleep.'

Controls on burial and burying grounds were also portrayed as a continuing political issue in Ireland. In 1780, responding to a public letter from John Wesley opposing rights for Catholics, Arthur O'Leary described how political intolerance even extended to controlling where Catholics could bury their dead:

> The penal laws offered the most galling insult to the Roman Catholic gentry, at the time of their being enacted. Their burying places were in the ruins of old abbeys, founded by their ancestors. A law was enacted, prohibiting to bury in those dreary haunts of cats and weasels, and a fine of ten shillings was to be levied on every person who assisted at the funeral.[24]

The public health aspects of Belfast's cluttered graveyards also resonated with medical opinion on hygiene and the management of disease. Again, in the 1780s, the Belfast press reported on public health issues raised by burial in churchyards and a prevalent scientific view that they were reservoirs of unhealthy 'elementary air'. Given the Society's innovative history in medicine and public health, and the Jacobin leanings of many of those associated with the Society, all these matters likely featured somewhere in the broader rationale for the Burying Ground.[25]

The remainder of this chapter will place Clifton Street cemetery in the context of the growing town by exploring burial practices and traditions throughout nineteenth-century Belfast, particularly those 'mystical and Gothic elements' that stood in contrast to the practices associated with the New Burying Ground, of which less is known.

BELFAST'S OFFICIAL BURIAL SPACES IN 1797

Prior to 1797, burial in Belfast was notionally confined to three medieval graveyards (see Figure 9.5). These were the established church cemeteries on High Street (where St George's now stands) and on the Shankill Road, as well as the Catholic burying ground at Friar's Bush. The word 'notionally'

Figure 9.5 Belfast burial grounds noted in the text: 1 New Burying Ground; 2 High Street; 3 Shankill; 4 Friar's Bush; 5 The Bastion; 6 Peter's Hill; 7 Death Pit; 8 Edward Street/Great Patrick Street; 9 The Felons Plot; 10 Beatty's Gut.

is used advisedly here as the three graveyards neither reflected the totality of spaces used for burial prior to 1797 nor the breadth of practices for disposing of the dead (as will be discussed further below).

The oldest of the burying grounds appears to be at Shankill, with its antiquity relative to the church on High Street presumed from the name (*Sean Cill* or 'Old Church'). An '*ecclesia alba*' and '*capella de vado*' are recorded as early as 1306, and as late as 1615 there is reference to '*ecclesia de Sancti Patricii de vado alba*'.[26] It is a reflection of the poverty of documentary records for Belfast prior to the seventeenth century that it is still not entirely clear which of these refers to Shankill, High Street or possibly even another church site entirely. The general consensus, though, is that 'ecclesia alba' is Shankill and 'capella de vado' is High Street.[27] Shankill was in ruins in 1604. A bullaun stone still lies within the site today, and Shankill was known to be used for burial through to its transfer to Belfast town council by order in 1776. Despite a handful of medieval references, little is known of its actual history other than it was well-established as a burying ground.

The High Street church was known as the Corporation Church when it was rebuilt in 1622, the Grand Fort in 1651, then the 'Church of Belfast' (1753) and the English Church (1757). It was demolished in 1774 and replaced by St George's, a chapel of ease for St Anne's, then the parish church for Belfast. The limits of the High Street burial ground are described in the *Town Book of the Corporation of Belfast*: 'The old burying-place was of considerable extent, being enclosed by High Street, Church Lane, Ann Street, and Forest Lane, now merged in Victoria Street.'[28] This is the trapezoidal plot shown on Thomas Philips' map, the earliest detailed survey of Belfast, dated to 1685.[29]

Burials of medieval and likely medieval date, clearly outside the High Street cemetery, are reported elsewhere in Belfast city centre, including Cornmarket and Castle Buildings, close to the former Belfast Castle. Reference to the discovery of human remains buried with short-bladed weapons on High Street could even suggest an early-medieval origin for the High Street site.[30]

Friar's Bush, to the south of Belfast city centre, was mainly used as a burying ground by Belfast's Catholic residents. As with Shankill and High Street, it had obscure medieval origins and continued in use until largely superseded by Milltown cemetery in the 1860s.[31]

BELFAST'S OFFICIAL NON-BURIAL SPACE IN 1797

A fourth official space for disposing of the dead also existed in 1797. This alternate space was not just sanctioned by the authorities but was intended for very specific use where the dead were to be deprived of formal burial within the rites subscribed to by their family and friends. This was generally a consequence of a death sentence, which, in effect, included punishment beyond death and demonstrates how the state, by denying access to funerary rites and customs, could also mobilise those 'mystical and gothic' aspects of death and burial.[32] Notably, this practice continued into the twentieth century, with the execution of prisoners generally being followed by burial within prison grounds.[33]

That such a burying plot existed in Belfast is only noted in a handful of sources, and none is sufficiently detailed to identify the exact location in the modern urban landscape. In 1861, Canon John Grainger noted that executed felons were buried along the Long Bank, which extended from Cornmarket out towards the Market district of Belfast. Decades later, in 1910, F.J. Bigger noted in the *Ulster Journal of Archaeology* that 'The late Henry S. Purdon, M.D., records the burial of many '98 victims in May's fields, a short distance beyond the termination of May Street. Here was a narrow strip of ground, with a row of graves, known as the croppies' burial ground.'[34]

The graves are also mentioned in a letter by W.S. Corken to *The Irish News* about Henry Joy McCracken.[35] He states that 'the burial place of the '98 men – his companions – was in May's Market where the spot was known as "The Felons Plot". The whereabouts of this sacred spot is unknown today in the Markets.'

Taking Bigger and Corken's accounts together, it can be determined that 'The Felons' Plot' lies somewhere beyond the eastern end of May Street, in the vicinity of May's Market.

BELFAST'S UNDOCUMENTED BURIAL SPACES

As well as Shankill and High Street, human remains of medieval date have been recorded from other locations around Belfast city centre including Castle Place, Castle Market and Cornmarket.[36] Thomas Phillips' 1685 map includes the burial ground on High Street (noted above). A 1696 map on linen, which is clearly based on the Phillips map, includes three further burial areas, two marked as enclosed spaces with crosses, with the third labelled as 'Death Pit'. All three of the sites indicated on the 1696 map are otherwise unrecorded amongst the eighteenth-century records of Belfast.[37] The various locations are shown in Figure 9.5.

It is possible to use their relative positions to identify their modern locations. The southernmost of the two burial grounds shown on the

1696 map lay close to the Edward Street/Great Patrick Street junction. The northernmost burial ground lies on the western corner of Peter's Hill and Millfield, extending as far as Boyd Street. The 'Death Pit' must then lie further north, possibly in the vicinity of Townsend Street. There is no additional evidence to be sure of the location of the Edward Street/Great Patrick Street burial ground. Both Peter's Hill and the 'Death Pit' have been the site of finds of human remains over the years and are discussed further below, along with other sites in Belfast where burials have been uncovered.

In 1859, the *Belfast News-Letter* reported that human bones had been found in Boyd Street when gas was being installed in a house there, at the location on Peter's Hill marked on the 1696 map. Ten years later, it was claimed that more human bones and a cannonball had been found in Boyd Street around 1864. Then, in 1871, Andrew Mairs, a grocer who lived at the corner of Boyd Street and Peter's Hill, was renovating his premises. After demolishing an old building on the site, the workmen cleared away debris and discovered 'within a distance of a few yards, and not more than a foot and a half beneath the surface, no less than nine human skulls, and as many bones as would go to make up nine human bodies ... the bones lay in a straight line from each skull in the manner in which bodies are interred in graveyards'.

These were laid out by a wall that had apparently been reused as the foundations of the old building.[38] Other reports of burials in the immediate vicinity include Carrick Court, on the opposite side of Peter's Hill, where, in 1894, workmen found 'the bones of a human arm from the shoulder blade to the fingernails', and apparently such discoveries had been 'frequent of late'. About fifty years ago, in the early 1970s, a further burial was found in Brennan's Sheet Metal Works at the top of Kent Street, on the other side of the road from Carrick Court.[39] Several months after the 1894 find, a grisly discovery was made in the lane between Library Street and Kent Street, where two young boys found the skeleton of a child.[40]

The Peter's Hill burial ground clearly merits further research. The 1696 Belfast map clearly labels Peter's Hill as 'St Peters Walk' while the name 'St Peters Hill' is also noted in Benn's *History of Belfast*.[41] There was even a street named 'Abbey Street' in the same block in the mid-nineteenth century (the origin of the name is not recorded). This area lies outside the ramparts erected around Belfast in 1642 and was not developed until the eighteenth century. Yet, Canon John Grainger, writing about the ramparts in 1861, noted that 'A portion of some of the outworks was existing until latterly on the site of Brown's Square.'[42] Brown Square defines the block in which this burial ground lies, so Grainger appears to be noting the presence of something that was believed to be of antiquity but the location suggests it was not the 1642 rampart. If it was some undocumented or simply unrecognised ecclesiastical site, possibly with an association with St Peter, its duration of use for burial is unclear. The find of the child skeleton nearby may hint that the site continued in use for child burials well into the nineteenth century.[43]

In 1897 old foundations were being pulled up at the end of Townsend Street, 200 metres further up Peter's Hill and away from the cluster of burials noted in the previous paragraphs. The workmen there also found a skull and bones. This location may be that marked as 'Death Pit' on the 1696 map. In the 1640s, it was recorded in Dublin, Drogheda and Cork that it was found necessary to appoint emergency burying grounds outside the towns on account of the terrific deaths of the people from disease.[44] During wartime in 1690, while there was no actual fighting in Belfast, Young reports a 'great mortality' in the town among fever-stricken soldiers, with both the Shankill and the High Street graveyards crowded, but he does not suggest the use of any other site for burial. While Belfast wasn't the scene of significant fighting in the 1640s either, it is possible that a 'Death Pit' was opened either then or in 1689–91 to deal with outbreaks of disease. Whether it was reused after that date is equally unknown.[45]

Burials are also known from the wide-open space at the crossroads of North Street and Royal Avenue. This was the site of Belfast's North Gate, with the line of Royal Avenue overlying the route of the 1642 rampart (see Figure 9.6). To the east of North Street, Royal Avenue replaced John Street which traced the line of a bastion in the rampart, and the area itself was apparently known as 'The Bastion'. Human remains have been reported from this area and some nearby locations, indicating the use of the area for burials.

In 1882 John Street was demolished to make way for Royal Avenue. During construction of the footpath at the junction with North Street,

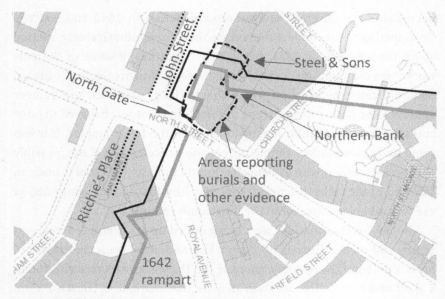

Figure 9.6 The Bastion burial ground, Royal Avenue.

at least twenty-one burials were identified (some had clearly been disturbed previously). In 1879 a further burial was found at Ritchie's Place, diagonally across the North Street–Royal Avenue junction. In 1883 construction of new buildings at the North Street corner uncovered more burials, as did work at Steel & Sons in 1894 (further burials were found in the footpath too). The description of the soils in which the burials were found suggest they were disturbed during construction of the 1642 rampart and are earlier in date, but the exact duration of use of a site here for burial is unclear. An archaeological excavation in the site to the rear off Church Street did not identify any human remains at this location.[46]

Other locations were clearly in use in the eighteenth and nineteenth centuries. In July 1869 a Mary Gunning was gathering cockles by a river called Beatty's Gut on the mudflats in Belfast Lough when she found a coffin buried in the sand and mud, held in place by four wooden stakes. Over the years there have been numerous reports of discoveries of human remains, both coffined burials and unprotected human remains from the shore of Belfast Lough. Along the lough shore, high tide covered up an extensive shelf of estuarine muds and sand that extended out for a

VIEW FROM THOMPSON'S BANK, SHORE ROAD.
From a Photo. in possession of Herbert Hughes.

Figure 9.7 Now built over and reclaimed, this is a view of the shoreline which was used for burials (after T. McTear and F.J. Bigger, 'Personal Recollections of the Beginning of the Century', *Ulster Journal of Archaeology*, vol. 5, no. 3 (1899), pp. 162–74).

considerable distance. Water courses like the River Milewater continued as channels through the muds and sand to reach the main channel in the centre of the lough. Beatty's Gut was the tidal creek that ran from the bottom of what is now Skegoneil Avenue (originally Buttermilk Loaning) and out to the middle of the lough (after 200 years of reclamation the foreshore of the lough is now utterly unrecognisable, although see an earlier view of this location in Figure 9.7).

Just after Mary Gunning's discovery in Beatty's Gut was reported, David McCormick, a compositor who lived in Durham Street in Belfast, wrote to the newspapers to explain:

> Sir – Having seen a paragraph in your issue today, regarding the finding of a coffin and human remains on the slob-land of the Shore Road, nearly opposite Boyd's public-house, I may mention, for the information of those not acquainted with the locality and its antecedents, that in by-gone days – so late as fifty or sixty years ago – the place, called 'Green's Barns' was set apart for the interment of suicidal cases, or, as it was termed in those days, persons who had 'put hands on themselves', and who were interred at high-water mark.[47]

Beatty's Gut lay just outside the municipal boundary of Belfast in the early nineteenth century. At the time, and probably since at least the seventeenth century, superstitions and taboos surrounded the remains of those who had committed suicide. Similarly, the remains of people who had been executed, and even murder victims, received different treatment in death than those who died naturally. Included amongst these are unbaptised children, who were excluded from being buried on consecrated ground (largely due to theological ideas propounded at the Council of Trent that ended in 1563).[48] This promulgated the theological underpinning that perpetuated a practice of burying unbaptised children in specific locations or designated areas of graveyards. This is often presented as a 'Catholic' tradition, but debates around the Catholic use of established church burial grounds and individual cases in England suggest it was an issue with the Anglican tradition (if not others) in the nineteenth century. O'Laverty names at least one such *cillín* (as they are known) outside Belfast, at Dunmurry, and there is ongoing research trying to identify further sites.[49] Older residents of the Shore Road claim that the space now known as 'Ringans Point' was also formerly a *cillín*. In 1846 the skeleton of a 'full-grown infant' was found in the grounds at the rear of Fortwilliam close to Buttermilk Loaning (i.e., Skegoneill Avenue). It is unclear if this is referencing the same location as Mary Gunning's find but is clearly located above the high-tide line. At least one reported find of a coffin below the high-tide line off the Shore Road included the remains of a male child. Other unexplained finds of children's remains include those at Castleton off Mount Collyer Road in 1890.[50]

THE NEW BURYING GROUND: FROM THE MYSTICAL AND GOTHIC TO PÈRE-LACHAISE

As was noted early in this chapter, the opening of the New Burying Ground by Belfast Charitable Society coincided with a significant moment in the evolution of cemeteries in Europe. It is not only early within the tradition of designed garden cemeteries erected on the urban margins but was explicitly non-denominational and constructed within the same ideological current from which Père-Lachaise was to famously emerge barely a decade later.

At that time, at the turn of the nineteenth century, Belfast had its official but unhygienic and cluttered church graveyards at Shankill, High Street and Friar's Bush. At the same time, burial took place at a series of other non-official venues, guided by superstition, taboo, folk-belief and religious doctrine. Whether the New Burying Ground was specifically articulated as a remedy or simply embodied Belfast's radical zeitgeist of the 1790s is unclear. Many of those who died unbaptised or by suicide can be found in the registry of the New Burying Ground from at least the 1830s onwards, even if specific spaces may have been retained for their burial. This does suggest some measure of success. Bridging the gaps between popular praxis, official policy and public need is arguably a core value that threads through the 'Enlightenment', the intellectual circles of late eighteenth-century Belfast and the Charitable Society.

It can at least be stated, though, that the reality of the minimal monetary impact it had on the income of Belfast Charitable Society suggests that the fundraising value of the New Burying Ground has been overstated in the past and that other motivations, such as speculated on here, may have been equally, if not more, important. That brings back into focus the innovative design and ideology embodied by the New Burying Ground which was in the vanguard of contemporary radical thought in the Western world.

CHAPTER TEN

'They had names too': Belfast in 1847

Christine Kinealy and Gerard MacAtasney

&

Unlike England, Scotland and Wales, Ireland did not have in place a national system of poor relief until the introduction of the Irish Poor Law in 1838. As previous chapters have explained, prior to 1838 the lack of a resident landlord class in the Belfast area had meant that the burden of caring for the poor fell upon a small number of benevolent individuals and philanthropic organisations. Chief amongst the latter was the Poorhouse, opened by the Belfast Charitable Society in 1775, with the aim of providing a refuge for the aged and infirm. The Poor Law entailed a compulsory tax for the care of the poor, who had no right to relief and had to prove themselves to be in a state of destitution. Central to the new legislation was the erection of workhouses, and by the mid-1840s, 130 of these huge, foreboding edifices had been erected throughout the country. The Belfast workhouse (the site of the present-day City Hospital on the Lisburn Road) was completed in March 1841 and had capacity for 1,000 inmates. Despite fears that it would be taken over by the Poor Law commissioners, the Charitable Society maintained its independence and continued to provide voluntary relief to the town's old and vulnerable. The Great Famine that rapidly followed the establishment of the Poor

Law would, however, put both statutory and voluntary welfare provision in Belfast under considerable pressure.

The first failure of the potato crop in the autumn of 1845 saw an average crop loss of one-third, and in the Belfast district distress was manifested in areas such as Ballymacarrett, which also suffered from structural economic problems. However, the blight of 1846 resulted in the complete decimation of the staple crop. In addition, that winter was one of the coldest on record, with heavy snowfalls, resulting in exceptionally large numbers applying for relief. By November, Belfast's workhouse had exceeded its original capacity and now contained 1,103 inmates.[1] Many applicants were already sick, sharply increasing the number of deaths in the establishment. Adding to the difficulties was the announcement by the committee of the town's fever hospital that, due to overcrowding, there would be no further admissions.[2] They urged the Poor Law board of guardians to admit all new and convalescent patients to the fever hospital attached to the workhouse. Although the guardians agreed, they were apprehensive, as the workhouse was feeling the mounting pressure created by the second failure of the potato crop and the attendant increase in disease and mortality.[3]

When the guardians sought an explanation from the medical officer regarding the sudden increase in mortality, he pointed to the inadequacy of workhouse facilities to deal with disease. The majority of deaths had occurred amongst young children who had been accommodated in cold and damp nursery wards. Also, because of overcrowding in the workhouse fever hospital, a number of patients had been placed in temporary sheds, which had few facilities and no heating. Moreover, due to poor construction, the wash-house did not operate efficiently, which meant that the inmates' clothes could be neither washed, fumigated nor dried adequately.[4] In the opinion of the medical officer, the spread of disease could be contained if these problems were addressed and if the floors of the sleeping areas – which were bare earth – were boarded over and fireplaces provided.[5]

The pressure on the workhouse and its fever hospital continued into the new year. On 12 January 1847, a deputation from the Belfast Relief Committee asked the guardians to increase the capacity of the workhouse hospital by renting more accommodation. The guardians rejected this request, pointing out that, under the provisions of the 1838 Poor Law Act, relief could only be provided to destitute paupers suffering from disease and not to any other category of sick persons.[6] Yet, following a recommendation by the Poor Law inspector, Edward Senior, that rented accommodation was preferable to temporary structures, the guardians sought more permanent accommodation for sick inmates.[7] Suitable buildings, however, proved to be difficult to procure. The guardians' attempt to rent the old House of Correction was unsuccessful, as the soup kitchen committee was already using it as a distribution centre.[8] Consequently, they were forced to continue to adapt the facilities already available to them. At the beginning of 1847, the piggery, stable and straw-house were converted into wards for the accommodation of 600 paupers. In addition, galleries were erected in the girls' upper dormitory, while training rooms were converted into sleeping areas. These changes meant that a further 200 people could be accommodated.[9]

By the end of January 1847, the number of workhouse inmates exceeded 1,500 and continuing problems with the wash-house led the master to admit that, as a result of this 'enormous evil', he could not ensure sanitation within the workhouse buildings.[10] His fears were borne out by the rapid spread of disease amongst inmates and staff. Both the training master and mistress contracted typhus fever, and the medical attendant, Dr Coffey, died from the disease.[11] By February 1847, there were 110 patients in the fever wards, compared with only thirty in the previous November.[12] The influx of sick paupers necessitated an increase in medical staff that, in turn, increased administrative expenses. The guardians had not anticipated the fever epidemic when negotiating their contracts in September 1846, so the master was forced to buy an additional ten tonnes of oatmeal in the market in February 1847, at a time when food prices were greatly inflated. The medical attendants had suggested that an improvement in diet was essential to the health of the inmates, amongst whom food deficiency-related diseases such as diarrhoea and dysentery were 'frequent'. Consequently, the adult breakfast and supper meals were changed from stirabout to milk with bread or rice. Also, as more than half of the deaths were occurring amongst children under the age of seven, they were provided with a more substantial diet. Instead of stirabout for breakfast and supper, young children received bread and soup four days a week, and rice and milk on the other days.[13] This measure necessitated the employment of an additional cook. The Poor Law commissioners disapproved of this extra expenditure, describing it as 'wholly without precedent', but reluctantly sanctioned it, 'given the conditions of the House'.[14]

By the beginning of March, numbers in the workhouse's fever hospital had reached 158, with eighteen of its beds containing two patients each. The inability to isolate fever patients from other sick inmates resulted in outbreaks of diarrhoea, dropsy, measles, scrofula and smallpox.[15] In a measure described by Dr Reid as 'the means of saving many lives', the guardians approached the committee of the Belfast General Hospital, a surgical institution which had been the town's main fever hospital until the opening of the workhouse infirmary, and asked them to accept all cases of smallpox and dysentery until the crisis had passed. The committee agreed to accept a limited number of patients at a cost of 1s per patient per day. Additionally, burying workhouse paupers who died in the general hospital – costing 1s 6d per burial – would be charged to the Union.[16] The guardians immediately removed forty-nine cases of dysentery and nineteen smallpox cases to the general hospital.[17] The workhouse infirmary was then able to concentrate on cases of fever, which were continuing to escalate. On 9 March, there were over 200 fever cases in the workhouse, with no sign of abatement.[18] At this stage, the guardians had been permitted by the central commissioners to build a larger, better-equipped fever hospital at a maximum cost of £3,500 – a loan that was to be repaid over twenty years.[19]

In addition to wrangles with the commissioners, the guardians were facing problems with the general hospital, as the number of removals from the workhouse exceeded the number agreed. The hospital authorities pointed out that workhouse inmates could only be accommodated by 'shutting out patients for whom the establishment was specially intended' and suggested that the guardians seek alternative accommodation.[20] This communication precipitated a desperate move by the guardians. On 23 March – with 253 patients in the fever hospital and demand increasing – they announced their determination to 'refuse admission into the workhouse of all cases of dysentery, under any circumstances – a decision that caused consternation amongst the medical officers within the town.[21] The doctors in the general hospital demanded that extra accommodation be provided by those authorities who were 'armed with the power of the law'. They warned that unless the decision was overturned immediately, 'awful mortality will take place.[22] Similar sentiments were expressed by the six district medical attendants who, in urging the guardians to obtain additional facilities, counselled that 'the vast numbers affected are in such abject poverty that it is perfectly impossible to treat them with any prospect of success'.[23] Taking cognisance of such warnings, the general hospital agreed to limit admissions of surgical patients to 'extraordinary cases only', thereby allowing for more dysentery patients to be treated.[24] Despite the gravity of the situation, at this stage most of the diseases within the town were confined to the workhouse and the various medical institutions, but the situation was deteriorating rapidly. In the spring and summer of 1847, the epidemic began to spill out onto the streets of Belfast.

FEVER FOLLOWS FAMINE

To those in the medical profession who had witnessed periods of food shortages – such as in 1816, 1822 and 1831 – it was clear that disease would follow.[25] Given the consecutive failures of the potato crop in 1845 and 1846, it was inevitable that 1847 would see 'infectious distemper increase by degrees and ravage every class in the community'.[26] Nevertheless, although reports of fever were noted in particular areas, the feeling was that these were localised and posed no threat to the general health of the town. The resultant lack of preparation caused much anxiety to those who believed that an outbreak was imminent. John Boyd of the Ballymacarrett Relief Committee warned the authorities in Belfast that if they did not address the spread of 'pestilential fever' on his side of the river, it would soon cross into the town and 'produce equally in its lanes and terraces, consequences the most deadly and disastrous'.[27]

Nevertheless, it took an unusual occurrence to alert the citizens of Belfast to the threat of fever. On 17 March 1847, an emigrant ship, the *Swatara*, was forced into port due to bad weather. It was on its way from Liverpool to Philadelphia and carried 296 passengers, most of whom were from Connacht. The ship had been damaged and required repairs that were estimated to take up to four weeks. Within days of its arrival, reports were circulating that the ship had been visited 'to an extraordinary extent' by typhus fever which, in the words of the *Belfast News-Letter*, caused 'a great sensation in the town'.[28] The local medical establishment moved quickly to provide aid. At a specially convened meeting on 2 April, the general hospital agreed to accept as many fever cases as possible from the ship. Within three days, thirty-five had been admitted, but the involvement was short-lived.[29] Only four days after the meeting, the guardians received a deputation from the hospital informing them that their funds were exhausted and that the Union would have to meet the expense of any further patients from the *Swatara*. They exhorted them to make swift provision for the remaining passengers. The guardians responded that they were only legally permitted to support inmates of the workhouse. In answer to the suggestion that they 'waive the strict letter of the law', the board agreed to meet such expenses if the commissioners in Dublin allowed them to do so.[30]

By 20 April, two passengers from the *Swatara* had died. As the disease was making 'rapid progress' in the town and its suburbs, further mortality was expected.[31] Both the general hospital in Frederick Street and the Union Fever Hospital were 'crowded to over-flowing', a situation which prompted the following comment in the *News-Letter*: 'There are many poor creatures in the back lanes of this town suffering from the dreadful disease, for whom there is no room in the hospitals. This is a dreadful calamity inasmuch as the contagion will, in consequence, spread, and perhaps infect the higher classes of society.'[32]

Whilst the prospect of disease amongst the higher classes appeared to be a possibility, the epidemic continued to be most virulent in the poorest districts. A reporter from the *Vindicator* described graphically a visit to Meek's Court, off Barrack Street, where the fever had been devastating the poorer classes for weeks. Its impact was heightened by overcrowding, lack of employment and inadequate relief. He cited examples of such poverty thus:

> Bernard Brennan, cobbler, with a wife and three young children, has been idle for five weeks; gets but two quarts of soup with bread. John Thompson, with an unhealthy wife and four young children,

earned during the week, but 3s. 6d. at breaking stones; gets two quarts of soup. Widow Mahoney, with three young children, one of which is very ill; gets but two quarts of soup with bread. John Smyth, confined to bed, has three young children, two of them apparently dying; gets three quarts of soup with bread.[33]

As fever spread in the town, the local institutions struggled to cope with the demands made on their limited resources. By the end of April, the general hospital contained only forty-five medical patients; the remaining 160 were suffering from fever, dysentery or smallpox.[34] In the same period, numbers in the workhouse hospital doubled from 254 on 25 March to 503 one month later. In many cases, up to four shared a bed, the healthy being forced to lie with the diseased.[35] The pressure on the general hospital was even greater. In May, the institution contained 710 fever patients but by July the number had reached 1,242. All other surgical cases and other patients were removed temporarily to the Charitable Society.[36]

'GREAT AND PECULIAR URGENCY'

Given the number of sick patients in the workhouse, it was not surprising that many staff became ill. During April alone, the schoolmistress, her replacement, the cook, two ward-masters, a nurse and the assistant master all suffered from fever, while in the general hospital the disease afflicted both the orderly and the house surgeon, Dr Anderson.[37] With numbers continuing to increase, extra accommodation was urgently sought. The attempt by the guardians to obtain the Lancastrian School as an auxiliary fever hospital was rejected by its custodians, the Ladies' Local Association.[38] The guardians also experienced difficulties in their efforts to construct a permanent fever building. The relief commissioners refused to provide the Union with a loan for this purpose. The Belfast guardians felt that they were not being treated as sympathetically as other unions and cited the precedent of the nearby Lurgan Union, which had received a government grant to construct a fever hospital. They commented: 'It is hoped that the wealth and liberality of Belfast will not be again given as a reason for refusing the requisite aid.' However, their opinions were dismissed by the commissioners who stated that the Lurgan situation was one of 'great and peculiar urgency'. The request by the Belfast guardians for external financial aid was again refused.[39]

Further discord with the Poor Law authorities arose when Edward Senior criticised the guardians for their 'liberal' policy of admitting fever patients to the workhouse, making it, in effect, a fever hospital. He insisted that all fever admissions be halted at once.[40] The guardians acquiesced and they were soon followed by the general hospital, which also stopped admitting fever patients when the official number of admissions had been reached.[41] The incident provided an insight into the prioritising of bureaucratic niceties over saving lives – an approach that was not confined to Belfast.

The consequence of such drastic action was to multiply fever in the poorest districts. Dr Anderson observed that because of this edict, hundreds of fever victims remained in their 'miserable dwellings' with little hope of recovery. He described how '[s]everal of these unfortunate creatures actually lay down before the Hospital in Frederick Street, hoping to be admitted into that asylum'. Anderson warned that unless action was immediately taken, Belfast would become 'a charnel-house, with infection in every corner and death in every street'.[42] His concern resulted in the general hospital requesting the mayor to hold a meeting to 'take into consideration the alarming progress of typhus fever'.[43] Ironically, the *News-Letter*, which only six months earlier had discounted the seriousness of the crisis, now campaigned vigorously for increased institutional responses within the town. Its primary concern, however, was for the wealthy rather than the poorer classes, but it made the practical suggestion for the immediate establishment of a board of health, as had been done in previous crises. The paper issued the following warning to those who doubted the severity of the situation:

> The calamity up to a very recent date has hitherto reached only the purses of the middle and wealthier classes; but the case is different now. The breath of pestilence is beginning to invade the houses of comfort and plenty and peace. Something of the misery which haunts the cottage of the poor is forcing its way into the castle of the rich.[44]

A subsequent town meeting held in the Commercial Buildings on 1 May repeated many grim details of the widespread suffering. The Catholic bishop Dr Denvir remarked that the extent of disease was 'hardly credible', while Dr McGee reported that deaths in the Union Fever Hospital had exceeded 600 in the first four months of the year. The Rev. William Johnston, a representative of the town soup kitchen committee, alleged that some landlords were more concerned with expense than with health, and a number of them had prevented the whitewashing of houses and lanes simply on the grounds of not wanting to incur any additional costs. In one case, the men employed by the soup committee to sanitise a court had been commanded to leave by the landlord. Johnston gave a brief account of the houses that required whitewashing:

> In one house there were lying ill of contagious diseases, four persons in one small room. The poor afflicted people had no straw to lie down upon, only a piece of dirty sackcloth. On this miserable bed nine persons, including the fever patients, were obliged to sleep every night ... In another part of the same room resided another family consisting of seven people, who also slept in the apartment – not near nine foot wide – four of whom were afflicted with a dangerous fever.[45]

Suggestions for increasing hospital capacity were put forward. Dr Marshall proposed that several houses be hired, while Dr Stevilly favoured the erection of sheds on the grounds of Frederick Street Hospital. The meeting concluded by agreeing to obtain further accommodation as a matter of urgency and to request that the government establish a local board of health. The latter application received immediate sanction.[46]

The newly established board of health introduced a number of measures which helped to ease the situation.[47] The Charitable Society agreed to provide accommodation for medical and surgical cases removed from the general hospital. Although the latter was responsible for all expenses incurred, the Charitable Society's consent was given reluctantly as their own accommodation was 'very limited'.[48] Moreover, the general hospital agreed to erect sheds within its grounds, while Dr Anderson (the hospital's surgeon) gave up his personal quarters to provide extra accommodation.[49] Having finally received the assent of Lord Donegall and the Ladies' Association to use the Lancastrian School, steps were taken to convert it into a fever hospital. A further temporary hospital was provided in the 'well-ventilated and clean' old military quarters in Barrack Street.[50]

Workhouse pressure was eased with the announcement that the central Board of Health in Dublin would pay for the treatment of all fever patients. The guardians also announced that smallpox and dysentery cases would be confined to the Union hospital while the other institutions in the town would concentrate on people suffering from fever.[51] Furthermore, 'overseers of the town' were made responsible for the cleansing of lanes and alleys throughout the district,[52] while, from 1 May, the Charitable Society prohibited any inmates from leaving their premises.[53] A few weeks later, the Night Asylum (established in November 1841), now accommodating 280 occupants on average, was temporarily closed to allow for fumigation. On one night, 25 May, fifty-seven fever patients had had to lie on bare boards without any treatment in what were described as 'deplorable conditions'. The asylum had, in effect, become an auxiliary fever hospital, and its inability to meet the demands placed on it led a correspondent of the *Northern Whig* to describe it as 'a hotbed of infection'. These conditions resulted in its eventual closure.[54]

By the spring of 1847 there were more than 1,300 fever patients in the various medical establishments, and each medical district elicited the same melancholy reports: 'Dock District – fever prevails to an unparalleled extent together with numerous cases of dysentery and diarrhoea; Shankill District – fever, dysentery and smallpox prevail to an alarming extent; Hospital and Cromac Districts – fever, dysentery, smallpox and measles prevalent.'

Reports from the College District verified what had been predicted by doctors some months earlier: 'Famine has been followed, and is now attended by, the usual result – a rapid spread of those diseases that ensue from insufficient nutrition.'[55] Under such circumstances, death became commonplace and visible. The following recorded examples from May and June 1847 demonstrated the high level of mortality outside the main relief institutions:

At noon in High Street, a mother with an emaciated child slumped down under a shop window on the south side of the street. The child died in her arms five minutes later. Her son had died in similar circumstances three weeks ago.[56]

Yesterday, a poor woman from Lisburn laid herself down on the footway in Chichester Street near Great Edward Street and died beside her husband and child. The latter were removed to the hospital.[57]

On Wednesday the 26th, a male and female were observed supporting one another in York Street. The woman sat down and the male stretched her on the footpath – she died in a few minutes. A poor woman had the same sad duty to do for her child on the same evening in May Street.[58]

Yesterday at three o'clock, a beggarman was found dead at the corner of Matier Street, Shankill Road – his name is unknown. At the same hour, a two-year-old child died in its mother's arms at May's Bridge. The cause of death is given as destitution.[59]

RISING MORTALITY AND MULTIPLE BURIALS

Although difficulties with burials only manifested themselves in the press in June, they had been evident to relief officials for some time. As early as 5 January, Belfast's board of guardians had acceded to an application from local magistrates to allow the burial in the workhouse grounds of unclaimed pauper bodies dying in and around the town.[60] The guardians were severely rebuffed by the Poor Law commissioners for this action. Moreover, the commissioners refused to sanction such an initiative, pointing out that it was open to abuse and 'contrary to the spirit and intention of the Irish Poor Relief Act'. Unable to challenge this assertion, the guardians reversed their decision.[61] Within weeks, the guardians found themselves unable to cope with the demands being placed on them by the workhouse dead – now averaging forty per week. Multiple burials were commonplace in the Union graveyard, with the master instructing that 'graves be not less than eight feet deep and a cover of not less than two feet be placed over the upper coffin'.[62] This order was opposed by Edward Senior, who stated that coffins should be covered with at least six feet of earth and that bodies be placed in individual graves. Unusually, the guardians challenged Senior, countering that 'however desirable separate interments may be' they were not practicable under the present circumstances.[63] They did, nevertheless, agree with Senior that the 'crowded state and objectionable site of the ground' made a new workhouse burial ground a pressing necessity.[64]

Under the provisions of the new Poor Relief Act, the guardians could purchase three acres of land for burials. The committee appointed to obtain a new burial site was directed to ensure that the site was situated away from the main building and the fever hospital.[65] The huge increase in mortality ensured that the guardians were not alone in seeking new grounds. However, the various charitable bodies had no legal right to purchase ground, and an act of parliament was required for a cemetery to be established by public subscription. On 27 March, the committee of the general hospital sent a 'strong memorial' to the town council urging the necessity of creating a suitable burial ground for the local poor.[66] On 10 April, the general hospital requested that the Charitable Society allow the burial of smallpox and dysentery sufferers in their cemetery. The Society had previously 'reluctantly' resolved to limit interments to those who died in the Poorhouse, as their burial ground was almost full. Notwithstanding this resolution, the Society acceded to the hospital's request on condition that it would only be until 1 June 1847.[67] The guardians were also experiencing difficulties in acquiring a suitable site. In July, they accepted a tender for three acres at the Blackstaff New Road, costing £300. Lamenting the high price, the guardians explained to Senior that the expenditure was unavoidable, 'as the pressure is very urgent and it will become incumbent on the board to make a selection without further delay'.[68]

Under these difficult circumstances, the Board of Health urged the guardians to allow general burials in the new Union ground. Given that no other public body was able either to purchase or to acquire a burial site, the onus was on the guardians to agree. Again, they were bound by the strict limitations placed on them by Poor Law legislation and the ever-vigilant central commissioners and their local inspector, Senior. Although the guardians acknowledged the 'calamitous consequences' of the lack of burial space, they pointed out that, even though they wished to open their new site to all, they had to adhere to the stipulations of the central commissioners.[69]

The consequences were quickly apparent. On 2 July, Friar's Bush graveyard was 'so much choked with the dead' that the sextons were obliged to dig deep square pits, each capable of holding forty coffins.[70] One week later, at the behest of the Board of Health, the Charitable Society resorted to the desperate measure of obtaining certificates from 'many of the most respectable medical practitioners', stating that it would be safe to open the graves of those who had died in the cholera epidemic of 1832–3.[71] This extraordinary development offered only a brief respite and, at a town meeting to discuss the issue held in early July, many harrowing details emerged of how Belfast was burying its dead. The Rev. Richard Oultan said of the Protestant Shankill graveyard: 'Coffins are heaped upon coffins until the last one often is not more than two inches under ground and in finding room for others, bodies that have not been long buried are often exhumed.' He added that if the matter was neglected any further, the population would have 'such scenes as are witnessed at Skibbereen brought home to their own doors'.[72] The meeting was also informed that the Charitable Society had purchased ten lots of ground but that they would ensure proper burials for another fortnight only. It was decided to maintain pressure on the guardians, and a memorial was sent pleading that all those dying in destitute circumstances be permitted to be buried in their new ground, irrespective of whether or not they were inmates of the workhouse.[73] The Poor Law commissioners were unmoved; they responded by reiterating that only those dying within the workhouse and Union fever hospital could be interred in the new graveyard.[74]

In addition to the difficulties attached to the burial of the poor, the general situation continued to deteriorate. Public concern was again voiced about the level of mendicancy in the town. The day asylum, originally established to combat the problem, was full and people were daily arriving from the impoverished country areas. In March 1847, James McAdam remarked that the town was 'swarming with beggars from all parts of the country'.[75] Yet, whilst many who came to Belfast were impoverished and seeking relief, a number who passed through the town were on their way to a new life outside Ireland – on 12 April alone, almost 1,000 passengers boarded vessels to travel to Quebec.[76] The unrelenting demands placed on the town's resources caused renewed consternation amongst Poor Law officials, leading Senior to suggest that the guardians should prevail on the local authorities to clear the streets of the 'immense floating mendicant population which now infect the town to the extent of thousands'. He asserted that they had been attracted to the town by the various charities therein, accusing them of being a 'source of contamination' and holding them responsible for causing the recent epidemic.[77] The absence of a Law of Settlement in the Irish Poor Law meant that admission to a workhouse could not be refused to paupers from outside the Union. However, the guardians restricted entry to the workhouse to those who were weakened and debilitated.[78] Similarly, the committee of the day asylum stipulated that admission to their premises was limited to those who could prove a long period of residence in Belfast.[79]

This new stringency was apparent in other ways. Further to these initiatives was the appointment of constables by the Charitable Society to apprehend vagrants and have them put to work or removed from the town. They were aided by the police committee, which allowed the male and female cells in the old Court House and House of Correction to be used for the confinement of vagrants.[80] This new co-ordinated policy had immediate effects and was lauded in the local press. The *Banner of Ulster* described the consequences thus:

> It is scarcely necessary to inform our readers in Belfast of the very happy change in the matter of street-begging which has been effected during the past few weeks. The drab-coated servants of the Charitable Society have done more to produce a healthy reaction in our own social condition than could be well credited. Hundreds of wretched beings who have left their still more wretched dwellings to spread contagion during the day throughout town have been picked up and carefully tended to by the Board of Health, while the sturdy vagrant and the insolent juvenile impostor have been shipped or sent by railroad or coach to the various places to which they allegedly belong.[81]

The reduction in the numbers on the streets resulting from the stricter treatment of vagrants paralleled a gradual diminution in fever levels. In July, there had been 2,200 fever patients in the various hospitals; by the end of August, this had fallen to 1,400.[82] However, mortality remained high, averaging seventy deaths per week. The shortage of burial sites continued to be a serious problem, leading the Board of Health to renew its attempts to obtain alternative locations. To this end, they convened a town meeting to discuss the matter on 23 August.[83] The gathering was highly critical of the Poor Law, especially what they regarded as the high-handed approach of the commissioners as regards burials. The meeting was informed that the commissioners had refused to allow the guardians to make their new ground available to all, despite the fact that the workhouse graveyard was the only one with vacant burial plots. The commissioners had also threatened to prosecute anyone attempting to bury people who were not inmates of the workhouse when they died.[84] Although the meeting attempted to find alternative ways of dealing with the town's dead, the scale of the problem hampered their efforts. Dr Stevilly estimated that, since June, approximately 2,000 had been interred, with no sign of abatement. The Catholic bishop Dr Denvir made the point that potential space in the existing graveyards was lost due to perpetuities for the families of 'the wealthy portion of the community'. Dr McGee observed that corpses had been left to lie in houses without coffins until the Board of Health paid for their burial, adding to the general level of disease. The influential Anglican clergyman, Dr Drew, claimed that the town's graveyards were 'shameful to any Christian community', relating gruesome details of a recent interment in the Shankill cemetery: 'A few days since I turned away in disgust when I observed the manner in which bones and skulls were thrown up and about and in which the spade was stuck into the coffins and dead bodies which had seemingly been but a very short time deposited.'[85]

The debate about the lack of burial space continued in the local press. The *Northern Whig* reported that a huge pit had been dug in the same graveyard, into which forty coffins were placed over the space of only a few days. The situation was not resolved until the following year when, with far less mortality, an extension to the Shankill graveyard was purchased, increasing its size by half.[86]

THE AMENDED POOR LAW

In August 1847, new relief measures were introduced, based on an extension of the existing Poor Law. Unlike earlier famine relief policies, the new measures were intended to be permanent rather than temporary. As a consequence of the Amended Poor Law Act, responsibility for all relief fell to the guardians and hence to the local ratepayers. Significantly also, for the first time, outdoor relief was now permitted under the Irish Poor Law. The new legislation was welcomed by the Belfast press, which argued that rural districts would now have to support their own poor, allowing the various institutions in Belfast to cater for local poverty.[87] The new legislation signalled the closure of the privately subsidised soup kitchens throughout the Union. The Howard Street kitchen ceased operations in July, while the Great George's Street kitchen, although still feeding 1,300 families, terminated on 27 August.[124] Consequently, all future applicants for relief were, in the words of the *Banner of Ulster*, to be 'thrown on the resources of the national treasury and the care and attention of the Poor Law Guardians'.[88]

The following weeks saw a gradual fall in the number of fever patients in hospitals. At the beginning of September, the figure was 1,287 with sixty-three fatalities; by October, it was 977 and forty-seven respectively.[89] Although deaths were mainly confined to those suffering 'severe dysentery', fever could still be fatal.[90] On 5 October, the death from typhus fever of Dr Anderson, house surgeon of the general hospital, was announced. The Rev. Richard Oultan was also reported as suffering from a 'dangerous attack' of fever, although he subsequently recovered.[91] In early November, the workhouse convalescent camp hospital was closed, the tents having been purchased by the guardians for future emergencies.[92] The day asylum continued to operate, the only alteration in its status being that both it and the old house of correction were placed under the control of the Belfast guardians.[93] Many of the inmates of the asylum were children, and this solution was seen as the best means of preventing their exposure to 'every species of physical and moral degradation'. The change in the nature of the establishment was noted by the *Banner of Ulster*, which declared: 'How pitiful was it a few months ago to enter the Asylum and contemplate the huddled mass of humanity and rags which presented itself and how pleasant the contrast now!'[94] Following the dissolution of the Board of Health on 30 November, the guardians assumed the main responsibility for public health in the town.[95] The various acquisitions by the guardians had increased workhouse capacity by 400, which did not include the extensions still being completed. By being able to provide such extended indoor accommodation, they were spared the necessity of having to offer outdoor relief, notwithstanding the continuing influx of paupers from neighbouring areas. At the end of 1847, the guardians pointed out that the 'great majority' of those seeking relief in the preceding months had come from distant parishes such as Toome, Drumall and Larne, where 'the whole population had been drafted by some means into Belfast'.[96]

The prospects for the harvest in 1848 were good, and it appeared that Belfast had passed through the worst of the Famine. Nevertheless, there were still many people in need of relief in the town and elsewhere. Dr A.G. Malcolm, in a lengthy letter to the *Northern Whig*, warned that other diseases would follow the fever epidemic, and he urged the establishment of a permanent sanitary association. In his view, no long-term benefits could be gained from initiating a board of health in times of severe distress only. He argued that those in positions of responsibility should ensure that the health of the Union would become a priority in the months ahead. He further observed that whilst the worst of the Famine appeared to be over, its legacy would continue to create difficulties for Belfast in subsequent years.[97]

A good local harvest in 1849 and a revival of industry in the northeast meant that demand for poor relief continued to fall. Simultaneously, a myth was being created that, due to the exceptionalism of the town of Belfast, they had weathered the crisis with relative ease. The introduction of the Rate-in-Aid tax in 1849 – a tax imposed on all Poor Law Unions but redistributed by the British treasury to the poorest ones – allowed for a narrative to emerge that focused on northern Protestant superiority, with one newspaper posing the question:

> It is true that the potato has failed in Connaught and Munster, but it has failed just as much in Ulster; therefore, if the potato has caused all the distress in the South and West, why has it not caused the

same misery here? It is because we are a painstaking, industrious, laborious people, who desire to work and pay our just debts, and the help of the Almighty is upon our labour. If the people of the South had been equally industrious with those of the North, they would not have had so much misery among them.[98]

The visit of Queen Victoria to Belfast later in the year – her first and only visit to the town – provided a further opportunity to demonstrate the loyalty of that portion of the empire to the monarchy and to the Union with Britain. The London *Times* opined: 'the intoxicating idea, cherished by so many, that there was strength in the Roman Catholic portion of Ireland to resist successfully the British power has proved to be a delusion'.[99] Already the tragic impact of the Famine on Belfast was being written out of history, a pattern that was repeated in the subsequent historiography. It would not be until the sesquicentenary of the appearance of the potato blight in 1995 that the work of recovery would gain momentum.

CHAPTER ELEVEN

'The moving spirit': Traversing Mary Ann McCracken's Belfast

Cathryn McWilliams

~~80~~

In Nicholas Joseph Crowley's oil painting *Fortune Telling by Cup Tossing* (1842), the older of the two models – generally agreed to be Mary Ann McCracken – plays the part of the tasseomancer, gazing into a teacup in search of the future (see Figure 11.1).[1] To her right side, an open window reveals Belfast's Cave Hill in the distance, with the town lying in the valley below. Upon closer inspection we see that the fortune teller's left arm is partially obscuring the lower corner of the window. The shades of blue and moss-green found on the sleeve of her dress seem to echo the colours in the landscape. Indeed, Cave Hill, the main body of the dress and the fortune teller's eyes are all a similar shade of stone blue. As a result, she appears to extend naturally into the land of the picture's exterior. Whether or not Crowley painted the scene in a house overlooking Belfast, or added in the view later, the blending of model and setting offers a fitting visualisation of McCracken's organic and unbreakable connection to the town and its landscape.

This chapter offers an opportunity to follow in the footsteps of one of the Belfast Charitable Society's most famous supporters and to explore her connections with the environs of Belfast as a whole. Mary Ann McCracken

Figure 11.1 *Fortune Telling by Cup Tossing* (1842) by Nicholas Joseph Crowley. (Courtesy of Sotheby's Picture Library)

(1770–1866) has become something of a Belfast icon during the century and a half since her death. However, it might just as easily be claimed that she achieved such status within her own lifetime. Born in Belfast on 8 July 1770 to Captain John McCracken and his second wife Ann (née Joy), Mary Ann was the fifth of six surviving children. The McCracken brood were raised in connection with Belfast's Third Presbyterian subscribing congregation and were educated at David Manson's co-educational school on Donegall Street, where corporal punishment was unheard of, boys and girls were taught as equals and learning was facilitated through play. This education, coupled with the family's status as part of the liberal middle class, produced children ideally fitted for intellectual openness and political radicalism.

Inspired by the ideals of the French Revolution and encouraged by the success of the American War of Independence, a Society of United Irishmen was founded in Belfast in 1791 with the goal of uniting 'all the people of Ireland' and achieving 'a complete and radical reform of the representation of the people in Ireland'.[2] Henry Joy McCracken was one of those in attendance at the first committee meeting, with his elder brothers William and Francis (Frank) swiftly joining him as sworn members. Indeed, Mary Ann's eagerness that her female friends join the society suggests that by 1797 she herself had already joined its ranks.[3] The society became more radical as it was forced underground, and a government crackdown resulted in many arrests. Both Henry and William were imprisoned in Dublin's Kilmainham Gaol, during which time Mary Ann regularly wrote to them about the developing situation in Belfast and on at least one occasion argued for equality of the sexes.[4] Following their release, Henry became heavily involved in the planning of a rebellion and went on to command the rebels at the Battle of Antrim in June 1798. Despite escaping into the Belfast hills, he was later captured and hanged outside the town's market house at the age of thirty-one. Mary Ann's own involvement in these events is vividly captured within both her correspondence and a transcribed interview. Although traditionally understood in light of her ill-fated brother, Mary Ann outlived her most cherished sibling by almost seventy years. In a bid to keep the memory of her brother and the cause alive, she assisted with and contributed to Irish historian Dr Richard Robert Madden's multi-volume corpus *The United Irishmen, Their Lives and Times* and other related works.

Mary Ann was also a keen promoter of the cultural revival of Ireland's ancient poetry, language and music, most notably assisting her close friend Edward Bunting with the gathering and processing of materials for his collection of Irish airs. In her early twenties, Mary Ann proposed a muslin business to her sister and by 1790 the operation had commenced. Her step-grandniece Anna McCleery revealed that 'her chief object in trying to make money was that she might have some of her own to give away as she wished'.[5] Although their workers' rights were given utmost priority, the sisters were forced to close the business sometime around 1815 owing to 'continued bankruptcies in all branches of the cotton industry'.[6]

From childhood, Mary Ann visited and assisted at the Poorhouse (later, the Belfast Charitable Society), which was 'the first public charitable institution in Belfast'.[7] Her uncles Robert and Henry Joy (two brothers who contributed significantly to the town's development) took an active part in its establishment. Indeed, her acquaintance with the institution began, in her own words, 'as soon as I could walk'.[8] Mary Ann and her sister Margaret sat on a small ladies' committee for the welfare of women and children, which had been inaugurated at the Belfast Charitable Society in March 1814. For reasons unknown, however, the committee was dissolved after two years. A more robust version of this committee was commenced on 27 July 1827, with Isabella Tennent as secretary. Upon the latter's withdrawal in 1832, Mary Ann took over the role. Her meticulous records consist of 'page after page of minutes written in plain, sensible handwriting in two very ordinary foolscap jotters, the lines on every page being ruled in pencil'.[9] Within these accounts, evidence abounds of Mary Ann's commitment to the needs and well-being of the women and children of the Poorhouse, such as her determination to establish an infant school, regardless of the disapproval of the gentlemen's committee. However, with a drop-off in ladies attending, the committee minutes came to an end in October 1851. This did not discourage Mary Ann, whose wider philanthropic activities were extensive and involved fundraising and organisational work for various charitable and humanitarian causes. Even into her last decades, she took on roles such as president of the Committee of the Belfast Ladies' Anti-Slavery Association.[10]

As far as can be discerned from the materials that survive, Mary Ann never travelled beyond the island of Ireland. Indeed, she rarely strayed beyond her hometown of Belfast. It was not until the age of twenty-six that Mary Ann (accompanied by her sister Margaret, brother John and Edward Bunting) first journeyed to Dublin with the express purpose of visiting her incarcerated brothers William and Henry Joy McCracken at Kilmainham Gaol. Whilst there, her mother Ann wrote to her, 'I was sorry to find by John's letter to his wife that you don't like Dublin, tho' I was sure it would be the case.'[11] Evidently, her first impression of the city was not a favourable one. Mary Ann and Margaret made the journey once again in October 1797, accompanied by their sister-in-law, Rose Ann (William McCracken's wife).[12] By 3 November 1797, the sisters had returned to Belfast, leaving Rose Ann with her husband at the jail.[13]

After his release in early December, Henry was heavily involved in the planning of a nationwide rebellion and led the rebels at the Battle of Antrim in June 1798, only to be driven into hiding following their defeat. On Mary Ann's twenty-eighth birthday, having received the news of her fugitive brother's capture and arrest, she and Captain McCracken 'went directly' to Carrickfergus jail to see the prisoner.[14] Father and daughter 'remained all night in Carrickfergus'[15] before returning home the following day.[16] Subsequently, on the morning of Henry's trial, Mary Ann 'arose at six, and set out in a carriage for the place where Miss Tomb was then staying with a lady, near Lisburn'[17] to persuade her cousin to give evidence at Henry's trial. These examples suggest that McCracken's earliest known travels were induced by dire circumstances and family crisis.

In the summer of 1813, Mary Ann was advised to go to a spa in order to recover from a persistent ailment. Anna McCleery later recalled that her step-grandaunt 'chose Ballynahinch as being the nearest, although informed that some other might be more speedily efficacious; but she wished to be where she could be quickly summoned home, should necessity arise'.[18] Even when she left the town, then, Mary Ann evidently remained in its orbit.

Nevertheless, several records of recreational excursions do exist. For instance, on 14 September 1809, the Belfast naturalist John Templeton noted in his journal: 'Went to Bangor with Miss Mary McCracken, found on the Rocks below Bangor: *Ligusticum Scoticum* with arenaria maritima, riccia glauca.'[19] From childhood, the Templeton and McCracken families had been close, and it is alleged that Mary Ann was a bridesmaid at John's wedding to Katherine Johnston on 21 December 1799.[20] Further reinforcing these connections, James Black's diary entry for 22 July 1838 observed that 'Miss Mary Ann Magee and Miss McCracken' – the latter described as 'the most benevolent being in the world'[21] – were visiting the Bangor residence of John's sister Eliza Templeton, perhaps Mary Ann's closest friend.[22] Indeed, Mary Ann referred to this trip in a letter of 1838, wherein she wrote to its unknown recipient, 'I delayed replying to the message you left for me with my niece until I should have an opportunity of reading your sermon, which I procured on my return from Bangor.'[23] Presumably, these social visits were of a regular nature until Eliza's death in 1839.[24]

MARY ANN MCCRACKEN'S RESIDENCES: A CHRONOLOGICAL SURVEY

In keeping with the above observations, Mary Ann's domestic residences were always to be found within Belfast's limits (see Figure 11.2), with the exception of several months spent in the neighbouring town of Holywood. The locations and properties in which she dwelled throughout her long life can be traced through street directories, committee reports and will calendars, but above all through her significant body of correspondence. Address details and superscriptions found within (and without) the letters reveal the trails she wove across the town.

39 High Street (1770–c. 1790s)

Between 1758 and 1772, all seven children of the McCracken children were born at this address. In 1784, at the age of twelve, Edward Bunting was welcomed into the McCracken household, having moved to Belfast to become an apprentice to William Ware, the organist of St Anne's Church.[25] At that time, the River Farset ran open through the centre of High Street, leading out into the docks where Captain McCracken berthed his ship. The house was demolished some time during the latter half of the nineteenth century, as Fred Heatley explains:

> It stood two doors from McKittrick's Entry, or Court, now Joy's Entry, and Dr. Madden, in his article on McCracken, states that Ogsden's confectioners at 39 High Street was the original house. Ogsden vacated the premises during the early 1860s and the Belfast Screw Steamer Coal Co. took possession. The last two decades of the century saw the removal of these old buildings but with the information we have, it is most likely that the site now occupied by St George's Hall is where the old McCracken house once stood.[26]

On 27 January 1999, a blue plaque was erected by the Ulster History Circle above Joy's Entry stating, 'Henry Joy McCracken 1767–1798, United Irishman, Born in a house near this site'.[27] Unfortunately, it fails to mention his arguably equally remarkable sister who was also born at this location.

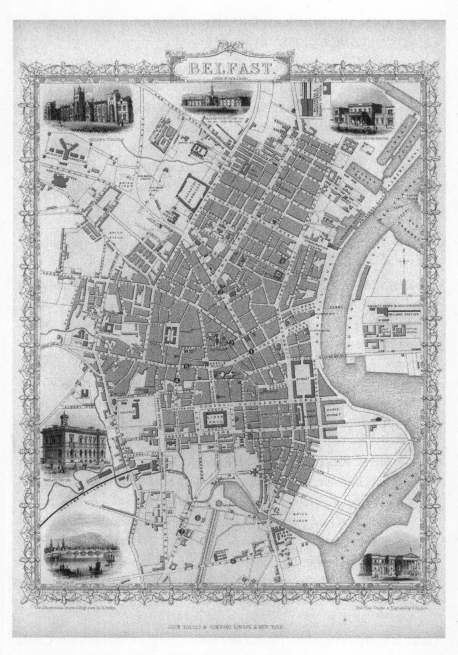

Figure 11.2 Map of Belfast by John Tallis from 1851 with the eight locations of McCracken's homes marked. (Courtesy of David Rumsey Map Collection Center, Stanford Libraries)

30 Rosemary Lane (c. 1790s–c. 1814)

At some point during the 1790s, the family relocated to 30 Rosemary Lane (later Rosemary Street), just a short distance from the previous property. McCleery vaguely suggests that the move occurred 'when she [Mary Ann] was past her childhood',[28] while historian John J. Marshall asserts that 'the McCracken family removed from High Street in the summer of 1796 to Rosemary Lane, next to Winecellar Entry'.[29] In any case, William McCracken's letter of 29 April 1797[30] is the first within Mary Ann's collection to be addressed to 'Rosemary Lane', while displaced United Irishman David Lyons' epistle dated 26 January 1804 is the final.[31] Evidence that Mary Ann and her sister operated their muslin business from this premises can be found within Belfast directories pertaining to the years 1806 and 1807.[32]

Shortly after Henry's execution on 17 July 1798, his illegitimate daughter Maria came to reside with the McCracken family at the property, having been (in Mary Ann's later words) 'left to our care'.[33] The house was affectionately referred to as 'Noah's Ark' owing to the 'numerous inmates', animals included.[34] Conveniently, the lane was also home to the McCracken family church; however, both buildings were destroyed during the Belfast Blitz of April 1941.

Waring Street (1808)

Sometime between 1807 and 1809, the sisters' place of business relocated from the family home to commercial premises on Waring Street.[35] It is unclear whether or not the siblings were living onsite; however, in McCracken's correspondence we do find a letter composed by Edward Bunting on 8 March 1809 addressed to 'Miss Mary McCracken/ Waring Street/ Belfast'.[36] Furthermore, an extant music notebook belonging to Mary Ann is inscribed, 'Nov. 15th 1808. Miss Mary McCracken Waring St, her book, Belfast'.[37] Mary McNeill, McCracken's biographer, refers to the Waring Street premises as the 'sisters' undertaking' rather than their place of residence, further noting, 'it seems likely that at this stage the sisters launched into production on a factory basis, continuing at the same time to employ weavers who worked in their own homes'.[38]

Donegall Street (c. 1814–43)

Following the death of Ann McCracken on 25 May 1814, those family members remaining at Rosemary Lane packed up and moved to Donegall Street. Indeed, two of Mary Ann McCracken's surviving epistles were written from 80 Donegall Street, the first dated 6/7 January 1843[39] and the second dated 1 April 1843.[40] Whilst living at this property, Mary Ann lost two siblings: Margaret on 11 December 1829, followed by Francis on 22 December 1842. In 1859, she reflected that 'at the time of my dear brother Frank's death we were much embarrassed by the house we were living in'.[41] Although keen to move, the 'avaricious & ill-tempered'[42] landlord refused to settle Francis' lease (of which eight years remained) for less than 200 pounds. Fortunately, friends and businessmen of the town rallied around to raise the required sum, as, in Mary Ann's own words, 'a testimonial to my brother's memory, bestowing it in the most delicate of manner so as not to hurt our feelings'.[43] The official surrender of the lease can be found within the Belfast Charitable Society's Mary Ann McCracken Collection.

7 Queen Street (1843–7)

Once free of the Donegall Street property, Mary Ann was quick to find alternative accommodation for herself and Maria. On 1 April 1843, she wrote to Dr Madden informing him that 'we are to leave Donegall St & expect to be fixed in our new habitation N°7 Queen St, before the end of the present month'.[44] Six of Mary Ann's remaining letters were penned from this address, where aunt and niece lived together for four years.

Holywood (c. July–November 1847)

Maria married the widower William McCleery in May 1847, instigating another move, albeit a temporary one. In a letter addressed from Holywood and dated 14 July 1847, Mary Ann explained, 'we are come to Holywood for a few months but I am generally in Belfast twice a week having duties to perform there which I cannot think of relinquishing'.[45] Evidently, McCracken could not be long separated from Belfast. The newly-weds, along with McCleery's four children and Mary Ann, resided there until November 1847, as outlined by the children's half second cousin, Jane Ellen Orr of Portaferry, in a letter to her brother John Malcolm Orr in Chicago: 'We had Anna and Mary McCleery down with us for three weeks last month, they liked being here very much indeed. They are all living in Holywood at present, and they intend remaining there until November, when they get settled in B'fast again.'[46]

28 Castle Street (1847–53)

A letter dated 27 September 1849 places the family at 28 Castle Street, which had presumably been their place of residence since November 1847. A total of ten extant epistles are addressed from this house, the final of which is dated 26 November 1851.[47]

Bankmore House (1853–62)

Mary Ann's remaining extant letters, dating between 27 February 1853 and 23 February 1861, are all addressed from 'Bankmore', a large house situated on the corner of the Dublin Road and Basin Lane. Indeed, between the years 1855 and 1862, the committee reports for the Belfast Ladies' Industrial National School for Girls consistently list Bankmore as McCracken's place of residence. Jonathan Bardon notes that 'Bankmore House, now the site of Bankmore Street, was in the country, outside the borough boundary'.[48] However, McNeill states that by the 1850s 'the McCleery's house with its garden and orchard was almost submerged by the tall warehouses spreading out behind the White Linenhall'.[49] Bankmore House was built by William McCleery's father, James, 'who came from the neighbourhood of Portaferry to work as an engineer and surveyor for the Lagan Navigation Company and Belfast Water Commissioners'.[50] It would seem that William moved his own family into the property shortly after James's death on 17 January 1852.[51]

In early 1859, Mary Ann wrote to Dr Madden from this address apologising for the delay, 'in consequence of small-pox being in the house as a cousin of Mr McCleery's who boards here had got smallpox, he did not know how & I found that no Lady would venture to enquire at the door & therefore I would not venture to write to anyone while there could be the most distant fear of danger'.[52]

At some point during 1862, the family inexplicably left the comfort of Bankmore House. The following year, a Belfast directory listed 'Bankmore House' as a 'Convent of Mercy'.[53] Indeed, within its 'Educational Institutions' section, the property is referred to as 'Bankmore Penitentiary', founded by the Sisters of Mercy 'for the reception of fallen and penitent females'.[54] Evidently, the establishment proved contentious as the house was attacked on 12 August 1864 by 'an Orange mob'.[55] By 1874, the publishing firm Marcus Ward & Co. had taken over the property and continued to be listed in directories alongside the Royal Ulster Works until 1887.[56]

80 Pakenham Place (1862–5)

The family did not stray far, however, settling in a nearby Victorian terrace house at 80 Pakenham Place, which bordered the grounds of Bankmore on the Dublin Road.[57] Accordingly, *The Sixteenth Report of the Committee for 1862–63 of the Belfast Ladies' Industrial National School for Girls* records 'Miss M'Cracken, Pakenham Place' as 'President' and 'Miss M'Cleery, Pakenham Place' as one of its 'secretaries'.[58] This information is echoed within both the seventeenth and eighteenth reports.

62 Donegall Pass (c. late 1865–26 July 1866)

The *Nineteenth Report of the Committee for 1865–66* sees a change in their circumstances. Whereas Miss McCracken is listed as 'President', residing at 'Pakenham Place', Miss McCleery's place of residence is given as 'Donegal Pass'.[59] Subsequently, the contributions section of the report states, 'Donegal Pass (Apsley Place): Miss M'Cracken'.[60] This would suggest that at some point between 1865 and 1866 Mary Ann and the McCleery family had moved to Donegall Pass. In consulting *The Belfast and Province of Ulster Directory for 1865* we find that 'Mrs Ellen Malcolmson' then resided at 'Apsley Place, Donegall Pass 62'.[61] Yet, the directory for 1868 lists 'McCleary [*sic*], William'[62] as inhabitant, confirming that the move took place in either late 1865 or early 1866. This would suggest that McCracken had resided at 62 Donegall Pass for less than a year when she died on 26 July 1866. Her last will and testament situates her as, 'late of Donegall Pass, Belfast, IRL, the County of Antrim',[63] where the McCleery family remained for at least a further two years.[64] The terrace house at 62 Donegall Pass still stands at the time of writing and on 27 January 1999, the Ulster History Circle unveiled a blue plaque at this location, reading, 'Mary Ann McCracken, 1770–1866, Social Reformer, Lived here'. As outlined above, however, she did so only for a matter of months.[65]

FROM THE BELFAST HILLS TO THE SCAFFOLD: ICONIC JOURNEYS OF 1798

One of Mary Ann's most celebrated journeys, described by her in an interview with Dr Madden (and later incorporated into his *The United Irishmen, Their Lives and Times*), was her expedition across the Belfast hills in search of her fugitive brother Henry Joy McCracken, who, just several days earlier, had led the rebels at the Battle of Antrim.[66] On this mission (undertaken at the age of twenty-seven) she was accompanied by Rose Ann. The pair set out from Belfast 'towards the White House',[67] a late sixteenth-century fortified farmhouse to the north of the town which, by 1798, had fallen into disrepair.[68] The distance between this building and the McCracken household at 30 Rosemary Lane was approximately four and a half miles. Having 'made some enquiries in the [Whitehouse] neighbourhood', the women met with James McGlathery (Rose Ann's brother) and proceeded to 'the country residence of Mr John Brown, a banker, then in England, whose gardener, Cunningham had given shelter occasionally to the wanderers'.[69] This was Merville House, a mere five-minute walk from the White House. Built in 1795 by John Brown, a partner in the so-called 'Bank of the Four Johns' on Ann Street, the house still stands today.

At dusk they continued to a house belonging to John Brice near Cave Hill, whom Mary Ann 'knew a little' and where they 'got a bed that night'.[70] The following day they 'continued their search and *at last* met with Gawin Watt and another person' who took them to 'a smith's house, on the lime-stone road leading to Antrim'.[71] It was at this house that Mary Ann encountered eight fugitives and advised them to return to their homes. Three of these men, 'Robert Henry, a schoolmaster, William Leith, and Robert Johnston' escorted the ladies further on their journey, travelling at a 'brisk' pace 'up hill, across fields, drains, and ditches for two hours' on the Black mountain before arriving at 'the Bowhill' where they eventually found Henry and six others 'sitting on the brow of the hill'.[72] In a letter to Dr Madden, dated 4 November 1859, Mary Ann referred to this location as 'Bowhill mountain',[73] which lies near Hannahstown, to the southwest of the Black mountain. Having been filled in on the men's 'adventures and escapes',[74] the women spent the night at a nearby house before making their way home the following day. James Hope was one of the six men whom they encountered on what he referred to as 'the Black Bohell'.[75] This meeting evidently stood out in Hope's memory as, some forty-five years later, he recalled how 'two ladies at this time arrived from Belfast at the risk of their lives'.[76] Hope's remark highlights the perilous nature of their journey and, indeed, historian Edna Fitzhenry considered it 'miraculous' that they 'made their way to Cave Hill unmolested' given that, at that time, 'Belfast was under the strictest martial law' and that 'many women met a worse fate than mere shooting'.[77] McNeill imagined the travellers constantly 'evading soldiers' while 'traversing country quite unknown to either of them with unusual courage and determination'.[78]

A year after Dr Madden published these details within the 'Memoir of Henry Joy McCracken',[79] Mary Ann made arrangements for the historian to visit the locations. In a letter dated 15 October 1844, she wrote to him, 'I look forward to the pleasure of seeing you both in Belfast, when Maria will be happy to accompany you & Mrs Madden to the Cavehill & old Jemmy will take us all to the Bowhill & Slemish'.[80] Evidence that the former excursion actually transpired can be found in Dr Madden's 1858 edition of *The United Irishmen*, wherein he states, 'I visited the spot on the Cave Hill where the same engagement was entered into, accompanied by the daughter of Henry Joy McCracken'.[81] Not only does the juxtaposition of these two quotations confirm the Cave Hill trip, it also acts to validate Maria's paternal parentage. Given this, it is likely that the latter excursion also took place, suggesting that at the age of seventy-four Mary Ann was willing and able to climb hills and trek through countryside once again, this time in the name of a United Irishmen tourism of sorts.

Arguably, her most famous journey was that taken arm-in-arm with her brother from the artillery barracks to the gallows which stood outside Belfast's old Market House. Indeed, this has become perhaps the most vivid image of Mary Ann in local cultural memory. She related Henry's fate to Thomas Russell the very next day, including the detail that 'I accompanied him to the place of execution.'[82] Notably, in the draft version of this letter she refers more explicitly to 'the scaffold'.[83] In retelling this event some forty-four years later, Mary Ann elaborated: 'I took his arm, and we walked together to the place of execution.'[84] That night, having 'learned that no relative of his was likely to attend the funeral',[85] she courageously defied expectation and joined the procession. McCracken recalled that 'I could not bear to think that no member of his family should accompany his remains, so I set out to follow them to the grave.'[86]

PACING THE TOWN: MOVEMENT, HEALTH AND 'OUT OF DOOR AVOCATIONS'

What is clear from studying Mary Ann McCracken's extant correspondence (ranging from 1796 to 1861), her interview with Dr Madden and her step-grandniece's biography is that she was a woman in constant motion. Upon considering her childhood, McCleery surmised that her step-grandaunt 'must have been a very active child, since she accomplished the feat of hopping three times across High Street without stopping'.[87] McCleery further described her as 'always energetic' and as 'the moving spirit [who] worked early and late' at her business endeavours.[88] Mary Ann herself recalled that at times when this work kept her 'close confined', her morning trips to the post office induced her 'to leap and dance with delight in the fresh morning air'.[89]

Following the closure of the sisters' business and the death of their mother in 1814, Mary Ann channelled her energies into outdoor charitable work, admitting to a friend at the time: 'I have allowed my out-of-door avocations to increase so much, that I have less command of time now than when I was occupied with business.'[90] Four decades on, her commitment remained steadfast, as, at the age of eighty-three, she pronounced, 'I am stronger than I was two years ago & able to walk for two or three hours & sometimes four every dry day in my usual avocations.'[91] It is perhaps little wonder that several months later, when 'particularly occupied with [her] usual out of door avocations', she suffered 'an attack of illness', which was diagnosed by Dr Drennan as a cold, exacerbated by 'overexertion'.[92] This scenario played out again three years later when what Mary Ann dismissed as 'only a cold' saw her 'confined to the house for more than a month'.[93] Writing to Dr Madden towards the end of this illness, she vented her frustration at 'not yet [being] allowed to go out but on a tolerably good day', considering it 'my bounden duty, as well as the greatest pleasure which this world can afford, to promote the happiness of others & therefore feel it a hardship to be restrained from exertion, thinking it preferable to wear out than to rust out but I do not wish to fret Maria; she has so much to bear'.[94] It would appear that, if not for Maria, Mary Ann would have worn out a lot quicker than she did in the service of other peoples' happiness. Indeed, it later became clear that Mary Ann had been underplaying the toll of these exertions:

> A year ago, when I had been out for three or four hours collecting for some of our charities, I suffered so much pain below the small of my back for near the half of the way in returning, that I had to press my hand with all my might on the bone for relief but now I can walk home nearly as fast as I did thirty years ago without the slightest pain, but only a sleepiness which I indulge after dinner in my easy chair.[95]

Presumably, this disclosure was only made as the pain had since passed. While her agility may have returned, Maria's anxieties remained, as is evident from Mary Ann's description of her daily routine later in the letter: 'after tea I have other interesting occupations & some times, whenever I have leisure, Maria reads to me as I hear her best & besides, I take up enough of the young people's time in walks as I am not allowed to go out alone'.[96]

Despite the apparent concerns over her independent walks, both the 1860–1 and 1861–2 committee reports for the Belfast Ladies' Industrial National School for Girls list 'Miss McCracken' as the sole collector for 'District No. 2'.[97] This area encompassed:

> Royal Terrace, Wilmont Terrace, Fitzwilliam Street, University Terrace, Botanic View, University Square, Queen's College, Botanic Cottage, Prospect Terrace, Claremont Terrace, Fountainville

Terrace, Botanic Road, Wesley Place, William's Place, Great Victoria St, Kensington Terrace, Balmoral Terrace, Mount Charles, Albion Place, The Crescent, Pakenham Place, Victoria Terrace, Victoria Place, Breadalbane Place, Glengall Place, Donegall Pass, Glenfield Place, Ormeau Road, Queen's Elms and Bankmore.[98]

Clearly, this was no mean feat for a woman beginning her tenth decade! The report for 1862–3 placed Mary Ann in this district once again; however, during this year she was accompanied by 'Miss M'Cleery', her step-grandniece Anna.[99] Although McCracken served as president of the committee from 1860 until her death, her role as a collector ceased in 1864.[100] In the committee report for 1866–7, she was eulogised as one 'whose place was never vacant at our weekly meetings, as long as she was able to attend'.[101] She was similarly remembered by the Belfast Ladies' Clothing Society as 'a most energetic collector of its funds'.[102]

It is perhaps unsurprising, then, that Mary Ann was often to be found reflecting on the value of mobility and bodily vitality, as she did in a letter of 1859:

> Exercise in the open air is necessary to promote health & I know many such, who devote the most of their time to similar objects, not one of whom is so entirely free from pain as I am, & consequently it is my peculiar duty to endeavour to be useful while I can, & from long habit, & tho' unsteady in my gait if alone, & much stooped & bent to one side, yet I can walk for an hour sometimes without once sitting down, & be out for two or three hours of almost every fair day without feeling any inconvenience.[103]

In the preceding decades, a similar regard for outdoor activity may have informed her approach to the health of others, with the minutes of the Belfast Charitable Society's ladies' committee from the 1820s, 1830s and 1840s recording her involvement in resolutions supporting increased opportunities for the Poorhouse children to participate in exercise, outdoor play and educational walks in the area.

In her final extant letter, Mary Ann expressed thankfulness for her seemingly boundless energy:

I am in better health than for many years previously & entirely free from bodily pain for which, at 90 years of age, I cannot be sufficiently thankful, tho' my sight & hearing are greatly impaired & I stoop much & lean to the one side but am still able to go out on a fine day to collect for four public charities & sometimes for cases of private distress, all which gives an unspeakable charm to life.[104]

Evidently, Mary Ann benefited both physically and mentally from the causes she championed, and perhaps this drive to remain 'useful' for as long as possible itself contributed to her longevity. Her attitude towards her age may also have been a factor, given that at seventy she professed to be merely 'middle-aged'.[105]

As well as bolstering some aspects of her reputation, Mary Ann's letters also occasionally provide an ironic contrast to the near-legendary walker described in 1914 by historian Alice Milligan, whose account records that 'some still living have seen Mary [Ann McCracken] passing along the streets of Belfast, an aged woman, clad in sombre gown, to whom Catholic artisans raised their caps reverently'.[106] A similar street scene was described in a letter to her niece Eliza Tennent in 1846 but with access to her own (rather flustered) inner thoughts:

A few days ago I met a very young Lady, with two or three little girls, who smiled & saluted me as we passed each other in a hurry & tho' I returned the salute & thought I should know the countenance, it was not till afterwards, I imagined her very like your niece Mary,[107] & on looking back I saw two of [the] little girls turn round, & thought them like yours, but supposed they were there in the country.[108] Were your young folks the party I passed? Will you apologize for my stupidity?[109]

Here she strides through the streets full of life and energy, but this rather less-intimidating version of Mary Ann suggests that her famously purposeful movement could occasionally come at the expense of social awareness.

LOVE LETTERS AND HATE MAIL: MARY ANN ON BELFAST

Through her correspondence, we are granted a unique insight into Mary Ann's views and opinions on Belfast and its inhabitants. Over the years, she documented and reflected upon the development of the growing town, the state of its philanthropic activity, the fluctuating mood of its people and the impact of significant events in its history. What emerges is a complex love-hate relationship of the kind which perhaps accompanies a true sense of belonging.

In 1798, Mary Ann bitterly described her hometown as a place where 'death and desolation stalk around', where 'the late enthusiasm of the public mind seems sinking almost to despair' and where 'human sacrifices are become so frequent as scarcely to excite any emotion'.[110] It is little wonder, then, that the day after her brother's execution she informed Thomas Russell that 'it is probable we may never meet again, as Frank intends leaving this unhappy Country in a few days & the rest of the family mean to follow him as soon as he can prepare a place of refuge in some distant land'.[111] Accordingly, Francis set sail from Cobh, County Cork, for Jamaica on 22 August 1798, though the family did not follow and he returned to Belfast in October 1800. That Belfast may have been deprived of Mary Ann McCracken now seems inconceivable, with the place and person appearing with hindsight to be inextricably linked. Yet, had the family followed through on their plan, the town would indeed have been bereft of its 'moving spirit'.[112]

On more than one occasion, Mary Ann took a dim view of the townsfolk's sense of charity. When raising funds for Thomas Russell's sister in July 1803, Mary Ann declared that she was 'ashamed of the little benevolence in spirit shown in the town of Belfast',[113] while in 1845, after attending a public meeting 'for the purpose of ameliorating the condition of the poor', she wrote the following scathing critique:

> It lasted, I think, three hours & many fine long speeches made, all evidencing very proper feelings, in which the expression Lower Class was never once made use of. How presumptuous & sinful is the useless drones of the community, who never endeavour by any exertion to promote the public good & think of nothing but their

own selfish gratification, to despise those whose poverty is caused by want of employment or insufficient remuneration for the labour which procures the idlers all the comforts & luxuries of life, while those who labour cannot obtain common necessities in return.[114]

Two years later, at the height of the Great Famine, Mary Ann did acknowledge the town's charitable endeavours, yet also raised concerns that these efforts were being made at the expense of its own poor:

The exertions of Belfast to relieve the general destitution, have been considered by many as having been highly injurious to our own poor, by causing such an influx of strangers from the inducements of the Night Asylum,[115] & Day Asylum,[116] to which such numbers flocked, that no[ugh]t out of five taken daily to the Fever Hospitals[117] belonged to Belfast & fever patients were known to have been frequently brought by the Railway Train & laid down in the street.[118]

Mary Ann also bemoaned the demise of the anti-slavery movement in the town. Despite Belfast's initial abolitionist efforts (the Belfast Anti-Slavery Society was established in 1830, while the Belfast Ladies' Anti-Slavery Association came into being in 1845),[119] by 1859 Mary Ann was one of only a handful of remaining campaigners. She lamented to fellow abolitionist Dr Madden: 'I am sorry to say that Belfast once so celebrated for its love of liberty is now so sunk in the love of filthy lucre, that there are but 16 or 17 female anti-slavery advocates for the good cause, paying 2/6 yearly, not one man, tho' several Quakers in Belfast & none to distribute papers to American Emigrants but an old woman within 17 days of 89'.[120] Several months later she reiterated this sentiment:

I am both ashamed & sorry to think Belfast has so far degenerated in regard to the Antislavery cause. I wish the people of Dublin would endeavour to rouse them, no doubt you are aware that the men of Belfast gave the matter up more than three years ago, all but the late Capt[n] Calder[121] who was one of the most perfect of human begins, & worthy M[r] Stanfield[122] who is now so lame that he is unable to walk about as formerly, who had noticed them monthly for two years, regularly to attend the monthly meetings, during which, not a single member made their appearance & now there are but 16 or 17 Ladies who meet occasionally & are the only advocates in Belfast of the good cause.[123]

Yet Mary Ann also took a degree of pride in her hometown. In 1849, she wrote to her niece Eliza Tennent in anticipation of her return from London, remarking, 'You will then see many great improvements in the appearance of Belfast, & in many other aspects of more importance than mere appearance.'[124] Several months later she further enthused, 'the health of the town is much improved of late & of course there is an increase of general happiness',[125] while in her final extant letter to her niece Mary Ann she wrote optimistically, 'I hope, my dear Eliza, that you continue recovering strength daily, & that on your return to Belfast you will be able to visit every part of the town, & see all the wonderful changes, (many of which are great improvements) which have taken place during your absence.'[126] Unfortunately, Eliza died five months later in London, dashing Mary Ann's hopes that her niece might experience these developments for herself. More specific examples of such improvements are provided in a letter of 1857 which saw her 'quite delighted'[127] with the latest additions to the town, namely the Belfast Model School and a nunnery.[128]

Over the course of her ninety-six years, Mary Ann made her mark through a variety of political, historiographical, educational, commercial and philanthropic activities. From her involvement with the United Irishmen and the preservation of their memory to her presidency of the Belfast Ladies' Anti-Slavery Association, Mary Ann proved an influential figure in many spheres and an indefatigable mainstay of the Society marked by the present volume.

Fittingly, she was interred in the Charitable Society's burial ground, now known as Clifton Street Cemetery. The grave remained unmarked until May 1909, when local antiquarians Francis Joseph Bigger and Robert May erected a small Mountcharles headstone over the plot. On that same occasion, May reinterred what were believed to be Henry Joy McCracken's remains:

A hermetically sealed phial was placed in the coffer, with the following inscription written on the parchment:– 'These bones were dug up in the old graveyard in High Street in 1902, and from several circumstances are believed to be those of Henry Joy McCracken. They were reverently treated and placed here by Robert May, of Belfast, 12 May, 1909, when the monument was placed to the memory of his beloved sister'.[129]

What is striking about the inscription on the monument is the emphasis on her status relative to Henry, with Mary described as his 'beloved sister' and as having 'wept by her brother's scaffold'. The ensuing epitaph 'Dileas go h-Eag' ('loyal until death') was perhaps intended as a reference to her commitment to her brother's memory. However, considering her mental and physical dedication to Belfast and the welfare of its people, it might just as easily be interpreted as honouring the longevity of what her obituary described as a truly 'active temperament'.[130]

Belfast Charitable Society in the Twenty-first Century

Paula Reynolds and David Watters

℘

The contributions to this volume provide us with valuable insights into the wider social, economic and political conditions prevailing at the time when the Belfast Charitable Society began its life and journeyed through the early and formative decades of its existence. On reading these essays we can understand how social and political changes within the wider world impacted on issues such as social welfare and reform, social justice, disadvantage and, crucially, on peoples' lives in the emerging city of Belfast. These same changes created challenges as well as opportunities for the Society, and, having faced them on numerous occasions, it emerged more resilient and steadfast in its purpose.

Two earlier pieces of work have successfully detailed the history and development of the Society: Dr Strain's detailed story of the organisation from its inception to the passing of the Poor Laws, and Dr Bardon's work which considered its first 250 years and was produced to mark that anniversary.[1] Both conclude by bringing their account of the organisation up to date at time of publication – 1960 and 2002 respectively. In part, their concluding chapters create a natural close to the authors' work but, more importantly, they begin to tell us about how the Society continues to transition and change form in order to meet the ever-changing needs of those 'appearing to the Society to be disadvantaged'.[2] They introduce new stages of the Society's life as it edges ever closer to its three-hundredth year.

In concluding, Strain advises us that societal changes were directly affecting the care and housing needs of older people even in the 1950s. He states that 'although no state income is received', some residents of Clifton House were reliant on the good will of local welfare institutions; however, there was a sense that those applying to move into the home faced a 'poverty of care and affection'.[3] The Society's own Annual Report of 1951 stated that 'Homes [for older people] have become more than ever a social necessity as families can no longer afford space for their older relatives in their houses.'[4] Bardon, reflecting on the period around the latter part of the twentieth century until 2002, emphasises how change in the regulation of care for older people was the key driver that led to the transformation of the Society and the use of Clifton House at that time.

This epilogue briefly considers the period from the mid-1990s to the present day, a time that has witnessed change at a rate and scale that can only be compared to the Society's early days. It has included the enactment of modernised governing legislation; large-scale building schemes, including the refurbishment and change of use of Clifton House; the end of delivery of direct care of older people; the introduction of a range of heritage services to tell the Society's story; the delivery of an enhanced programme of philanthropy; and the establishment of a new foundation to celebrate the life and work of Mary Ann McCracken. All of this was led and managed by a series of dedicated and committed presidents, boards, committees and staff.

TOWARDS THE MILLENNIUM

In the early years of this period, those leading up to the new millennium, the Society was faced with the challenge of having to react to changes in the delivery of care for older people, as well as to demographic changes in the local area. In the area of older people's care, regulation was changing rapidly and, at the same time, increasing demands were being placed on services as needs and expectations became more complex and varied.

This all took place without any additional external resources or support. The area of Belfast in which Clifton House sits, on the edge of North Belfast, was and remains an area of high socio-economic deprivation. The area was severely affected by the length and ferocity of the Troubles and the legacy of that conflict remains visible in the widespread segregation of the local community. Yet, in the period under discussion, many positive conversations had begun to take place in which regeneration opportunities and possibilities are being explored.

It was against this backdrop that, in 1995, the Society took decisive action to change how and where it delivered care to older people to ensure that the organisation would survive the upheaval in social care and the changes in the world around it. Bardon concurs that 'the decision that the [Society's] Board came to at its meeting on 23 May 1995 was as important as the decision to establish the Society some 243 years earlier'.[5] He was referring to the decision to build a new nursing home, which would allow the Society to continue to deliver the same high standard of care that it had been doing for more than 200 years, whilst operating within the new regulatory requirements. Staying true to its ethos and reflecting past building projects, such as the Poorhouse, the Society chose to build a state-of-the-art nursing home nearby at Carlisle Circus – future-proofing the provision of care for older people while creating an important catalyst for local physical and economic regeneration.

As with most charities, large-scale capital ventures of this scale require organisational change. Essentially, this came in the form of a need to modernise the act of parliament that governed the Society, as discussed in an earlier chapter in this volume. On 18 July 1996, the House of Lords passed the fifth piece of legislation pertaining to the Society in what was its 244-year history. In doing so, the Belfast Charitable Society Act 1996 was enacted into law and modernised the objects, powers, constitution and management of the Society. The original mission was re-enforced through the statement of the objects: 'to pursue all or any charitable activities which advance the interests or are for the benefit of persons appearing to the Society to be disadvantaged ... including the care of the elderly, the relief of poverty, homelessness, distress, infirmity and sickness ... and to participate in all forms of co-operation ... to achieve any of the objects'.[6]

Guided by the new legislation, the Society could now go about making its building project a reality. It approved an investment of £5 million of its own funds into the new nursing home project but required a further £1 million to complete the task. It enlisted the support and expertise of Lady Moyra Quigley, who rose to the challenge by spearheading the Society's third ever public fundraising appeal – the Home from Home appeal. She encouraged private subscriptions, business donations, fundraising efforts such as abseiling, and secured grants including £400,000 from the National Lottery Charities Board. In total, over £1m was raised, ensuring the project's viability, and so building began almost immediately. Clifton Nursing Home was opened on 21 June 2001, catering for the housing and care needs of 100 older people and supporting 100 jobs in a state-of-the-art care facility.

The board's decision in May 1995 not only precipitated the need for legislative change and culminated in the new building project but it also meant that Clifton House, the Society's home since 1752, could be reoriented. As per its second object, the Society looked to 'co-operate' with another strategic partner, the local housing association Belfast Improvement Housing (BIH). This partnership approach ensured this substantial asset could still meet the housing needs of older people. A seventy-year lease of the house and grounds was granted to BIH, with exclusive access to the boardroom and subsequently the central part of the building being retained by the Society. The housing association then went about a major refurbishment of the Grade 'A' listed building to build fifty sheltered housing units: thirty-nine in Clifton House, the refurbished Gate Lodge and ten in new-build mews; and a twenty-seven-bed residential supported care unit. BIH met the accommodation refurbishment project cost, which was completed in 2002.

Once re-opened, the Society took on the operational management of the residential care unit, delivering the contract on behalf of the housing association and ensuring that the care, housing and social needs of the residents were met. With the new-build nursing home located at Carlisle Circus and a totally refurbished Clifton House in close proximity, the Society started the new century (and millennium) again at the forefront of provision of tailored care for some of the most vulnerable in Belfast's population.

MOVING OUT OF CARE

As noted, the Society retained exclusive access to the central historic core of Clifton House. It now invested almost £300,000 of its own funds and secured grant aid from the Heritage Lottery Fund to create the interpretative centre, which opened in May 2003. This was an important move as, in addition to its role in looking after those in need, the Society recognised the need to do more to profile its 'interesting and honourable history'.[7] The development of Clifton House as one of Belfast's key heritage sites, the protection and development of built and cultural heritage in this part of Belfast more widely and the public dissemination of Belfast Charitable Society's fascinating and important history were now recognised as something worth investing in if the potential of this rich heritage to promote the social regeneration of the area was to be realised.

By September 2005, as the Society's accounts for that year reveal, its main focus was on developing the role of Clifton House 'both in areas of education and heritage promotion ... [and] to involve itself to a greater extent in the community either solely or in partnership'.[8] It is also evident from these accounts that the massive undertaking of establishing the nursing home and operating it in tandem with the residential care unit was working efficiently, which perhaps explains why the board was confident enough to establish heritage as its new focus of attention at this time. As the decade progressed, however, the scale and challenges of the nursing home venture became more apparent. The burden of increasing care dependencies, regulatory and related management requirements, service delivery and rising costs meant that the nursing home started to create significant financial pressure. The Society's history of being a considerable and considerate employer now also started to affect the bottom line, as the costs associated with defined benefit pension schemes soared. The Society had endeavoured to look after its employees throughout their lifetimes with generous employment terms, but this was beginning to have detrimental implications for the sustainability of the organisation.

In November 2007 the members elected a new president, Lady Quigley, and new chairperson, Lorna Anderson. They were about to encounter some of the most trying times the organisation has had to face in its long history. By late 2008 nursing care costs had increased dramatically due to the introduction of new minimum requirements for healthcare and a series of staff-related costs. The latter included the need to police check new staff, the related dependency on agency costs and the rising employers' contribution to the pension scheme. The Society's own investments also suffered due to the impact of the 2008 financial crash. The problems continued to escalate, and in November 2010 the 239th annual general meeting was advised that costs had risen by 27 per cent and further losses were anticipated in the coming year. By November 2013, it was reported that the Society had made '£2 million of its own money available to support the nursing home'.[9] The burden of governance and management had become too complex and challenging. The minutes note that the members and the board 'therefore reached the unavoidable conclusion that the Society should step back from its involvement in the Care Home business and should negotiate an agreement with a professional care home provider'.[10]

On 14 January 2014, Belfast Charitable Society transferred the responsibility of care provision by leasing the nursing home and entire service to a third-party provider. The scale of this decision should not be underestimated, and it was not taken lightly; however, it was considered to have been in the best interests of residents, staff and the organisation itself. The Society did retain the responsibility of the operation of the residential unit at Clifton House but noted in its accounts of 2014 that this, too, would be transferred to a third-party provider in the near future.[11] The benefits of the move away from direct care provision became immediately clear. The level of risk and threat had been removed and a substantial annual income stream had been created through the very commercial nursing home lease.

MAKING OUR PAST OUR FUTURE

The board then embarked on a new strategic direction, visioning for the future while remaining steadfast to the original objects and mission – to address disadvantage. The first sizable step the Society took in shaping its new strategy came in the form of a £250,000 grant to the Northern Ireland Hospice: £100,000 capital costs allocation for its Research and

Education Centre and the reminder supporting ongoing costs over a three-year period. This covered a range of costs including vital training for staff in holistic palliative dementia care; respite for teenagers; and a transformational change project to adapt service delivery to prevent hospital admissions and to ensure end-of-life care at home. In September 2015, the board appointed its first chief executive officer and soon after launched its new strategic plan, 'Making Our Past Our Future'.[12] The plan's vision was (and remained to 2022) 'to be the recognised leader in the provision of progressive, relevant and philanthropic charitable work in Belfast and the wider community'. Its mission committed the organisation 'to preserving, promoting and utilising the philanthropic heritage of the Society to address disadvantage'. These high-level aspirations were translated into a set of operational aims focused on philanthropy, heritage, care of older people and, latterly, the Mary Ann McCracken Foundation, to be delivered through a range of projects and partnerships.

Regarding its work 'to lead and influence on how philanthropy is delivered and developed', the Society invested in the Building Better Futures Fund which provided loans to grassroots groups who address disadvantage, encouraging them to move away from complete grant dependency. It manages the funds of other philanthropic organisations, such as the Barbour Fund, which supports people from less well-off backgrounds to improve their lives by enhancing their employability, providing activities to reduce the isolation felt by older people and developing educational resources for young people outside of mainstream education. The Society delivers its own annual programme of grants that has included providing bursaries for young adults from low-income backgrounds and direct financial support for families in crisis. The latter is reminiscent of some elements of the Society's outdoor relief scheme that ran 200 years ago.

The Society also provides financial support, skills and expertise to a local heritage-led regeneration project in north Belfast – working to transform the physical environment, local economy, community engagement and image of the area, while building the resilience of fourteen local organisations. It was instrumental in establishing the North Belfast Heritage Cluster and now leads its Great Place North Belfast Project, funded by the National Lottery Heritage Fund.[13] The Cluster has been extremely successful in helping to bring the diverse group of voluntary organisations who have responsibility for the stewardship of sixteen heritage buildings and sites in an area stretching just over one mile from the city centre. The Great Place project has resourced an array of activities including the development of urban design guidelines for potential developers in Clifton Street; the redesign of the road and streetscape to accommodate the needs of pedestrians, cyclists and road users and the creation of places such as small urban parklets; archival management tools and improved access to the massive social history associated with the Cluster members, while telling their intriguing stories through a comprehensive social media campaign; development of local tourism opportunities through the creation of a heritage trail; and working with partner organisations to develop a weekend programme of events to celebrate the heritage and culture of north Belfast.

At Clifton House, the Society educates and informs visitors about philanthropy, the influence it has had on the development of Belfast and its role in addressing disadvantage. This has created and sustained jobs and volunteer posts. Interlinked with this, it fulfils its custodial role by preserving and safeguarding the House and its vast archive collection.

Today's Belfast Charitable Society works hard to remain true to the original ethos and values of 1752. It remains self-reliant and independent from government, enabling it to take well-measured and informed risks and to be flexible to address emerging need. This was very evident in March 2020 when COVID-related restrictions led to enforced home schooling. Within a matter of days, the Society had offered a £10,000 grant, leveraged an additional £40,000 and purchased 225 laptops for pupils from less well-off backgrounds in north Belfast.

Later in 2020, and in response to the international outcry about inequality and racism after the death of George Floyd and the Black Lives Matter campaigns, the Society decided to use its keynote event, the launch of the Mary Ann McCracken Foundation, to open a discussion about 'Legacies of Slavery'. In January 2021, over 400 people engaged via an online platform in a thought-provoking session delivered by the award-winning Professor David Olusoga. The audience was confronted with the complexities and contradictions of philanthropy and slavery in the past and the continued relevance of these issues today. The Foundation will take forward discussions of this nature to ensure that the social reform advocated for by figures such as Mary Ann McCracken lives on.

The Society has other exciting plans to transform the local economic and physical environment through the purchase and renovation of property and its lobbying role for substantial urban improvement projects. Moving forward, it will use its own physical assets to continue to care for the needs of older people. It will use its base at Clifton House to facilitate discussion that will educate and agitate thinking about poverty and inequality. And it will work with a wide range of strategic and trusted partners to keep the needs of the disadvantaged to the fore, with 'determination to endeavour to do the right thing at all times'.

Endnotes

☙

INTRODUCTION

1   Jonathan Jeffrey Wright, *The 'Natural Leaders' and Their World: Politics, Culture and Society in Belfast c. 1801–1832* (Liverpool, 2012), p. 21.

2   Dominic Bryan and S.J. Connolly, with John Nagle, *Civic Identity and Public Space: Belfast Since 1780* (Manchester, 2019), p. 36.

3   For a discussion of the rise of urban gentry in the late seventeenth to mid-eighteenth centuries, see Jon Stobart, 'Who were the urban gentry? Social elites in an English provincial town, c. 1680–1760', *Continuity and Change*, vol. 26, pt 1 (2011), pp. 89–112.

4   W.H. Crawford 'The Belfast middle classes in the late eighteenth-century', in David Dickson, Dáire Keogh and Kevin Whelan (eds), *The United Irishmen: Republicanism, Radicalism and Rebellion* (Dublin, 1993), p. 64.

5   Pieter Tesch, 'Presbyterian radicalism', in Dickson, Whelan and Keogh (eds), *The United Irishmen*, pp. 33–48.

6   Quoted in S.J. Connolly, 'Improving town 1750–1820', in S.J. Connolly (ed.), *Belfast 400: People, Place and History* (Liverpool, 2012), p. 182.

7   Ibid.

8   Ibid., p. 184.

9   R.J. Morris, 'Voluntary societies and British urban elites, 1780–1850: An analysis', *The Historical Journal*, vol. 26, no. 1 (1983), pp. 95–118.

10 J.R.R. Adams, *The Printed Word and the Common Man: Popular Culture in Ulster 1700–1900* (Belfast, 1987), p. 9.

11 Alice Johnson, 'The civic elite of nineteenth-century Belfast', *Irish Economic and Social History*, vol. 43, iss. 1 (2016), p. 66.

12 Ian Budge and Cornelius O'Leary, *Belfast: Approach to Crisis. A Study of Belfast Politics 1613–1970* (London, 1973), p. 16.

13 Ibid., p. 8.

14 Ibid., p. 28.

15   Connolly, 'Improving town', pp. 162–4, 178.

16   Ibid., p. 179.

17   R.W.M. Strain, *Belfast and its Charitable Society: A Story of Urban Social Development* (London, 1961), p. 13.

18   For a discussion of poverty in pre-Famine Ireland, see Joel Mokyr, 'Industrialization and poverty in Ireland and the Netherlands', *The Journal of Interdisciplinary History*, vol. 10, no. 3 (Winter 1980), pp. 429–58.

19   Douglas Larmar Jones, 'The strolling poor: Transiency in eighteenth-century Massachusetts', *Journal of Social History*, vol. 8, no. 3 (Spring 1975), pp. 28–54.

20   Ciarán McCabe, *Begging, Charity and Religion in pre-Famine Ireland* (Liverpool, 2018), p. 1.

21   Ibid., p. 3.

22   Raymond Gillespie, 'Making Belfast, 1600–1750', in Connolly (ed.), *Belfast 400*, p. 158.

23   Ibid.

24   Strain, *Belfast and its Charitable Society*, pp. 23–4.

25   R.M.W. Strain, 'The history and associations of the Belfast Charitable Society'. Address given to the Ulster Medical Society, 13 November 1952, printed in *Ulster Medical Journal*, vol. 22, no. 1 (May 1953), p. 34.

26   13 and 14 Geo. 3 c46 (Ir) (1774), Quoted in Strain, 'The history and associations', p. 36.

27   Belfast Charitable Society website, https://belfastcharitablesociety.org/about-us/our-mission/ (accessed 08/10/ 2021).

28   Strain, *Belfast and its Charitable Society*.

29   Jonathan Bardon, *An Interesting and Honourable History: The Belfast Charitable Society, the First 250 Years, 1752–2002* (Belfast, 2002).

30   Anna Clark, 'Wild workhouse girls and the Liberal imperial state in mid-nineteenth century Ireland', *Journal of Social History*, vol. 39, no. 2 (2005), pp. 389–409; Virginia Crossman, *Politics, Power and Pauperism in Late Nineteenth-century Ireland* (Manchester, 2006); Mel Cousins, 'Registration of the religion of children under the Irish Poor Law, 1838–1870', *Journal of Ecclesiastical History*, vol. 61, no. 1 (2010), pp. 107–24; essays in Virginia Crossman and Peter Gray (eds), *Poverty and Welfare in Ireland 1838–1948* (Dublin, 2011); Virginia Crossman and Donnacha Seán Lucey, '"One huge abuse": The Cork Board of Guardians and the expansion of outdoor relief in post-Famine Ireland', *English Historical Review*, vol. 126, no. 523 (2011), pp. 1408–29; Virginia Crossman, *Poverty and the Poor Law in Ireland 1850–1914* (Liverpool, 2013); Olwen Purdue, '"A gigantic system of casual pauperism": The contested role of the workhouse in late nineteenth-century Belfast', in Beate Althammer, Andreas Gestrich and Jens Gründler (eds), *The Welfare State and the 'Deviant Poor' in Europe, 1870–1933* (Basingstoke, 2014); Olwen Purdue, 'Surviving the industrial city: The female poor and the workhouse in late nineteenth-century Belfast', *Urban History*, vol. 44, no. 1 (2017), pp. 69–90; Olwen Purdue, 'Nineteenth-century Nimbys, or what the neighbour saw? Poverty, surveillance, and the boarding-out of Poor Law

children in late nineteenth-century Belfast', *Family & Community History*, vol. 23, no. 2 (2020), pp. 119–135; Simon Gallaher, 'Children and childhood under the Irish Poor Law, *c*. 1850–1914' (PhD thesis, Cambridge University, 2019).

31   McCabe, *Begging, Charity and Religion*; Alison Jordan, *Who Cared? Charity in Victorian and Edwardian Belfast* (Belfast, 1992); Maria Luddy, *Women and Philanthropy in Nineteenth-century Ireland* (Cambridge, 1995); Margaret H. Preston, *Charitable Words: Women, Philanthropy and the Language of Charity in Nineteenth-century Dublin* (Westport, 2004); essays in Laurence M. Geary and Oonagh Walsh (eds), *Philanthropy in Nineteenth-century Ireland* (Dublin, 2015).

32   Ronald Cassell, *Medical Charities, Medical Politics: The Irish Dispensary System and the Poor Law, 1836–1872* (Woodbridge, 1997); Greta Jones and Elizabeth Malcolm (eds), *Medicine, Disease and the State in Ireland, 1650–1940* (Cork, 1999); Greta Jones, *'Captain of all these men of death': The History of Tuberculosis in Nineteenth and Twentieth Century Ireland* (Amsterdam, 2001); L.M. Geary, *Medicine and Charity in Ireland 1718–1851* (Dublin, 2004); essays in Catherine Cox and Maria Luddy (eds), *Cultures of Care in Irish Medical History, 1750–1970* (Basingstoke, 2010); essays in Donnacha Séan Lucey and Virginia Crossman (eds), *Healthcare in Ireland and Britain from 1850: Voluntary, Regional and Comparative Perspectives* (London, 2014); Ciara Breathnach, 'Medical officers, bodies, gender and weight fluctuation in Irish convict prisons, 1877–95', *Medical History*, vol. lviii, no. 1 (2014), pp. 67–86; Ciara Breathnach, 'Handywomen and birthing in rural Ireland, 1851–1955', *Gender & History*, vol. xxviii, no. 1 (2016), pp. 34–56; Robyn Lori Atcheson, 'Poverty, poor relief and public health in Belfast *c*. 1800–1851', (PhD thesis, Queen's University Belfast, 2018); Ida Milne, *Stacking the Coffins: Influenza, War and Revolution in Ireland 1918–19* (Manchester, 2018).

33   Virginia Crossman, 'Cribbed, contained and confined? The care of children under the Irish Poor Law, 1850–1920', *Éire-Ireland*, vol. xliv (2009); essays in Alice Mauger and Anne MacLellan (eds), *Growing Pains: Childhood Illness in Ireland, 1750–1950* (Dublin, 2013); C.J. Gilleard, *Old Age in Nineteenth-century Ireland: Ageing under the Union* (London, 2017).

34   Jacinta Prunty, *Dublin Slums, 1800–1925: A Study in Urban Geography* (Dublin, 1998).

35   T.W. Guinnane and Cormac Ó Gráda, 'Mortality in the North Dublin Union during the Great Famine', *The Economic History Review*, vol. lv, no. 3 (2002), pp. 487–506.

36   Connolly (ed.), *Belfast 400*; David Dickson, *Dublin: The Making of a Capital City* (London, 2014); John Cunningham, *A Town Tormented by the Sea: Galway, 1790–1914* (Dublin, 2004); David Dickson, *Old World Colony: Cork and South Munster 1630–1830* (Cork, 2005); Matthew Potter, *The Government and the People of Limerick: The History of Limerick Corporation/City Council, 1197–2006* (Limerick, 2006); Bradley and Michael O'Dwyer (eds), *Kilkenny Through the Centuries: Chapters in the History of an Irish City* (Kilkenny, 2009).

37   John Lynch, *A Tale of Three Cities: Comparative Studies in Working-Class Life* (London, 1998); Raymond Gillespie, *Early Belfast: The Origins and Growth of an Ulster Town to 1750* (Belfast, 2007); W.A. Maguire, *Belfast: A History* (Lancaster,

new ed. 2009); essays in Olwen Purdue (ed.), *Belfast, The Emerging City 1850–1914* (Dublin, 2012); Kyle Hughes, *The Scots in Victorian and Edwardian Belfast: A Study in Elite Migration* (Edinburgh, 2013); Sean Farrell, 'Feed my lambs: The Reverend Thomas Drew and Protestant children in early Victorian Belfast', *New Hibernia Review*, vol. 19, no. 2 (Summer 2015), pp. 43–58; Diarmid A. Finnegan and Jonathan Jeffrey Wright, 'Catholics, science and civic culture in Victorian Belfast', *British Journal for the History of Science*, vol. 48, no. 2 (2015), pp. 261–87; Lesley E.E. Donaldson, '"A street of butchers": An economic and social profile of Hercules Place and Hercules Street, Belfast 1860–90', *Irish Economic and Social History*, vol. 44 (2017) pp. 102–21; essays in Georgina Laragy, Olwen Purdue and Jonathan Jeffrey Wright (eds), *Urban Spaces in Nineteenth-century Ireland* (Liverpool, 2018); Stuart Irwin, 'Managing a mature industrial city: Belfast Corporation 1874–96' (PhD thesis, Queen's University Belfast, 2019); Alice Johnson, *Middle-class Life in Victorian Belfast* (Liverpool, 2020).

38 Kenneth L. Dawson, *The Belfast Jacobin: Samuel Neilson and the United Irishmen* (Newbridge, 2017).

39 Radical MP, J.A. Roebuck, writing in 1868. Quoted in Lauren M.E. Goodlad, '"Making the working man like me": Charity, pastorship, and middle-class identity in nineteenth-century Britain; Thomas Chalmers and Dr. James Phillips Kay', *Victorian Studies*, vol. 43, no. 4 (Summer 2001), p. 591.

40 John Ó Neill, see Chapter 9 in this volume.

41 Cathryn McWilliams, see Chapter 11 in this volume.

CHAPTER ONE: BELFAST CHARITABLE SOCIETY AND LEGISLATION

1 13 and 14 Geo. 3 c46 (Ir) (1774). Early legislation may be referred to by the regnal year and a chapter number and a long title. Some early acts were later given formal short titles and some acts have acquired popular short titles.

2 11 and 12 Geo. 3 c30 (Ir) (1772).

3 Richard Woodward, Dean of Clogher (1764–81) published pamphlets in the 1760s advocating county poorhouses and hospitals and a system of badging beggars and punishment for those fit for labour. Mel Cousins, 'The Irish Parliament and relief of the poor: The 1772 legislation establishing houses of industry', *Eighteenth-Century Ireland*, vol. 28 (2013), pp. 95–115.

4 33 Hen 8 c15 (Ir) (1542) dealing with begging and vagrancy and 10 & 11 Chas 1 c4 (Ir) (1634–5) dealing with houses of correction. Workhouses were established in Dublin by 2 Anne c19 (Ir) (1703) and in Cork by 9 Geo. 2 c6 (Ir) (1735).

5 For a history of the Society see R.W.M. Strain, *Belfast and its Charitable Society: A Story of Urban Social Development* (Oxford, 1961).

6 Belfast Charitable Society [hereafter BCS] Archive, Committee Minute Books, 1771–4, p. 217.

7 7 Geo. 3 c3 (Ir) (1768) established eight-year parliaments to replace parliaments for the life of the monarch.

8   33 Hen. 8 c1 (Ir) (1541).

9   10 Hen. 7 c4 (Ir) (1494). Sir Edward Poynings (1459–1521) was Lord Deputy of Ireland in 1494–5.

10   James Kelly, *Poynings' Law and the Making of Law in Ireland 1660–1800* (Dublin, 2007) p. 8.

11   6 Geo. 1 c5 (1719).

12   R.F.G. Holmes, *Our Irish Presbyterian Heritage* (Belfast, 1985) p. 58.

13   Arthur Chichester (1739–99), MP at Westminster for a Wiltshire constituency 1768–74, became the first marquis of Donegall in 1791.

14   George Hamilton (1732–93), son of Alexander Hamilton, MP for Killyleagh for twenty years to 1759. Henry Skeffington (1744–1811) succeeded by his brother Chichester as the 4th earl of Masserene.

15   William Bristow (1735–1808). Waddell Cunningham (1729–97), president of the Belfast Chamber of Commerce and Belfast Harbour Board.

16   The First and Third Presbyterian were non-subscribing churches. James Makay was minister of First from 1756 until he died in 1781. James Cromby (1730–90) joined Makay in 1769 and remained until his death. Rev. John McBride, minister of First in 1704, refused to take the oath of abjuration and went into exile in Scotland. He fared better than Rev. McCracken of Lisburn, as he returned to Belfast in 1708 to take charge of Second. William Laird was minister of Third from 1747 to 1791, and Mary Ann and Henry Joy and the McCracken family were members.

17   John Barkley, 'Late Eighteenth Century Belfast and St Mary's Chapel Lane 1784–1831', *Ulster Genealogical Review*, vol. 2, no. 2 (1986), p. 82.

18   Dr Cornelius Denvir (1791–1865) held the chair of natural philosophy and mathematics at Maynooth College and later combined work as the parish priest at Downpatrick and teaching duties at St Malachy's College before becoming bishop of Down and Connor.

19   BCS Archive, Committee Minute Books, 1771–4.

20   BCS Archive, Committee Minute Books, 1775–6.

21   40 Geo. 3 c37 (Ir) (1800).

22   The Irish parliament passed the Act of Union (Ireland) 1800 (40 Geo. 3 c38 (Ir)) and the Great Britain parliament passed the Union with Ireland Act 1800 (39 & 40 Geo. 3 c67).

23   Edward May (1751–1814) became manager of the Donegall properties. William John Skeffington (1747–1811), MP for Antrim 1768–1800.

24   George Chichester (1769–1844). W.A. Maguire, *Living Like a Lord: The Second Marquis of Donegall 1769–1844* (Belfast, 2002), p. 7.

25   25 Geo. 3 c64 (Ir) (1785).

26   Fred Heatley, *Henry Joy McCracken and His Times* (Belfast, 1967), pp. 45–7.

27   Mary McNeill, revised by Cathryn McWilliams, *Mary Ann McCracken 1770–1786: A Belfast Panorama* (first published 1960; revised ed., Dublin, 2019).

28   Geo. 3 c57 (1817).

29 Sir Stephen May (1781–1845) was one of Bonaparte's 'detenus'. In the war with Napoleon, the British placed an embargo on French vessels in their ports. The response was the seizure of British citizens in France who were imprisoned or granted parole in local areas and were known as Bonaparte's detenus.

30 Strain, *Belfast and its Charitable Society*, pp. 212–41.

31 Representation of the People (Ireland) Act 1832 (2 and 3 Will. 4 c88), known as The Great Reform Act. The boundaries were changed by the Parliamentary Boundaries (Ireland) Act 1832 (2 and 3 Will. 4 c89).

32 Municipal Corporations (Ireland) Act 1840 (3 & 4 Vict. c108).

33 Brian Griffin, *The Bulkies: Police and Crime in Belfast 1800–1865* (Dublin, 1997), p. 6.

34 3 Vict. c88 (1840).

35 Belfast Water Act 1840 (3 Vict. c79).

36 The Poor Relief (Ireland) Act 1938 (42 Vict. c56).

37 BCS Archive, Committee Minute Books, 1835–45. Lord Morpeth (1802–64), chief secretary 1835–41.

38 BCS Archive, General Board Minutes 1828–89.

39 A.R. Hart, *A History of the King's Serjeants at Law in Ireland* (Dublin, 2000), pp. 167 and 184.

40 See Olwen Purdue '"A gigantic system of casual pauperism": The contested role of the workhouse in late nineteenth-century Belfast', in Beate Althammer, Andreas Gestrich and Jens Gründler (eds), *The Welfare State and the 'Deviant Poor' in Europe, 1870–1933* (Basingstoke, 2014); 'Surviving the industrial city: The female poor and the workhouse in late nineteenth-century Belfast', *Urban History*, vol. 44, no. 1 (2017), pp. 69–90.

41 BCS Archive, Annual Report 1845.

42 Maguire, *Living like a Lord*, p. 90.

43 Belfast Charitable Society Act 1996 (Chapter vi).

CHAPTER TWO: A HOUSE DIVIDED

1 BCS Archive, Committee Minute Books, 1791–4, 17 December 1791. Equiano is recorded as Gustavus Vasa [*sic*], his slave name and the one used in the frontispiece of the London (1789) and New York (1791) editions of his *Narrative*.

2 N. Rodgers, *Equiano and Anti-slavery in Eighteenth-century Belfast* (Belfast, 2000), pp. 6–12; *Belfast News-Letter*, 16–20 December 1791; O. Equiano, *The Interesting Narrative and Other Writings* (London, 2003 ed.), p. 235. Neilson was a subscriber to the Irish edition of Equiano's narrative, taking five copies (list of subscribers p. 380). At the Belfast commemoration of the fall of the Bastille on 14 July 1791, a banner proclaimed the message 'Can the African Slave Trade, tho' morally wrong, be politically right', and at a dinner that evening in the White Linen Hall, the nineteenth of twenty-eight toasts was 'To the society for abolishing the slave trade',

Belfast News-Letter, 15–19 July 1791. Thomas Russell and Mary Ann McCracken were well known for their refusal to consume sugar.

3   William Drennan to Martha McTier, 17 May 1806, in J. Agnew (ed.), *The Drennan-McTier Letters III* (Dublin, 1998), p. 480. Cunningham, one of Belfast's wealthiest businessmen, owned a slave plantation in Dominica which he named 'Belfast'.

4   While Cunningham's scheme had been halted, Belfast imported raw cotton and sugar in large quantities from plantations in North America and the West Indies, triggering the consciences of some of the inhabitants. A contributor (signed BC) to Neilson's newspaper, *The Northern Star* (hereafter *NS*), in April 1792 proclaimed, 'Now if it be admitted that the consumption of West India produce (especially rum and sugar) is the sole support of this trade, every individual, as far as he consumes, becomes accessory to the guilt', *NS*, 14–18 April 1792. William Cowper's famous poem 'The Negro's Complaint' was published in the second edition of *NS*, 4–7 January 1792.

5   R.J. Morris, 'Voluntary societies and British urban elites, 1780–1850: An analysis', *The Historical Journal*, vol. 26, no. 1 (1983), pp. 95–118.

6   J. Killen, *A History of the Linen Hall Library, 1788–1988* (Belfast, 1990), pp. 1–13.

7   A.T.Q. Stewart, *Belfast Royal Academy: The First Century, 1785–1885* (Antrim, 1985), p. 3. All of those mentioned were Volunteers. Sinclaire, the Simms and Magee were all future United Irishmen.

8   *Belfast Mercury* [hereafter *BM*], 20 March 1786; *The Belfast Evening Post* [hereafter *BEP*], 26 June 1786. By June, 270 children were attending.

9   *BEP*, 22 June 1786.

10   R.W.M. Strain, *Belfast and its Charitable Society: A Story of Urban Social Development* (London, 1961), p. 52.

11   BCS Archive, General Board Minutes, 6 May 1778.

12   BCS Archive, Committee Minutes, 31 October 1781; 14 December 1782 for O'Neill's donation. O'Neill later became one of the two reformist MPs for County Antrim. He was killed by an insurgent at the battle of Antrim on 7 June 1798.

13   William Brown was a merchant and banker as well as a Volunteer, *NS*, 27 November–1 December 1794. For Greg, Hamilton and Cunningham, *NS*, 23–26 December 1796 and 27 February–3 March 1797; *Belfast News-Letter* [hereafter *BNL*], 18 December 1797.

14   *BM*, 6 March 1786. Other performances in aid of the Poorhouse included the comic opera *The Maid of the Mill* and a staging of *Romeo and Juliet*, *NS*, 3–6 June 1796; 23–27 April 1795.

15   *BM*, 6 March 1786.

16   *BM*, 19 October 1786.

17   *BNL*, 26–29 October 1790; *NS*, 14–18 April 1792.

18   *NS* 16–20 June 1792.

19   BCS Archive, Committee Minute Books, 1791–4, 12 March 1791. Four of the five attendees at this meeting (Neilson, John Haslett, William McCleery and Gilbert McIlveen Jr) were United Irishmen.

20   A list of members of the Belfast First Volunteer Company is published in George Benn, *A History of the Town of Belfast*, vol. 1 (Belfast, 2008), pp. 754–5. Many of this corps served in the committee of the Belfast Charitable Society. The first captain of the company was Stewart Banks and one of the lieutenants (later captain) was Waddell Cunningham.

21   BCS Archive, Committee Minutes, 30 June 1781; 28 July 1781. Francis Annesley, the 2nd Lord Glerawly (later 1st Earl Annesley), had been elected colonel of the Rathfriland Volunteers in October 1780 but resigned in December, most likely because he opposed the politicisation of the Volunteers and the influence of the town's Presbyterian minister, Rev. Samuel Barber, in the company. It may be that Glerawly had resumed his position by 1781. BCS Committee Minutes, 30 June 1781; Ulster Museum, 603-1914, Minute Book of Rathfriland Volunteers; A. Morrow, 'The Rev. Samuel Barber AM and the Rathfriland Volunteers', *Ulster Journal of Archaeology*, Second Series, vol. 14, no. 2/3 (May–August 1908), pp. 104–19; A. Blackstock, 'Samuel Barber of Rathfriland: The interaction of national and local politics', *Eighteenth-Century Ireland*, vol. 30 (2015), pp. 122–39.

22   BCS Archive, Committee Minutes, 7 July 1781.

23   BCS Archive, Committee Minutes, 23 March 1782; 15 June 1782.

24   See, for example, the editorial comment that 'the spirit of volunteering is as lively as ever', *BM*, 17 April 1786.

25   *BM*, 12 August 1783.

26   E.M. Johnston-Liik, *History of the Irish Parliament, 1692–1800*, vol. III (Belfast, 2002), pp. 567–8; G. Chambers, *Faces of Change: The Belfast and Northern Ireland Chambers of Commerce and Industry, 1783–1983* (Belfast, 1983), pp. 42–4.

27   BCS Archive, General Board Minutes, 5 November 1788; 10 March 1790; 16 February 1791. Tennent was treasurer in 1788 and Neilson was elected to the same post in 1790 and 1791.

28   T.W. Tone, 'Memoirs', in T. Bartlett (ed.), *Life of Theobald Wolfe Tone: Memoirs, Journals and Political Writings, compiled and arranged by William T.W. Tone, 1826* (Dublin, 1998), p. 39.

29   T.W. Tone [A Northern Whig], *An Argument on Behalf of the Catholics of Ireland* (August 1791).

30   K. Whelan, *The Tree of Liberty: Radicalism, Catholicism and the Construction of Irish Identity, 1760–1830* (Cork, 1996), p. 100.

31   William Drennan to Samuel McTier, 21 May 1791, in Agnew (ed.), *The Drennan-McTier Letters I*, p. 357.

32   For Neilson's role in forming and developing the strategy of the of the United Irishmen, see K.L. Dawson, *The Belfast Jacobin: Samuel Neilson and the United Irishmen* (Dublin, 2017). Interestingly, Neilson met with Drennan in Dublin on the day that the latter wrote his oft-quoted letter to Samuel McTier.

33   *NS*, 21–25 January 1792.

34   For example, Thomas Milliken was a regular attender at Charitable Society committee meetings in the 1790s. He also served as chairman of the First Belfast Society of

United Irishmen in 1793. Secretary to the same at this time was Neilson's one-time business partner James Hyndman, who attended numerous meetings of the general board. David Bigger, a merchant with premises on High Street, began attending meetings of the BCS committee in September 1792. He was secretary of the Third Belfast United Irish Society. Bigger was the grandfather of the famous Belfast lawyer and antiquarian Francis Joseph Bigger. His involvement with the committee and general board lasted into the nineteenth century. *NS*, 29 September–3 October 1793; 3–6 October 1793.

35   *NS*, 28 January–1 February 1792.

36   *BNL*, 31 January–3 February 1792.

37   BCS Archive, Committee Minutes, 30 June 1792.

38   Journal of Wolfe Tone, 13 July 1792, quoted in Bartlett (ed.), *Life of Theobald Wolfe Tone*, p. 133.

39   *NS*, 11–14 July 1792.

40   BCS Archive, General Board Minutes, 10 March 1790; 16 February 1791; 23 July 1795. Neilson resigned in April 1792 and was replaced by John Haslett, another United Irishman and original subscriber to the *NS*. It is likely that Neilson's editorial duties forced his resignation.

41   BCS Archive, Committee Minutes, 29 December 1792.

42   For Simms' involvement in the early stages of the *NS*, see National Archives of Ireland (NAI), Rebellion Papers, 620/15/8/1 *Northern Star* Minute Book, 1791–3.

43   NAI, Rebellion Papers, 620/4/54, Examination of prisoners in Belfast, 16 July 1798; 620/39/14, Examination of Samuel Orr, 3 July 1798.

44   Simms had married a Miss Gilliland from the Collin district in 1786. *BNL*, 8–11 August 1786; Chambers, *Faces of Change*, p. 91.

45   BCS Archive, General Board Minutes, 1782–3, 1793.

46   J.J. Wright, *The 'Natural Leaders' and Their World: Politics, Culture and Society in Belfast c.1801–1832* (Liverpool, 2012).

47   PRONI, T/3541/5/3, 'Particulars of History of a North County Irish Family: Autobiographical account of John Caldwell jr'.

48   NAI, Rebellion Papers, 620/125/197, Thomas Whinnery to John Lees, 29 October 1796. Lees' information generally ended up on the desk of Edward Cooke, the under-secretary in Dublin Castle and head of intelligence; 620/3/32/1, Anonymous to Thomas Pelham (chief secretary) and Cooke, 25 February 1798.

49   *BNL*, 8 June 1798; NAI, Rebellion Papers, 620/39/97, Crown Solicitor John Pollock (Belfast) to Edward Cooke, no date 1798. We know that Tennent was in custody on 24 August 1798. 620/39/203, list of United Irish prisoners in Belfast. It is possible that Tennent had bought the silence of John Hughes, a bookseller, United Irishman and government informer on whose evidence several suspects were interned. See PRONI, T/3541/5/3, 'Particulars of History of a North County Irish Family: Autobiographical account of John Caldwell jr'.

50   *BM*, 10 January 1786; *BNL*, 3–7 April 1789 and 9–12 February 1790.

51   Chambers, *Faces of Change*, pp. 75–6; Dawson, *The Belfast Jacobin*, pp. 114–15.

52 *BNL*, 8 June 1798; 15 June 1798; BCS Archive, General Board Minutes, 15 February 1803.

53 BCS Archive, General Board Minutes, 1781; PRONI, Pelham MSS, General Lake to Thomas Pelham, 3 July 1797; W. Roulston, 'John Campbell White of Baltimore', in P. Gilmore, T. Parkhill and W. Roulston (eds), *Exiles of '98: Ulster Presbyterians and the United States* (Belfast, 2018), pp. 92–5.

54 Strain, *Belfast and its Charitable Society*, p. 81; NAI, Rebellion Papers, 620/19/45, Pledge of Belfast citizens to subscribe to a second newspaper, 19 September 1791; *BNL*, 4 June 1798 and 15 June 1798.

55 Kent History and Library Centre, Camden MSS, U840/0147/4/2.

56 G. Chambers, 'Divided loyalties in the business community of Belfast in 1798', *Familia*, vol. 2, no. 16 (1994).

57 *BNL*, 3 July 1798.

58 For Getty's marriage in 1793, see *BNL* 1–5 February 1793. Grimshaw's son, Nicholas jr, was a member of the Belfast Yeomanry Cavalry, *BNL*, 18 June 1798.

59 Chambers, *Faces of Change*, pp. 64–6. Crawford was in partnership with the leading United Irishman Robert Simms in Crumlin Mills. The partnership was dissolved in August 1798, *BNL*, 31 August 1798.

60 Hughes' evidence should be treated with caution since he was motivated by self-preservation, *BNL*, 14 September 1798. Details of Crawford's contribution to the yeomanry fund is found in the *BNL*, 3 July 1798. Five years after the rebellion, another informer, 'SK', noted that Crawford, by this time a lieutenant in the loyalist yeomanry, was the reverse in his views. 'He is brother-in-law to the Simms whose politics he has ever supported', NAI, Rebellion Papers, 620/65/126, statement of SK, 23 May 1803.

61 *BNL*, 3 July 1798; 16 October 1798.

62 BCS Archive, Committee Minutes 1791–4. Stevenson was still serving on the committee after the rebellion. For his enrolling as a yeoman, *BNL*, 8 June 1798.

63 Martha McTier to William Drennan, 9 October 1797 and 15 January 1798 in Jean Agnew (ed.), *The Drennan-McTier Letters 2* (Dublin, 1998), pp. 340–1, 360.

64 *NS*, 2–5 December 1796.

65 Martha McTier to William Drennan, n.d. October 1803; Drennan to Mrs McTier, n.d. November 1803, in Jean Agnew (ed.), *The Drennan-McTier Letters 3* (Dublin, 1999), pp. 158, 170.

66 BCS Archive, General Board Minutes, Memorial to Lord Cornwallis, 27 October 1798, 4 January 1799, 8 January 1799, 25 January 1799, 26 January 1799.

67 BCS Archive, BCS Letter from John Hughes to the Governors of the Poorhouse, 4 March 1799. I would like to thank Aaron McIntyre, Archive and Heritage Co-ordinator for the Belfast Charitable Society, for sharing this reference.

68 PRONI T/1210/42, Henry Joy McCracken to Mary Ann McCracken, 12 June 1798.

69 Wright, *The 'Natural Leaders' and Their World*.

CHAPTER THREE: FROM NEW ORLEANS TO CLIFTON STREET

1   I am grateful to Mark Doyle, W.A. Hart and Nik Ribianszky for comments on this chapter, and to Aaron McIntyre, Archive and Heritage Co-ordinator for the Belfast Charitable Society, for advice on sources.

2   Samuel Cunningham to John Cunningham, 9 August 1792, PRONI, D1108/A/3; *Belfast News-Letter* [hereafter *BNL*], 16 January 1797.

3   Will of Samuel Cunningham, PRONI, D1108/A/10. Cunningham's will, and his career in the Caribbean, is discussed in Nini Rodgers, 'Belfast and the Black Atlantic', in Nicholas Allen and Aaron Kelly (eds), *The Cities of Belfast* (Dublin, 2003), pp. 27–40 at 30–1.

4   'Killead Presbyterian Church', available online at http://glenavyhistory.com/places-of-worship/killead-places-of-worship/killead-presbyterian-church/ (accessed 7/6/2021).

5   Rodgers, 'Belfast and the Black Atlantic', p. 31.

6   The description is Rodgers', but Cunningham's will also refers to his property in 'slaves'. Rodgers, 'Belfast and the Black Atlantic', p. 31; Will of Samuel Cunningham, PRONI, D1108/A/10.

7   Thomas M. Truxes (ed.), *Letterbook of Greg & Cunningham 1756–57: Merchants of New York and Belfast* (Oxford, 2001), pp. 40, 362, 366; Rodgers, 'Belfast and the Black Atlantic', pp. 31–2; Nini Rodgers, 'Making history in Belfast: The tale of Francis Joseph Bigger, Samuel Shannon Millin and Waddell Cunningham', in Sabine Wichert (ed.), *From the United Irishmen to Twentieth-century Unionism* (Dublin, 2004), pp. 24–34. See also, Bill Rolston, '"A lying old scoundrel": Waddell Cunningham & Belfast's role in the slave trade', *History Ireland*, vol. 11, no. 1 (2003), pp. 24–7 and Aaron McIntyre, 'International day for the remembrance of the slave trade and its abolition 2020', available online at https://belfastcharitablesociety.org/international-day-for-the-remembrance-of-the-slave-trade-and-its-abolition-2020/ (accessed 10/6/2021).

8   Kenneth Morgan 'Colston, Edward (1636–1721)', in *Oxford Dictionary of National Biography*, available online at www.oxforddnb.com (accessed 10/6/2021). For Colston's statue, see Bristol Museum's 'The Colston statue: what next?' website, available online at https://exhibitions.bristolmuseums.org.uk/the-colston-statue/?utm_source=whatson&utm_medium=referral&utm_campaign=colston (accessed 10/6/2021).

9   Mary McNeill, *The Life and Times of Mary Ann McCracken, 1770–1866: A Belfast Panorama* (Belfast, 1997), pp. 257–87, 293–5. See also, Cathryn McWilliams, 'The letters and legacy of Mary Ann McCracken' (PhD, Åbo Akademi University, 2021), pp. 85–97.

10 *BNL*, 16 December 1791; John J. Monaghan, 'The rise and fall of the Belfast Cotton Industry', *Irish Historical Studies*, iii, 9 (1942), pp. 1–17 at 3; Nini Rodgers, 'Equiano in Belfast: A study of the anti-slavery ethos in a Northern town', *Slavery & Abolition*, vol. 18, no. 2 (1997), pp. 73–89 (esp. 73, 75, 76, 80); Rodgers, 'Making history', p. 26; Kenneth L. Dawson, *The Belfast Jacobin: Samuel Neilson and the United*

Irishmen (Newbridge, 2017), pp. 18–19, 23–5; McIntyre, 'International day for the remembrance of the slave trade'.

11 Vincent Carretta, 'Olaudah Equiano: African British abolitionist and founder of the American slave narrative', in Audrey Fisch (ed.), *The Cambridge Companion to the African American Slave Narrative* (Cambridge, 2007), pp. 44–60 at 45.

12 R.W.M. Strain, *Belfast and its Charitable Society: A Story of Urban Social Development* (London, 1961), pp. 242–5 (243 for quote).

13 See, however, Aaron McIntyre, 'Black History Month: William John Brown and his escape from slavery', available online at https://cliftonbelfast.com/black-history-month-william-john-brown-and-his-escape-from-slavery/ (accessed 09/08/21) and [Glenravel History Project], 'The records of Clifton Street Cemetery', available online at www.culturenorthernireland.org/features/heritage/records-clifton-street-cemetery (accessed 09/08/21).

14 See, in addition to the works by Rodgers and Truxes cited in notes 3, 7 and 10 above, Norman E. Gamble, 'The business community and the trade of Belfast, 1767–1800' (PhD, University of Dublin, 1978), pp. 290–1; Douglas Cameron Riach, 'Ireland and the campaign against slavery, 1830–60' (PhD, University of Edinburgh, 1975), passim; Nini Rodgers, *Ireland, Slavery and Anti-slavery, 1612–1865* (Basingstoke, 2007), passim; Daniel Ritchie, '"The stone in the sling": Frederick Douglass and Belfast abolitionism', *American Nineteenth-Century History*, vol. 18, no. 3 (2017), pp. 245–72; Sean Farrell, 'Going to extremes: Anti-Catholicism and anti-slavery in early-Victorian Belfast', *European Romantic Review*, vol. 28, no. 4 (2017), pp. 461–72; Daniel Ritchie, *Isaac Nelson: Radical Abolitionist, Evangelical Presbyterian, and Irish Nationalist* (Liverpool, 2018), pp. 54–5; Krysta Beggs-McCormick, '"Methinks I see grim slavery's gorgon form": Abolitionism in Belfast, 1775–1865' (PhD, Ulster University, 2018).

15 W.A. Hart, 'Africans in eighteenth-century Ireland', *Irish Historical Studies*, vol. xxxiii, no. 120 (2002), pp. 19–32; Mark Doyle, 'Those the empire washed ashore: Uncovering Ireland's multiracial past', in Timothy McMahon, Michael de Nie and Paul Townend (eds), *Ireland in an Imperial World* (Cambridge, 2017), pp. 55–61.

16 Raymond Gillespie and Stephen A. Royle, *Belfast, Part 1, to 1840* (Irish Historic Towns Atlas no. 12) (Dublin, 2003), pp. 6–8, 10; S.J. Connolly, 'Improving town, 1750–1820', in S.J. Connolly (ed.), *Belfast 400: People, Place and History* (Liverpool, 2012), pp. 161–97 at 172–3, 195; Monaghan, 'Rise and fall', p. 1.

17 Gillespie and Royle, *Belfast*, p. 6 and maps 9 and 11; Raymond Gillespie, *Early Belfast: The Origins and Growth of an Ulster Town to 1750* (Belfast, 2007), pp. 1–2.

18 Gillespie and Royle, *Belfast*, map 11.

19 Belfast Night Watch Reports, 12 May 1812 to 19 May 1816, PRONI, D/46/1A, pp. 191, 301, 432.

20 *Northern Whig* [hereafter *NW*], 16 August 1830; *BNL*, 20 August 1830, 7 January 1831.

21 *BNL*, 2 December 1825, 20 January 1826, 2 January 1827, 7 January 1831.

22 *BNL*, 1 September 1826, 14 September 1827; Narcissus G. Batt, 'Belfast sixty years

ago: Recollections of a septuagenarian', *Ulster Journal of Archaeology*, 2nd series, ii, 2 (1896), pp. 92–5 at 92.

23   *BNL*, 1 September 1826, 14 September 1827; *List of the subscribers to the Belfast Charitable Society with a statement of accounts from November 1, 1829 – to November 1, 1830* (Belfast, 1830), pp. 3, 9.

24   *BNL*, 2 December 1825, 20 August 1830.

25   *NW*, 16 August 1830.

26   *BNL*, 20 August 1830; Brian Griffin, *The Bulkies: Police and Crime in Belfast 1800–1865* (Dublin, 1998), p. 51; Jonathan Jeffrey Wright, *Crime and Punishment in Nineteenth-century Belfast: The Story of John Linn* (Dublin, 2020), p. 35.

27   *BNL*, 20 August 1830.

28   Kenneth Morgan, *Slavery and the British Empire: From Africa to America* (Oxford, 2008), p. 156; Kirsten Sword, 'Remembering Dinah Nevil: Strategic deceptions in eighteenth-century antislavery', *Journal of American History*, vol. 97, no. 2 (2010), pp. 315–43 at 317, 321, 323; Gretchen Holbrook Gerzina, *Black London: Life before Emancipation* (New Brunswick, 1995), pp. 116–32.

29   This account is based on Patricia Hagler Minter, '"The state of slavery": Somerset, the Slave, Grace, and the rise of pro-slavery and anti-slavery constitutionalism in the nineteenth-century Atlantic World', *Slavery & Abolition*, vol. 36, no. 4 (2015), pp. 603–17 at 604–6 (605 for quotes). See also Gerzina, *Black London*, pp. 78–9.

30   Minter, '"The state of slavery"', p. 606.

31   *BNL*, 13 November 1827.

32   Minter, '"The state of slavery"', p. 605.

33   *BNL*, 20 August 1830.

34   Brown's case was first publicised by the *Belfast Commercial Chronicle* in a report which was later reprinted in the *Northern Whig* and, with some minor alterations, the *Belfast News-Letter*. See *NW*, 16 August 1830; *BNL*, 20 August 1830.

35   *NW*, 16 August 1830.

36   Edward Muir and Guido Ruggiero, 'Introduction: The crime of history', in Edward Muir and Guido Ruggiero (eds), *History from Crime* (Baltimore, 1994), pp. vii–xviii at ix.

37   Ibid.

38   *NW*, 16 August 1830.

39   Ibid.; Registry Books, p. 4, available online at www.belfasthistoryproject.com/cliftonstreetcemetery (accessed 09/08/21).

40   *NW*, 16 August 1830.

41   Martha S. Jones, *Birthright Citizens: A History of Race and Rights in Antebellum America* (Cambridge, 2018), p. 21; Richard Bell, 'Counterfeit kin: Kidnappers of color, the reverse underground railroad, and the origins of practical abolition', *Journal of the Early American Republic*, vol. 38, no. 2 (2018), pp. 199–230 at 200–1. See also, Julie Winch, 'Philadelphia and the other underground railroad', *The Pennsylvania Magazine of History and Biography*, vol. 111, no. 1 (1987), pp. 3–25.

42   Bell, 'Counterfeit kin', pp. 201, 206.

43 Jones, *Birthright Citizens*, pp. 21, 25, 77; Martha S. Jones, 'The case of *Jean Baptiste, un Créole de Saint-Domingue*: Narrating slavery, freedom, and the Haitian Revolution in Baltimore City', in Brian Ward, Martyn Bone and William A. Link (eds), *The American South and the Atlantic World* (Gainesville, 2013), pp. 104–28 at 105.

44 Winch, 'Philadelphia and the other underground railroad', p. 5.

45 Bell, 'Counterfeit kin', p. 207.

46 *NW*, 16 August 1830.

47 Bell, 'Counterfeit kin', pp. 202–3. See also Winch, 'Philadelphia and the other underground railroad'.

48 Jones, 'The case of *Jean Baptiste*', p. 120. One of a group of around twenty enslaved people carried from Saint Domingue in 1796 by a widow named Volunbrun, Baptiste was kidnapped while a Baltimore court was considering his freedom suit (pp. 104, 105, 108, 120).

49 Aaron McIntyre, 'Black History Month'.

50 *NW*, 16 August 1830.

51 *BNL*, 20 August 1830.

52 *NW*, 16 August 1830.

53 *BNL*, 20 August 1830.

54 *NW*, 16 August 1830.

55 Ibid.; *BNL*, 20 August 1830.

56 'Historical Notaries' Indexes, by Decade' ('Boswell, William 1828 Volume 05'; 'De Armis, Felix 1828 Volume 13'; 'Duncan, John N. 1828 Volume 03'; 'Pollock, Carlile 1828 Volume 23'), available online at www.orleanscivilclerk.com/notarychrono.htm (accessed 21/07/2021); Bertram W. Korn, 'Jews and Negro slavery in the Old South, 1789–1865', *Publications of the American Jewish Historical Society*, vol. 50, no. 3 (1961), pp. 172, 172 n.74.

57 Rashauna Johnson, *Slavery's Metropolis: Unfree Labour in New Orleans during the Age of Revolution* (Cambridge, 2016), pp. 1–2, 11, 14, 15. See also, Eric Arnesen, *Waterfront Workers of New Orleans: Race, Class and Politics, 1863–1923* (Urbana and Chicago, 1994), p. 14.

58 Johnson, *Slavery's Metropolis*, pp. 3, 7–8, 12; Arnesen, *Waterfront Workers*, p. 13; Lorena Walsh, 'Work and the slave economy', in Gad Heuman and Trevor Burnard (eds), *The Routledge History of Slavery* (London, 2011), pp. 101–18 at 109; *BNL*, 20 August 1830.

59 *BNL*, 20 August 1830.

60 Johnson, *Slavery's Metropolis*, p. 14.

61 Ibid., pp. 60–1; James Sidbury, 'Resistance to slavery', in Heuman and Burnard (eds), *The Routledge History of Slavery*, pp. 204–19 at 211. See also, for seaborne escape, Marcus Rediker, 'Serendipity in the archives: Or, a lost freedom story I found while looking for something else', available online at https://publicseminar.org/essays/serendipity-in-the-archives/ (accessed 8/10/2021).

62 Cawdon advert quoted in McNeill, *The Life and Times of Mary Ann McCracken*,

p. 294 (see also 322 n.10 for date); Hart, 'Africans in eighteenth-century Ireland', p. 24; 'Notebook', PRONI, D3113/4/14; Gamble, 'Business community', p. 291.

63   Oliver Goldsmith, *An History of the Earth, and Animated Nature* (8 vols, London, 1774), vi, pp. 241–2.

64   Quoted in Riach, 'Ireland and the campaign against American slavery', p. 3. See also, Marcus Rediker, 'History from below the water line: Sharks and the Atlantic slave trade', *Atlantic Studies*, vol. 5, no. 2 (2008), pp. 285–97 at 293 and Farrell, 'Going to extremes', p. 461.

65   The original report is printed alongside Starks' letter in *BNL*, 23 June 1818. This episode is also discussed briefly in Beggs-McCormick, 'Methinks I see', p. 65.

66   *BNL*, 23 June 1818.

67   Ibid.

68   *BNL*, 25 December 1818.

69   *BNL*, 6 November and 8 December 1818.

70   This was not unusual. For the employment of enslaved Barbadians at sea, see Philip D. Morgan, 'British encounters with Africans and African-Americans, circa 1600–1780', in Bernard Bailyn and Philip D. Morgan (eds), *Strangers within the Realm* (Williamsburg, 1991), pp. 157–219 at 195; Trevor Burnard, 'British West Indies and Bermuda', in Robert L. Paquette and Mark M. Smith (eds), *The Oxford Handbook of Slavery in the Americas* (New York, 2010), pp. 134–53 at 140.

71   *BNL*, 5 September 1828.

72   *Guardian and Constitutional Advocate* [hereafter *GCA*], 5 September 1828.

73   Ibid.; *BNL*, 5 September 1828. See also, for this episode, Beggs-McCormick, 'Methinks I see', p. 65 and Sam Hanna Bell, *Within our Province: A Miscellany of Ulster Writing* (Belfast, 1972), pp. 38–7.

74   Sarah Hannon and Neil Kennedy, '"Slavery wears the mildest aspect": Imagining mastery and emancipation in Bermuda's House of Assembly', *Journal of Caribbean History*, vol. 53, no. 1 (2019), pp. 60–81 at 69 (for quote); *Anti-Slavery Monthly Reporter*, vol. ii, 17 (Oct. 1828), p. 327; *The Friend*, vol. iv, 1 (1830), p. 8.

75   Amelia Murray MacGregor, *History of the Clan Gregor from Public Records and Private Collections* (2 vols, Edinburgh 1898–1901), pp. ii, 296–7, 301; Lorenzo Sabine, *The American Loyalists, or Biographical Sketches of Adherents to the British Crown in the War of the Revolution; Alphabetically Arranged; with a Preliminary Historical Essay* (Boston, 1847), pp. 615–16; Susan E. Klepp and Roderick A. McDonald, 'Inscribing experience: An American working woman and an English gentlewoman encounter Jamaica's slave society, 1801–1805', *William and Mary Quarterly*, vol. 58, no. 3 (2001), pp. 637–60 at 640; A.T.Q. Stewart, *The Summer Soldiers: The 1798 Rebellion in Antrim and Down* (Belfast, 1995), p. 81.

76   Lord Dungannon to marquess of Downshire, 1 September 1796, PRONI, MIC565/8; *BNL*, 5 September and 12 December 1796, 9 January 1797.

77   Klepp and McDonald, 'Inscribing experience', pp. 638–9, 640, 652; Stewart, *Summer Soldiers*, p. 81.

78   Klepp and McDonald, 'Inscribing experience', pp. 637, 637 n.1, 653.

79   *BNL*, 26 July 1808.

80   *NW*, 16 August 1830.

81   *NW*, 4 September 1828. See also *BNL*, 5 September 1828 and *GCA*, 5 September 1828.

82   *BNL*, 11 April 1826; Bill Jackson, *Ringing True: The Bells of Trummery and Beyond – 350 Years of an Irish Quaker Family* (York, 2005), pp. 77–8. For a revealing analysis of Quaker anti-slavery activity in the late eighteenth century, see Sword, 'Remembering Dinah Nevil'.

83   *GCA*, 5 September 1828.

84   *BNL*, 17 September 1830.

85   *BNL*, 22 February 1831. I am grateful to W.A. Hart for bringing Oveton to my attention.

86   Richard S. Harrison, *A Biographical Dictionary of Irish Quakers*, 2nd ed. (Dublin, 2008), p. 48.

87   Ibid., pp. 4–9; *The Friend*, new series, vol. xi, 124 (1871), p. 96; Jackson, *Ringing True*, pp. 76–89 (esp. 76, 81). For Bell and the *Irish Friend*, see also Riach, 'Ireland and the campaign against American slavery', pp. 95–100, 111, 116 n.3, 119, 120, 122, 257–8, 260–2; Bill Jackson (ed.), *The Irish Friend: Excerpts from the Pioneer Quaker Newspaper* (Belfast, 2016), esp. pp. ix–xii; Beggs-McCormick, 'Methinks I see', pp. 8 n.38, 144–50, 262.

88   Sword, 'Remembering Dinah Nevil', p. 318.

89   Morgan, *Slavery and the British Empire*, p. 177; Catherine Hall, *Macaulay and Son: Architects of Imperial Britain* (New Haven, 2012), pp. 79–80.

90   *The Friend*, new series, xi, 124 (1871), p. 96; Harrison, *A Biographical Dictionary*, p. 48.

91   Morgan, *Slavery and the British Empire*, pp. 182, 184–5.

92   *BNL*, 14 and 17 September 1830; Beggs-McCormick, 'Methinks I see', pp. 67–8.

93   *BNL*, 13 April and 27 July 1830; Morgan, *Slavery and the British Empire*, p. 186; Beggs-McCormick, 'Methinks I see', pp. 66–7.

94   *BNL*, 17 September 1830.

95   Ritchie, *Isaac Nelson*, pp. 54–5; Morgan, *Slavery and the British Empire*, p. 186. See also, for the development of abolition in Belfast in the early 1830s, Riach, 'Ireland and the campaign against American slavery', pp. 44–9; Beggs-McCormick, 'Methinks I see', pp. 68–74.

96   *BNL*, 26 November 1830.

97   Registry Books, p. 4; Gillespie and Royle, *Belfast*, map 11.

98   Registry Books, p. 4.

99   *BNL*, 5 September 1828.

100 *BNL*, 6 January 1826; Stephen A. Royle, *Portrait of an Industrial City: 'Clanging Belfast', 1750–1914* (Belfast, 2011), p. 114.

101 Strain, *Belfast and its Charitable Society*, p. 249.

CHAPTER FOUR: POVERTY AND THE MAKING OF
THE BELFAST CHARITABLE SOCIETY

1 John Gamble, *Society and Manners in Early Nineteenth-century Ireland*, edited by Breandán Mac Suibhne (Dublin, 2011), pp. 268–71.

2 Patricia Craig (ed.), *The Belfast Anthology* (Belfast, 1999), p. 175.

3 *Belfast News-Letter* [hereafter *BNL*], 1 June 1810.

4 William Bruce and Henry Joy, *Belfast Politics*, edited by John Bew (Dublin, 2005), pp. 126–7.

5 James Quinn, 'The United Irishmen and social reform', in *Irish Historical Studies*, vol. xxxi, no. 122 (Nov. 1998), pp. 195–201.

6 Kenneth Dawson, *The Belfast Jacobin: Samuel Neilson and the United Irishmen* (Newbridge, 2017), pp. 18–19; C.J. Woods (ed.), *Journals and Memoirs of Thomas Russell* (Dublin, 1991), p. 36.

7 *Rules and Regulations for the House of Industry, Belfast ...* (Belfast, 1810) reproduced in Public Record Office of Northern Ireland, *Problems of a Growing City: Belfast 1780–1870* (Belfast, 1973), pp. 55–60.

8 Henry Joy, 'Remarks on public charity with an account of the rise, progress and state of charitable foundations in Belfast, 1818', edited by Jim Smyth, in *Analecta Hibernica*, vol. 51 (2020), pp. 202–3.

9 For instance, see Alan Blackstock, 'Loyalist associational culture and civic identity in Belfast, 1793–1835', in Jennifer Kelly and R.V. Comerford (eds), *Associational Culture in Ireland and Abroad* (Dublin, 2010), pp. 47–66.

10 Joy, 'Remarks', p. 203.

11 *BNL*, 25, 29 Jan. 1771. The practice may have gone on for some time as it was commented in 1783 that 'Wadell [Cunningham, a prominent Belfast merchant] has been blessed by the poor for selling cheap meal bought by the public subscriptions', Jean Agnew (ed.), *The Drennan-McTier letters, 1, 1776–1793* (Dublin, 1998), p. 79. See also R.W.M. Strain, *Belfast and its Charitable Society: A Story of Urban Social Development* (Oxford, 1961), pp. 93–4.

12 Raymond Gillespie and Roibeard Ó Gallachóir (eds), *Preaching in Belfast, 1747–72: A Selection of the Sermons of James Saurin* (Dublin, 2015), pp. 98–9.

13 Gillespie and Ó Gallachóir (eds), *Preaching in Belfast*, pp. 207–8. Saurin used the word 'society' in its modern sense frequently in his sermons, and it is at least as probable that the Belfast merchant John Black learned the word from hearing these than Jim Livesey's suggestion that he became familiar with it in France. Jim Livesey, *Civil Society and Empire: Ireland and Scotland in the Eighteenth-century Atlantic World* (London, 2009), p. 149. For the earlier use of the word, see Phil Withington, 'Plantation and civil society', in Éamonn Ó Ciardha and Micheál Ó Siochrú (eds), *The Plantation of Ulster: Ideology and Practice* (Manchester, 2012), pp. 64–7.

14 This paragraph is based on Raymond Gillespie, 'Making Belfast, 1600–1750', in S.J. Connolly (ed.), *Belfast 400: People, Place and History* (Liverpool, 2012), pp. 140–1.

15 David Dickson, *Arctic Ireland: The Extraordinary Story of the Great Frost and Forgotten Famine of 1740–1* (Belfast, 1997), pp. 18, 29, 32.

16 *Dublin Gazette*, 23–26 June, 10–14 July, 4–7 August 1733.

17 Raymond Gillespie and Alison O'Keeffe (eds), *Register of the Parish of Shankill, Belfast* (Dublin, 2006).

18 Gillespie and Ó Gallachóir (eds), *Preaching in Belfast*, pp. 30–1.

19 Ibid., p. 204. The quotation is from Proverbs 11.26.

20 James Kelly, *Food Rioting in Ireland in the Eighteenth and Nineteenth centuries* (Dublin, 2017), pp. 98–9, 185, 186–7, 196; Eoin Magennis, 'In search of the "moral economy": Food scarcity in 1756–7 and the crowd', in Peter Jupp and Eoin Magennis (eds), *Crowds in Ireland, c. 1720–1920* (Basingstoke, 2000), pp. 198–200, 203–4, 205–6.

21 Public Record Office of Northern Ireland [hereafter PRONI], D 354/839, 840, 842, 844, 846, 850, 851, 854, 856, 863–6, 870, 872.

22 Gillespie and O'Keeffe (eds), *Register of the Parish of Shankill*, pp. 33–5; Gillespie and Ó Gallachóir (eds), *Preaching in Belfast*, pp. 30–1.

23 St Anne's Cathedral, Belfast, MS sermons of James Saurin, vol. 5, pp. 201–31.

24 *A Proposal for the Support and Regulation of the Poor by subjecting them to the Case and maintaining them at the Charge of their Respective Parishes* (Belfast, 1763).

25 Gillespie and O'Keeffe (eds), *Register of the Parish of Shankill*, passim.

26 Isaac Ward, 'The Black family', *Ulster Journal of Archaeology*, 2nd ser., vol. viii, no. 4 (Oct. 1902), pp. 181–2.

27 W.A. Seaby and T.G.F. Paterson, 'Ulster beggars' badges', *Ulster Journal of Archeology*, 3rd ser., vol. xxx (1970), pp. 101–6.

28 *BNL*, 27 Aug. 1756.

29 Gillespie, 'Making Belfast', p. 139.

30 William Tisdall, *An Account of the Charity School in Belfast* (1720), pp. 3–4.

31 Based on Raymond Gillespie, 'Religion and politics in a provincial town: Belfast 1660–1720', in Salvador Ryan and Clodagh Tait (eds), *Religion and Politics in Urban Ireland, c. 1500–c. 1750: Essays in Honour of Colm Lennon* (Dublin, 2016), pp. 173–92.

32 For a broad outline of poor relief, see David Dickson, 'In search of the old Irish poor law', in Rosalind Mitchison and Peter Roebuck (eds), *Economy and Society in Scotland and Ireland, 1500–1939* (Edinburgh, 1988) pp. 149–59.

33 Strain, *Belfast and its Charitable Society*, pp. 18–23.

34 Ward, 'The Black family', p. 183.

35 T.G.F. Paterson (ed.), 'Belfast in 1738', *Ulster Journal of Archaeology*, 3rd ser., vol. ii (1939), p. 122.

36 Agnew (ed.), *The Drennan-McTier Letters*, 1, p. 20.

37 Gillespie and Ó Gallachóir (eds), *Preaching in Belfast*, pp. 230–8, 257–66.

38 James Kelly, 'Charitable societies: Their genesis and development, 1720–1800', in James Kelly and Martyn Powell (eds), *Clubs and Societies in Eighteenth-century Ireland* (Dublin, 2010), pp. 89–100.

39 Andrew Sneddon, 'State intervention and provincial health care: The county infirmary system in late eighteenth-century Ulster', in *Irish Historical Studies*, vol. xxxviii, no. 149 (May 2012), pp. 5–21; Mel Cousins, 'The Irish parliament and the relief of the poor: The 1772 legislation establishing houses of industry', *Eighteenth Century Ireland*, vol. xxviii (2013), pp. 95–115.

40 Strain, *Belfast and its Charitable Society*, pp. 18–24.

41 I am grateful to Aaron McIntyre, Archive and Heritage Co-ordinator for the Belfast Charitable Society, for providing this information.

42 Reproduced in Raymond Gillespie and Stephen Royle, *Belfast, Part 1 to 1840* (Irish Historic Towns Atlas no. 12) (Dublin, 2003), map 8.

43 Ward, 'The Black family', p. 178.

44 Jean Agnew (ed.), *The Drennan-McTier Letters, 2, 1794–1801* (Dublin, 1998), p. 20.

45 J.R.R. Adams (ed.), *Merchants in Plenty: Joseph Smyth's Belfast Directories of 1807 and 1808* (Belfast, 1991).

46 PRONI, D509/792.

47 For example, C.E.B. Brett, *Roger Mulholland, Architect of Belfast, 1740–1818* (Belfast, 1976), pp. 12–13.

48 Arthur Young, *A Tour in Ireland, 1776–9*, edited by J.B. Ruane (2 vols, Shannon, 1970), i, p. 146.

49 C.J. Woods (ed.), *Charles Abbot's Tour through Ireland and North Wales* (Dublin, 2019), p. 31.

50 Gamble, *Society and Manners*, p. 268.

51 Agnew (ed.), *The Drennan-McTier Letters*, 1, p. 179.

52 Ward, 'The Black family', p. 179.

53 Strain, *Belfast and its Charitable Society*, p. 24.

54 Ibid., pp. 33–6. Dunlop would design a cupola that was never built: see ibid., p. 43.

55 Mylne's elevation is reproduced in Paul Larmour, *Belfast: An Illustrated Architectural Guide* (Belfast, 1987), p. xii.

56 Strain, *Belfast and its Charitable Society*, p. 43.

57 Quoted in ibid., p. 64.

58 Ibid., pp. 65–7.

59 For this see Blackstock, 'Loyalist associational culture', passim; Norman Gamble, 'The business community and trade of Belfast, 1767–1800' (PhD thesis, Trinity College Dublin, 1978), pp. 156–83.

CHAPTER FIVE: 'DOING THE NEEDFUL'

1 P.D. Hardy, *Twenty-One Views in Belfast and its Neighbourhood: Reprinted, with notes and an introduction by C.E.B. Brett* (Belfast, 2005 [1837]).

2 S.J. Connolly, 'Improving town, 1750–1820', in S.J. Connolly (ed.), *Belfast 400: People, Place and History* (Liverpool, 2012), p. 169.

3 Belfast Charitable Society [hereafter BCS] Archive, Committee Minute Books, 1776–9, 25 July 1778, 11 July 1778.

4   Burials, Belfast, St Anne's (Shankill), Connor and Antrim, September 1784–
    March 1799, Public Record Office Northern Ireland [hereafter PRONI] T679/224,
    p. 123.
5   BCS Archive, Committee Minute Books, 1776–9, 28 February 1778.
6   Ibid., 28 September 1776.
7   Ibid., 5 April 1777.
8   BCS Archive, Committee Minute Books, 1775–6, 31 August 1776, 'Catherine
    Connolly "entitled to 3s 3d or her choice to come into the house"'.
9   Ibid., 5 April 1777.
10 Ibid., 19 July 1777.
11 R.W.M. Strain, *Belfast and its Charitable Society: A Story of Urban Development*
    (London, 1961), p. 95.
12 George Benn, *A History of the Town of Belfast from the Earliest Times to the Close of
    the Eighteenth Century* (London, 1877), p. 512.
13 BCS Archive, Committee Minute Books, 1776–9.
14 See Strain, *Belfast and its Charitable Society*, p. 69.
15 BCS Archive, Committee Minute Books, 1776–9, 31 May 1777; ibid., 7 March 1778.
16 M. Cousins, 'The Irish Parliament and relief of the poor: The 1772 legislation
    establishing houses of industry', *Eighteenth-Century Ireland*, vol. 28 (2013), pp. 101.
17 BCS Archive, Committee Minute Books, 1775–6, 15 February 1775.
18 See Benn, *A History of the Town of Belfast*, p. 514.
19 Raymond Gillespie, 'Making Belfast 1600–1750', in Connolly, *Belfast 400*, p. 140.
20 Ibid.
21 BCS Archive, Committee Minute Books, 1775–6, 20 March 1775.
22 BCS Archive, Committee Minute Books, 1776–9, 18 April 1778.
23 BCS Archive, Committee Minute Books, 1779–83, 15 January 1780.
24 BCS Archive, Committee Minute Books, 1775–6, 3 April 1775; ibid., 1 May 1775.
25 Ibid., 19 June 1775.
26 BCS Archive, Committee Minute Books, 1776–9, 9 May 1778.
27 See Strain, *Belfast and its Charitable Society*, p. 74.
28 BCS Archive, Committee Minute Books, 1775–6, 13 July 1776.
29 Ibid.
30 BCS Archive, Committee Minute Books, 1779–83, 3 January 1778.
31 BCS Archive, Committee Minute Books, 1776–9, 5 July 1777.
32 Ibid.
33 Ibid., 4 April 1778.
34 BCS Archive, Committee Minute Books, 1775–6, 4 December 1775; ibid., 2 January
    1776.
35 Ibid., 26 October 1776.
36 BCS Archive, Committee Minute Books, 1776–9, 10 May 1777.
37 Ibid., 4 October 1777.
38 Ibid., 20 December 1777.
39 Ibid., 17 January 1778.

40   BCS Archive, Committee Minute Books, 1775–6, 3 February 1776.

41   Ibid., 17 February 1776.

42   BCS Archive, Committee Minute Books, 1776–9, 2 January 1779.

43   V. Smith, *Clean: A History of Personal Hygiene and Purity* (New York, 2007).

44   BCS Archive, Committee Minute Books, 1791–4, 3 September 1791.

45   See Strain, *Belfast and its Charitable Society*, p. 161.

46   BCS Archive, Committee Minute Books, 1776–9, 26 October 1776.

47   BCS Archive, Committee Minute Books, 1775–6, 10 July 1775.

48   BCS Archive, Committee Minute Books, 1776–9, 30 January 1779.

49   BCS Archive, Committee Minute Books, 1779–83, 9 February 1782.

50   Ibid., 18 July 1778.

51   Ibid., 15 May 1779.

52   Ibid., 15 May 1779.

53   BCS Archive, Committee Minute Books, 1775–6, 6 January 1776.

54   BCS Archive, Committee Minute Books, 1776–9, 5 October 1776.

55   Ibid., 12 October 1776.

56   BCS Archive, Committee Minute Books, 1775–6, 3 April 1775.

57   BCS Archive, Committee Minute Books, 1776–9, 12 July 1777.

58   Ibid., 19 July 1777.

59   Ibid., 17 February 1776.

60   BCS Archive, Committee Minute Books, 1776–9, 26 July 1777.

61   BCS Archive, Committee Minute Books, 1775–6, 24 April 1775.

62   Ibid., 20 January 1776.

63   Ibid., 3 February 1776.

64   BCS Archive, Committee Minute Books, 1776–9, 24 April 1778.

65   BCS Archive, Committee Minute Books, 1775–6, 3 April 1775.

66   BCS Archive, Committee Minute Books, 1779–83, 4 December 1779.

67   BCS Archive, Committee Minute Books, 1775–6, 24 July 1775.

68   BCS Archive, Committee Minute Books, 1779–83, 30 September 1780.

69   BCS Archive, Committee Minute Books, 1776–9, 9 September 1777.

70   Ibid., 17 October 1778.

71   Ibid., 24 October 1778, 16 December 1778, 30 January 1779.

72   BCS Archive, Committee Minute Books, 1779–83, 26 February 1780, 20 October 1781, 14 December 1782.

73   Ibid., 18 January 1783.

74   BCS Archive, Committee Minute Books, 1776–9, 8 March 1777.

75   Ibid., 26 April 1777.

76   BCS Archive, Committee Minute Books, 1779–83, 1 January 1780.

77   BCS Archive, Committee Minute Books, 1776–9, 4 April 1778.

78   Ibid., 16 January 1779.

79   Ibid., 23 January 1779.

80   Ibid., 12 April 1777.

81   A. Winter and T. Lambrecht, 'Migration, poor relief and local autonomy: settlement

policies in England and the Southern Low Countries in the eighteenth century', *Past & Present*, vol. 218 (2013), p. 91.

82 Ibid.

83 BCS Archive, Committee Minute Books, 1779–83, 29 May 1779.

84 Ibid., 24 March 1781, 11 August 1781, 28 September 1782.

85 BCS Archive, Committee Minute Books, 1775–6, 6 July 1776.

86 BCS Archive, Committee Minute Books, 1779–83, 2 June 1781.

87 BCS Archive, Committee Minute Books, 1776–9, 20 February 1779.

88 BCS Archive, Committee Minute Books, 1779–83, 15 April 1780.

89 BCS Archive, Committee Minute Books, 1775–6, 6 January 1776.

90 Ibid., 13 January 1776.

91 BCS Archive, Committee Minute Books, 1776–9, 27 June 1778.

92 Ibid., 28 February 1778.

93 M. Quane, 'The Hibernian Marine School Dublin', *Dublin Historical Record*, vol. 21, no. 2 (March 1967), p. 72.

94 BCS Archive, Committee Minute Books, 1776–9, 18 April 1778, 13 June 1778.

95 W.A. Maguire, 'Lords and Landlords: The Donegall Family', in J.C. Beckett (ed.), *Belfast: The Making of the City* (Belfast, 1988), p. 30.

96 BCS Archive, Committee Minute Books, 1775–6, 8 May 1775.

97 BCS Archive, Committee Minute Books, 1779–83, 24 February 1781.

98 Ibid., 4 July 1778.

99 See Strain, *Belfast and its Charitable Society*, p. 93.

100 BCS Archive, Committee Minute Books, 1779–83, 28 June 1783.

101 Ibid.

102 Ibid., 8 July 1783.

103 Ibid.

104 Ibid.

105 Ibid.

106 BCS Archive, Cash Book, 1787–1811, Cash Book March 1798; T. Pakenham, *The Year of Liberty: The History of the Great Irish Rebellion of 1798* (London, 1992), pp. 57–8.

107 Ibid., October 1798.

108 BCS Archive, Committee Minute Books, 1800–5, 10 May 1800.

109 Ibid., 7 May 1801.

110 See Strain, *Belfast and its Charitable Society*, p. 279.

111 BCS Archive, Committee Minute Books, 1805–11, 23 September 1809; see also Strain, *Belfast and its Charitable Society*, p. 279.

112 A.G. Malcolm, *The History of the General Hospital, Belfast and the Other Medical Institutions of the Town* (Belfast, 1851), p. 53.

113 See Malcolm, *The History of the General Hospital, Belfast*, p. 63.

114 *Belfast News-Letter*, 28 April 1801.

115 See Strain, *Belfast and its Charitable Society*, p. 172.

116 Ibid.

117 Ibid., p. 175.

118 *Belfast News-Letter*, 31 October 1809.

119 A. Jordan, *Who Cared? Charity in Victorian & Edwardian Belfast* (Belfast, 1992).

120 See Benn, *The History of the General Hospital, Belfast*, p. 77.

121 Quoted in Strain, *Belfast and its Charitable Society*, p. 179.

CHAPTER SIX: CHARITABLE SOCIETIES AND THE WELFARE
LANDSCAPE IN PRE-FAMINE BELFAST

1 I wish to thank Professor Olwen Purdue for assistance in the preparation of this chapter, as well as Sir Ronnie Weatherup for clarity on points respecting eighteenth-century legislation.

2 Henry Cooke, *A Sermon, Preached in the Meeting-house of the Third Presbyterian Congregation, Belfast, on Sunday, the 18th December, 1814, in aid of the funds of the House of Industry* (Belfast, 1815), p. 13.

3 Ibid., p. 22.

4 For a discussion of these themes, see Ciarán McCabe, *Begging, Charity and Religion in Pre-Famine Ireland* (Liverpool, 2018), pp. 105–24.

5 An expansion of Belfast's municipal boundary also contributed to the town's (later, the city's) growth.

6 S.J. Connolly, 'Improving town, 1750–1820', in S.J. Connolly (ed.), *Belfast 400: People, Place and History* (Liverpool, 2012), pp. 178–80; Peter Froggatt, 'Industrialisation and health in Belfast in the early nineteenth century', in David Harkness and Mary O'Dowd (eds), *The Town in Ireland. Historical Studies XIII* (Belfast, 1981), pp. 155–85.

7 Cooke, *A Sermon, Preached, in aid of the House of Industry*, pp. 21–2.

8 Register of the Second Presbyterian congregation, Belfast (PA), 6 February 1820, Public Record Office of Northern Ireland [hereafter PRONI], CR4/9/A/1; ibid., 6 August, 3 September 1820, 6 June 1824, 4 March 1827.

9 For instance, see *Belfast News-Letter* [hereafter *BNL*], 27 April 1832. For a discussion of vestries' welfare duties in this period, see McCabe, *Begging, Charity and Religion*, Chapter 4.

10 Rev. Abraham Dawson, 'The annals of Christ Church, Belfast, from its Foundation in 1831', typescript copy, 1858, PRONI, Records of Christ Church, Belfast, CR1/13/D/2, pp. 5–6, 11, 60. See Sean Farrell, 'Feed my lambs: the Reverend Thomas Drew and Protestant children in early Victorian Belfast', *New Hibernia Review*, vol. 19, no. 2 (summer 2015), pp. 43–58.

11 Alison Jordan, *Who Cared? Charity in Victorian and Edwardian Belfast* (Belfast, n.d. [1992]), pp. 196–7.

12 R.J. Morris, 'Voluntary societies and British urban elites, 1780–1850: An analysis', *Historical Journal*, vol. 26, no. 1 (March 1983), p. 109.

13 Connolly, 'Improving town', p. 169.

14 Jonathan Jeffrey Wright, *The 'Natural Leaders' and Their World: Politics, Culture and Society in Belfast, c. 1801–1832* (Liverpool, 2012), p. 201.

15 Quoted in Jonathan Bardon, *An Interesting and Honourable History: The Belfast Charitable Society, the First 250 Years, 1752–2002* (Belfast, 2002), p. 12. Despite the Society's establishment in 1752, it was another twenty-two years before the poorhouse at the northwestern end of Donegall Street opened.

16 *Belfast Commercial Chronicle* [hereafter *BCC*], 13 February 1811. The reference to the sermon being held in 'the Church of this town' suggests an Anglican place of worship, in contrast to a Dissenting meeting house or a Catholic chapel.

17 These themes are discussed in Laurence M. Geary, '"The best relief the poor can receive is from themselves": The Society for Promoting the Comforts of the Poor', in Laurence M. Geary and Oonagh Walsh (eds), *Philanthropy in Nineteenth-Century Ireland* (Dublin, 2015), pp. 40–1; McCabe, *Begging, Charity and Religion*, pp. 149–50.

18 The names of the Belfast House of Industry's directors are to be found in *BNL*, 4 May 1810; their occupations are identified in J.R.R. Adams, *Merchants in Plenty: Joseph Smyth's Belfast Directories of 1807 and 1808* (Belfast, 1991). For the names of the Dublin committee, see: *Report of the Association for the Suppression of Mendicity in Dublin, for the Year 1818* (Dublin, 1819); their occupations are identified in contemporary street and trade directories, such as *Watson's*.

19 W.H. Crawford, 'The Belfast middle classes in the late eighteenth century', in David Dickson, Dáire Keogh and Kevin Whelan (eds), *The United Irishmen: Republicanism, Radicalism and Rebellion* (Dublin, 1993), p. 64.

20 For the Marine Society, see: Joy Manuscripts, vol. 7, pp. 207–08 (Linen Hall Library, Belfast, Joy manuscripts). For the other institutions, see the useful appendix III in Wright, *The 'Natural Leaders' and Their World*, pp. 245–6.

21 *Martin's Belfast Directory, 1841*, pp. 246–7.

22 R.W.M. Strain, *Belfast and its Charitable Society: A Story of Urban Development* (London, 1961), pp. 82–95, 199–201; Bardon, *An Interesting and Honourable History*, pp. 28–9.

23 *BNL*, 17 June 1817; P. Frederick Gallaher [*sic*] to William Cunningham, 30 December 1831, PRONI, Cunningham and Clarke papers, D1108/A/28A; ibid., D1108/A/28B.

24 For the Belfast Charitable Society in this regard, see *BCC*, 29 May, 4 December 1805. For the House of Industry, see *BNL*, 17 June 1817, 7 January 1820.

25 *BNL*, 13 June 1809.

26 Ibid., 8 February 1811.

27 *BCC*, 30 December 1809.

28 *BNL*, 11 March 1817.

29 Ibid., 17 November 1815.

30 *BNL*, 13 June 1809. See also ibid., 4 March 1808.

31 Ciarán McCabe, 'The early years of the Strangers' Friend Society, Dublin: 1790–1845', *Bulletin of the Methodist Historical Society*, 19 (2014), pp. 65–93, at 66–9.

32 *BNL*, 18–21 March 1796.

33   John Joseph Monaghan, 'A social and economic history of Belfast, 1801–1825' (unpublished PhD thesis, Queen's University Belfast, 1940), pp. 446–7.

34   BCS Archive, Committee Minute Books, 17 June 1809. The Society's records, currently held at Clifton House, Belfast, were consulted by the present author while they were in the care of the Linen Hall Library, Belfast.

35   Dublin Mendicity Institution Minute Book, 13 July 1830, NLI, Dublin Mendicity Institute papers, MS 32,599/4; [Robert Perceval], *An Attempt Toward a Plan for Rendering the Charitable Institutions of Dublin More Effective by Cooperation* (Dublin, 1818), available in National Archives of Ireland, Chief Secretary's Office Registered Papers, CSORP 1160/10.

36   For these men's involvement with the SFS, see *BNL*, 30 December 1808. For their association with the House of Industry, see ibid., 14 July 1809.

37   *BNL*, 29 January, 9 September 1828, 19 August 1836. However, the society is not mentioned in the detailed outline of Belfast charitable institutions contained in the reports of the (Whately) Poor Inquiry of 1833–6: *Poor Inquiry (Ireland). Appendix (C.)–Parts I and II. Part I. Reports on the State of the Poor, and on the Charitable Institutions in Some of the Principal Towns; With Supplement Containing Answers to Queries. Part II. Report on the City of Dublin, and Supplement Containing Answers to Queries; With Addenda to Appendix (A.)., and Communications*, pp. 7–17, H.C. 1836 [Cd 35], xxx, 35.

38   BCS Archive, Committee Minute Books, 12 September 1774.

39   Ibid., 20 March 1775.

40   Steve Hindle, 'Dependency, shame and belonging: Badging the deserving poor, *c.* 1550–1750', *Cultural and Social History*, vol. 1, no. 1 (2004), pp. 6–35. Writing in 1737, Jonathan Swift observed that pride prevented many Dublin beggars from wearing badges: 'They are too lazy to work, they are not afraid to steal, not ashamed to beg; and yet are too proud to be seen with a Badge, as many of them have confessed to me, and not a few in very injurious Terms, particularly the Females. They all look upon such an Obligation as a high Indignity done to their Office.' See [Jonathan Swift], *A Proposal for Giving Badges to the Beggars in all the Parishes of Dublin* (London, 1737), p. 8.

41   Mel Cousins, 'The Irish parliament and relief of the poor: The 1772 legislation establishing houses of industry', *Eighteenth-Century Ireland*, vol. 28 (2013), 95–115; David Fleming and John Logan (eds), *Pauper Limerick: The Register of the Limerick House of Industry 1774–93* (Dublin, 2011), pp. xi–xxiv. For a broader discussion, see McCabe, *Begging, Charity and Religion*, pp. 134–8.

42   Quoted in Strain, *Belfast and its Charitable Society*, p. 57.

43   11 & 12 Geo. III [Ire.], c. 30. The 1774 legislation that incorporated the Belfast Charitable Society also extended to the Society the powers in respect of the poor that had already been granted to counties, county boroughs and cities under the 1772 statute: 13 & 14 Geo. III [Ire.], c. 46.

44   BCS Archive, Committee Minute Books, 23 September 1809.

45   F[rancis] Barker and J[ohn] Cheyne, *An Account of the Rise, Progress, and Decline of*

the Fever Lately Epidemical in Ireland ... vol. 1 (2 vols, Dublin and London, 1821), p. 60.

46 For the long-standing association of beggars with disease, see McCabe, *Begging, Charity and Religion*, pp. 105–14.

47 *Ireland. An Account of All Sums of Money Levied in the Several Parishes of Ireland, by Authority of Vestry ... Part I* (n.p., n.d. [*c.* 1824]), p. 354 (consulted at NLI, ref. Ir274108il).

48 Ibid., p. 377.

49 BCS Archive, Committee Minute Books, 8 March 1817.

50 Ibid., 26 April 1817. For a wider discussion of the early history of the town's police, see Brian Griffin, *The Bulkies: Police and Crime in Belfast, 1800–1865* (Dublin, 1998), pp. 1–22.

51 Barker and Cheyne, *Account of the Rise, Progress, and Decline of the Fever*, vol. 1, p. 460.

52 11 & 12 Geo. III, c. 30 [Ire.] (2 June 1772); 13 & 14 Geo. III, c. 46 [Ire.] (2 June 1774).

53 For the Dublin and London societies, see Audrey Woods, *Dublin Outsiders: A History of the Mendicity Institution 1818–1998* (Dublin, 1998); M.J.D. Roberts, 'Reshaping the gift relationship: The London Mendicity Society and the suppression of begging in England 1818–1869', *International Review of Social History*, 36 (1991), pp. 201–31. The wider movement is considered in detail in McCabe, *Begging, Charity and Religion*, pp. 146–84.

54 Raymond Gillespie and Stephen A. Royle, *Belfast, Part I, to 1840* (Irish Historic Towns Atlas, no. 12) (Dublin, 2003), p. 22; *BNL*, 14 July 1809.

55 John Dubourdieu, *Statistical Survey of the County of Antrim, with Observations on the Means of Improvement; Drawn up for the Consideration, and by Direction of the Dublin Society* (Dublin, 1812), pp. 410–11.

56 Anon., 'Abolition of mendicity', *Belfast Monthly Magazine*, vol. 2, no. 11 (30 June 1809), p. 436.

57 'Rules and regulations for the House of Industry, in Belfast, laid before a general meeting of the town for their approbation, and unanimously agreed to', *Belfast Monthly Magazine*, vol. 4, no. 21 (30 April 1810), p. 263.

58 *Second Report of Geo. Nicholls, Esq., to Her Majesty's Principal Secretary of State for the Home Department, on Poor Laws, Ireland*, p. 11, H.C. 1837–38 [Cd 104], xxxviii, p. 667.

59 *Poor Inquiry (Ireland). Appendix (C.) ... Part I. Reports on the State of the Poor, and on the Charitable Institutions in Some of the Principal Towns; With Supplement Containing Answers to Queries*, p. 11, H.C. 1836 [Cd 35], xxx, p. 47.

60 'Rules and regulations for the House of Industry, Belfast', p. 261.

61 *Leinster Journal*, 19 April 1820.

62 *BNL*, 14 July 1809.

63 *BNL*, 15 September 1809.

64 *BNL*, 14 July 1809; *Poor Inquiry. First Report, 1836, Appendix C, Part I*, p. 11; Jordan, *Who Cared?*, pp. 20–21; *Martin's Belfast Directory for 1841–42*, pp. 246–7.

65 *Poor Inquiry. First Report, 1836, Appendix C, Part I*, p. 13.

66 *BNL*, 15 May 1810; 'Rules and regulations for the House of Industry, Belfast', p. 267.

67 *Poor Inquiry. First Report, 1836, Appendix C, Part I*, p. 12.

68 Ibid., pp. 13, 12.

69 Wright, *The 'Natural Leaders' and Their World*, pp. 202–3.

70 *Poor Inquiry. First Report, 1836, Appendix C, Part I*, pp. 13–14. See also *The Sixth Report of the General Committee of the Mendicity Association, Instituted in Londonderry, 13th May, 1825 … (Derry, 1831)*, pp. 6–7.

71 *BCC*, 19 September 1838. In Dublin, Master Connor of the Mendicity Association appealed to similar sensibilities, telling a gathering of the charity's managers and supporters, 'If this work-house system be adopted as the sole remedy for distress, then would an end be put to those voluntary charities – those voluntary acts of kindness and benevolence which have conferred honour on those by whom I am surrounded (hear, hear)': *The Freeman's Journal*, 21 February 1838.

72 Ciarán McCabe, '"The going out of the voluntary and the coming in of the compulsory": The impact of the 1838 Irish Poor Law on voluntary charitable societies in Dublin city', *Irish Economic and Social History*, vol. 45 (2018), pp. 47–69.

73 McCabe, *Begging, Charity and Religion*, pp. 169–84.

74 *The Northern Whig*, 9 February 1839. See also Strain, *Belfast and its Charitable Society*, pp. 294–9.

75 *The Newry Examiner & Louth Advertiser*, 19 August 1840.

76 *BCC*, 10 August 1839.

77 *Appendices B. to F. to the Eighth Annual Report of the Poor Law Commissioners*, Appendix E, no. 10, p. 384, H.C. 1842 [Cd 399], xix, 396.

78 *BNL*, 4 June 1841.

79 *BNL*, 9 February 1841.

80 *BNL*, 25 December 1840.

81 *BNL*, 23 December 1842. For this period in Belfast, including the decline of the Belfast House of Industry, see Christine Kinealy and Gerard MacAtasney, *The Hidden Famine: Poverty, Hunger and Sectarianism in Belfast, 1840–50* (London, 2000), pp. 24–32.

82 Strain, *Belfast and its Charitable Society*, pp. 298–9.

83 Ibid., p. 299. See also Bardon, *An Interesting and Honourable History*, p. 34.

84 W.E. Vaughan and A.J. Fitzpatrick (eds), *Irish Historical Statistics. Population, 1821–1971* (Dublin, 1978), p. 36.

85 The full first report is published in *BNL*, 6 January 1843.

86 Kinealy and MacAtasney, *The Hidden Famine*, p. 92.

87 R.J. Morris, 'Civil society and the nature of urbanism: Britain, 1750–1850', *Urban History*, vol. 25, no. 3 (1998), pp. 289–301; Morris, 'Voluntary societies and British urban elites'.

CHAPTER SEVEN: CHILD WELFARE AND EDUCATION
IN THE INDUSTRIALISING TOWN

1   Belfast Charitable Society [hereafter BCS] Archive, Committee Minute Books, 1775–6.
2   Ibid.
3   Alysa Levene, *Childcare, Health and Mortality at the London Foundling Hospital, 1741–1800: 'Left to the mercy of the world'* (Manchester, 2007); Frances Miley and Andrew Read, 'Go gentle babe: Accounting and the London Foundling Hospital 1757–97', *Accounting History*, vol. 21, nos 2–3 (2016), pp. 167–84.
4   Lesley Hulonce, *Pauper Children and Poor Law Childhoods in England and Wales, 1834–1910* (Swansea, 2016), available online at Cronfra-Swansea University open access repository, https://cronfraswan.ac.uk/Record/cronfa29574 (accessed 16/06/2021); Katrina Honeyman, *Child Workers in England, 1780–1820: Parish Apprentices and the Making of the Early Industrial Labour Force* (Aldershot, 2007).
5   Maria Luddy, *Women and Philanthropy in Nineteenth-century Ireland* (Cambridge, 1995).
6   Olwen Purdue, 'Nineteenth-century NIMBYs, or what the neighbour saw? Poverty, surveillance, and the boarding-out of poor law children in late nineteenth-century Belfast', *Family and Community History*, vol. 23, no. 2 (2020), pp. 119–35; Sarah-Anne Buckley, *The Cruelty Man: Child Welfare, the NSPCC and the State of Ireland, 1889–1956* (Manchester, 2013).
7   R.W.M. Strain, *Belfast and its Charitable Society: A Story of Urban Social Development* (London, 1961), p. 18; S.J. Connolly, 'Improving town, 1750–1820', in S.J. Connolly (ed.), *Belfast 400: People, Place and History* (Liverpool, 2012), p. 168.
8   *Belfast News-Letter* [hereafter *BNL*], 6 July 1752.
9   Ibid.; Connolly, 'Improving town, 1750–1820', p. 168.
10 BCS Archive, Committee Minute Books, 1775–6.
11 Ibid., p. 97.
12 Francis Duke, 'Pauper education', in Derek Fraser (ed.), *The New Poor Law in the Nineteenth Century* (London, 1976), p. 67; Claire Marie Rennie, 'The education of children in London's foundling hospital, c. 1800–1825', *Childhood in the Past*, vol. 11, no. 1 (2018), p. 9; Deborah Simonton, 'Schooling the poor: Gender and class in eighteenth-century England', *British Journal for Eighteenth-Century Studies*, vol. 23 (2000), pp. 183–93.
13 Irish Poor Relief Act, 1838, 1 and 2 Vic., c. 56.
14 Harry Hendrick, *Children, Childhood and English Society 1880–1990* (Cambridge, 1997), pp. 36–8.
15 Factory Inspector's Report 1857, quoted in Marjorie Cruickshank, 'Factory children and compulsory education: The short-time system in the textile areas of north-west England 1833–64', *The Vocational Aspect of Education*, vol. 30, no. 77 (1978), p. 114.
16 Ray Pallister, 'Workhouse education in County Durham: 1834–1870', *The British Journal of Educational Studies*, vol. 16, no. 3 (October 1968), p. 279.

17   Jane Humphries, 'Care and cruelty in the workhouse: Children's experience of residential poor relief in eighteenth- and nineteenth-century England', in Nigel Goose and Katrina Honeyman (eds), *Childhood and Child Labour in Industrial England: Diversity and Agency, 1750–1914* (Surrey, 2013), p. 125.

18   Alysa Levene, 'Charity apprenticeship and social capital in eighteenth-century London', in Nigel Goose and Katrina Honeyman (eds), *Childhood and Child Labour*, p. 61.

19   Jane Humphries, *Childhood and Child Labour in the British Industrial Revolution* (Cambridge, 2010), pp. 329–30.

20   Cruickshank, 'Factory children and compulsory education', p. 112.

21   W.B. Stephens, *Education in Britain 1750–1914* (Basingstoke, 1998), p. 4; Elaine Brown, 'Working-class education and illiteracy in Leicester, 1780–1870' (PhD thesis, University of Leicester, 2002), p. 23.

22   Stephens, *Education in Britain 1750–1914*, p. 4.

23   Brown, 'Working-class education and illiteracy in Leicester, 1780–1870', p. 24.

24   Malcolm McKinnon Dick, 'English conservatives and schools of the poor c. 1780–1870' (PhD thesis, University of Leicester, 2002), p. 184.

25   Ibid., pp. 184–218.

26   Dick, 'English conservatives and schools of the poor', p. 211.

27   Kenneth Milne, 'Irish Charter Schools', *The Irish Journal of Education/ Iris Eireannach an Oideachais*, vol. 8, no. 1 (Summer, 1974), p. 5.

28   Ibid.

29   Ibid., p. 17.

30   Ibid.

31   Ibid.

32   Deborah Simonton, 'Schooling the poor: Gender and class in eighteenth-century England', *British Journal for Eighteenth-Century Studies*, no. 23 (2000), p. 185.

33   Ibid.

34   Simonton, 'Schooling the poor', p. 186.

35   BCS Archive, Committee Minute Books, 1775–6.

36   Hendrick, *Children, Childhood and English Society*, p. 38.

37   Heather Shore, *Artful Dodgers: Youth and Crime in early 19th-century London* (London, 1999), p. 35.

38   S.J. Connolly and Gillian McIntosh, 'Whose city? Belonging and exclusion in the nineteenth-century urban world', in S.J. Connolly (ed.), *Belfast 400* (Liverpool, 2012), p. 237.

39   BCS Archive, Orderly Book, 1775–7.

40   BCS Archive, Committee Minute Books, 1776–9.

41   BCS Archive, Orderly Report Book, 1803–20.

42   BCS Archive, Committee Minute Books, 1805–11.

43   BCS Archive, Committee Minute Books, 1776–9; Orderly Book, 1775–7.

44   BCS Archive, Committee Minute Books, 1776–9.

45   Dick, 'English conservatives and schools of the poor', p. 25.

46 Connolly and McIntosh, 'Whose city?', p. 245.

47 Ibid.

48 BCS Archive, Orderly Report Book, 1803–20.

49 BCS Archive, Orderly Book, 1775–7.

50 BCS Archive, Committee Minute Books, 1805–11.

51 Ibid.

52 Kenneth Milne, *The Irish Charter Schools, 1730–1830* (Dublin, 1997), p. 20.

53 Ernst Guggisberg, 'The reduction of poverty starts with children: Swiss societies for educating the poor in the nineteenth and twentieth centuries', in Beate Althammer, Lutz Raphael and Tamara Stazic-Wendt (eds), *Rescuing the Vulnerable: Poverty, Welfare and Social Ties in Modern Europe* (New York, 2016), p. 100.

54 Tom Walsh, 'The national system of education, 1831–2000', in Brendan Walsh (ed.), *Essays in the History of Irish Education* (London, 2016), p. 7; Patrick John Dowling, *The Hedge Schools of Ireland* (Dublin, 1935), pp. 45–9.

55 S.J. Connolly, 'Improving town, 1750–1820', p. 175.

56 Claire Allen, 'Urban elites, civil society and governance in early nineteenth-century Belfast, c. 1800–1832' (PhD thesis, Queen's University Belfast, 2010), p. 232.

57 BCS Archive, Orderly Report Book, 1803–20.

58 Ibid.

59 Ibid.

60 Ibid.

61 Brown, 'Working-class education and illiteracy in Leicester', p. 15.

62 Hendrick, *Children, Childhood and English Society*, p. 39.

63 BCS Archive, Orderly Report Book, 1803–20.

64 Ibid.

65 Ibid.

66 Brown, 'Working-class education and illiteracy in Leicester', pp. 15–16.

67 BCS Archive, Report of the committee of industry: Regulation for the sewing girls, 22 May 1813.

68 Ibid.

69 Ibid.

70 Ibid.

71 Caitriona Clear, *Social Change and Everyday Life in Ireland, 1850–1922* (Manchester, 2009), p. 64.

72 *BNL*, 8 April–11 April 1783.

73 BCS Archive, Committee Minute Books, 1776–9.

74 Honeyman, *Child Workers in England, 1780–1820*, p. 17.

75 Alysa Levene, 'Parish apprenticeship and the old poor law in London', *Economic Review History*, vol. 63, no. 4 (2010), p. 939.

76 Honeyman, *Child Workers in England, 1780–1820*, p. 128.

77 Levene, *Childcare, Health and Mortality*, p. 195.

78 Honeyman, *Child Workers in England, 1780–1820*, p. 128.

79 Quoted in Olwen Purdue, 'Poverty and power: The Irish poor law in a north Antrim town, 1861–1921', *Irish Historical Studies*, vol. 37, no. 148 (November 2011), p. 568.

80 Levene, 'Parish apprenticeship and the old poor law in London', p. 919.

81 BCS Archive, Committee Minute Books, 1771–4 (Clifton House, MS1/2015/002/0003); BCS Archive, Committee Minute Books, 1775–6 (Clifton House, MS1/2015/002/0004); BCS Archive, Committee Minute Books, 1776–9 (Clifton House; MS1/2015/002/0005); BCS Archive, Committee Minute Books, 1800–5 (Clifton House, MS1/2015/003/0008); BCS Archive, Committee Minute Books, 1805–11 (Clifton House, MS1/2015/004/0009); BCS Archive, Committee Minute Books, 1811–18 (Clifton House, MS1/2015/004/0010); BCS Archive, Admission Record, 1798–1837 (Clifton House, MS12/2015/002/0047).

82 Pamela Sharpe, 'Poor children as apprentices in Colyton, 1598–1830', *Continuity and Change*, vol. 6, pt 2 (1991), p. 255; Levene, 'Parish apprenticeship and the old poor law in London', p. 924.

83 BCS Archive, Examiner's report of the boy's school, 2 October 1813.

84 Ibid.

85 BCS Archive, Committee Minute Books, 1811–18.

86 Allen, 'Urban elites, civil society and governance', p. 227.

87 Ibid.

88 Levene, 'Parish apprenticeship and the old poor law in Law', p. 916.

89 BCS Archive, Committee Minute Books, 1771–4 (Clifton House, MS1/2015/002/0003); BCS Archive, Committee Minute Books, 1775–6 (Clifton House, MS1/2015/002/0004); BCS Archive, Committee Minute Books, 1776–9 (Clifton House; MS1/2015/002/0005); BCS Archive, Committee Minute Books, 1800–5 (Clifton House, MS1/2015/003/0008); BCS Archive, Committee Minute Books, 1805–11 (Clifton House, MS1/2015/004/0009); BCS Archive, Committee Minute Books, 1811–18 (Clifton House, MS1/2015/004/0010); BCA Archive, Admission Record, 1798–1837 (Clifton House, MS12/2015/002/0047).

90 Jonathan Bardon, *Belfast: An Illustrated History* (Belfast: Blackstaff Press, 1982), p. 31.

91 Levene, 'Parish apprenticeship and the old poor law in London', p. 927.

92 Andy Bielenberg, 'The Irish economy, 1815–1880: Agricultural transition, the communications revolution and the limits of industrialisation', in James Kelly (ed.), *The Cambridge history of Ireland, Volume 3: 1730–1880* (Cambridge, 2018), p. 180; Ina Scherder, 'Galway workhouses in the nineteenth and twentieth centuries: Function and strategy', in Andreas Gestrich, Steven King and Lutz Raphael (eds), *Being Poor in Modern Europe: Historical Perspectives 1800–1940* (Oxford, 2006), p. 188; Katharina Brandes, 'Orphans, pauper children or wayward children? The lives of children cared for by public institutions in Hamburg, 1892–1914', in Beate Althammer, Lutz Raphael and Tamara Stazic-Wendt (eds), *Rescuing the Vulnerable*, p. 77.

93 Clear, *Social Change and Everyday Life*, p. 34.

94 Honeyman, *Child Workers in England, 1780-1820*, p. 151.

95 Ibid., p. 151.

96 Levene, *Childcare, Health and Mortality*, p. 204.

97 Honeyman, 'Compulsion, compassion and consent', pp. 74–5.

98 Levene, *The Childhood of the Poor*, pp. 73–4.

99 BCS Archive, Committee Minute Books, 1800–5.

100 Ibid.

101 Ibid.

102 Ibid.

103 Honeyman, *Child Workers in England, 1780-1820*, p. 176.

CHAPTER EIGHT: POORHOUSE TO PANDEMIC

1 David Kennedy, 'The early eighteenth century', in J.C. Beckett and R.E. Glasscock (eds), *Belfast: The Origin and Growth of an Industrial City* (London, 1967), p. 51.

2 J.L. McCracken, 'Early Victorian Belfast', in Beckett and Glasscock (eds), *Belfast*, p. 92.

3 J.B. Bryan, *A Practical View of Ireland, from the Period of the Union: With plans for the permanent relief of her poor, and the improvement of her municipal organization: To which is annexed, a comparative survey of the laws and institutions of foreign states, for the maintenance, education, and protection of the working classes* (Dublin, 1831), p. 64.

4 Catherine Cox, 'Discursive essay: A better known territory? Medical history and Ireland', *Proceedings of the Royal Irish Academy. Section C: Archaeology, Celtic Studies, History, Linguistics, Literature*, vol. 113 (2013), p. 343.

5 Richard Clarke, *The Royal Victoria Hospital Belfast: A History 1797-1997* (Belfast, 1997); J.F. O'Sullivan, *Belfast City Hospital: A Photographic History* (Donaghadee, 2003).

6 Laurence M. Geary, *Medicine and Charity in Ireland* (Dublin, 2004), p. 2.

7 Ronald Cassell, *Medical Charities, Medical Politics: The Irish Dispensary System and the Poor Law, 1836-1872* (Woodbridge, 1997); Mark Finnane, *Insanity and the Insane in Post-Famine Ireland* (London, 1981); Catherine Cox, *Negotiating Insanity in the South East of Ireland, 1820-1900* (Manchester, 2012); Margaret Preston and Margaret Ó hÓgartaigh (eds), *Gender and Medicine in Ireland, 1700-1950* (Syracuse, 2012); Catherine Cox and Maria Luddy (eds), *Cultures of Care in Irish Medical History, 1750-1970* (Basingstoke, 2010).

8 S.J. Connolly (ed.), *Belfast 400: People, Place and History* (Liverpool, 2012); S.A. Royle, *Portrait of an Industrial City: 'Clanging Belfast', 1750-1914* (Belfast, 2011); David Hempton and Myrtle Hill, *Evangelical Protestantism in Ulster Society 1740-1890* (London, 1992); Michael Farrell, *The Poor Law and the Workhouse in Belfast 1838-1948* (Belfast, 1978); Olwen Purdue (ed.), *Belfast, The Emerging City: 1850-1914* (Dublin, 2012).

9   R.W.M. Strain, *Belfast and its Charitable Society: A Story of Urban Social Development* (London, 1961).

10   G.M. Beale, 'Treating Ulster's rural poor: The county infirmaries of Armagh and Down 1766–1851', *The Ulster Medical Journal*, vol. 71, no. 2 (2002), p. 111; Pierce Grace, 'Patronage and health care in eighteenth-century Irish county infirmaries', *Irish Historical Studies*, vol. 41, no. 159 (2017), p. 5.

11   *Poor Inquiry (Ireland), Appendix B, containing general reports upon the existing system of public medical relief in Ireland; local reports upon dispensaries, fever hospitals, county infirmaries, and lunatic asylums; with supplement, Parts i and ii containing answers to questions from the officers, &c. of medical institutions,* [369] H.C. 1835 xxxii, 24–5.

12   Beale, 'Treating Ulster's rural poor', p. 115; Grace, 'Patronage and health care', p. 17.

13   Andrew Sneddon, 'State intervention and provincial health care: The county infirmary system in late eighteenth-century Ulster', *Irish Historical Studies*, vol. 38, no. 149 (2012), pp. 8–12; Grace, 'Patronage and health care', p. 9.

14   Beale, 'Treating Ulster's rural poor', p. 111.

15   Sneddon, 'State intervention and provincial health care', p. 20.

16   Grace, 'Patronage and health care', pp. 5, 17, 19.

17   G.M. Beale, 'Dispensaries in counties Armagh and Down in the pre-Famine years', *The Ulster Medical Journal*, vol. 66, no. 2 (1997), p. 123.

18   Ibid., pp. 130–1.

19   Ibid., pp. 123, 132.

20   Geary, *Medicine and Charity in Ireland*, pp. 76, 86.

21   Ibid., p. 89.

22   Ibid., p. 66.

23   Cassell, *Medical Charities, Medical Politics*, pp. 7, 10.

24   Strain, *Belfast and its Charitable Society*, p. 54.

25   Ibid., p. 74.

26   Ibid.

27   Ibid., p. 75.

28   T.H. Mullin, *Coleraine in Georgian Times* (Belfast, 1977), pp. 58–9.

29   Laurence M. Geary, '"The wages of sin is death": Lock hospitals, venereal disease, and gender in pre-famine Ireland', in Preston and Ó hÓgartaigh (eds), *Gender and Medicine in Ireland, 1700–1950*, p. 161; Katherine Fennelly, 'The institution and the city: The impact of hospitals and workhouses on the development of Dublin's north inner city, c. 1773–1911', *Urban History*, vol. 47 (2020), p. 674.

30   James Kelly, 'Charitable societies: Their genesis and development, 1720–1800', in James Kelly and Martyn J. Powell (eds), *Clubs and Societies in Eighteenth-century Ireland* (Dublin, 2010), p. 90.

31   Strain, *Belfast and its Charitable Society*, p. 76.

32   Ibid., p. 80.

33   Margaret Preston, *Charitable Words: Women, Philanthropy, and the Language of Charity in Nineteenth-century Dublin* (Westport, 2004), pp. 175–6.

34 Peter Mandler, 'Poverty and charity in the nineteenth-century metropolis: An introduction', in Peter Mandler (ed.), *The Uses of Charity: The Poor on Relief in the Nineteenth-century Metropolis* (Philadelphia, 1990), p. 20.

35 Mary McNeill, *The Life and Times of Mary Ann McCracken: A Belfast Panorama* (Belfast, 1960), p. 254.

36 Feeonagh Chambers, 'Calendar of the minute book entries of the ladies' committee of the Belfast Charitable Society 1827–51' (MA calendar, QUB, 2001), p. 1.

37 McNeill, *The Life and Times of Mary Ann McCracken*, p. 263; Chambers, 'Calendar of the minute book entries of the ladies' committee', p. 12.

38 McNeill, *The Life and Times of Mary Ann McCracken*, pp. 281–2.

39 Chambers, 'Calendar of the minute book entries of the ladies' committee', pp. 13–32.

40 BCS Archive, Steward's Reports 1814–16, 26 March 1814.

41 BCS Archive, Orderly Book, 1821–53, 1 November 1823.

42 BCS Archive, Steward's Notebook 1805–10, 10 August 1805, 30 August 1806, 6 December 1806.

43 Clarke, *The Royal Victoria Hospital*, p. 5.

44 M.E. Rose, 'The doctor in the industrial revolution', *British Journal of Industrial Medicine*, vol. 28, no. 1 (1971), p. 23.

45 Clarke, *The Royal Victoria Hospital*, p. 14.

46 J.S. Logan, 'The working man of the profession', *The Ulster Medical Journal*, vol. 43, no. 1 (1974), p. 24.

47 H.G. Calwell, *Andrew Malcolm of Belfast 1818–1856: Physician and Historian* (Belfast, 1977), p. 25.

48 Strain, *Belfast and its Charitable Society*, p. 74.

49 Ibid., p. 77.

50 Clarke, *The Royal Victoria Hospital*, p. 3.

51 Geary, *Medicine and Charity in Ireland*, p. 20.

52 J.V. Pickstone, *Medicine and Industrial Society: A History of Hospital Development in Manchester and its Region, 1752–1946* (Manchester, 1985), p. 35.

53 BCS Archive, Ladies' Committee Minute Books, 3 September 1828.

54 BCS Archive, Orderly Book, 23 March 1822.

55 McNeill, *The Life and Times of Mary Ann McCracken*, pp. 270–1.

56 Joshua R. Eyler, 'Introduction breaking boundaries, building bridges', in Joshua Eyler (ed.), *Disability in the Middle Ages: Reconsiderations and Reverberations* (Farnham, 2010), p. 3.

57 David M. Turner, 'Picturing disability in eighteenth-century England', in Michael Rembis, Catherine J. Kudlick and Kim E. Nielson (eds), *The Oxford Handbook of Disability History* (New York, 2018), p. 345.

58 BCS Archive, Steward's Notebook, 1810–14, 8 December 1810, 19 January 1811, 21 September 1811, 20 June 1812.

59 Strain, *Belfast and its Charitable Society*, p. 61.

60 For further reading on the insane and the rise of asylums, see Catherine Cox, *Negotiating Insanity in the Southeast of Ireland 1830–1900* (Manchester, 2012); Mark

Finnane, *Insanity and the Insane in Post-Famine Ireland* (London, 1981); Joseph Robins, *Fools and Mad: A History of the Insane in Ireland* (Dublin: Institute of Public Administration, 1986).

61   Oonagh Walsh, 'Cure or custody: Therapeutic philosophy at the Connaught District Lunatic Asylum', in Preston and Ó hÓgartaigh (eds), *Gender and Medicine in Ireland, 1700–1950*, p. 81.

62   Alice Mauger, *The Cost of Insanity in Nineteenth-century Ireland: Public, Voluntary and Private Asylum Care* (Cham, 2018), p. 152.

63   Strain, *Belfast and its Charitable Society*, pp. 79, 287.

64   Pauline Prior, 'Gender and criminal lunacy in nineteenth-century Ireland', in Preston and Ó hÓgartaigh (eds), *Gender and Medicine in Ireland, 1700–1950*, p. 87.

65   Strain, *Belfast and its Charitable Society*, p. 287.

66   BCS Archive, Steward's Notebook, 1810–14.

67   BCS Archive, Steward's Notebook, 1810–14.

68   Walsh, 'Cure or custody', p. 77.

69   Fennelly, 'The institution and the city', p. 675.

70   BCS Archive, Steward's Notebook, 1810–14, 16 June 1810.

71   BCS Archive, Steward's Notebook, 1810–14, 25 June, 16 July 1814.

72   Eoin O'Brien, 'Chronology of the House of Industry and the Richmond, Whitworth and Hardwicke Hospitals', in Eoin O'Brien, Lorna Browne and Kevin O'Malley (eds), *The House of Industry Hospitals 1772–1987* (Monkstown, 1988), p. 291.

73   BCS Archive, Letter from Lord Lieutenant to Belfast Charitable Society, 25 February 1819.

74   Strain, *Belfast and its Charitable Society*, p. 288.

75   Ibid., p. 289.

76   *Belfast Almanack* [hereafter *BA*], 1831, p. 47.

77   A.G. Malcolm, *The History of the General Hospital, Belfast, and the Other Medical Institutions of the Town; with chronological notes and biographical reminiscences connected with its rise and progress* (Belfast: W. & G. Agnew, 1851), p. 91; Proceedings Book of Belfast District Lunatic Asylum, 20 May 1829, PRONI, HOS28/1/2/1.

78   J.A. Pilson, *History of the Rise and Progress of Belfast, and Annals of the County Antrim, from the Earliest Period till the Present Time* (Belfast, 1846), p. 49.

79   Finnane, *Insanity and the Insane in Post-Famine Ireland*, p. 27.

80   Walsh, 'Cure or custody', pp. 84–5.

81   *Fifteenth Annual Report of the Belfast District Lunatic Asylum for the Insane Poor of the Counties of Antrim and Down, and County of the Town of Carrickfergus, for the Year ended the 31st of March, 1845* (Belfast, 1845), p. 15.

82   *Twelfth Annual Report of the Belfast District Lunatic Asylum for the Insane Poor of the Counties of Antrim and Down, and County of the Town of Carrickfergus, for the Year ended the 31st of March, 1842* (Belfast, 1842), p. 10.

83   Malcolm, *The History of the General Hospital*, p. xxix.

84   Mauger, *The Cost of Insanity in Nineteenth-century Ireland*, pp. 231–3.

85   4 October 1830, Proceedings Book of Lunatic Asylum.

86 6 May 1833, Proceedings Book of Lunatic Asylum; Denis Phelan, *A Statistical Inquiry into the Present State of the Medical Charities of Ireland; with suggestions for a medical poor law, by which they may be rendered much more extensively efficient* (Dublin, 1835), p. 234.

87 *Poor Inquiry, Appendix B*, p. 31.

88 Walsh, 'Cure or custody', p. 72.

89 *Eighth Annual Report of the Belfast District Asylum for the Insane Poor of the Counties of Antrim and Down, and County of the Town of Carrickfergus, for the Year ended the 31st of March, 1838* (Belfast, 1838), p. 6.

90 Malcolm, *The History of the General Hospital*, p. 91.

91 *Fourteenth Annual Report of the Belfast District Asylum for the Insane Poor of the Counties of Antrim and Down, and County of the Town of Carrickfergus, for the Year ended the 31st of March, 1844* (Belfast, 1844), pp. 11–12; P.M. Prior, 'Murder and madness: Gender and the insanity defence in nineteenth-century Ireland', *New Hibernia Review*, vol. 4, no. 4 (2005), p. 20.

92 6 February 1832, Proceedings Book of Lunatic Asylum.

93 Malcolm, *The History of the General Hospital*, p. 93; Finnane, *Insanity and the Insane in Post-Famine Ireland*, p. 40.

94 *Fourteenth Annual Report of the Belfast District Asylum*, p. 27.

95 *Fifteenth Annual Report of the Belfast District Asylum*, pp. 21–2.

96 Ian Campbell Ross, 'The early years of the Dublin Lying-in Hospital', in Ian Campbell Ross (ed.) *Public Virtue, Public Love: The Early Years of the Dublin Lying-in Hospital* (Dublin, 1986), p. 14.

97 Geary, *Medicine and Charity in Ireland*, p. 20.

98 Campbell Ross, 'The early years of the Dublin Lying-in Hospital', p. 14.

99 J.F. O'Sullivan, 'Two hundred years of midwifery 1806–2006', *The Ulster Medical Journal*, 75, 3 (2006), p. 214.

100 Malcolm, *The History of the General Hospital*, p. 44.

101 *BA*, 1805, p. 40.

102 Malcolm, *The History of the General Hospital*, pp. 44–5.

103 O'Sullivan, 'Two hundred years of midwifery', p. 216; Strain, *Belfast and its Charitable Society*, pp. 164–5.

104 Strain, *Belfast and its Charitable Society*, p. 163.

105 *Report of the Late Committee of the Lying-in Hospital, Belfast; together with a statement of accounts, and a list of the subscribers, for the year ending 31st December, 1829* (Belfast, 1830), p. 9.

106 BCS Archive, Steward's Notebook, 1810–14, 22 August 1812.

107 Strain, *Belfast and its Charitable Society*, p. 167.

108 Ibid., p. 168.

109 Ibid., p. 169.

110 Pickstone, *Medicine and Industrial Society*, pp. 32–4.

111 Calwell, *Andrew Malcolm of Belfast 1818–1856*, p. 13.

112 Geary, *Medicine and Charity in Ireland*, pp. 140–1.

113 Figures taken from *BA*, 1809–1828 and Minute Books of the Lying-in Hospital Belfast 1829–1835, PRONI, HOS32/1/1.

114 O'Sullivan, 'Two hundred years of midwifery', p. 216.

115 Malcolm, *The History of the General Hospital*, p. 46; *Belfast General and Commercial Directory for 1819 containing an alphabetical list of the merchants, manufacturers and inhabitants in general: And a history of Belfast and its institutions* (Belfast, 1819); *Henderson's new Belfast directory and northern repository for 1843–44 containing information relating to the Counties of Antrim, Armagh and Down with lists of the inhabitants of the chief towns, also an alphabetical list of the inhabitants of Belfast together with a street directory and a classification of trades and professions also a plan of Belfast, map of Antrim, and distance table of Ireland* (Belfast, 1843).

116 Malcolm, *The History of the General Hospital*, p. 46.

117 J.K. Feeney, *The Coombe Lying-in Hospital* (Dublin, 1983), p. 25.

118 Cormac Ó Gráda, 'Dublin's demography in the early nineteenth century: Evidence from the Rotunda', *Population Studies*, vol. 45, no. 1 (1991), p. 46.

119 Malcolm, *The History of the General Hospital*, Appendix xxx.

120 Clarke, *The Royal Victoria Hospital*, p. 3.

121 *BA*, 1805, p. 39; *The Census of Ireland for the Year 1851. Part V. Tables of Deaths. Vol. II. Containing the tables and index*, 261 [2087] H.C. 1856, xxix, p. 167.

122 McNeill, *The Life and Times of Mary Ann McCracken*, p. 53.

123 Geary, *Medicine and Charity in Ireland*, pp. 70, 75.

124 Malcolm, *The History of the General Hospital*, p. 57.

125 T.P. O'Neill, 'Fever and public health in pre-Famine Ireland', *The Journal of the Royal Society of Antiquaries of Ireland*, vol. 103 (1973), p. 7; Strain, *Belfast and its Charitable Society*, p. 158.

126 Malcolm, *The History of the General Hospital*, p. 41.

127 George Benn, *A History of the Town of Belfast from 1799 till 1810, together with some incidental notices on local topics and biographies of many well-known families, Volume II* (London and Belfast, 1880), pp. 26, 162.

128 Pilson, *History of the Rise and Progress of Belfast*, p. 45.

129 *BA*, 1818, p. 41.

130 *BA*, 1809–1851.

131 *Belfast 1819 Directory*; Strain, *Belfast and its Charitable Society*, p. 154.

132 BCS Archive, Letters from Fever Hospital to Belfast Charitable Society, 16 June 1822; 30 June 1822; 20 July 1822.

133 Strain, *Belfast and its Charitable Society*, p. 157.

134 Ibid.

135 Ibid., p. 158.

136 Ibid.

137 Geary, *Medicine and Charity in Ireland*, p. 27; Pickstone, *Medicine and Industrial Society*, p. 46.

138 Strain, *Belfast and its Charitable Society*, p. 158.

139 *Belfast Newsletter* [hereafter *BNL*], 10 June 1828.

140 *BNL*, 10 May, 17 May, 4 June 1833.

141 *BA*, 1818, p. 41; Queries for Belfast Fever Hospital and Dispensary, PRONI, D1923/3/15; *Poor Inquiry, Appendix B*, p. 30; Phelan, *A Statistical Inquiry into the Present State of the Medical Charities of Ireland*, p. 139.

142 William Mateer, 'Statistics of fever, with general observations on its nature, causes and treatment', *The Dublin Journal of Medical Science; exhibiting a comprehensive view of the latest discoveries in medicine, surgery, and the collateral science*, vol. 10 (1836), p. 34.

143 Phelan, *A Statistical Inquiry into the Present State of the Medical Charities of Ireland*, Table IX.

144 *Poor Inquiry, Appendix B*, p. 325.

145 Geary, '"The wages of sin is death"', pp. 155–6.

146 Ibid., p. 156.

147 Queries for Belfast Fever Hospital and Dispensary.

148 Malcolm, *The History of the General Hospital*, Appendix xxv.

149 Pilson, *History of the Rise and Progress of Belfast*, p. 46.

150 Calwell, *Andrew Malcolm of Belfast 1818–1856*, p. 21.

151 Clarke, *The Royal Victoria Hospital*, p. 3.

152 Ibid., p. 9.

153 Hugh Fenning, 'Typhus epidemic in Ireland, 1817–1819: Priests, ministers, doctors', *Collectanea Hibernica*, 41 (1999), p. 117.

154 G.M. Beale, 'Fever hospitals in counties Armagh and Down: 1817–39', *The Ulster Medical Journal*, vol. 69, no. 1 (2000), p. 44.

155 Fenning, 'Typhus epidemic in Ireland, 1817–1819', p. 117.

156 Clarke, *The Royal Victoria Hospital*, p. 9; Malcolm, *The History of the General Hospital*, p. 76.

157 W.E. Vaughan and A.J. Fitzpatrick (eds), *Irish Historical Statistics: Population, 1821–1971* (Dublin, 1978), p. 11.

158 Malcolm, *The History of the General Hospital*, p. 82.

159 *BA*, 1823, p. 42.

160 *BNL*, 13 February 1835, 21 August 1835.

161 *The Census of Ireland for the Year 1851. Part III. Report on the Status of Disease*, 1 [1765] H.C. 1854, lviii, 44.

162 *Poor Inquiry (Ireland). Appendix C, Part i: Reports on the state of the poor, and on the charitable institutions in some of the principal towns; with supplement containing answers to queries*, 35 [35], H.C. 1836, xxx, 15; *BNL*, 18 February 1831.

163 *BNL*, 4 September 1832.

164 *The Third Report of the Belfast Society for Relief of the Destitute Sick; adopted at the annual general meeting of the society, on Tuesday, the 25th of August, 1829; with a list of subscribers* (Belfast, 1829), p. 5.

165 *BA*, 1828–1833.

166 *BA*, 1828, p. 48.

167 *Poor Inquiry, Appendix B*, p. 200.

168   *BA*, 1831, p. 50.

169   *BNL*, 6 April 1830.

170   Malcolm, *The History of the General Hospital*, p. 94.

171   *Poor Inquiry, Appendix B*, p. 200.

172   Pilson, *History of the Rise and Progress of Belfast*, p. 46.

173   O'Neill, 'Fever and public health in pre-Famine Ireland', p. 17.

174   Letter from Dr James McDonnell to Dr Wilson, Belfast, 13 February 1832, PRONI D3819/A/5/9; Letter from Dr James McDonnell to Dr John Thomson, Belfast, 27 March 1832, PRONI D3819/A/5/10.

175   Henry McCormac, *Cholera Morbus. Short outline of its History, while in Belfast* (Belfast, 1832), p. 3.

176   Clarke, *The Royal Victoria Hospital*, p. 11.

177   O'Neill, 'Fever and public health in pre-Famine Ireland', p. 18; Strain, *Belfast and its Charitable Society*, p. 259.

178   Strain, *Belfast and its Charitable Society*, p. 260.

179   O'Neill, 'Fever and public health in pre-Famine Ireland', p. 20; *BNL*, 15 November 1831.

180   *BNL* 17 February, 24 February 1832.

181   *The Orthodox Presbyterian*, vol. 3, no. 23 (June 1832), p. 302; *Religious Consideration of Pestilence, by a Minister; and Medical Treatment of Cholera, by a Physician of the Cholera Hospital, Belfast* (Belfast, 1832).

182   Malcolm, *The History of the General Hospital*, p. 18.

183   Ibid., p. 98.

184   Ibid., p. 99.

185   Strain, *Belfast and its Charitable Society*, p. 260.

186   Ibid.

187   BCS Archive, Orderly Book, 15 September 1832.

188   BCS Archive, Orderly Book, 18 August 1832.

189   Strain, *Belfast and its Charitable Society*, p. 262.

190   6 August 1832, Proceedings Book of Lunatic Asylum.

191   11 August 1832, Proceedings Book of Lunatic Asylum.

192   Proceedings Book of Lunatic Asylum, 3 September 1832.

193   *Report of the Late Committee of the Lying-in Hospital, Belfast; together with a statement of accounts, and a list of the subscribers, for the year ending 31st December, 1832* (Belfast, 1833).

194   *BA*, 1804–1828; Minute Book of Lying-in Hospital Belfast.

195   Calwell, *Andrew Malcolm of Belfast 1818–1856*, p. 103.

196   *BNL*, 13 July 1832.

197   Malcolm, *The History of the General Hospital*, p. 101.

198   McCormac, *Cholera Morbus*, p. 11.

199   Thomas Thompson, *Practical Remarks on the Epidemic Cholera, which at present prevails in Belfast and its Vicinity* (Belfast, 1832), p. 6.

200   Malcolm, *The History of the General Hospital*, p. 106.

CHAPTER NINE: THE NEW BURYING GROUND AND BURIAL
IN NINETEENTH-CENTURY BELFAST

1   In the text hereafter, the Society is used as shorthand for Belfast Charitable Society.

2   As quoted in R.M.W. Strain, *Belfast and its Charitable Society: A Story of Urban Social Development* (1961), p. 243.

3   Advert text reported in George Benn's *A History of the Town of Belfast from the Earliest Times to the Close of the Eighteenth Century* (London, 1877), p. 551.

4   Strain, *Belfast and its Charitable Society*, p. 243.

5   Quoted in Strain, *Belfast and its Charitable Society*, p. 244.

6   For instance, see discussions by Fewer in 'An apparent funerary anomaly from seventeenth-century Waterford', *Journal of the Royal Society of Antiquaries of Ireland*, vol. 128 (1998), pp. 17–25 or T. Allen in 'Abingdon', *Current Archaeology*, 121 (1990), pp. 24–7.

7   Strain, *Belfast and its Charitable Society*, p. 245.

8   For instance, see discussion of relative value of guineas and paper money in *Saunders's Newsletter*, 6 May 1811.

9   Strain, *Belfast and its Charitable Society*, p. 243.

10   A drawing of the gatehouse was published in Joe Baker, *Clifton Street Cemetery: North Belfast's Historic Gem* (Belfast, 2006), p. 21.

11   *Northern Whig*, 24 December 1875.

12   The date of 1810 is given for the Luke Mausoleum by both James Stevens Curl in *The Egyptian Revival: Ancient Egypt as the Inspiration for Design Motifs in the West* (Abingdon, 2013), p. 292 and Paul Larmour in *Belfast: An Illustrated Architectural Guide* (Friar's Bush Press, 1987), p. 1. Newspaper reports on modifications in 1858 note that the design is by Thomas Jackson and stonework by William Graham and the original was conceived and erected by Edmund Getty (*Belfast Morning News*, 1 January 1858). Curl and Larmour's date of 1810 is clearly too early, and a design by Getty appears to be unlikely to date from earlier than perhaps 1830. The latter date was previously assigned by Curl in *The Egyptian Revival: An Introductory Study of a Recurring Theme in the History of Taste* (Allen & Unwin, 1982), p. 162. However, both Curl and Larmour do seem to believe that Egyptian style themes, which were fashionable in the 1810s, were evident in the New Burying Ground (such as that in the Jones plot, purchased in 1806).

13   Quoted in Strain *Belfast and its Charitable Society*, pp. 261–5.

14   See Baker, *Clifton Street Cemetery*, p. 21. The burial register began in 1831 and notes 11,230 burials after that date. This was to include many of Belfast's key figures throughout this period. Many of these individuals are recounted in Baker, *Clifton Street Cemetery* and Strain, *Belfast and its Charitable Society*.

15   See debate on the need for a new burial ground in Belfast in *Belfast Protestant Journal*, 17 July 1847. For City Cemetery and Milltown, see Tom Hartley's books *Belfast City Cemetery: The History of Belfast, Written in Stone* (Blackstaff Press,

2010) and *Milltown Cemetery: The History of Belfast, Written in Stone* (Blackstaff Press, 2014).

16   These are mentioned by Strain, *Belfast and its Charitable Society*.

17   *Belfast News-Letter* and *The Northern Whig*, 17 & 24 December 1875.

18   It is possible to identify other potential burials of suicide victims in this plot, such as John Shaw who committed suicide in 1842 and was buried in the New Burying Ground but is not listed in the Register (*Northern Whig*, 28 September 1842). Burials where suicide is noted appear in the Register from 1836 onwards, so burial within the New Burying Ground itself was not proscribed for suicide victims.

19   See: Strain, *Belfast and its Charitable Society*; A.C.W. Merrick and R.S.J. Clarke, *Gravestone Inscriptions: Old Belfast Families and the New Burying Ground from Gravestone Inscriptions, with Wills and Biographical Notes*, vol. 4 (Ulster Historical Foundation, 1991); Baker, *Clifton Street Cemetery*; also available online at www.belfasthistoryproject.com/cliftonstreetcemetery/ (accessed 18/8/2021).

20   See Christopher Wren's *Letter of Advice to the Commissioners for Building Fifty New City Churches* (1711).

21   The history is given in J.H. Benham, *History of the City Burial Ground in New Haven, together with The Names of the Owners of the Lots Therein* (New Haven, 1863).

22   See Ken Worpole, *Last Landscapes: The Architecture of the Cemetery in the West* (Reaktion, 2004) and James Stevens Curl, 'The design of the early British cemeteries', *Journal of Garden History* (1984), vol. 4, no. 3, pp. 223–54.

23   For example, see Curl, 'Design of the early British cemeteries', Worpole, *Last Landscapes*, D. Tulla Lightfoot, *The Culture and Art of Death in 19th Century America* (McFarland, 2019).

24   Arthur O'Leary remarks on John Wesley's letter to the Committee for conducting the Free Press appeared in *The Freeman's Journal*, 14 March 1780.

25   Comments by Doctor O'Ryan and Dr Kelso on the qualities of air and the danger of burying in churchyards were reported in the *Belfast News-Letter*, 5 December 1786.

26   '*Ecclesia alba*' or 'white church'; '*capella de vado*' or 'chapel of the ford'; '*ecclesia de Sancti Patricii de vado alba*' or 'St Patrick's white church of the ford'.

27   For instance, see Raymond Gillespie and Stephen Royle's *Belfast, Part I, to 1840* (Irish Historic Towns Atlas no. 12) (Dublin, 2003) or Raymond Gillespie's *Early Belfast* (UHF, 2007). Earlier discussions of the ecclesiastical history of the Belfast area appear in Reeves' *Ecclesiastical Antiquities of Down, Connor and Dromore* (1847), p. 186, and in George Benn's *History of the Town of Belfast* (1823), p. 252.

28   R.M. Young, *The Town Book of the Corporation of Belfast, 1613–1813* (1892), p. 316.

29   See Philips maps included with Gillespie and Royle, *Belfast, Part I, to 1840*.

30   Some of the medieval burials and finds in Belfast city centre are discussed in John Ó Néill's 'A medieval ring brooch and other nineteenth-century discoveries at High Street, Belfast', *Ulster Journal of Archaeology* 65 (2006), pp. 63–6.

31   See Eamon Phoenix, *Two Acres of Irish History* (Ulster Historical Foundation, 1988). Further out from Belfast other burial grounds were also used, like Hannahstown.

32 The phrase 'mystical and gothic' (also quoted earlier) is taken from Worpole, *Last Landscapes*, p. 11.

33 Nor was this practice universal or consistent – two men, one a Catholic, one a Protestant – were hanged for the rape and murder of Cicely Robinson in Ballymaccarret then returned to their families for burial. Belfast was scandalised by their funerals at the end of April 1827 as large crowds held separate boisterous wakes in Shankill and then, following a dispute over the degree of consecration of the ground, another for the Catholic in Hannahstown. These were reported in the press, such as *Belfast News-Letter*, 30 April 1827.

34 F.J. Bigger notes this information in the *Ulster Journal of Archaeology* 16 (1910), p. 96.

35 See *The Irish News*, 2 January 1971.

36 See Ó Néill, 'A Medieval Ring Brooch'.

37 The maps are all included in Gillespie and Royle, *Belfast, Part I, to 1840* and Gillespie, *Early Belfast*.

38 The various discoveries were noted in the *Belfast News-Letter*, 8 January 1859, *Belfast Weekly News*, 9 October 1869 and *Belfast Telegraph*, 22 May 1871.

39 Information from a local resident Liam McFarlane.

40 These were reported in *The Irish News*, 23 June 1894.

41 See Benn, *History of Belfast*.

42 J. Grainger, 'Results of Excavations in High Street, Belfast', *Ulster Journal of Archaeology* (1861), pp. 113–21.

43 It may not be coincidental that during the court case over the New Burying Ground in 1875 Peter's Hill is implied to be another site from which soil was transported in which there may have been human bone (see *The Northern Whig*, 24 December 1875).

44 R.M. Young, *Historical Notices of Old Belfast and its Vicinity* (1896), p. 206.

45 Reports of the Townsend Street find were given in the *Belfast Telegraph* and *The Irish News* on 22 June 1897. The reference to Schomberg is in Young, *The Town Book*, p. 243.

46 C. McSparron and E. Murray 'Excavations at Church Street, Belfast', *Ulster Journal of Archaeology*, 63 (2004), pp. 114–22.

47 *Belfast News-Letter*, 31 July 1869; this is corroborated elsewhere by memoirs of Narcissus Batt 'Belfast sixty years ago: Recollections of a septuagenarian', *Ulster Journal of Archaeology*, vol. 2, no. 2 (1896), pp. 92–5.

48 Eileen Murphy, 'Children's Burial Grounds in Ireland (Cillíní) and Parental Emotions Toward Infant Death', *International Journal of Historical Archaeology*, vol. 15, no. 3 (2011), pp. 409–28. While Murphy identifies the different treatment of the remains of unbaptised children as a Catholic issue, there remained issues in the Anglican tradition until at least the 1870s and 1880s in Ireland (see reports on debate by the Irish Protestant bishops of Revision Bills in *Cork Constitution*, 11 May 1876) and local cases in Britain such as at Bedale (see *Worcester Herald*, 12 July 1879) and Gwinear (*Cornish Telegraph*, 2 June 1883).

49   J. O'Laverty, *An Historical Account of the Diocese of Down and Connor, Ancient and Modern*, vol. 2 (1878), p. 341.

50   The male child found in a coffin on the mud flats off the Shore Road was reported by the *Ballymena Observer* 26 June 1880. The 1846 discovery was reported in the *Belfast Protestant Journal*, 20 June 1846. The remains found at Castleton were reported in the *Belfast Weekly News* on 8 February 1890.

CHAPTER TEN: 'THEY HAD NAMES TOO'

1   Minutes of Belfast Board of Guardians [hereafter BBG], Public Record Office of Northern Ireland [hereafter PRONI] BG/7A/5, p. 16, 17 November 1846.

2   Minutes of Belfast General Hospital Committee [hereafter BGHC], PRONI, Mic. 514/1/1/5, 17 October 1846.

3   Minutes of BBG, p. 16, 20 October 1846.

4   Ibid., p. 107, 15 December 1846; pp. 114–15, 22 December 1846.

5   Ibid., pp. 149–50, 12 January 1847.

6   Ibid., p. 96, 18 December 1846; p. 128, 29 December 1846; pp. 157–8, 19 January 1847.

7   Ibid., p. 170, 26 January 1847.

8   Ibid., p. 171.

9   Ibid., p. 175.

10   Ibid., p. 176.

11   Ibid., p. 136; p. 169, 26 January 1847; p. 183, 2 February 1847.

12   Ibid., p. 183, 2 February 1847.

13   Ibid., p. 201, 9 February 1847.

14   Ibid., p. 218, 23 February 1847; p. 246, 9 March 1847.

15   Ibid., p. 228, 2 March 1847.

16   Ibid., p. 249, 9 March 1847; Minutes of BGHC, Mic. 514/1/1/5, 27 February 1847, 6 March 1847, 8 March 1847.

17   Minutes of BBG, BG/7/A/5, p. 256, 16 March 1847; p. 278, 23 March 1847.

18   Ibid., p. 243, 9 March 1847.

19   Ibid., p. 197, 9 February 1847.

20   Ibid., p. 277, 23 March 1847; Minutes of BGHC, Mic. 514/1/1/5, 20 March 1847.

21   Minutes of BBG, BG/7/A/5, p. 278, 23 March 1847.

22   Ibid., pp. 298–9, 30 March 1847.

23   Ibid., p. 301.

24   Ibid., p. 300.

25   See Christine Kinealy and Gerard Moran, *Famines Before and After the Great Hunger* (Cork, 2020); Gerard MacAtasney, *The Other Famine: The 1822 Crisis in County Leitrim* (Dublin, 2010).

26   *Belfast News-Letter* [hereafter, *BNL*], 20 April 1847.

27   John Boyd to Relief Commissioners, National Archives, Dublin, Relief Commission Papers, 3/2/8/9, 27 January 1847.

28 *BNL*, 6 April 1847.

29 Minutes of BGHC, Mic. 514/1/1/5, 2 April 1847; *Banner of Ulster* [hereafter *BOU*], 9 April 1847.

30 Minutes of BBG, BG/A/7/5, pp. 307–8, 3 April 1847.

31 *BNL*, 23 April 1847.

32 Ibid.

33 *Belfast Vindicator*, 21 April 1847.

34 *BOU*, 30 April 1847.

35 Minutes of BBG, BG/7/A/5, p.302, 25 March 1847; p. 345, 27 April 1847.

36 Annual Report of the Belfast General Hospital for the year ending 31 March 1848. Available at the Wellcome Library online: https://wellcomelibrary.org/collections/browse/collections/digasylum/ (accessed 10/06/2021).

37 Minutes of BBG, BG/7/A/5, p. 315, 6 April 1847; p. 327, 13 April 1847; Minutes of BGHC, 514/1/1/5, 10 April 1847.

38 *BNL*, 26 March 1847; Minutes of BBG, BG/7/A/5, pp. 318–19, 6 April 1847.

39 Minutes of BBG, BG/7/A/5, p. 340, 20 April 1847; p. 367, 4 May 1847.

40 Ibid., p. 353, 27 April 1847.

41 Ibid.

42 *BOU*, 30 April 1847.

43 Ibid.

44 *BNL*, 30 April 1847.

45 Ibid., 4 May 1847.

46 *BOU*, 4 May 1847.

47 *BNL*, 7 May 1847.

48 Minutes of BGHC, MIC/514/1/1/5, 7 May 1847; Minutes of Charitable Society [hereafter, CS], PRONI, MIC/61/6/32, 8 May 1847, 15 May 1847.

49 *BNL*, 7 May 1847.

50 Ibid., 25 May 1847.

51 Minutes of BBG, BG/7/A/5, p. 380, 4 May 1847.

52 *BNL*, 11 May 1847.

53 Minutes of CS, MIC/61/6/32, 1 May 1847.

54 *The Northern Whig* [hereafter *NW*], 3 June 1847.

55 Ibid., 8 June 1847.

56 *BNL*, 7 May 1847.

57 Ibid., 25 May 1847.

58 Ibid., 28 May 1847.

59 Ibid., 8 June 1847; 20 July 1847.

60 Minutes of BBG, BG/7/A/5, p.132, 5 January 1847.

61 Ibid., pp. 159–61, 19 January 1847.

62 Ibid., p. 192, 9 February 1847.

63 Ibid., p. 280, 23 March 1847; p. 303, 30 March 1847.

64 Ibid., p. 247, 9 March 1847.

65   Ibid., BG/7/A/6, 5 May, 25 May 1847.

66   Minutes of BGHC, MIC/514/1/1/4, 27 March 1847.

67   Ibid., 10 April 1847; Minutes of CS, MIC/61/6/32, 10 April 1847.

68   Minutes of BBG, BG/7/A/6, pp. 86–7, 14 July 1847; p. 97, 21 July 1847.

69   Ibid., p. 7, 25 May 1847; p. 41, 15 June 1847.

70   *BNL*, 16 July 1847.

71   Minutes of CS, MIC/61/6/32, 9 July 1847.

72   *BOU*, 16 July 1847; *BNL*, 16 July 1847.

73   Ibid.

74   Minutes of BBG, BG/7/A/6, pp. 106–7, 28 July 1847.

75   *BNL*, 23 July 1847.

76   Diary of James MacAdam, PRONI, D/2930/7/6, 5 March 1847.

77   Report of A.C. Buchanan, Chief Agent, Government Emigration Office, Quebec, PRONI, T/3168/3, 11 May 1847.

78   Minutes of BBG, BG/7/A/6, p.68, 30 June 1847.

79   *BNL*, 29 June 1847.

80   Ibid., 13 August 1847.

81   Ibid., 30 July 1847.

82   *BOU*, 6 July 1847.

83   Ibid., 20 July 1847; *BNL*, 20 July 1847, 31 August 1847.

84   *BNL*, 20 August 1847.

85   Ibid.

86   Ibid., 24 August 1847; *BOU*, 24 August 1847.

87   *NW*, 3 August 1847.

88   *BOU*, 27 August 1847.

89   Ibid.

90   Ibid., 7 September 1847; *BNL*, 7 September, 19 October 1847.

91   *BOU*, 21 September 1847.

92   *BNL*, 5 October 1847.

93   *NW*, 28 October 1847.

94   *BOU*, 28 December 1847.

95   Ibid.

96   *BNL*, 16 November 1847.

97   *NW*, 25 December 1847.

98   *The Newry Telegraph*, 6 March 1849.

99   *The Times* (London), 30 August 1849.

CHAPTER ELEVEN: THE MOVING SPIRIT

1   See Figure 1, *Fortune Telling by Cup Tossing* (1842) by Nicholas Joseph Crowley. Photograph courtesy of Sotheby's Picture Library. For a detailed evaluation of the claim that Mary Ann modelled for Crowley, see C. McWilliams, 'The letters and

legacy of Mary Ann McCracken (1770–1866)' (PhD thesis, Åbo, Finland: Åbo Akademi University Press, 2021), pp. 67–9.

2   'The United Irishmen (1791)', in J.L. Altholz (ed.), *Selected Documents in Irish History* (New York & London, 2000), p. 70.

3   TCD, Madden MSS 873/151, Mary Ann McCracken to Henry Joy McCracken, 16 March 1797.

4   Ibid.

5   A. McCleery, 'Life of Mary Ann McCracken, Sister of Henry Joy McCracken', in R.M. Young (ed.), *Historical Notices of Old Belfast* (Belfast, 1896), p. 177.

6   Mary McNeill, *The Life and Times of Mary Ann McCracken 1770–1866: A Belfast Panorama* (Dublin, 1960), p. 245.

7   TCD, Madden MSS 873/81, Mary Ann McCracken to Madden, 13 February 1859.

8   Young, *Old Belfast*, p. 193.

9   McNeill, *The Life and Times of Mary Ann McCracken*, p. 286.

10   McWilliams, 'The letters and legacy of Mary Ann McCracken (1770–1866)', p. 90.

11   Ann McCracken, Belfast to Mary Ann McCracken, Dublin, 16 November 1796, in R.M. Young (ed.), *Ulster in '98: Episodes and Anecdotes* (Belfast, 1893), p. 93; McNeill, *The Life and Times of Mary Ann McCracken*, pp. 114–15.

12   See TCD, Madden MSS 873/135, Rose Ann McCracken and Mary Ann McCracken to Henry Joy McCracken, 27 September 1797; 873/136 Mary Ann McCracken to Henry Joy McCracken, October 1797, wherein the forthcoming trip is alluded to.

13   TCD, Madden MSS 873/137, Mary Ann McCracken to Henry Joy McCracken, 3 November 1797.

14   TCD, Madden MSS 873/146, Mary Ann McCracken to Margaret McCracken, 8 July 1798.

15   R.R. Madden, *The United Irishmen, Their Lives and Times*, 2nd Series, vol. 2 (London, 1843), p. 485.

16   On the morning of 9 July 1798, Mary Ann and Captain John McCracken were denied entry back into the jail but they did manage to talk to Henry through the window of his cell.

17   Madden, *The United Irishmen, Their Lives and Times*, 2nd Series, vol. 2, p. 487.

18   Young, *Old Belfast*, p. 192.

19   NMNI, History Collection, BELUM.S56.4, John Templeton's Journal 1809. The plants they discovered growing on the rocks are more commonly known as Scots lovage, sea thrift and Glaucous Crystalwort.

20   See Byrne, 'Templeton, John', in J. McGuire and J. Quinn (eds), *Dictionary of Irish Biography*, vol. 9 (Cambridge, 2009), p. 303.

21   See PRONI, McKisack deposited genealogical papers D1725/18, James Black, personal diary, November 1837–October 1844.

22   Eliza relocated to Bangor following her sister's marriage to Mr McGee of that town. See NMNI, History Collection, BELUM.S56.6, John Templeton's Journal 1811.

23   Mary Ann McCracken to unknown, 1838, in Young, *Old Belfast*, pp. 194–5.

24   Her death and burial at Bangor are noted in James Black's diary entry of 7 February
     1839. See PRONI, McKisack deposited genealogical papers D1725/18, James Black,
     personal diary, November 1837–October 1844.

25   Edward Bunting continued to lodge with the McCrackens until his marriage to
     Marianne Chapman in 1819.

26   F. Heatley, *Henry Joy McCracken* (Belfast, 1967), pp. 12–13.

27   'Henry Joy McCracken', Ulster History Circle, available online at http://
     ulsterhistorycircle.org.uk/henry-joy-mccracken/ (accessed 04/05/2014). Joy's Entry
     was named after Mary Ann's grandfather Francis Joy, whose warehouse once stood
     on the site.

28   Young, *Old Belfast*, p. 177.

29   J. J. Marshall, 'Miscellanea: Old Belfast signboards (note by Isaac W. Ward)', *Ulster
     Journal of Archaeology*, vol. 12 (1906), p. 189.

30   TCD, Madden MSS 873/119, William McCracken to Mary Ann and Margaret
     McCracken, 29 April 1797.

31   PRONI, Records of the Young Family Belfast, D2930/3/2/1, David Lyons to Mary
     Ann McCracken, 26 January 1804.

32   '1806 Belfast Traders Directory', Street Directories, Lennon Wylie, available online
     at www.lennonwylie.co.uk/1806.htm (accessed 11/02/2021); '1807 Belfast/Ulster
     Street Directory', Street Directories, Lennon Wylie, available online at www.
     lennonwylie.co.uk/1807.htm (accessed 11/02/2021).

33   Madden, *The United Irishmen, Their Lives and Times*, 2nd Series, vol. 2, p. 497.

34   Young, *Old Belfast*, p. 177.

35   *Belfast Directory for 1808* (Belfast, 1808), p. 30; *Holden's Triennial Directory, for 1809,
     1810, 1811* (London, 1811).

36   LHL, Beath MSS, Box 1, Letter 1, Edward Bunting to Mary Ann McCracken, 8
     March 1809.

37   QUBSC, Bunting Collection MS4/19, Miss Mary McCracken, Manuscript Psalms
     and Old Airs.

38   McNeill, *The Life and Times of Mary Ann McCracken*, p. 244.

39   TCD, Madden MSS 873/94, Mary Ann McCracken to Madden, 6 and 7 January
     1843.

40   TCD, Madden MSS 873/666, Mary Ann McCracken to Madden, 1 April 1843.

41   TCD, Madden MSS 873/82, Mary Ann McCracken to Madden, 22 February 1859.

42   TCD, Madden MSS 873/79, Mary Ann McCracken to Madden, 23 June 1859.

43   TCD, Madden MSS 873/82, Mary Ann McCracken to Madden, 22 February 1859.
     The brother to whose memory she is referring is Francis McCracken.

44   See TCD, Madden MSS 873/666, Mary Ann McCracken to Madden, 1 April 1843.

45   RIA, Richard Robert Madden Collection 24 O 10/ 22 (i&ii), Mary Ann McCracken
     to Madden, 14 July 1847.

46   Private Collection of John Orr McCleery, Jane Ellen Orr to John Malcolm Orr, 30
     August 1847.

47   TCD, Madden MSS 873/71, Mary Ann McCracken to Madden, 26 November 1851.

48 Jonathan Bardon, *Belfast: An Illustrated History* (Belfast, 1982), p. 76.

49 McNeill, *The Life and Times of Mary Ann McCracken*, p. 307.

50 PRONI, Benn Papers D3113/7/8, Charles H. Brett to George Benn, 7 October 1874. James McCleery's role on the Water Pipe Committee is outlined throughout R.W.M. Strain's *Belfast and its Charitable Society: A Story of Urban Social Development* (London, 1961).

51 See McWilliams, 'The letters and legacy of Mary Ann McCracken (1770–1866)', pp. 936–9.

52 TCD, Madden MSS 873/80, Mary Ann McCracken to Madden, 2 February 1859. The lodger (William McCleery's cousin) was William Henry Orr.

53 *The Belfast and Province of Ulster Directory 1863–64* (Belfast, 1863), p. 119.

54 Ibid., p. 535; *The Belfast and Province of Ulster Directory for 1865–66* (Belfast, 1865), p. 577.

55 J. Magee, *Barney. Bernard Hughes of Belfast, 1808–1878: Master Baker, Liberal and Reformer* (Belfast, 2001), p. 118.

56 See PRONI, Benn Papers D3113/7/8, Charles H. Brett to George Benn, 7 October 1874, in which Brett passes on a message from Mr John Ward explaining the manner in which 'their manufactory' derived the name Bankmore.

57 See *The Belfast and Province of Ulster Directory 1865–66* (Belfast, 1865), p. 421.

58 *The Sixteenth Report of the Committee for 1862–63 of the Belfast Ladies' Industrial National School for Girls conducted in the Lancasterian School-House, Frederick-Street, being the First Ragged School established in Ireland* (Belfast, 1863), p. 2.

59 *The Nineteenth Report of the Committee for 1865–66 of the Belfast Ladies' Industrial National School for Girls* (Belfast, 1866), p. 2.

60 Ibid., p. 12. Mary Ann's contribution was 2s 6d.

61 *The Belfast and Province of Ulster Directory for 1865–66*, p. 49.

62 'The Belfast and Province of Ulster Directory for 1868' Street Directories, Lennon Wylie, available online at www.lennonwylie.co.uk/alphanames1868mc.htm (accessed 07/05/2014).

63 PRONI, 'Will Calendars', https://apps.proni.gov.uk/willscalendar_ie/willsSearch ResultsDetails.aspx. A transcription of McCracken's last will and testament can be found within McWilliams, 'The letters and legacy of Mary Ann McCracken (1770–1866)', pp. 899–900.

64 By 1870 the McCleery family had moved from this address to 70 Donegall Pass. See *The Belfast and Province of Ulster Directory for 1870* (Belfast, 1868), p. 261. At the time of his death on 1 September 1874, William McCleery's will states that he was living at 55 University Street.

65 Guy Beiner raises the point that the plaque fails to mention her connection to the United Irishmen. However, there are also countless other epithets which could have competed for inclusion. It is possible that the plaque's placement on a late residence may have influenced the description. See G. Beiner, *Forgetful Remembrance: Social Forgetting and Vernacular Historiography of a Rebellion in Ulster* (Oxford, 2018), p. 580.

66   Madden, *The United Irishmen, Their Lives and Times*, 2nd Series, vol. 2, pp. 479–99. The page range here indicates the interview portion of the 'Memoir of Henry Joy McCracken' (Chapter 24). Within this publication, Mary Ann McCracken's account is indexed as 'M'Cracken, H.J., his sister, interview with her'. McCracken later provided Madden with a list of corrections to this memoir (complete with page numbers) within two letters; the first dated 2 August 1859 (TCD Madden MSS 873/83) and the second dated 4 November 1859 (TCD Madden MSS 873/87).

67   Madden, *The United Irishmen, Their Lives and Times*, 2nd Series, vol. 2, p. 479.

68   S. Millsopp, 'The White House at Newtownabbey', Bangor Historical Society, 13 October 2006, www.bangorhistoricalsocietyni.org/DATABASE/ARTICLES/articles/000026/002689.shtml. In recent years, the White House Preservation Trust restored the building and in 2015 gifted it to Antrim and Newtownabbey Borough Council. It currently functions as a historical visitor centre.

69   Madden, *The United Irishmen, Their Lives and Times*, 2nd Series, vol. 2, p. 479.

70   Ibid. Within this publication, Madden mistakenly referred to this individual as 'John Brier.' However, in a later letter to the historian, Mary Ann highlighted this error: 'Page 479: John *Brice* was the name of the man at whose home we stopped near the Cavehill on our way in search of my brother.' TCD Madden MSS 873/87, Mary Ann McCracken to Madden, 4 November 1859.

71   Ibid., p. 480. It is possible that the other person was John Queery of Belfast, owing to the fact that both Watt and Queery were with Henry Joy McCracken when he was arrested.

72   Ibid.

73   TCD, Madden MSS 873/87, Mary Ann McCracken to Madden, 4 November 1859. Commonly spelt 'Bohill'.

74   Madden, *The United Irishmen, Their Lives and Times*, 2nd Series, vol. 2, p. 480.

75   Ibid., p. 458. This is indexed as 'Hope's account of the Battle of Antrim'.

76   Ibid.

77   Edna Fitzhenry, *Henry Joy McCracken* (Dublin, 1936), pp. 130–1.

78   McNeill, *The Life and Times of Mary Ann McCracken*, p. 175.

79   'Hope's account of the Battle of Antrim' and Mary Ann's 'interview' transcript within Madden, *The United Irishmen, Their Lives and Times*, 2nd Series, vol. 2, pp. 389–506.

80   TCD, Madden MSS 873/156, Mary Ann McCracken to Madden, 15 October 1844.

81   Madden, *The United Irishmen, Their Lives and Times*, 2nd Series, 2nd Edition (Dublin, 1858), p. 30.

82   NAI, Rebellion Papers Collection NRA 620/16/3/8, microfilm, Mary Ann McCracken to Thomas Russell, 18 July 1798.

83   TCD Madden MSS 873/645, draft manuscript, Mary Ann McCracken to Thomas Russell, 18 July 1798.

84   Madden, *The United Irishmen, Their Lives and Times*, 2nd Series, vol. 2, p. 493.

85   Ibid., p. 495.

86   Ibid.

87   Young, *Old Belfast*, pp. 176–7.

88   Ibid., p. 177.

89   Ibid.

90   Mary Ann McCracken to unknown, *c.* 1815, in Young, *Old Belfast*, p. 193.

91   TCD, Madden MSS 873/73, Mary Ann McCracken to Madden, 16 December 1853.

92   TCD, Madden MSS 873/75, Mary Ann McCracken to Madden, 25 February 1854.
      Her niece being Maria McCleery, née McCracken.

93   TCD, Madden MSS 873/76, Mary Ann McCracken to Madden, 21 January 1857.

94   Ibid.

95   TCD, Madden MSS 873/70, Mary Ann McCracken to Madden, 13 November 1857.

96   Ibid.

97   *Fourteenth Report of the Committee for 1860–61 of the Belfast Ladies' Industrial
      National School for Girls* (Belfast, 1861), p. 10; *Fifteenth Report of the Committee for
      1861–62 of the Belfast Ladies' Industrial National School for Girls* (Belfast, 1862), p. 15.

98   Ibid.

99   *Sixteenth Report of the Committee for 1862–63 of the Belfast Ladies' Industrial
      National School for Girls* (Belfast, 1863), p. 11. 'Miss M'Cleery's' address is listed
      as 'Pakenham Place', where Mary Ann McCracken and the McCleery family were
      accommodated at that time. Although there were two Miss McCleerys within the
      household, Anna and her younger sister Mary McCracken McCleery, the latter
      married Christopher Aitchison on 23 July 1862, thus becoming Mrs Aitchison.
      Furthermore, the reports show that 'Miss M'Cleery' continued to serve on the
      committee and to collect for District 2 until 1870. Anna McCleery never married
      and died on 11 October 1888.

100   *Seventeenth Report of the Committee for 1863–64 of the Belfast Ladies' Industrial
      National School for Girls* (Belfast, 1864), p. 11.

101   *Twentieth Report of the Committee for 1866–67 of the Belfast Ladies' Industrial
      National School for Girls* (Belfast, 1867), p. 4.

102   Young, *Old Belfast*, p. 195.

103   TCD, Madden MSS 873/81, Mary Ann McCracken to Madden, 13 February 1859.

104   RIA, Richard Robert Madden Collection 24 O 10/ 48, Mary Ann McCracken to
      Madden, 23 February 1861.

105   Young, *Old Belfast*, p. 197.

106   Milligan, 'Irish Heroines', in J. Dunn and P.J. Lennox (eds), *The Glories of Ireland*
      (Washington D.C., 1914), p. 167.

107   Mary Brown McCracken (16 August 1827–9 July 1885), daughter of Henry Joy
      McCracken Junior (John McCracken Junior's son) and Eliza Duffin. Mary Brown
      McCracken and Eliza Tennent (her aunt) were close friends.

108   Eliza Tennent's surviving daughters were Annie (who married Nicholas de la
      Cherois of Ballywilliam in 1864), Evelyn Margaret (who married James Owens of
      Holestone, Antrim in 1861) and Letitia (who married Henry Harrison in 1860 and
      was mother to artist Sarah Cecilia (1863–1941) and Henry Harrison (17 December
      1867–20 February 1954)). Letitia married Henry Hartley Withers in 1896, after the
      death of her first husband.

109 PRONI, Tennent Papers D1748/H/29/2, Mary Ann McCracken to Eliza Tennent, 14 May 1846.

110 TCD, Madden MSS 873/147, Mary Ann McCracken to Francis McCracken, c. 18/19 July 1798.

111 NAI, Rebellion Papers Collection NRA 620/16/3/8, Mary Ann McCracken to Thomas Russell, 18 July 1798.

112 Young, *Old Belfast*, p. 177.

113 PRONI, McNeill Papers D3732/3/3, 5 volumes of notes for Life and Times of Mary Ann McCracken, Notebook 3, Mary Ann McCracken to Bernard Coile, 8 July 1803. Handwritten transcription.

114 RIA, Richard Robert Madden Collection 24 O 10/ 22 (iii), Mary Ann McCracken to Madden, 14 May 1845.

115 Belfast's night asylum opened in November 1841. Due to overcrowding and unsanitary conditions, it closed in 1847.

116 Belfast's day asylum was established in early 1847. Christine Kinealy notes that in that year it 'admitted 569 people in one day alone, three-quarters of whom were reported to be from the south and west of Ireland'. C. Kinealy, *This Great Calamity: The Irish Famine 1845–52* (Dublin, 1994), p. 171.

117 These included the Union Fever Hospital and the general hospital on Belfast's Frederick Street. Temporary fever hospitals were also set up in the workhouse infirmary, the Lancasterian school, the old military quarters in Barrack Street and at the Academical Institution.

118 RIA, Richard Robert Madden Collection 24 O 10/ 22 (i&ii), Mary Ann McCracken to Madden, 14 July 1847.

119 See Boston Public Library, 'Address from the Committee of the Belfast Ladies' Anti-Slavery Association to the Ladies of Ulster', 23 September 1846, https://archive.org/details/addressfromcommi00unse (accessed 12/03/2014).

120 TCD, Madden MSS 873/84, Mary Ann McCracken to Madden, 22 June 1859.

121 Commander Francis Anderson Calder (1787–7 November 1855), born in Edinburgh, Royal Navy sailor, agent for the Sunday School Society of Ireland, founder and honorary secretary of the Belfast Society for the Prevention of Cruelty to Animals and joint secretary to the Belfast Anti-Slavery Society.

122 James Stanfield (c. 1782–4 January 1867), grocer, member of the Evangelical Alliance, committee member of the Belfast Charitable Society and joint secretary to the Belfast Anti-Slavery Society.

123 TCD, Madden MSS 873/83, Mary Ann McCracken to Madden, 2 August 1859.

124 PRONI, Tennent Papers D1748/H/29/3, Mary Ann McCracken to Eliza Tennent, 3 October 1849.

125 PRONI, Tennent Papers D1748/H/29/4, Mary Ann McCracken to Eliza Tennent, 6 December 1849.

126 PRONI, Tennent Papers D1748/H/29/5, Mary Ann McCracken to Eliza Tennent, 26 December 1849.

127 TCD, Madden MSS 873/70, Mary Ann McCracken to Madden, 13 November 1857.

128 The Belfast Model School opened in Divis Street on 19 May 1857, while the Our Lady of Mercy Convent (later Saint Paul's) was opened on the Crumlin Road in the autumn of 1857.

129 F.J. Bigger, 'Memorials of the patriot dead', *Ulster Journal of Archaeology*, vol. 15 (1909), p. 94.

130 *Weekly Northern Whig*, 4 August 1866.

EPILOGUE

1   R.W.M. Strain, *Belfast and its Charitable Society: A Story of Urban Development* (London, 1961), pp. 315–19; Jonathan Bardon, *An Interesting and Honourable Society: The Belfast Charitable Society, the First 250 Years, 1750–2002* (Belfast, 2003), pp. 38–40.

2   Belfast Charitable Society Act 1996 – *An Act to make provision as to the objects, powers, constitution and management of the Belfast Charitable Society and for connected purposes.*

3   Strain, *Belfast and its Charitable Society*, pp. 315–19.

4   BCS Archive, Annual Report, 1951.

5   See Bardon, *An Interesting and Honourable Society.*

6   See Belfast Charitable Society Act 1996 – Objects.

7   The title of Bardon's history of the Society.

8   Belfast Charitable Society audited accounts to end September 2005.

9   *The Two Hundredth and Forty Second Report of the Belfast Charitable Society and the Account of the Proceedings at the AGM for Year ended September 2012.*

10   Ibid.

11   Belfast Charitable Society audited accounts to end September 2014.

12   Belfast Charitable Society strategic plan September 2015, 'Making Our Past Our Future'.

13   North Belfast Heritage Cluster members at August 2021 include: Annesley St Synagogue, Belfast Charitable Society, Belfast Orange Hall, Carnegie Oldpark Library, Duncairn Complex, Dunlewey Addiction Services, Indian Community Centre, Frederick Street Quaker Meeting House, North Belfast Working Men's Club, Redeemer Central, St Anne's Cathedral, St Malachy's College, St Patrick's Parish Church and The Jesuit Order.

Index

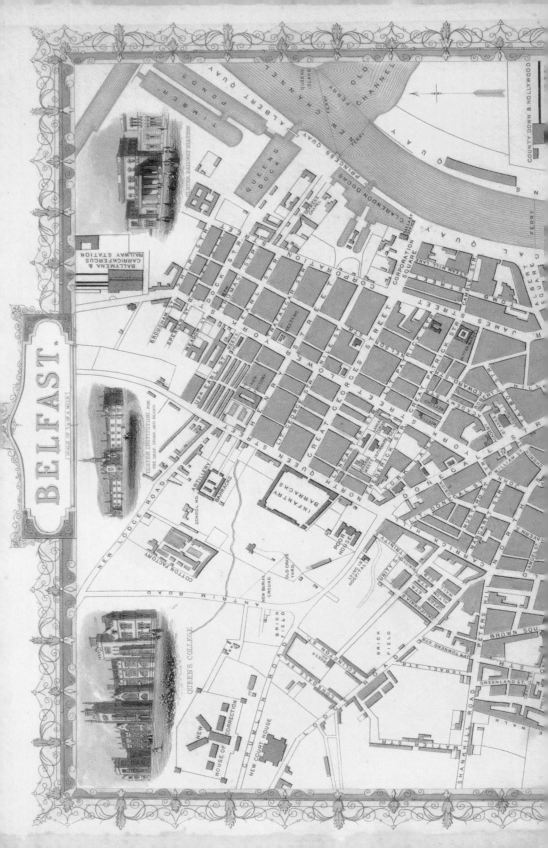

BELFAST.

SCALE OF 1/2 A FURLONG

OLD CHANNEL

NEW CHANNEL

QUEENS FERRY QUAY

PRINCESS QUAY

ALBERT QUAY

QUAY

COUNTY DOWN & HOLLYWOOD FERRY

CLARENDON DOCKS

CORPORATION QUAY

TIMBER PONDS

QUEENS DOCK

ULSTER RAILWAY STATION

BALLYMENA & CARRICKFERGUS RAILWAY STATION

ULSTER INSTITUTION FOR THE DEAF, DUMB AND BLIND

QUEENS COLLEGE

NEW HOUSE OF CORRECTION

NEW COURT HOUSE

ANTRIM ROAD

NEW LODGE ROAD

ARTILLERY BARRACKS

SCHOOL HO.

COTTON FACTORY

INFANTRY BARRACKS

POOR HOUSE

OLD GRAVE YARD

NEW BURIAL GROUND

BRICK FIELD

BRICK FIELD

LYING IN HOSPITAL

CRUMLIN ROAD

CORPORATION STREET

DOCK STREET

BROUGHAM STREET

MEADOW STREET

TRAFALGAR STREET

THOMAS STREET

GREAT PATRICK STREET

UP EARL STREET

HENRY STREET

YORK STREET

GEORGES STREET

LOWER DONEGAL STREET

NORTH QUEEN STREET

GREAT GEORGES STREET

STEAM MILL LANE

TOMB STREET

JAMES STREET

CAMBR. STREET

ALBERT STR.

PATRICK STREET

HILL STREET

EDWARD STREET

DONEGAL STREET

TALBOT STREET

ACADEMY STREET

NELSON STREET

VICTORIA STREET

DONEGAL STREET

WILLIAM STREET

JOHN STREET

MUSGRAVE STREET

CARRICK HILL

TRINITY

STREET

PETERS HILL

BROWN SQU.

GREENLAND ST.

SHANKHILL ROAD

PETERS HILL

WALL STREET